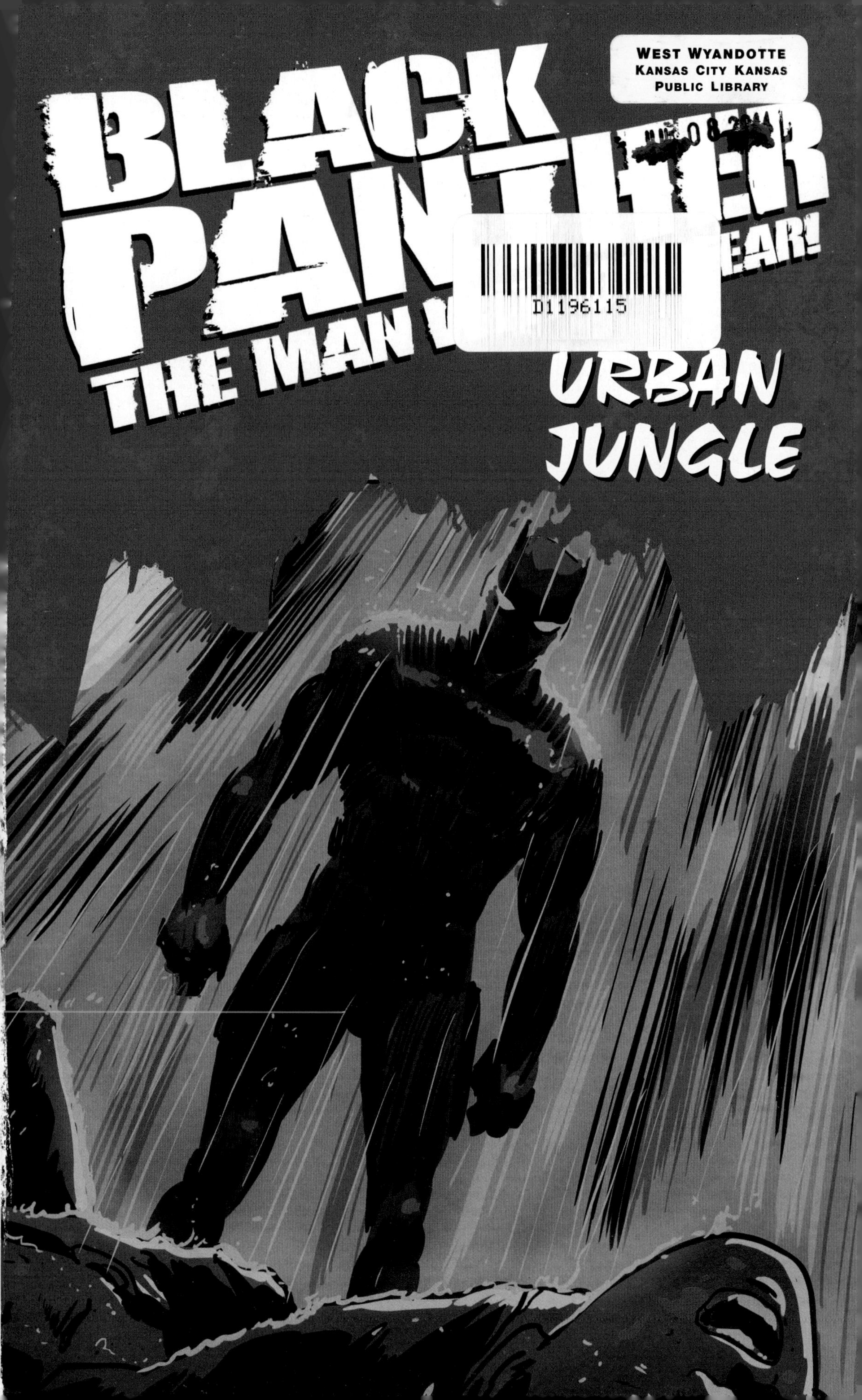
BLACK
PAN
EAR!
THE MAN
URBAN
JUNGLE

BLACK PANTHER
THE MAN WITHOUT FEAR!

URBAN JUNGLE

WRITER: **DAVID LISS**

ARTISTS: **FRANCESCO FRANCAVILLA** (ISSUES #513-515 & 517-518)

WITH **JEFTE PALO** (ISSUE #516)

COLORIST (ISSUE #516): **JEAN-FRANCOIS BEAULIEU**

LETTERER: **VC'S JOE CARAMAGNA**

COVER ARTISTS: **SIMONE BIANCHI** & **SIMONE PERUZZI**

ASSISTANT EDITORS: **RACHEL PINELLAS** & **JOHN DENNING**

EDITOR: **BILL ROSEMANN**

COLLECTION EDITOR & DESIGN: **CORY LEVINE**

EDITORIAL ASSISTANTS: **JAMES EMMETT** & **JOE HOCHSTEIN**

ASSISTANT EDITORS: **MATT MASDEU, ALEX STARBUCK** & **NELSON RIBEIRO**

EDITORS, SPECIAL PROJECTS: **JENNIFER GRÜNWALD** & **MARK D. BEAZLEY**

SENIOR EDITOR, SPECIAL PROJECTS: **JEFF YOUNGQUIST**

SENIOR VICE PRESIDENT OF SALES: **DAVID GABRIEL**

SVP OF BRAND PLANNING & COMMUNICATIONS: **MICHAEL PASCIULLO**

EDITOR IN CHIEF: **AXEL ALONSO**

CHIEF CREATIVE OFFICER: **JOE QUESADA**

PUBLISHER: **DAN BUCKLEY**

EXECUTIVE PRODUCER: **ALAN FINE**

BLACK PANTHER: THE MAN WITHOUT FEAR VOL. 1 — URBAN JUNGLE. Contains material originally published in magazine form as BLACK PANTHER: THE MAN WITHOUT FEAR #513-518 and X-MEN: CURSE OF THE MUTANTS SPOTLIGHT. First printing 2011. ISBN# 978-0-7851-4523-3. Published by MARVEL WORLDWIDE, INC., a subsidiary of MARVEL ENTERTAINMENT, LLC. OFFICE OF PUBLICATION: 135 West 50th Street, New York, NY 10020. Copyright © 2010 and 2011 Marvel Characters, Inc. All rights reserved. $16.99 per copy in the U.S. and $18.50 in Canada (GST #R127032852); Canadian Agreement #40668537. All characters featured in this issue and the distinctive names and likenesses thereof, and all related indicia are trademarks of Marvel Characters, Inc. No similarity between any of the names, characters, persons, and/or institutions in this magazine with those of any living or dead person or institution is intended, and any such similarity which may exist is purely coincidental. **Printed in the U.S.A.** ALAN FINE, EVP - Office of the President, Marvel Worldwide, Inc. and EVP & CMO Marvel Characters B.V.; DAN BUCKLEY, Publisher & President - Print, Animation & Digital Divisions; JOE QUESADA, Chief Creative Officer; JIM SOKOLOWSKI, Chief Operating Officer; DAVID BOGART, SVP of Business Affairs & Talent Management; TOM BREVOORT, SVP of Publishing; C.B. CEBULSKI, SVP of Creator & Content Development; DAVID GABRIEL, SVP of Publishing Sales & Circulation; MICHAEL PASCIULLO, SVP of Brand Planning & Communications; JIM O'KEEFE, VP of Operations & Logistics; DAN CARR, Executive Director of Publishing Technology; JUSTIN F. GABRIE, Director of Publishing & Editorial Operations; SUSAN CRESPI, Editorial Operations Manager; ALEX MORALES, Publishing Operations Manager; STAN LEE, Chairman Emeritus. For information regarding advertising in Marvel Comics or on Marvel.com, please contact John Dokes, SVP Integrated Sales and Marketing, at jdokes@marvel.com. For Marvel subscription inquiries, please call 800-217-9158. **Manufactured between 6/9/11 and 6/28/11 by QUAD/GRAPHICS, DUBUQUE, IA, USA.**

10 9 8 7 6 5 4 3 2 1

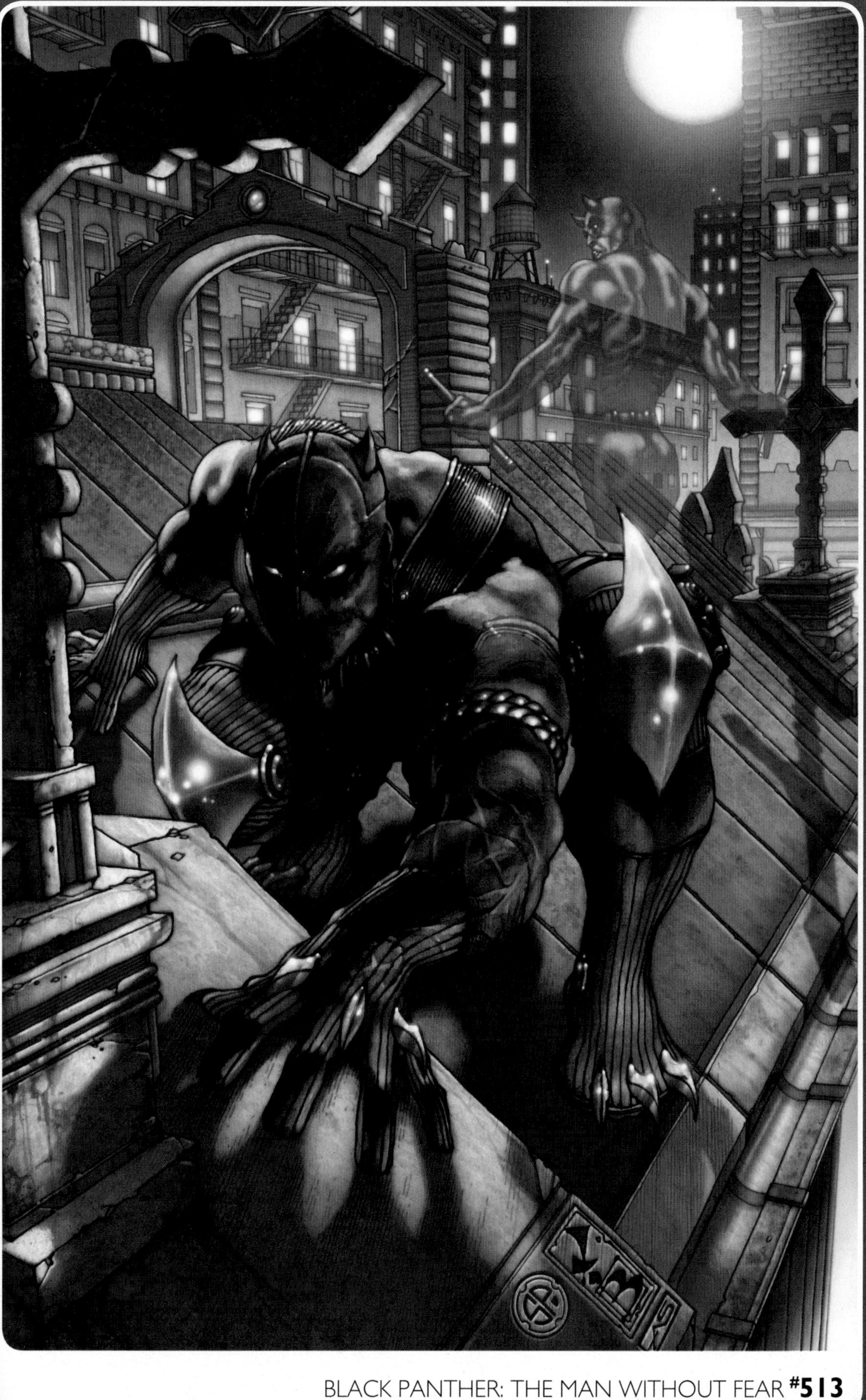

BLACK PANTHER: THE MAN WITHOUT FEAR #513

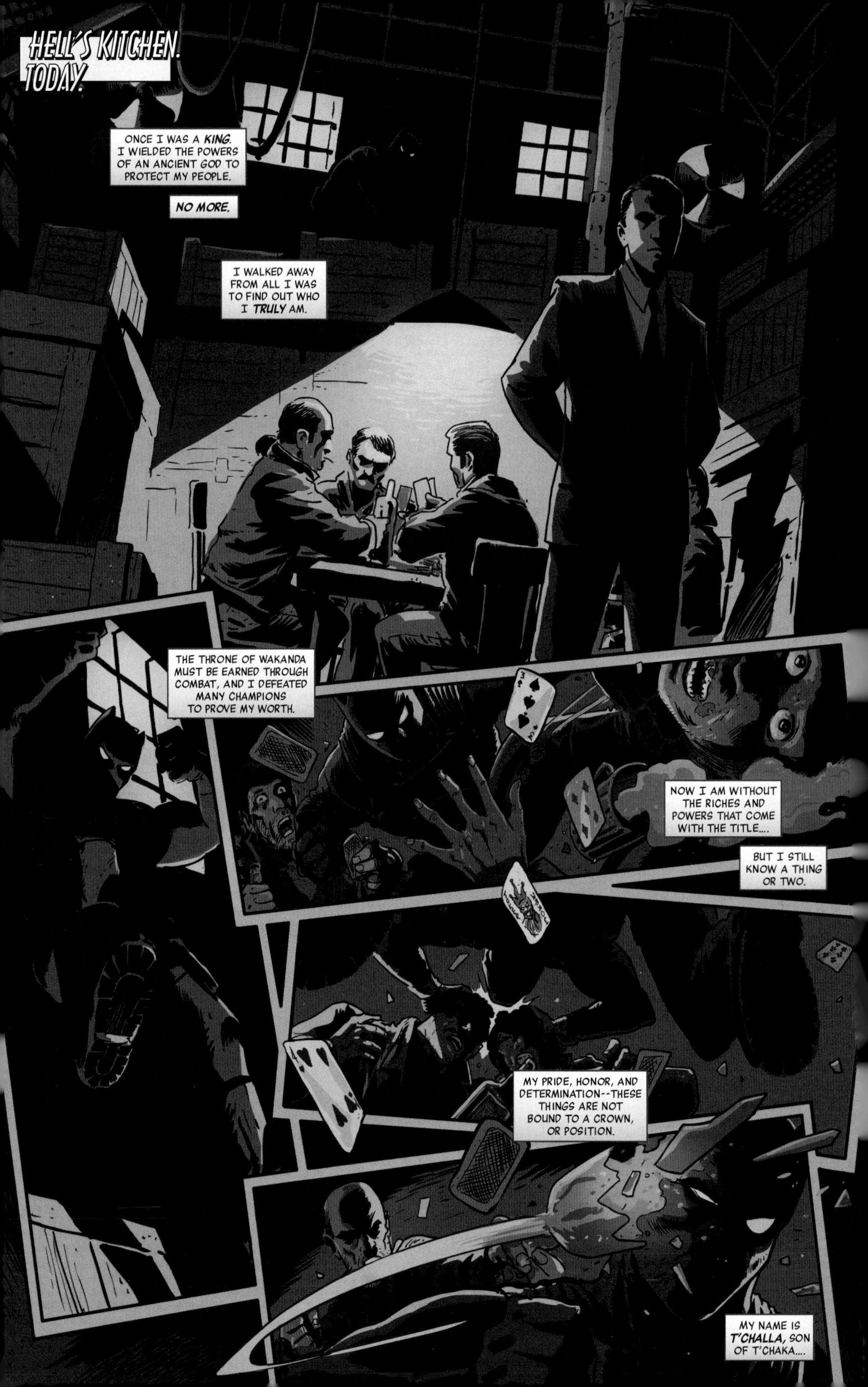
HELL'S KITCHEN. TODAY.
ONCE I WAS A KING. I WIELDED THE POWERS OF AN ANCIENT GOD TO PROTECT MY PEOPLE.
NO MORE.
I WALKED AWAY FROM ALL I WAS TO FIND OUT WHO I TRULY AM.
THE THRONE OF WAKANDA MUST BE EARNED THROUGH COMBAT, AND I DEFEATED MANY CHAMPIONS TO PROVE MY WORTH.
NOW I AM WITHOUT THE RICHES AND POWERS THAT COME WITH THE TITLE....
BUT I STILL KNOW A THING OR TWO.
MY PRIDE, HONOR, AND DETERMINATION--THESE THINGS ARE NOT BOUND TO A CROWN, OR POSITION.
MY NAME IS T'CHALLA, SON OF T'CHAKA....

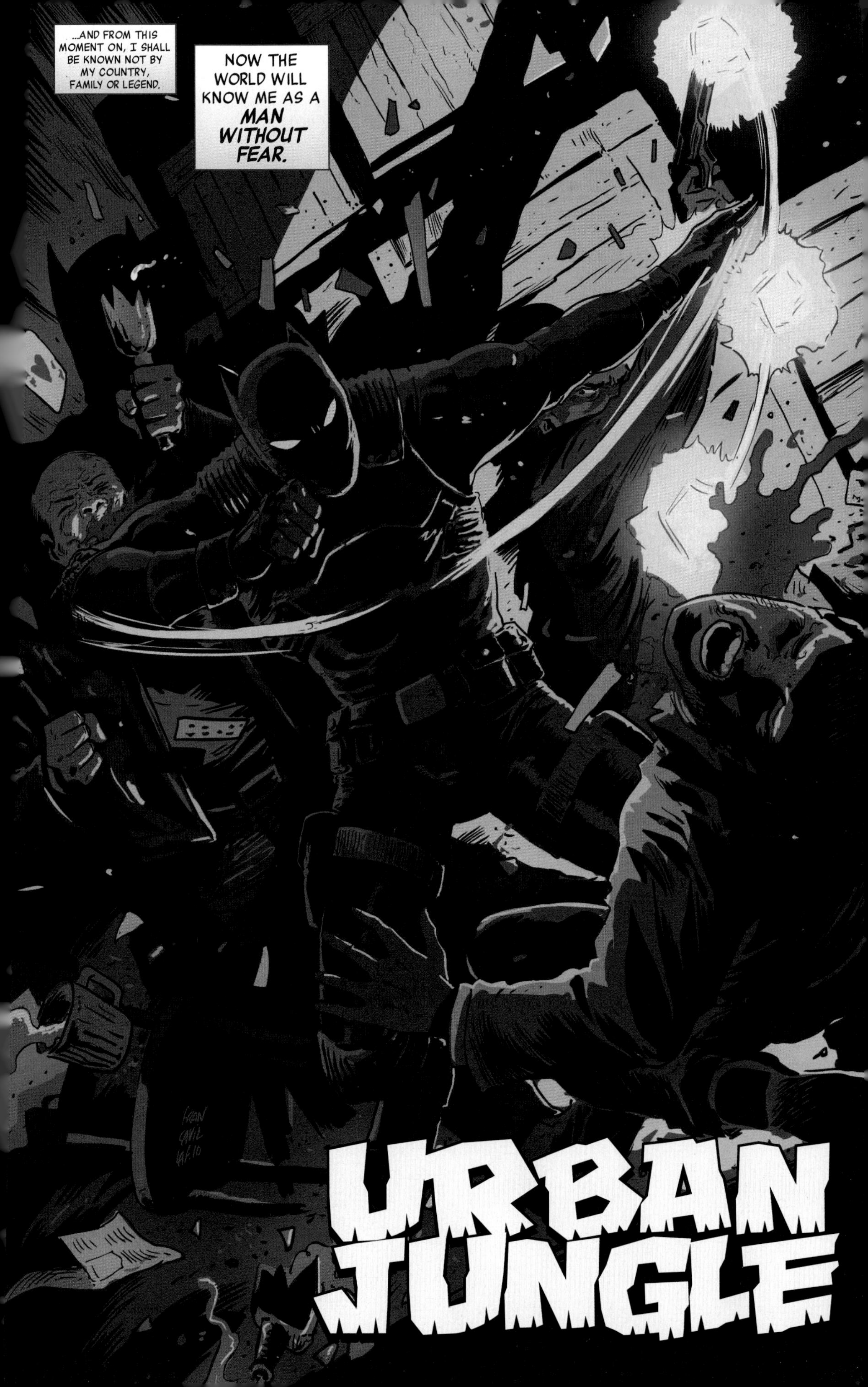
...AND FROM THIS MOMENT ON, I SHALL BE KNOWN NOT BY MY COUNTRY, FAMILY OR LEGEND.
NOW THE WORLD WILL KNOW ME AS A MAN WITHOUT FEAR.
URBAN JUNGLE

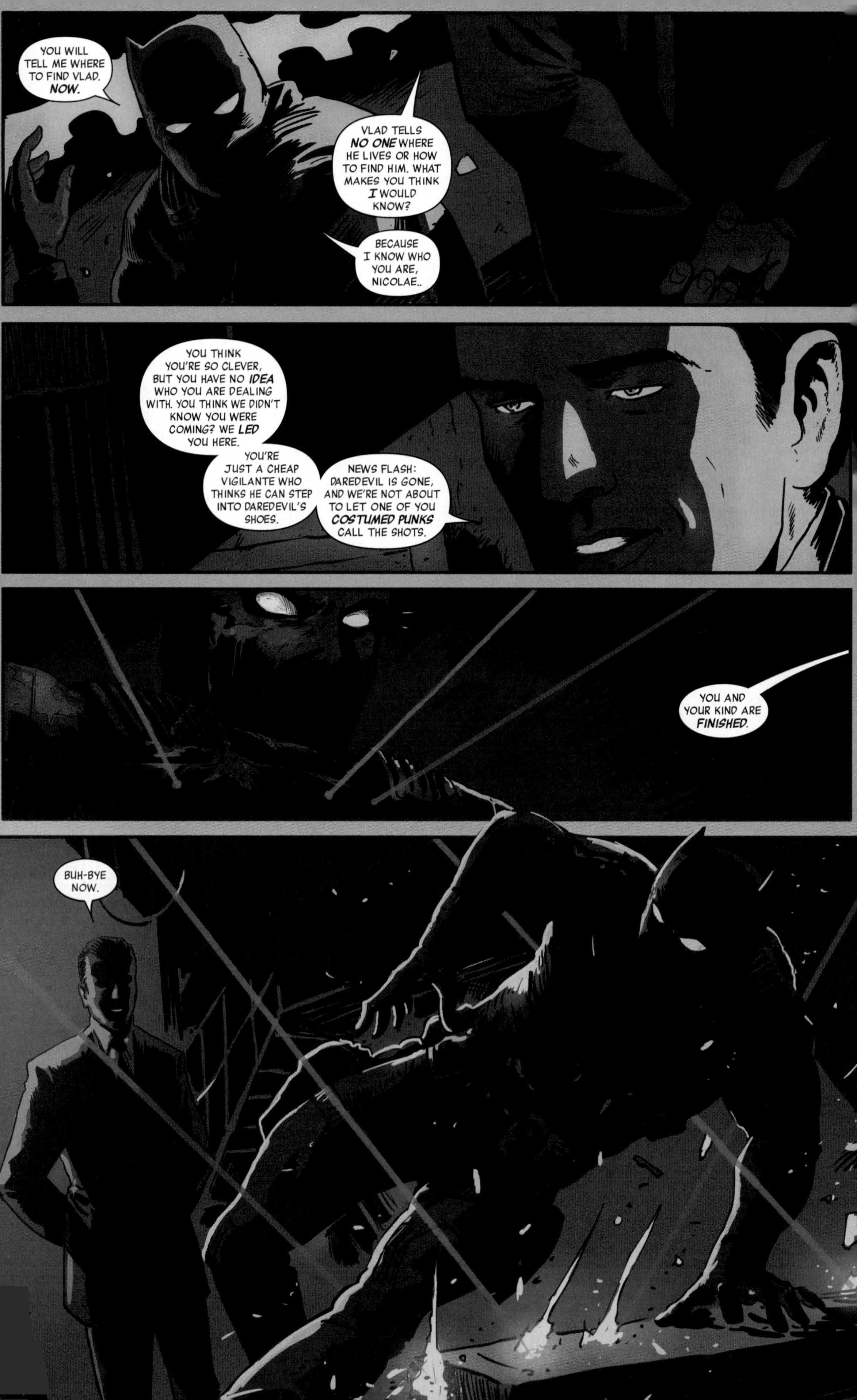
YOU WILL TELL ME WHERE TO FIND VLAD. NOW.
VLAD TELLS NO ONE WHERE HE LIVES OR HOW TO FIND HIM. WHAT MAKES YOU THINK I WOULD KNOW?
BECAUSE I KNOW WHO YOU ARE, NICOLAE..
YOU THINK YOU'RE SO CLEVER, BUT YOU HAVE NO IDEA WHO YOU ARE DEALING WITH. YOU THINK WE DIDN'T KNOW YOU WERE COMING? WE LED YOU HERE.
YOU'RE JUST A CHEAP VIGILANTE WHO THINKS HE CAN STEP INTO DAREDEVIL'S SHOES.
NEWS FLASH: DAREDEVIL IS GONE, AND WE'RE NOT ABOUT TO LET ONE OF YOU COSTUMED PUNKS CALL THE SHOTS.
YOU AND YOUR KIND ARE FINISHED.
BUH-BYE NOW.

After seizing control of the ancient Ninja cult known as The Hand, Matt Murdock (a.k.a. the vigilante called Daredevil) attempted to use the evil organization as a force of good in his quest to guard the mean streets of New York City's Hell's Kitchen. But instead of redeeming The Hand, Matt was himself corrupted. After a brutal stand-off with the city's heroes, Matt purged himself of the cult's influence...but may have lost his own soul in the process.

Half a world away, T'Challa, the spiritual leader and warrior king of the African nation Wakanda, engaged in a fierce battle of wills with the iron-fisted despot known as Dr. Doom. T'Challa eventually succeeded in defeating the tyrant...but in the process destroyed his nation's stockpile of valuable Vibranium, the source of Wakandan wealth and power. In the aftermath of this crisis, T'Challa relinquished his role as Black Panther, giving up the technology and metahuman abilities associated with that title.

Two good men, in their neverending war against evil, fell. This is the story of one of them attempting to rise.

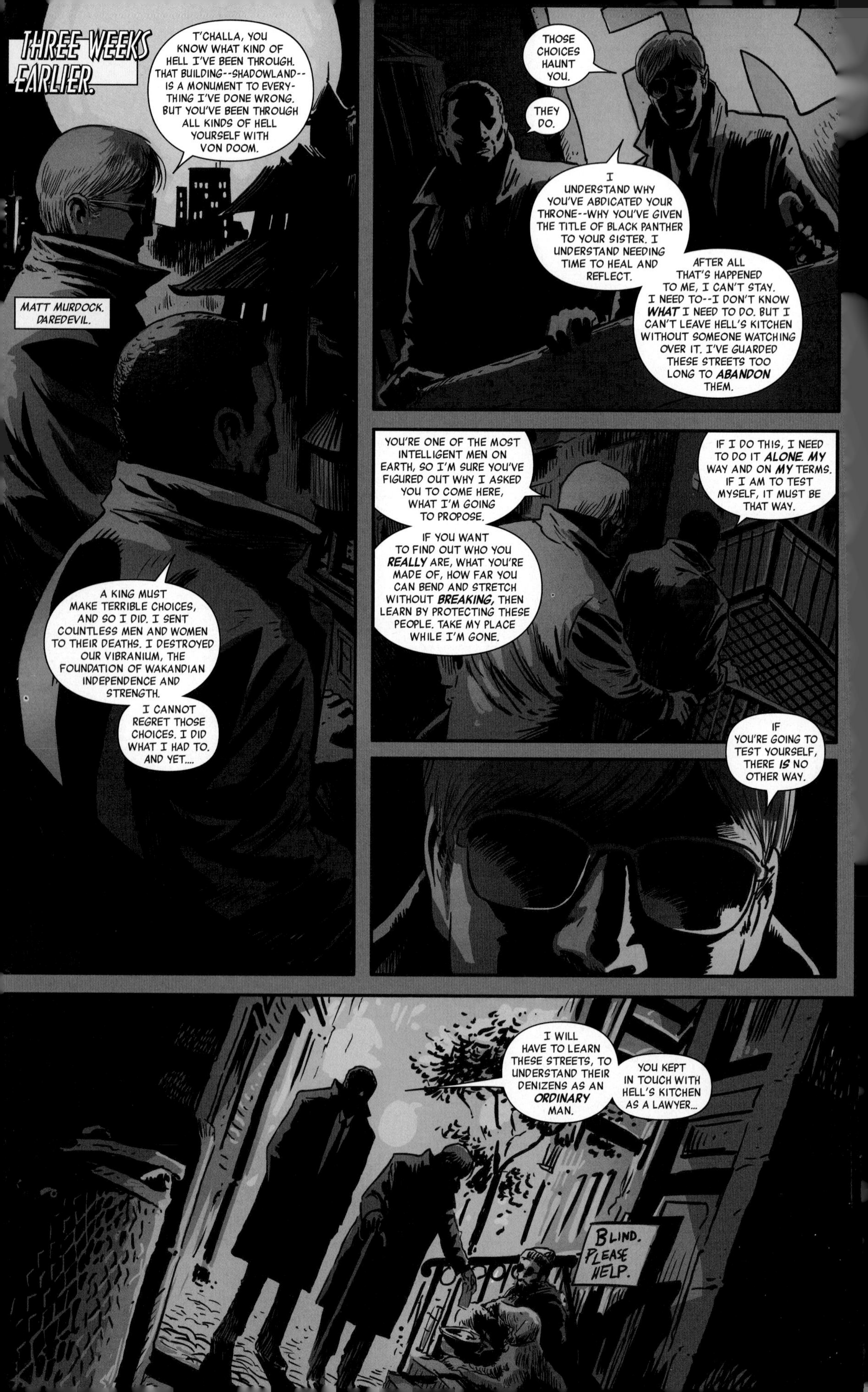
THREE WEEKS EARLIER.
T'CHALLA, YOU KNOW WHAT KIND OF HELL I'VE BEEN THROUGH. THAT BUILDING--SHADOWLAND--IS A MONUMENT TO EVERYTHING I'VE DONE WRONG. BUT YOU'VE BEEN THROUGH ALL KINDS OF HELL YOURSELF WITH VON DOOM.
MATT MURDOCK. DAREDEVIL.
A KING MUST MAKE TERRIBLE CHOICES, AND SO I DID. I SENT COUNTLESS MEN AND WOMEN TO THEIR DEATHS. I DESTROYED OUR VIBRANIUM, THE FOUNDATION OF WAKANDIAN INDEPENDENCE AND STRENGTH.
I CANNOT REGRET THOSE CHOICES. I DID WHAT I HAD TO. AND YET....
THOSE CHOICES HAUNT YOU.
THEY DO.
I UNDERSTAND WHY YOU'VE ABDICATED YOUR THRONE--WHY YOU'VE GIVEN THE TITLE OF BLACK PANTHER TO YOUR SISTER. I UNDERSTAND NEEDING TIME TO HEAL AND REFLECT.
AFTER ALL THAT'S HAPPENED TO ME, I CAN'T STAY. I NEED TO--I DON'T KNOW WHAT I NEED TO DO. BUT I CAN'T LEAVE HELL'S KITCHEN WITHOUT SOMEONE WATCHING OVER IT. I'VE GUARDED THESE STREETS TOO LONG TO ABANDON THEM.
YOU'RE ONE OF THE MOST INTELLIGENT MEN ON EARTH, SO I'M SURE YOU'VE FIGURED OUT WHY I ASKED YOU TO COME HERE, WHAT I'M GOING TO PROPOSE.
IF YOU WANT TO FIND OUT WHO YOU REALLY ARE, WHAT YOU'RE MADE OF, HOW FAR YOU CAN BEND AND STRETCH WITHOUT BREAKING, THEN LEARN BY PROTECTING THESE PEOPLE. TAKE MY PLACE WHILE I'M GONE.
IF I DO THIS, I NEED TO DO IT ALONE. MY WAY AND ON MY TERMS. IF I AM TO TEST MYSELF, IT MUST BE THAT WAY.
IF YOU'RE GOING TO TEST YOURSELF, THERE IS NO OTHER WAY.
I WILL HAVE TO LEARN THESE STREETS, TO UNDERSTAND THEIR DENIZENS AS AN ORDINARY MAN.
YOU KEPT IN TOUCH WITH HELL'S KITCHEN AS A LAWYER...
BLIND. PLEASE HELP.

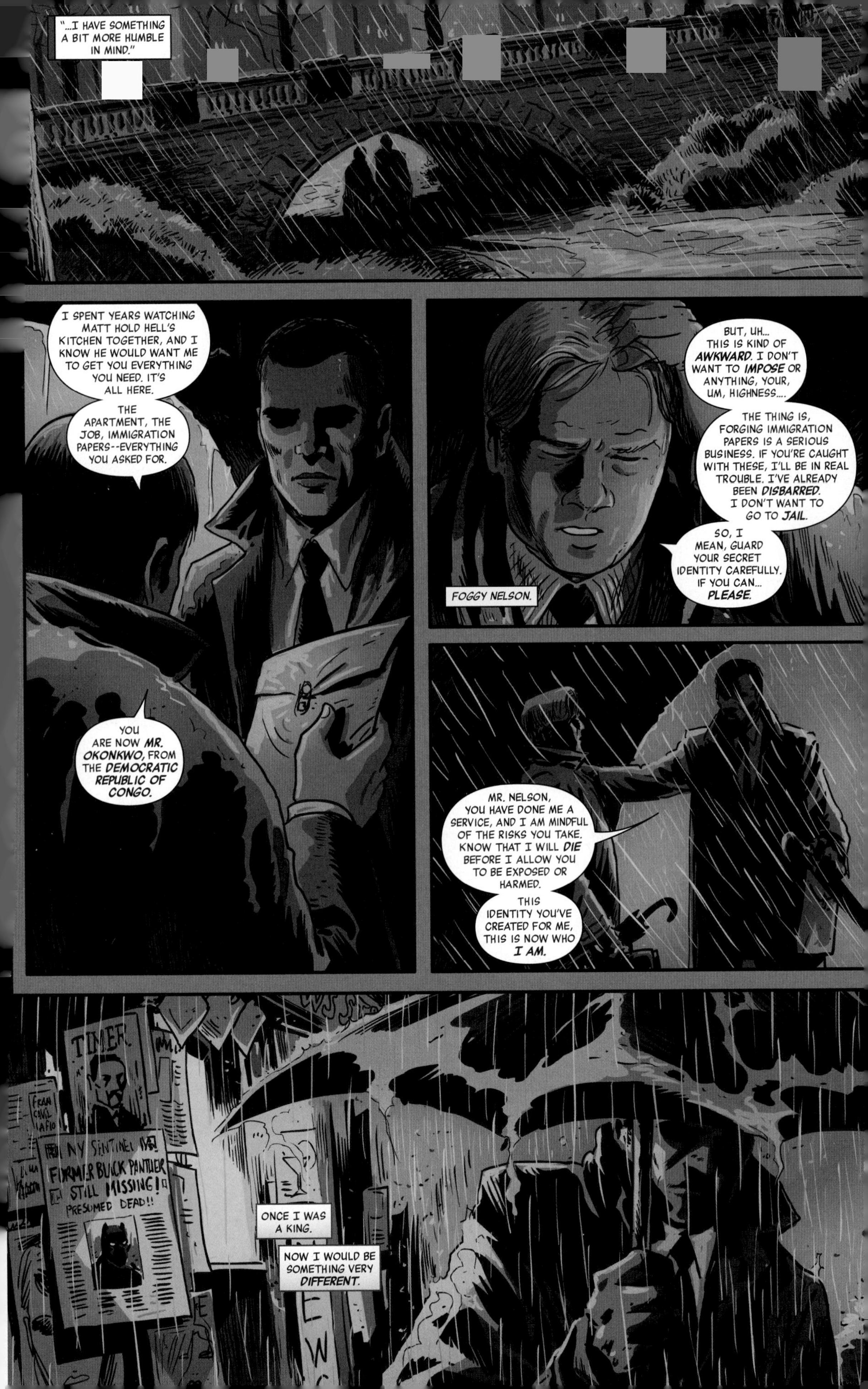
"...I HAVE SOMETHING A BIT MORE HUMBLE IN MIND."
I SPENT YEARS WATCHING MATT HOLD HELL'S KITCHEN TOGETHER, AND I KNOW HE WOULD WANT ME TO GET YOU EVERYTHING YOU NEED. IT'S ALL HERE.
THE APARTMENT, THE JOB, IMMIGRATION PAPERS--EVERYTHING YOU ASKED FOR.
YOU ARE NOW MR. OKONKWO, FROM THE DEMOCRATIC REPUBLIC OF CONGO.
BUT, UH... THIS IS KIND OF AWKWARD. I DON'T WANT TO IMPOSE OR ANYTHING, YOUR, UM, HIGHNESS....
THE THING IS, FORGING IMMIGRATION PAPERS IS A SERIOUS BUSINESS. IF YOU'RE CAUGHT WITH THESE, I'LL BE IN REAL TROUBLE. I'VE ALREADY BEEN DISBARRED. I DON'T WANT TO GO TO JAIL.
SO, I MEAN, GUARD YOUR SECRET IDENTITY CAREFULLY. IF YOU CAN... PLEASE.
FOGGY NELSON.
MR. NELSON, YOU HAVE DONE ME A SERVICE, AND I AM MINDFUL OF THE RISKS YOU TAKE. KNOW THAT I WILL DIE BEFORE I ALLOW YOU TO BE EXPOSED OR HARMED.
THIS IDENTITY YOU'VE CREATED FOR ME, THIS IS NOW WHO I AM.
TIMER
NY SENTINEL
FORMER BLACK PANTHER STILL MISSING!
PRESUMED DEAD!!
ONCE I WAS A KING.
NOW I WOULD BE SOMETHING VERY DIFFERENT.

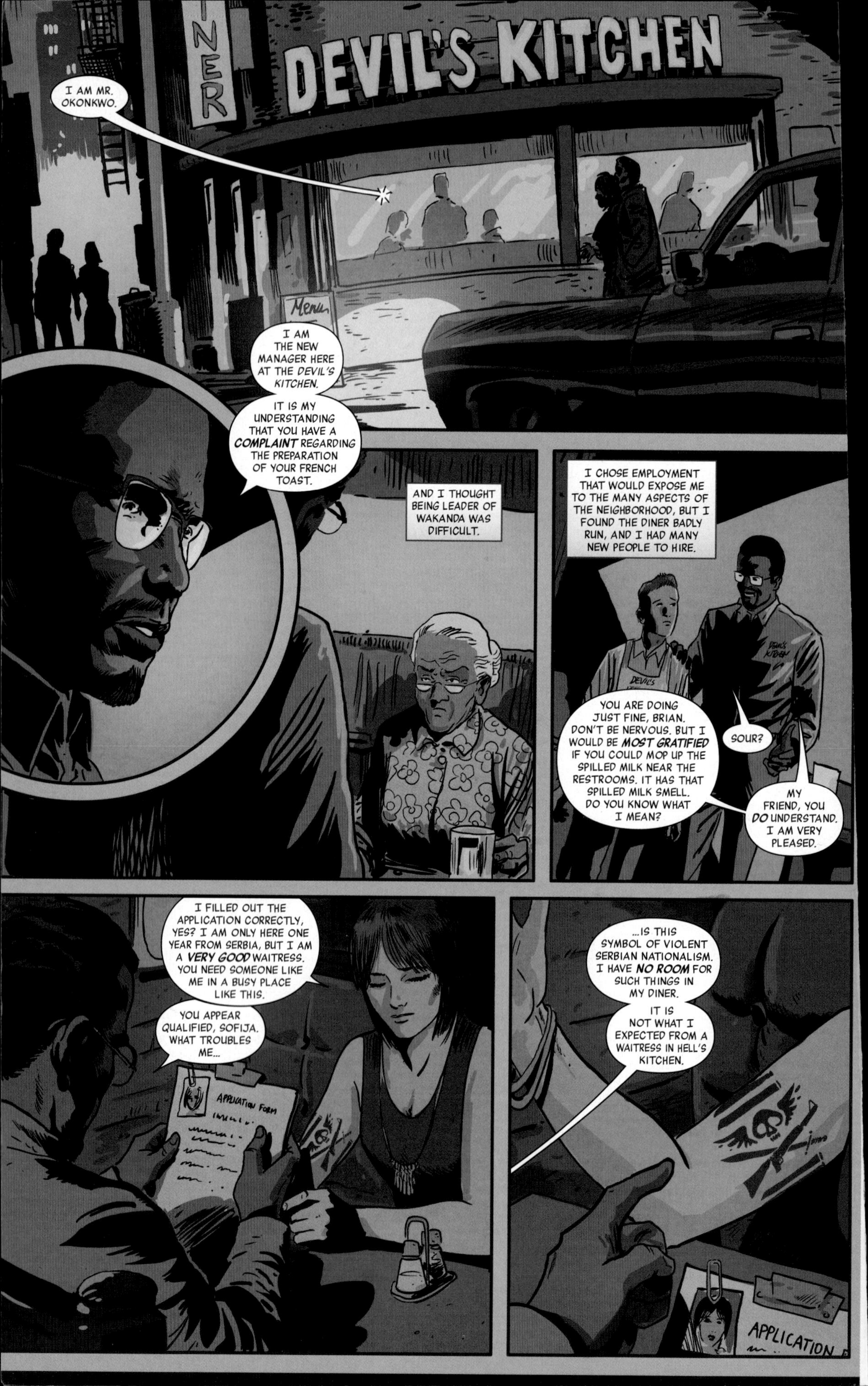
DINER
DEVIL'S KITCHEN
I AM MR. OKONKWO.
Menu
I AM THE NEW MANAGER HERE AT THE DEVIL'S KITCHEN.
IT IS MY UNDERSTANDING THAT YOU HAVE A COMPLAINT REGARDING THE PREPARATION OF YOUR FRENCH TOAST.
AND I THOUGHT BEING LEADER OF WAKANDA WAS DIFFICULT.
I CHOSE EMPLOYMENT THAT WOULD EXPOSE ME TO THE MANY ASPECTS OF THE NEIGHBORHOOD, BUT I FOUND THE DINER BADLY RUN, AND I HAD MANY NEW PEOPLE TO HIRE.
YOU ARE DOING JUST FINE, BRIAN. DON'T BE NERVOUS. BUT I WOULD BE MOST GRATIFIED IF YOU COULD MOP UP THE SPILLED MILK NEAR THE RESTROOMS. IT HAS THAT SPILLED MILK SMELL. DO YOU KNOW WHAT I MEAN?
SOUR?
MY FRIEND, YOU DO UNDERSTAND. I AM VERY PLEASED.
I FILLED OUT THE APPLICATION CORRECTLY, YES? I AM ONLY HERE ONE YEAR FROM SERBIA, BUT I AM A VERY GOOD WAITRESS. YOU NEED SOMEONE LIKE ME IN A BUSY PLACE LIKE THIS.
YOU APPEAR QUALIFIED, SOFIJA. WHAT TROUBLES ME...
APPLICATION FORM
...IS THIS SYMBOL OF VIOLENT SERBIAN NATIONALISM. I HAVE NO ROOM FOR SUCH THINGS IN MY DINER.
IT IS NOT WHAT I EXPECTED FROM A WAITRESS IN HELL'S KITCHEN.
APPLICATION

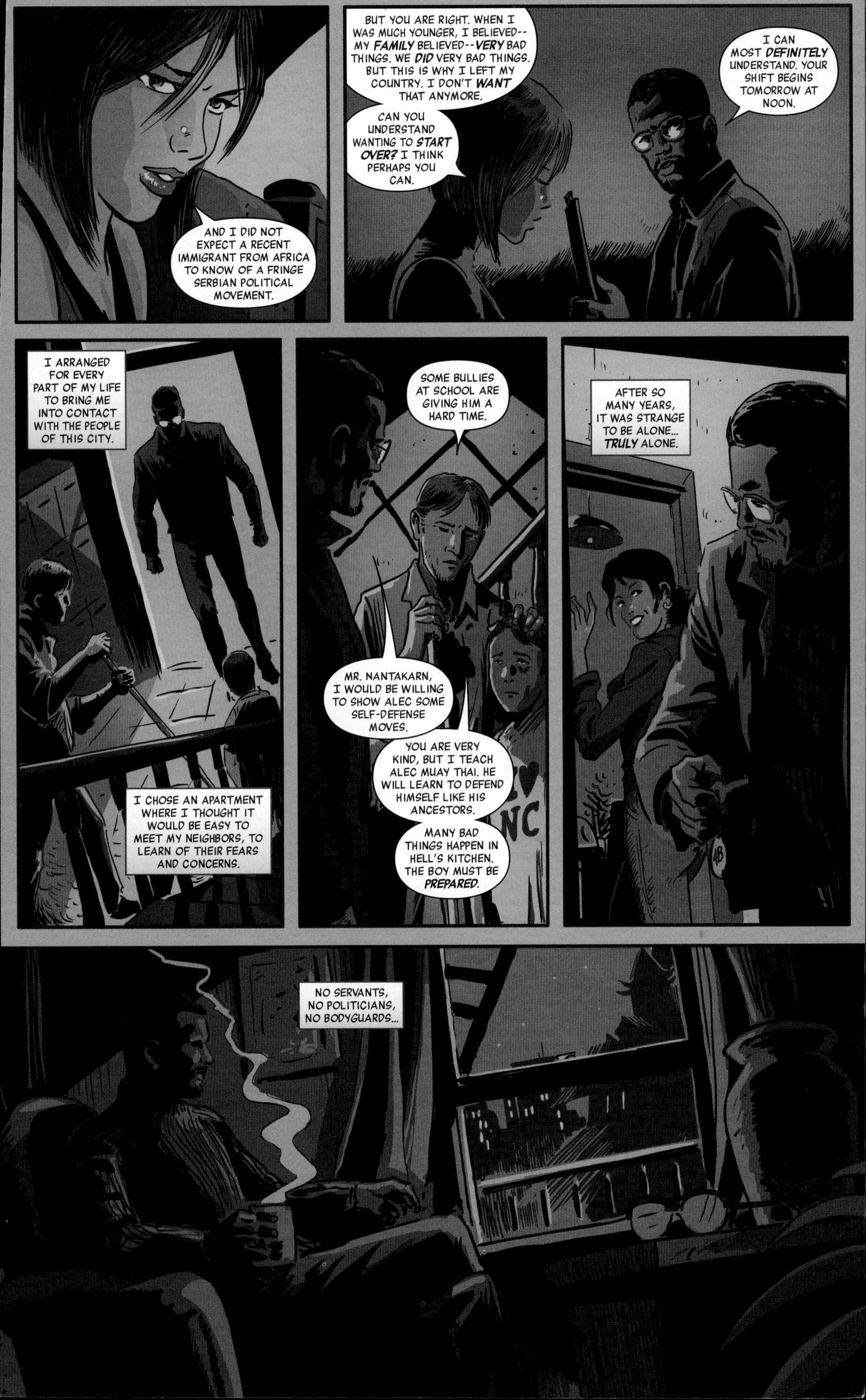
AND I DID NOT EXPECT A RECENT IMMIGRANT FROM AFRICA TO KNOW OF A FRINGE SERBIAN POLITICAL MOVEMENT.
BUT YOU ARE RIGHT. WHEN I WAS MUCH YOUNGER, I BELIEVED-- MY FAMILY BELIEVED--VERY BAD THINGS. WE DID VERY BAD THINGS. BUT THIS IS WHY I LEFT MY COUNTRY. I DON'T WANT THAT ANYMORE.
CAN YOU UNDERSTAND WANTING TO START OVER? I THINK PERHAPS YOU CAN.
I CAN MOST DEFINITELY UNDERSTAND. YOUR SHIFT BEGINS TOMORROW AT NOON.
I ARRANGED FOR EVERY PART OF MY LIFE TO BRING ME INTO CONTACT WITH THE PEOPLE OF THIS CITY.
I CHOSE AN APARTMENT WHERE I THOUGHT IT WOULD BE EASY TO MEET MY NEIGHBORS, TO LEARN OF THEIR FEARS AND CONCERNS.
SOME BULLIES AT SCHOOL ARE GIVING HIM A HARD TIME.
MR. NANTAKARN, I WOULD BE WILLING TO SHOW ALEC SOME SELF-DEFENSE MOVES.
YOU ARE VERY KIND, BUT I TEACH ALEC MUAY THAI. HE WILL LEARN TO DEFEND HIMSELF LIKE HIS ANCESTORS.
MANY BAD THINGS HAPPEN IN HELL'S KITCHEN. THE BOY MUST BE PREPARED.
AFTER SO MANY YEARS, IT WAS STRANGE TO BE ALONE... TRULY ALONE.
4B
NO SERVANTS, NO POLITICIANS, NO BODYGUARDS...

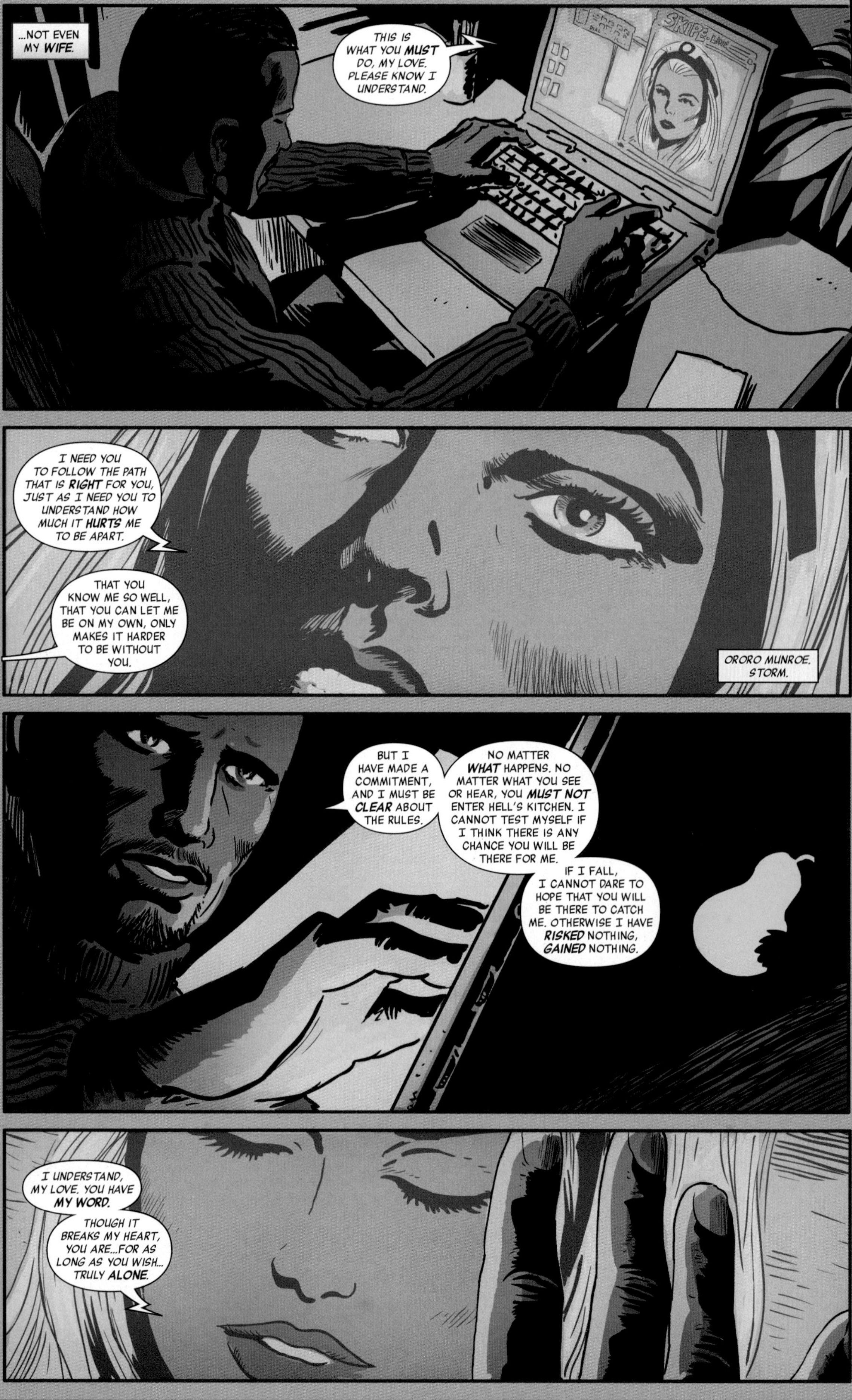

...NOT EVEN MY WIFE.
THIS IS WHAT YOU MUST DO, MY LOVE. PLEASE KNOW I UNDERSTAND.
I NEED YOU TO FOLLOW THE PATH THAT IS RIGHT FOR YOU, JUST AS I NEED YOU TO UNDERSTAND HOW MUCH IT HURTS ME TO BE APART.
THAT YOU KNOW ME SO WELL, THAT YOU CAN LET ME BE ON MY OWN, ONLY MAKES IT HARDER TO BE WITHOUT YOU.
ORORO MUNROE. STORM.
BUT I HAVE MADE A COMMITMENT, AND I MUST BE CLEAR ABOUT THE RULES.
NO MATTER WHAT HAPPENS. NO MATTER WHAT YOU SEE OR HEAR, YOU MUST NOT ENTER HELL'S KITCHEN. I CANNOT TEST MYSELF IF I THINK THERE IS ANY CHANCE YOU WILL BE THERE FOR ME.
IF I FALL, I CANNOT DARE TO HOPE THAT YOU WILL BE THERE TO CATCH ME. OTHERWISE I HAVE RISKED NOTHING, GAINED NOTHING.
I UNDERSTAND, MY LOVE. YOU HAVE MY WORD.
THOUGH IT BREAKS MY HEART, YOU ARE...FOR AS LONG AS YOU WISH... TRULY ALONE.

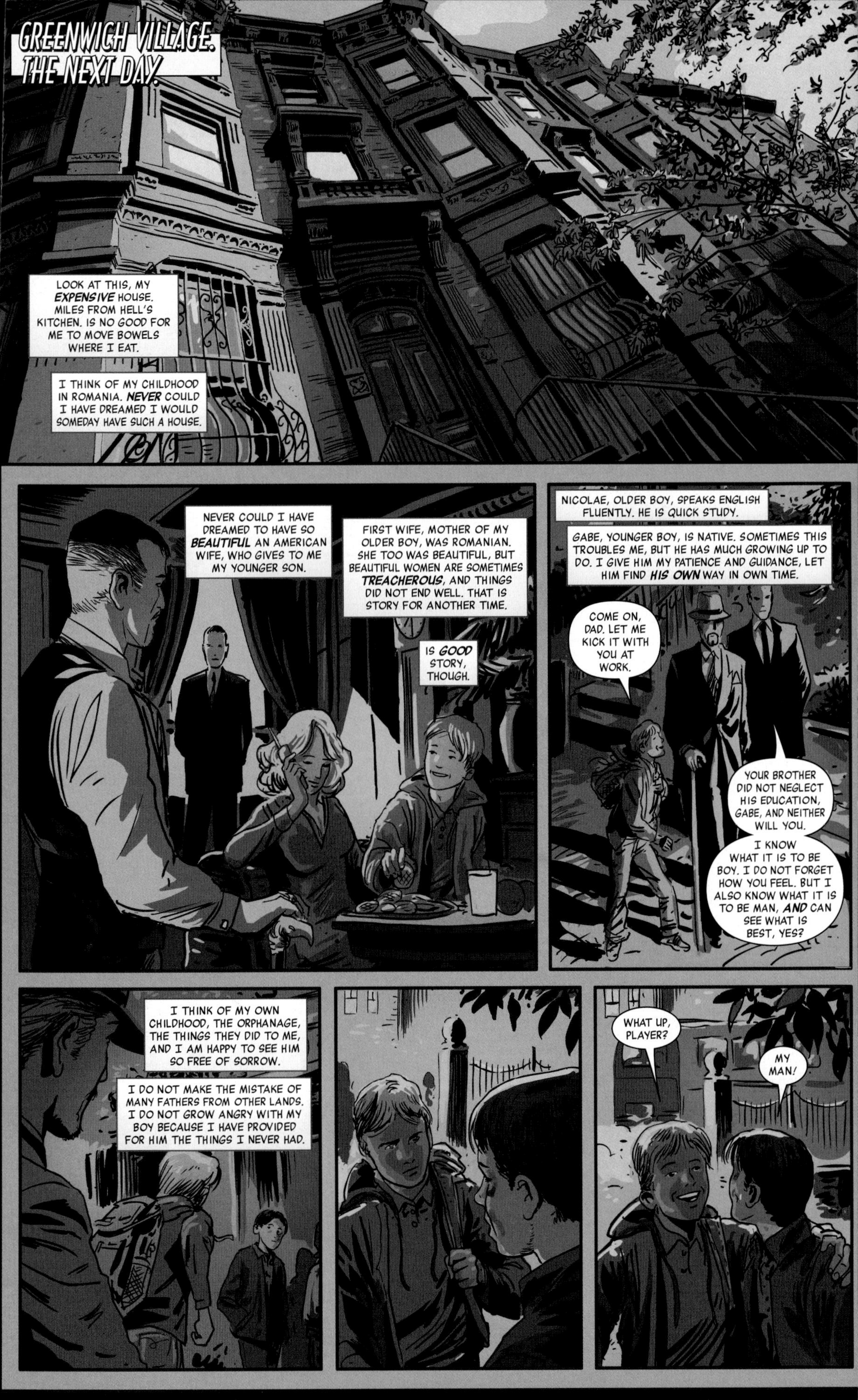
GREENWICH VILLAGE. THE NEXT DAY.
LOOK AT THIS, MY EXPENSIVE HOUSE. MILES FROM HELL'S KITCHEN. IS NO GOOD FOR ME TO MOVE BOWELS WHERE I EAT.
I THINK OF MY CHILDHOOD IN ROMANIA. NEVER COULD I HAVE DREAMED I WOULD SOMEDAY HAVE SUCH A HOUSE.
NEVER COULD I HAVE DREAMED TO HAVE SO BEAUTIFUL AN AMERICAN WIFE, WHO GIVES TO ME MY YOUNGER SON.
FIRST WIFE, MOTHER OF MY OLDER BOY, WAS ROMANIAN. SHE TOO WAS BEAUTIFUL, BUT BEAUTIFUL WOMEN ARE SOMETIMES TREACHEROUS, AND THINGS DID NOT END WELL. THAT IS STORY FOR ANOTHER TIME.
IS GOOD STORY, THOUGH.
NICOLAE, OLDER BOY, SPEAKS ENGLISH FLUENTLY. HE IS QUICK STUDY.
GABE, YOUNGER BOY, IS NATIVE. SOMETIMES THIS TROUBLES ME, BUT HE HAS MUCH GROWING UP TO DO. I GIVE HIM MY PATIENCE AND GUIDANCE, LET HIM FIND HIS OWN WAY IN OWN TIME.
COME ON, DAD. LET ME KICK IT WITH YOU AT WORK.
YOUR BROTHER DID NOT NEGLECT HIS EDUCATION, GABE, AND NEITHER WILL YOU.
I KNOW WHAT IT IS TO BE BOY. I DO NOT FORGET HOW YOU FEEL. BUT I ALSO KNOW WHAT IT IS TO BE MAN, AND CAN SEE WHAT IS BEST, YES?
I THINK OF MY OWN CHILDHOOD, THE ORPHANAGE, THE THINGS THEY DID TO ME, AND I AM HAPPY TO SEE HIM SO FREE OF SORROW.
I DO NOT MAKE THE MISTAKE OF MANY FATHERS FROM OTHER LANDS. I DO NOT GROW ANGRY WITH MY BOY BECAUSE I HAVE PROVIDED FOR HIM THE THINGS I NEVER HAD.
WHAT UP, PLAYER?
MY MAN!

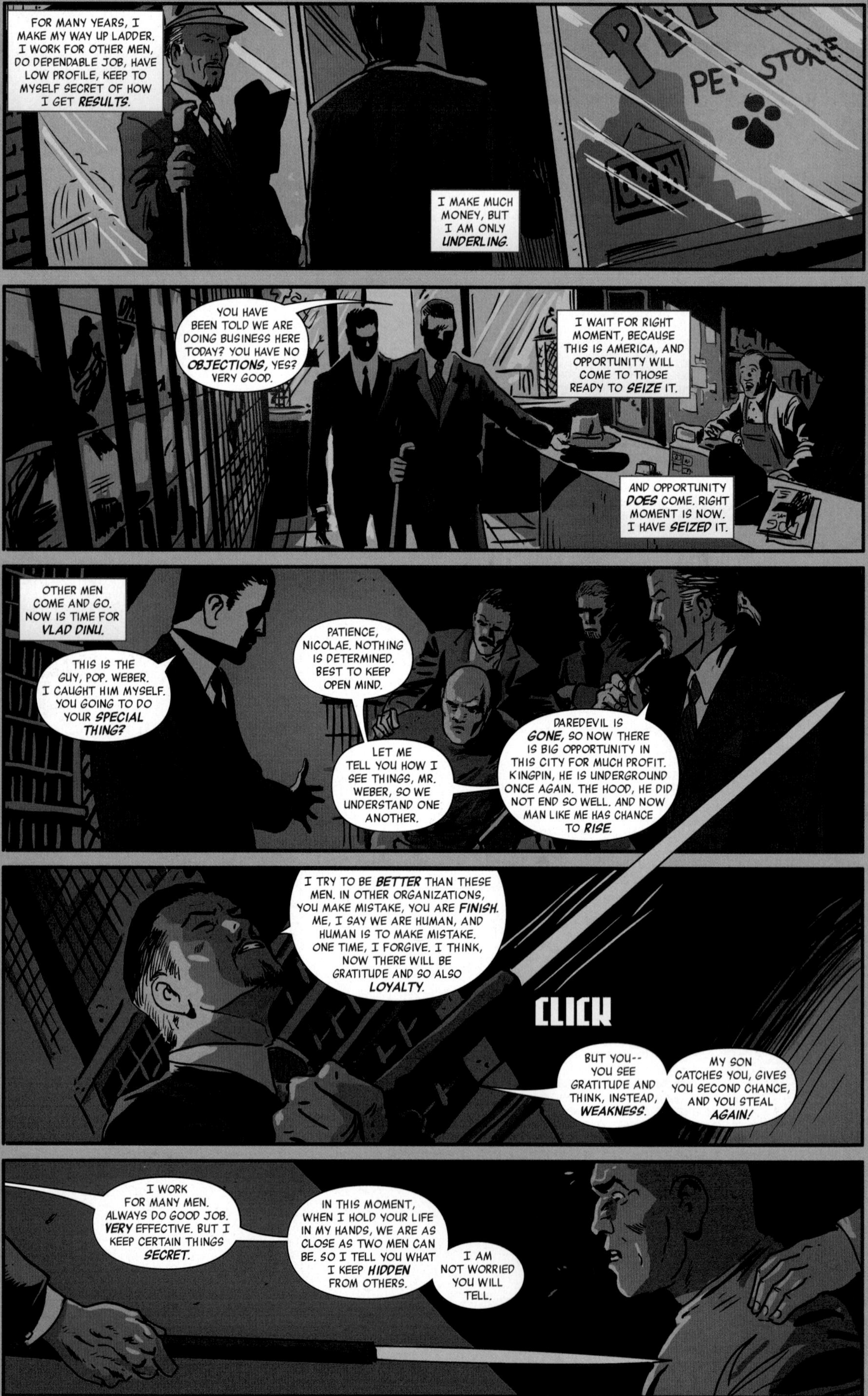
FOR MANY YEARS, I MAKE MY WAY UP LADDER. I WORK FOR OTHER MEN, DO DEPENDABLE JOB, HAVE LOW PROFILE, KEEP TO MYSELF SECRET OF HOW I GET RESULTS.
PET STORE
I MAKE MUCH MONEY, BUT I AM ONLY UNDERLING.
YOU HAVE BEEN TOLD WE ARE DOING BUSINESS HERE TODAY? YOU HAVE NO OBJECTIONS, YES? VERY GOOD.
I WAIT FOR RIGHT MOMENT, BECAUSE THIS IS AMERICA, AND OPPORTUNITY WILL COME TO THOSE READY TO SEIZE IT.
AND OPPORTUNITY DOES COME. RIGHT MOMENT IS NOW. I HAVE SEIZED IT.
OTHER MEN COME AND GO. NOW IS TIME FOR VLAD DINU.
THIS IS THE GUY, POP. WEBER. I CAUGHT HIM MYSELF. YOU GOING TO DO YOUR SPECIAL THING?
PATIENCE, NICOLAE. NOTHING IS DETERMINED. BEST TO KEEP OPEN MIND.
LET ME TELL YOU HOW I SEE THINGS, MR. WEBER, SO WE UNDERSTAND ONE ANOTHER.
DAREDEVIL IS GONE, SO NOW THERE IS BIG OPPORTUNITY IN THIS CITY FOR MUCH PROFIT. KINGPIN, HE IS UNDERGROUND ONCE AGAIN. THE HOOD, HE DID NOT END SO WELL. AND NOW MAN LIKE ME HAS CHANCE TO RISE.
I TRY TO BE BETTER THAN THESE MEN. IN OTHER ORGANIZATIONS, YOU MAKE MISTAKE, YOU ARE FINISH. ME, I SAY WE ARE HUMAN, AND HUMAN IS TO MAKE MISTAKE. ONE TIME, I FORGIVE. I THINK, NOW THERE WILL BE GRATITUDE AND SO ALSO LOYALTY.
CLICK
MY SON CATCHES YOU, GIVES YOU SECOND CHANCE, AND YOU STEAL AGAIN!
BUT YOU-- YOU SEE GRATITUDE AND THINK, INSTEAD, WEAKNESS.
I WORK FOR MANY MEN. ALWAYS DO GOOD JOB. VERY EFFECTIVE. BUT I KEEP CERTAIN THINGS SECRET.
IN THIS MOMENT, WHEN I HOLD YOUR LIFE IN MY HANDS, WE ARE AS CLOSE AS TWO MEN CAN BE. SO I TELL YOU WHAT I KEEP HIDDEN FROM OTHERS.
I AM NOT WORRIED YOU WILL TELL.

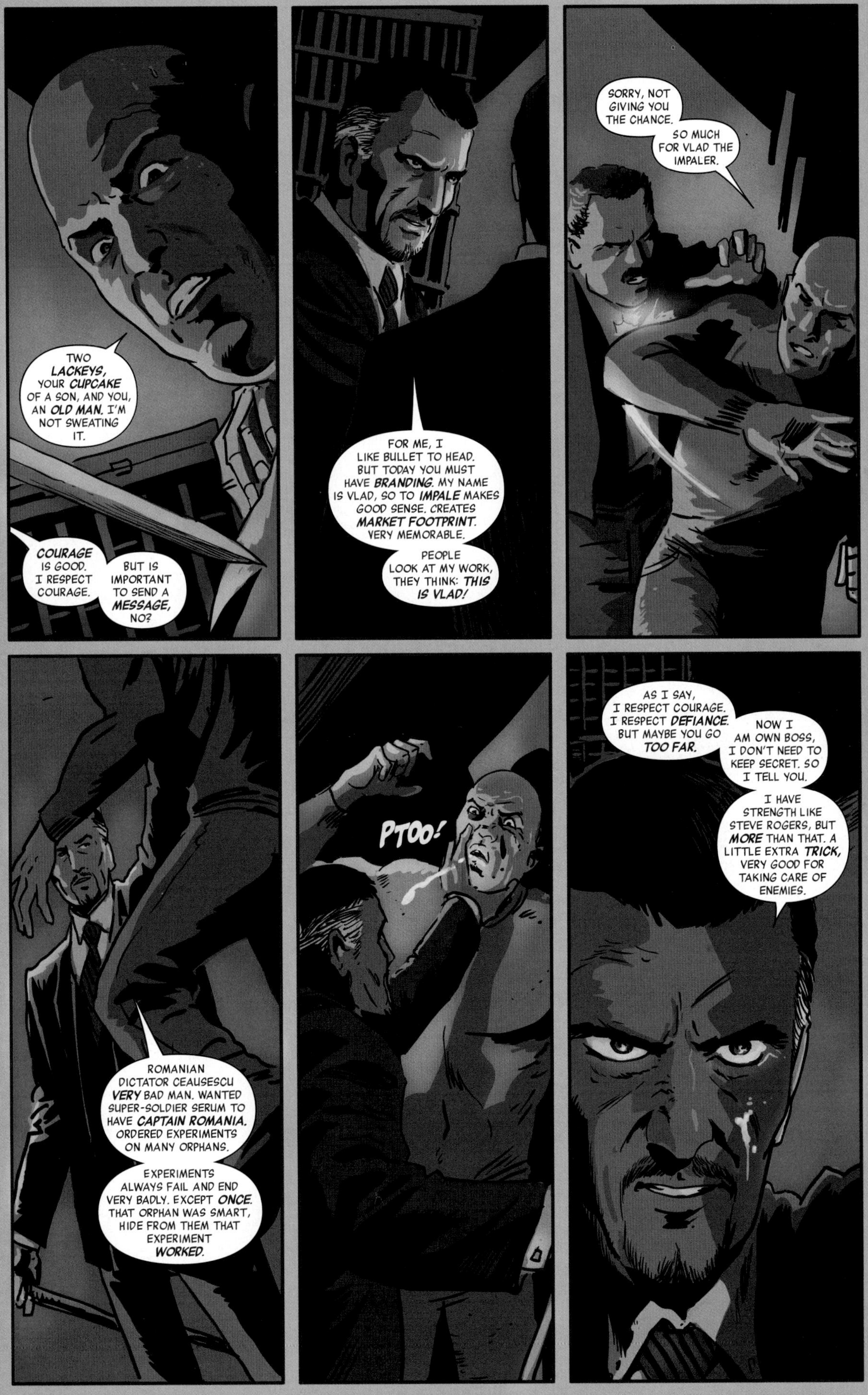
TWO LACKEYS, YOUR CUPCAKE OF A SON, AND YOU, AN OLD MAN. I'M NOT SWEATING IT.
COURAGE IS GOOD. I RESPECT COURAGE.
BUT IS IMPORTANT TO SEND A MESSAGE, NO?
FOR ME, I LIKE BULLET TO HEAD. BUT TODAY YOU MUST HAVE BRANDING. MY NAME IS VLAD, SO TO IMPALE MAKES GOOD SENSE. CREATES MARKET FOOTPRINT. VERY MEMORABLE.
PEOPLE LOOK AT MY WORK, THEY THINK: THIS IS VLAD!
SORRY, NOT GIVING YOU THE CHANCE.
SO MUCH FOR VLAD THE IMPALER.
ROMANIAN DICTATOR CEAUSESCU VERY BAD MAN. WANTED SUPER-SOLDIER SERUM TO HAVE CAPTAIN ROMANIA. ORDERED EXPERIMENTS ON MANY ORPHANS.
EXPERIMENTS ALWAYS FAIL AND END VERY BADLY. EXCEPT ONCE. THAT ORPHAN WAS SMART, HIDE FROM THEM THAT EXPERIMENT WORKED.
PTOO!
AS I SAY, I RESPECT COURAGE. I RESPECT DEFIANCE. BUT MAYBE YOU GO TOO FAR.
NOW I AM OWN BOSS, I DON'T NEED TO KEEP SECRET. SO I TELL YOU.
I HAVE STRENGTH LIKE STEVE ROGERS, BUT MORE THAN THAT. A LITTLE EXTRA TRICK, VERY GOOD FOR TAKING CARE OF ENEMIES.

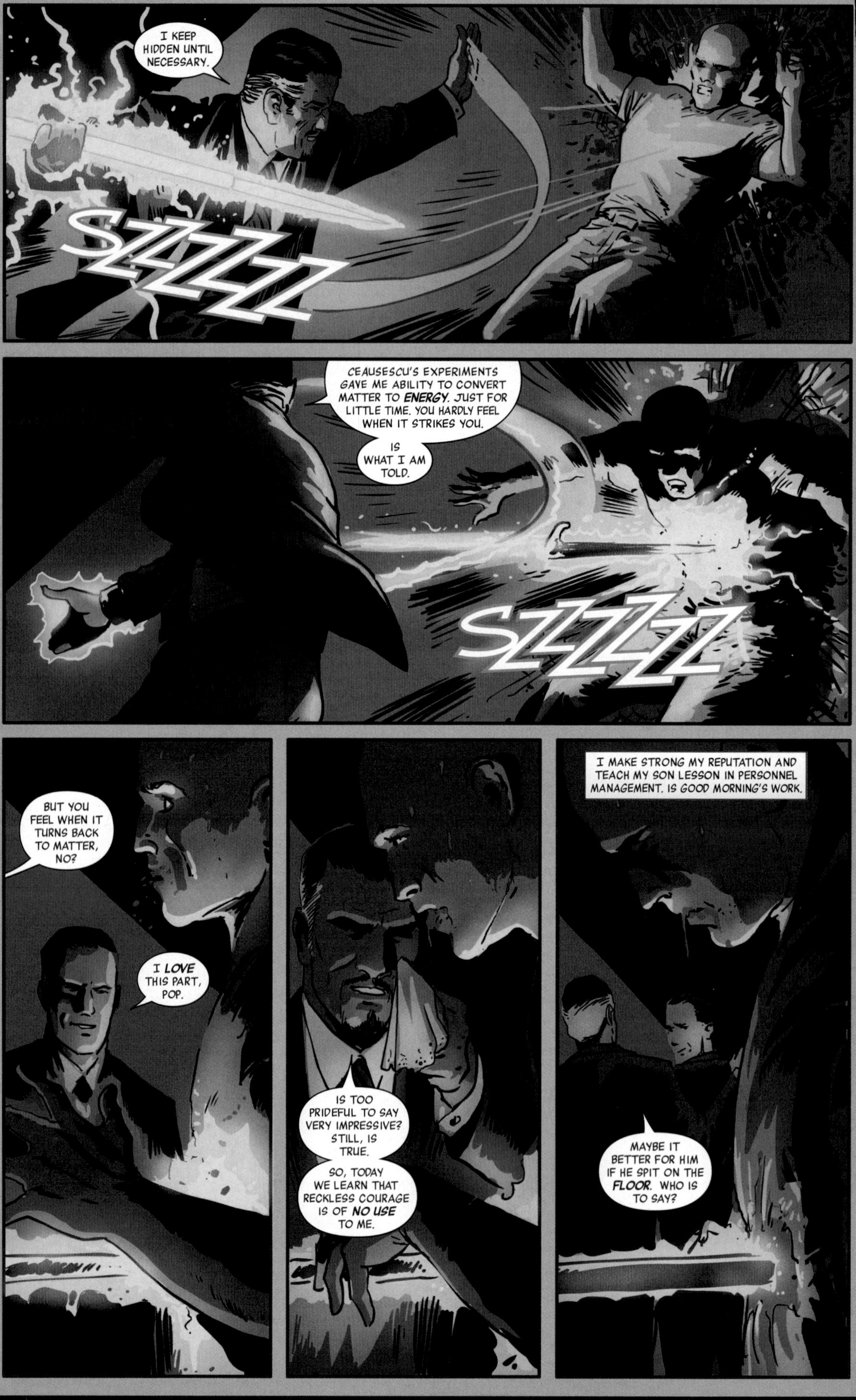
I KEEP HIDDEN UNTIL NECESSARY.
SZZZZZ
CEAUSESCU'S EXPERIMENTS GAVE ME ABILITY TO CONVERT MATTER TO ***ENERGY***. JUST FOR LITTLE TIME. YOU HARDLY FEEL WHEN IT STRIKES YOU.
IS WHAT I AM TOLD.
SZZZZZ
BUT YOU FEEL WHEN IT TURNS BACK TO MATTER, NO?
I ***LOVE*** THIS PART, POP.
IS TOO PRIDEFUL TO SAY VERY IMPRESSIVE? STILL, IS TRUE.
SO, TODAY WE LEARN THAT RECKLESS COURAGE IS OF ***NO USE*** TO ME.
I MAKE STRONG MY REPUTATION AND TEACH MY SON LESSON IN PERSONNEL MANAGEMENT. IS GOOD MORNING'S WORK.
MAYBE IT BETTER FOR HIM IF HE SPIT ON THE ***FLOOR***. WHO IS TO SAY?

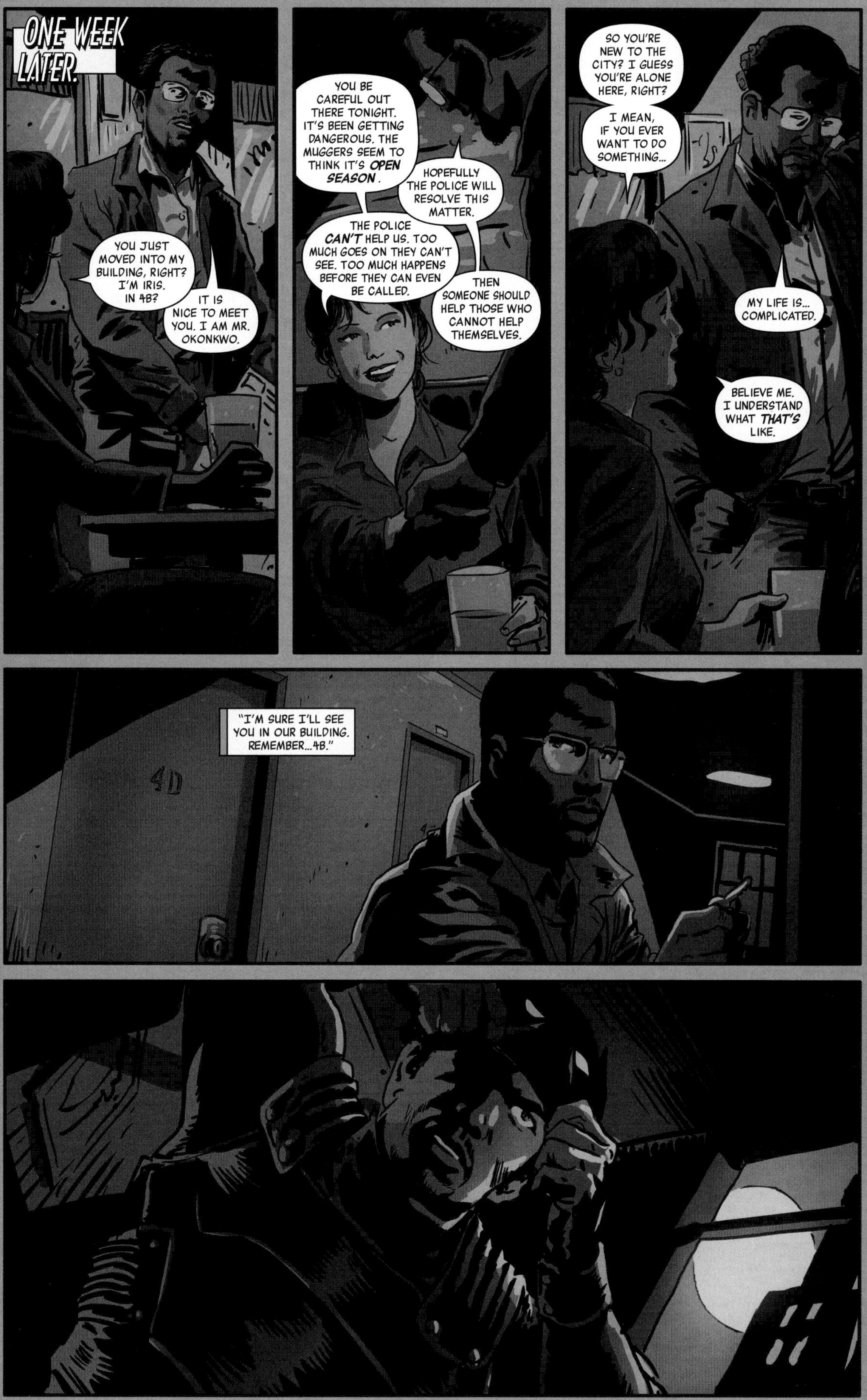
ONE WEEK LATER.
YOU JUST MOVED INTO MY BUILDING, RIGHT? I'M IRIS. IN 4B?
IT IS NICE TO MEET YOU. I AM MR. OKONKWO.
YOU BE CAREFUL OUT THERE TONIGHT. IT'S BEEN GETTING DANGEROUS. THE MUGGERS SEEM TO THINK IT'S OPEN SEASON.
HOPEFULLY THE POLICE WILL RESOLVE THIS MATTER.
THE POLICE CAN'T HELP US. TOO MUCH GOES ON THEY CAN'T SEE. TOO MUCH HAPPENS BEFORE THEY CAN EVEN BE CALLED.
THEN SOMEONE SHOULD HELP THOSE WHO CANNOT HELP THEMSELVES.
SO YOU'RE NEW TO THE CITY? I GUESS YOU'RE ALONE HERE, RIGHT?
I MEAN, IF YOU EVER WANT TO DO SOMETHING...
MY LIFE IS... COMPLICATED.
BELIEVE ME. I UNDERSTAND WHAT THAT'S LIKE.
"I'M SURE I'LL SEE YOU IN OUR BUILDING. REMEMBER...4B."
4D

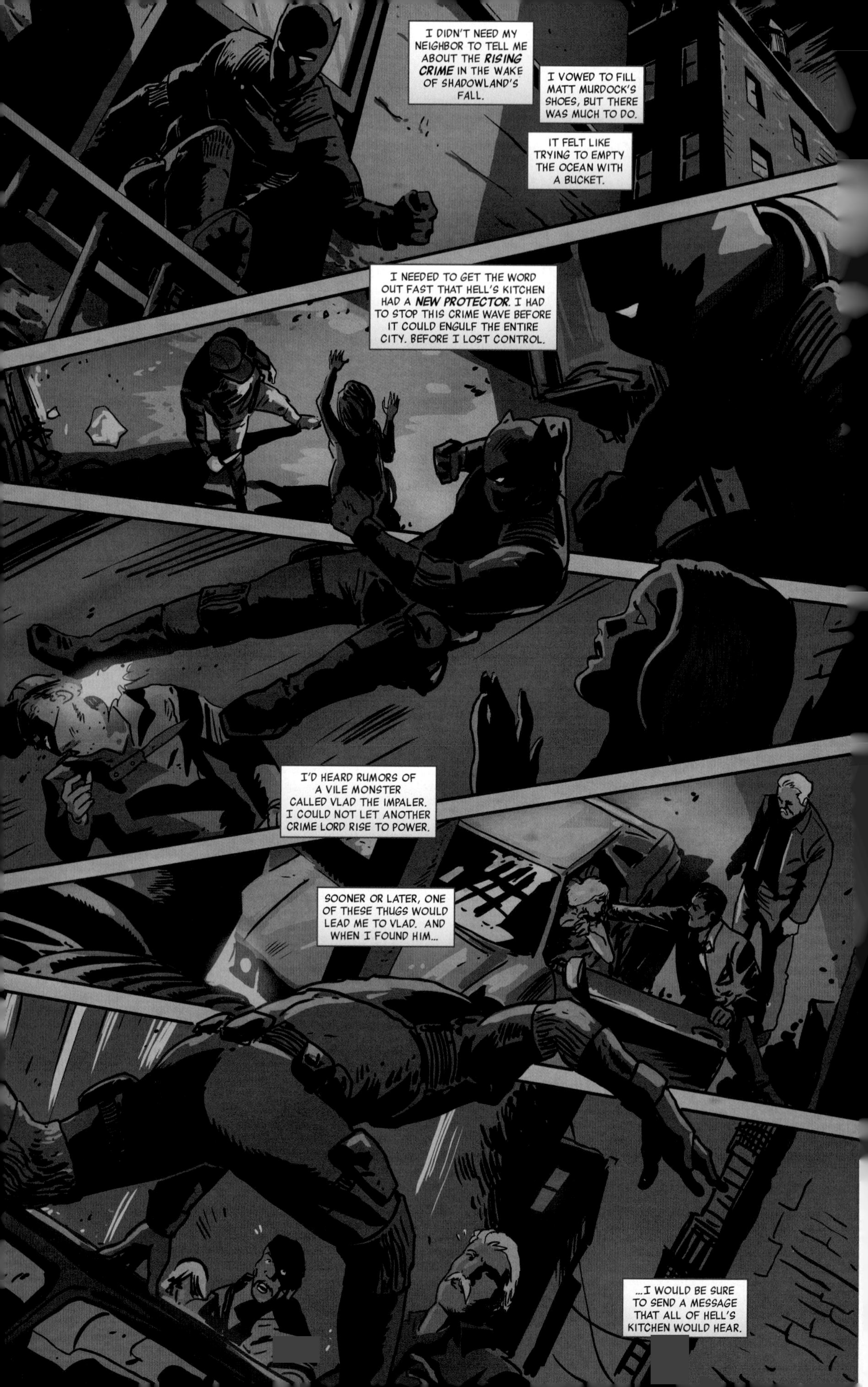
I DIDN'T NEED MY NEIGHBOR TO TELL ME ABOUT THE ***RISING CRIME*** IN THE WAKE OF SHADOWLAND'S FALL.
I VOWED TO FILL MATT MURDOCK'S SHOES, BUT THERE WAS MUCH TO DO.
IT FELT LIKE TRYING TO EMPTY THE OCEAN WITH A BUCKET.
I NEEDED TO GET THE WORD OUT FAST THAT HELL'S KITCHEN HAD A ***NEW PROTECTOR***. I HAD TO STOP THIS CRIME WAVE BEFORE IT COULD ENGULF THE ENTIRE CITY. BEFORE I LOST CONTROL.
I'D HEARD RUMORS OF A VILE MONSTER CALLED VLAD THE IMPALER. I COULD NOT LET ANOTHER CRIME LORD RISE TO POWER.
SOONER OR LATER, ONE OF THESE THUGS WOULD LEAD ME TO VLAD. AND WHEN I FOUND HIM...
...I WOULD BE SURE TO SEND A MESSAGE THAT ALL OF HELL'S KITCHEN WOULD HEAR.

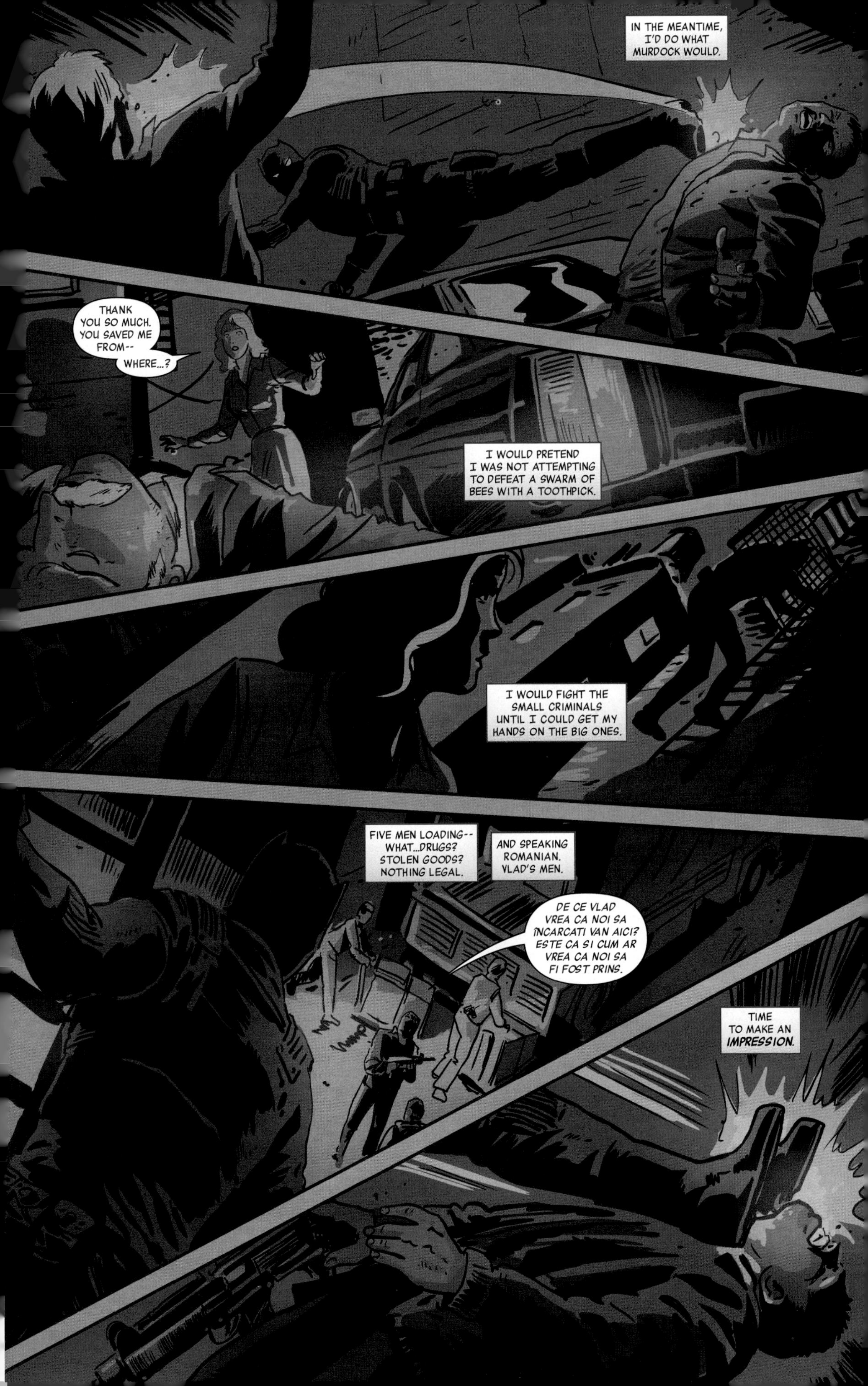
IN THE MEANTIME, I'D DO WHAT MURDOCK WOULD.
THANK YOU SO MUCH. YOU SAVED ME FROM--
WHERE...?
I WOULD PRETEND I WAS NOT ATTEMPTING TO DEFEAT A SWARM OF BEES WITH A TOOTHPICK.
I WOULD FIGHT THE SMALL CRIMINALS UNTIL I COULD GET MY HANDS ON THE BIG ONES.
FIVE MEN LOADING-- WHAT...DRUGS? STOLEN GOODS? NOTHING LEGAL.
AND SPEAKING ROMANIAN. VLAD'S MEN.
DE CE VLAD VREA CA NOI SA ÎNCARCATI VAN AICI? ESTE CA SI CUM AR VREA CA NOI SA FI FOST PRINS.
TIME TO MAKE AN *IMPRESSION*.

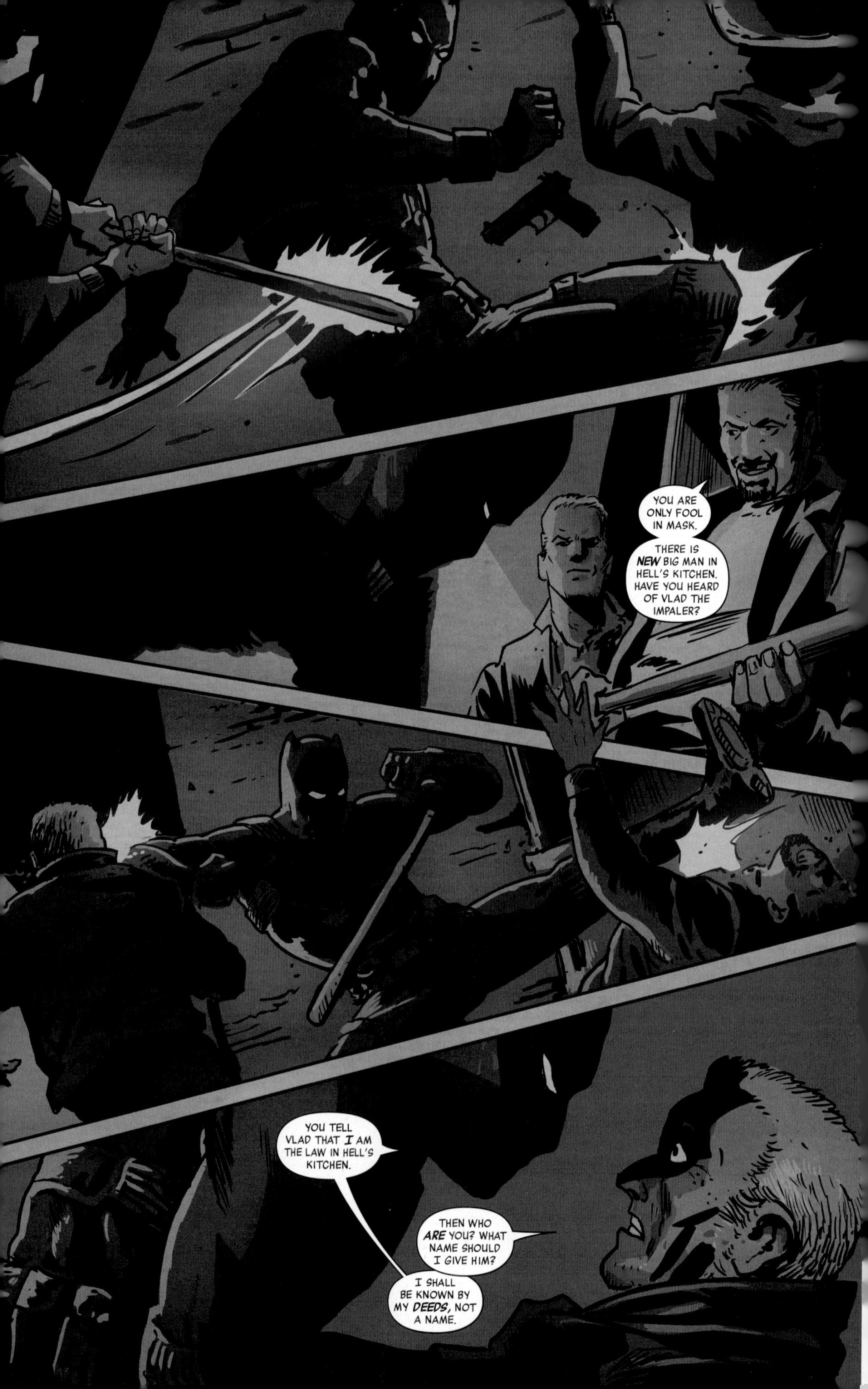
YOU ARE ONLY FOOL IN MASK.
THERE IS NEW BIG MAN IN HELL'S KITCHEN. HAVE YOU HEARD OF VLAD THE IMPALER?
YOU TELL VLAD THAT I AM THE LAW IN HELL'S KITCHEN.
THEN WHO ARE YOU? WHAT NAME SHOULD I GIVE HIM?
I SHALL BE KNOWN BY MY DEEDS, NOT A NAME.

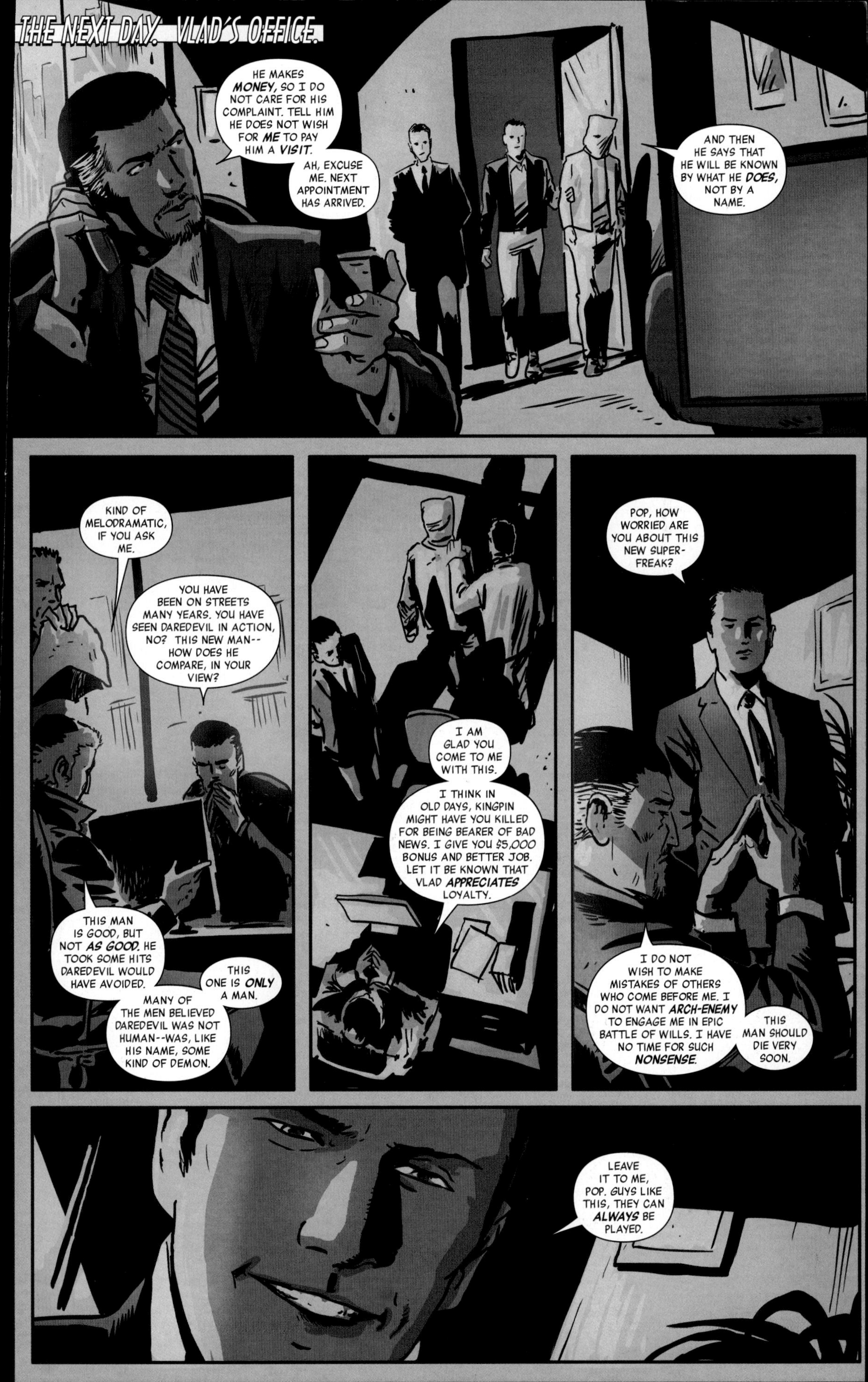
THE NEXT DAY. VLAD'S OFFICE.
HE MAKES MONEY, SO I DO NOT CARE FOR HIS COMPLAINT. TELL HIM HE DOES NOT WISH FOR ME TO PAY HIM A VISIT.
AH, EXCUSE ME. NEXT APPOINTMENT HAS ARRIVED.
AND THEN HE SAYS THAT HE WILL BE KNOWN BY WHAT HE DOES, NOT BY A NAME.
KIND OF MELODRAMATIC, IF YOU ASK ME.
YOU HAVE BEEN ON STREETS MANY YEARS. YOU HAVE SEEN DAREDEVIL IN ACTION, NO? THIS NEW MAN--HOW DOES HE COMPARE, IN YOUR VIEW?
THIS MAN IS GOOD, BUT NOT AS GOOD. HE TOOK SOME HITS DAREDEVIL WOULD HAVE AVOIDED.
THIS ONE IS ONLY A MAN.
MANY OF THE MEN BELIEVED DAREDEVIL WAS NOT HUMAN--WAS, LIKE HIS NAME, SOME KIND OF DEMON.
I AM GLAD YOU COME TO ME WITH THIS.
I THINK IN OLD DAYS, KINGPIN MIGHT HAVE YOU KILLED FOR BEING BEARER OF BAD NEWS. I GIVE YOU $5,000 BONUS AND BETTER JOB. LET IT BE KNOWN THAT VLAD APPRECIATES LOYALTY.
POP, HOW WORRIED ARE YOU ABOUT THIS NEW SUPER-FREAK?
I DO NOT WISH TO MAKE MISTAKES OF OTHERS WHO COME BEFORE ME. I DO NOT WANT ARCH-ENEMY TO ENGAGE ME IN EPIC BATTLE OF WILLS. I HAVE NO TIME FOR SUCH NONSENSE.
THIS MAN SHOULD DIE VERY SOON.
LEAVE IT TO ME, POP. GUYS LIKE THIS, THEY CAN ALWAYS BE PLAYED.

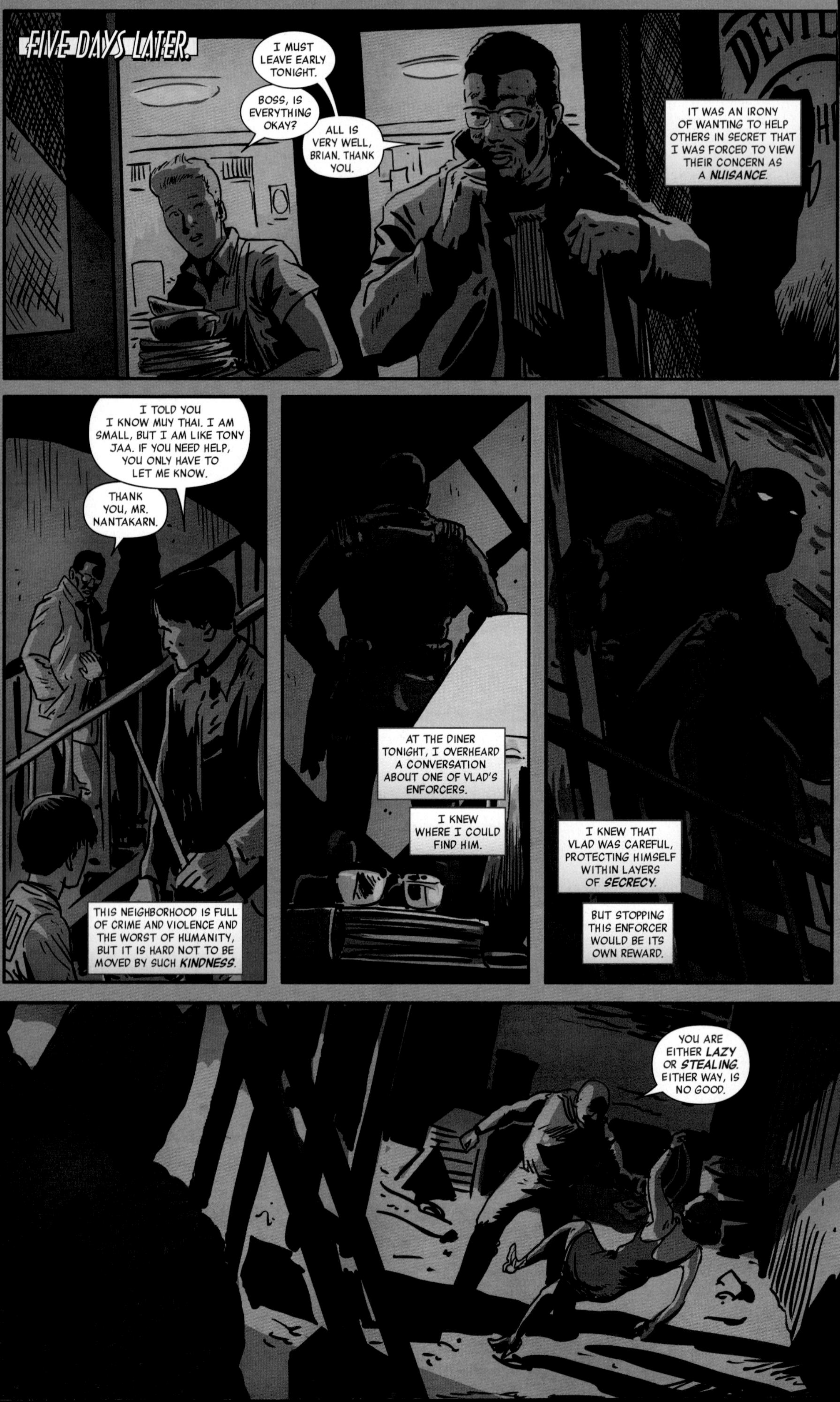
FIVE DAYS LATER.
I MUST LEAVE EARLY TONIGHT.
BOSS, IS EVERYTHING OKAY?
ALL IS VERY WELL, BRIAN. THANK YOU.
IT WAS AN IRONY OF WANTING TO HELP OTHERS IN SECRET THAT I WAS FORCED TO VIEW THEIR CONCERN AS A NUISANCE.
I TOLD YOU I KNOW MUY THAI. I AM SMALL, BUT I AM LIKE TONY JAA. IF YOU NEED HELP, YOU ONLY HAVE TO LET ME KNOW.
THANK YOU, MR. NANTAKARN.
THIS NEIGHBORHOOD IS FULL OF CRIME AND VIOLENCE AND THE WORST OF HUMANITY, BUT IT IS HARD NOT TO BE MOVED BY SUCH KINDNESS.
AT THE DINER TONIGHT, I OVERHEARD A CONVERSATION ABOUT ONE OF VLAD'S ENFORCERS.
I KNEW WHERE I COULD FIND HIM.
I KNEW THAT VLAD WAS CAREFUL, PROTECTING HIMSELF WITHIN LAYERS OF SECRECY.
BUT STOPPING THIS ENFORCER WOULD BE ITS OWN REWARD.
YOU ARE EITHER LAZY OR STEALING. EITHER WAY, IS NO GOOD.

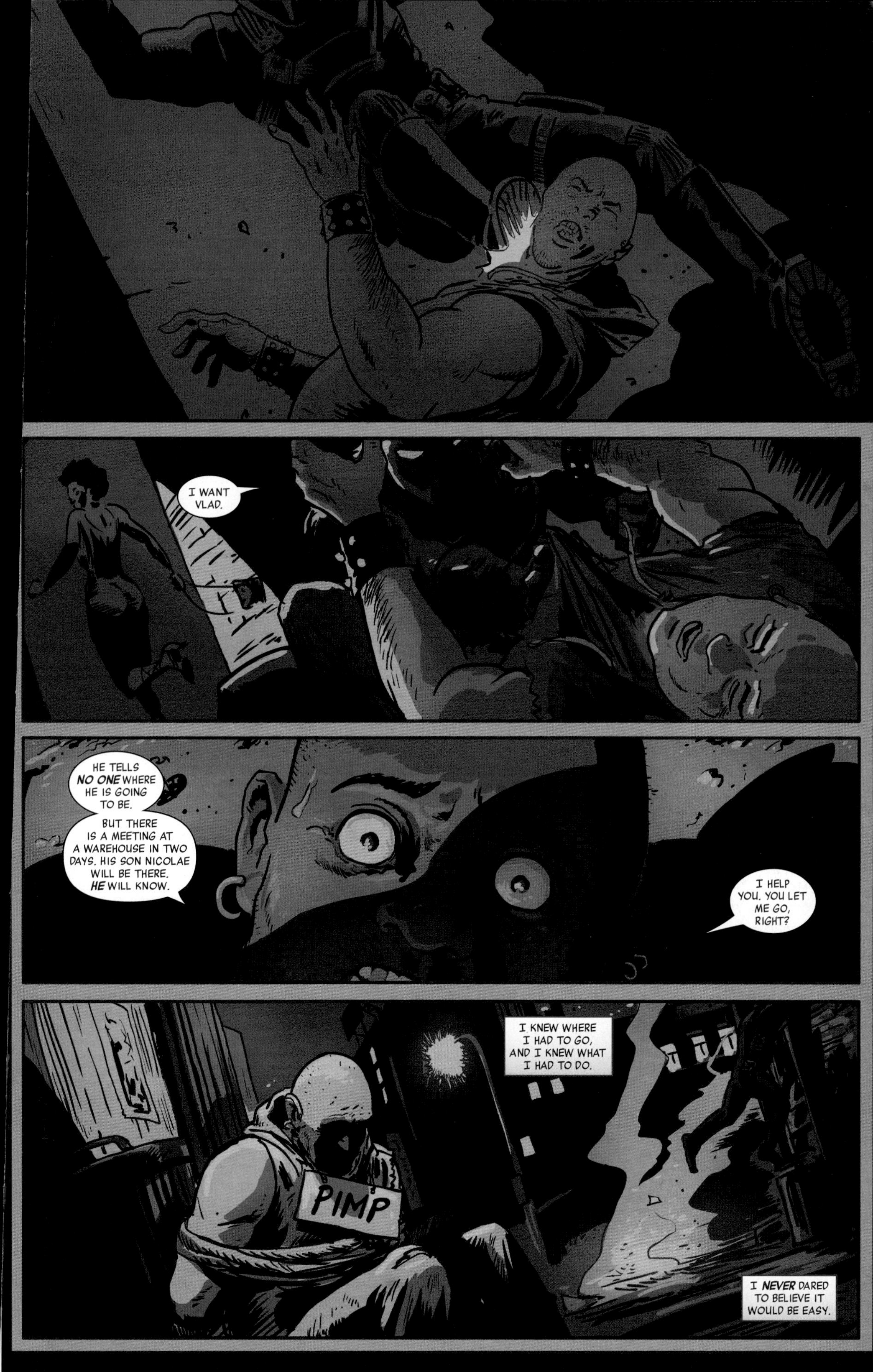
I WANT VLAD.
HE TELLS *NO ONE* WHERE HE IS GOING TO BE.
BUT THERE IS A MEETING AT A WAREHOUSE IN TWO DAYS. HIS SON NICOLAE WILL BE THERE. *HE* WILL KNOW.
I HELP YOU. YOU LET ME GO, RIGHT?
I KNEW WHERE I HAD TO GO, AND I KNEW WHAT I HAD TO DO.
PIMP
I *NEVER* DARED TO BELIEVE IT WOULD BE EASY.

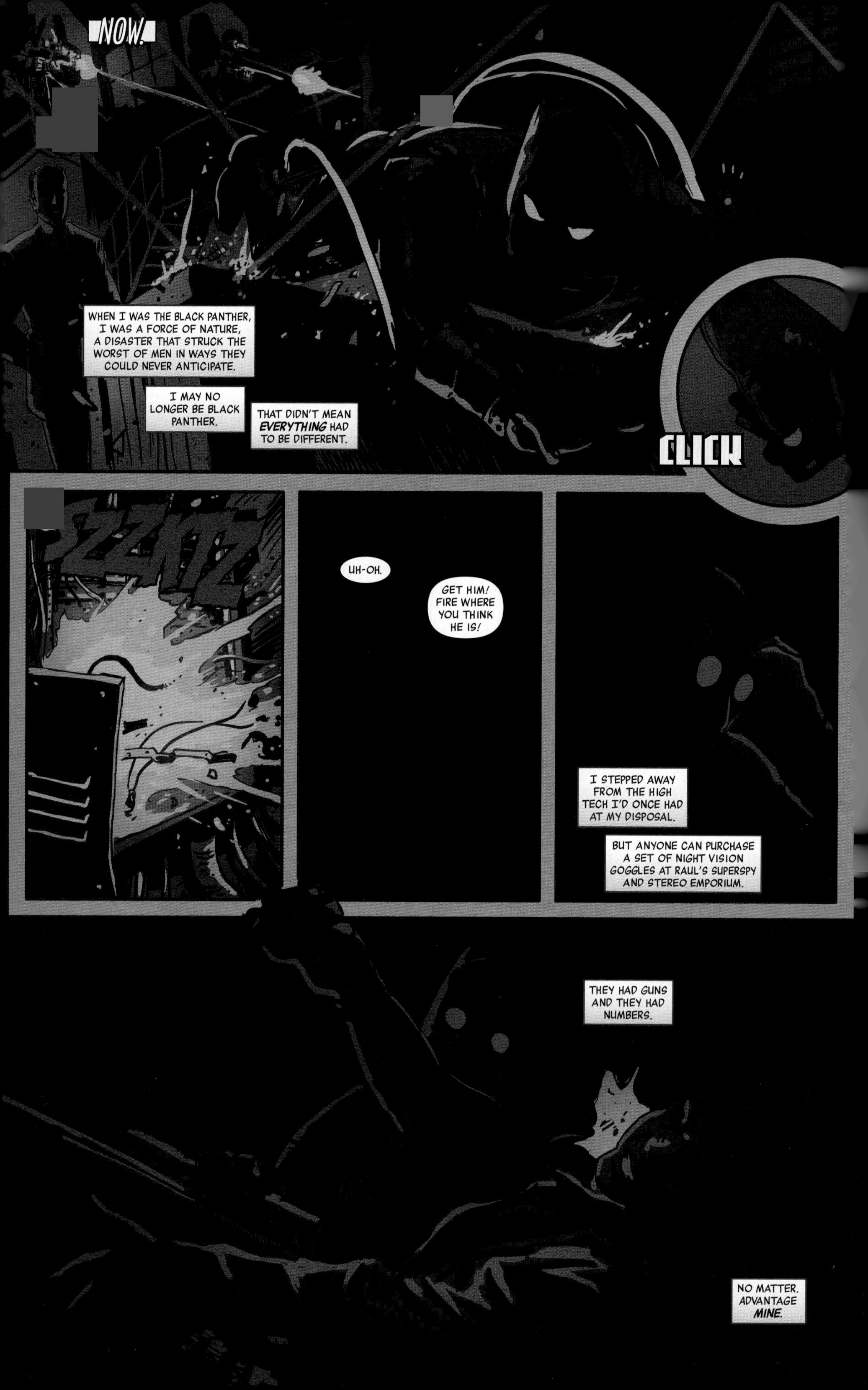
NOW!
WHEN I WAS THE BLACK PANTHER, I WAS A FORCE OF NATURE, A DISASTER THAT STRUCK THE WORST OF MEN IN WAYS THEY COULD NEVER ANTICIPATE.
I MAY NO LONGER BE BLACK PANTHER.
THAT DIDN'T MEAN *EVERYTHING* HAD TO BE DIFFERENT.
CLICK
UH-OH.
GET HIM! FIRE WHERE YOU THINK HE IS!
I STEPPED AWAY FROM THE HIGH TECH I'D ONCE HAD AT MY DISPOSAL.
BUT ANYONE CAN PURCHASE A SET OF NIGHT VISION GOGGLES AT RAUL'S SUPERSPY AND STEREO EMPORIUM.
THEY HAD GUNS AND THEY HAD NUMBERS.
NO MATTER. ADVANTAGE *MINE*.

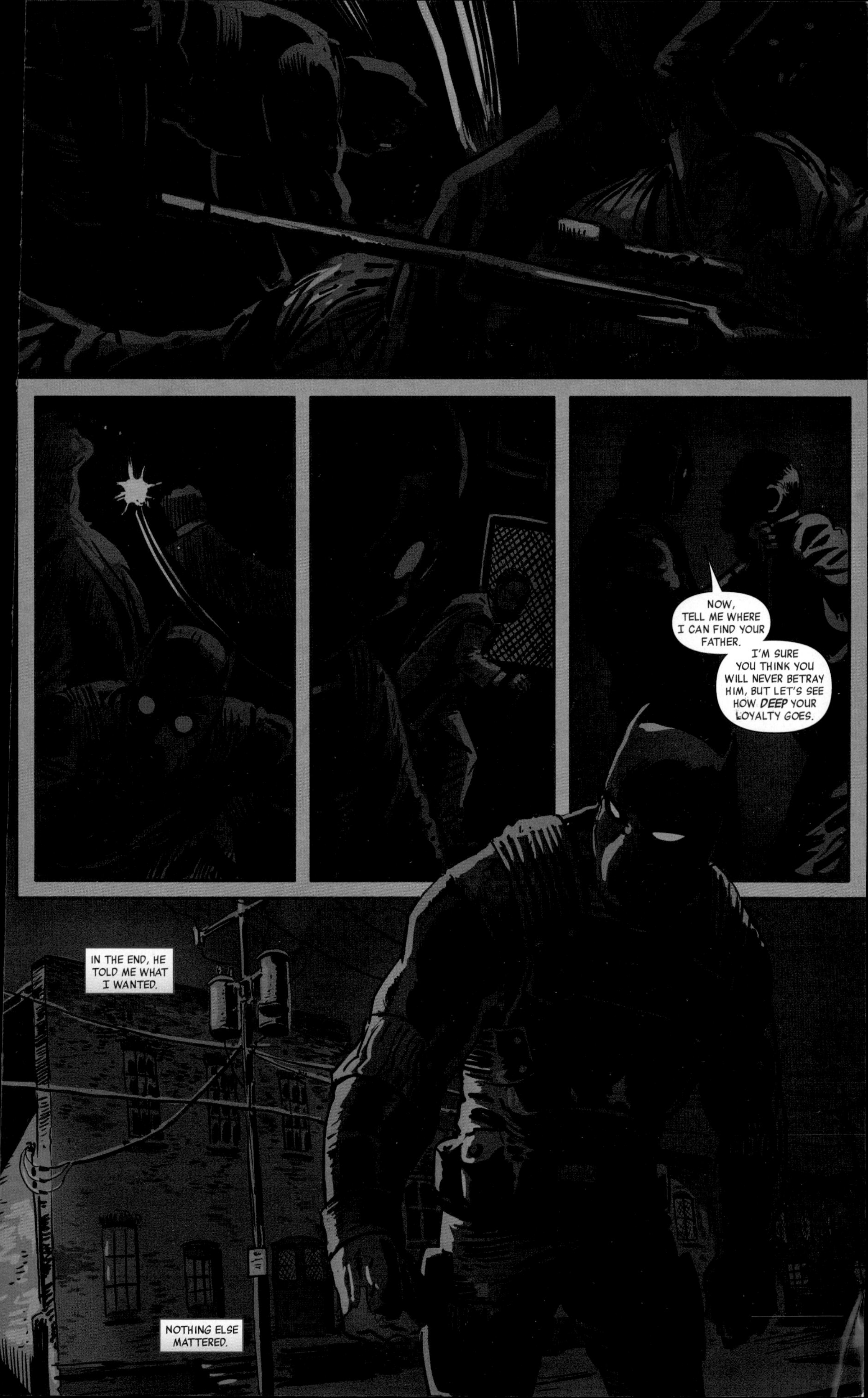
NOW, TELL ME WHERE I CAN FIND YOUR FATHER.
I'M SURE YOU THINK YOU WILL NEVER BETRAY HIM, BUT LET'S SEE HOW DEEP YOUR LOYALTY GOES.
IN THE END, HE TOLD ME WHAT I WANTED.
NOTHING ELSE MATTERED.

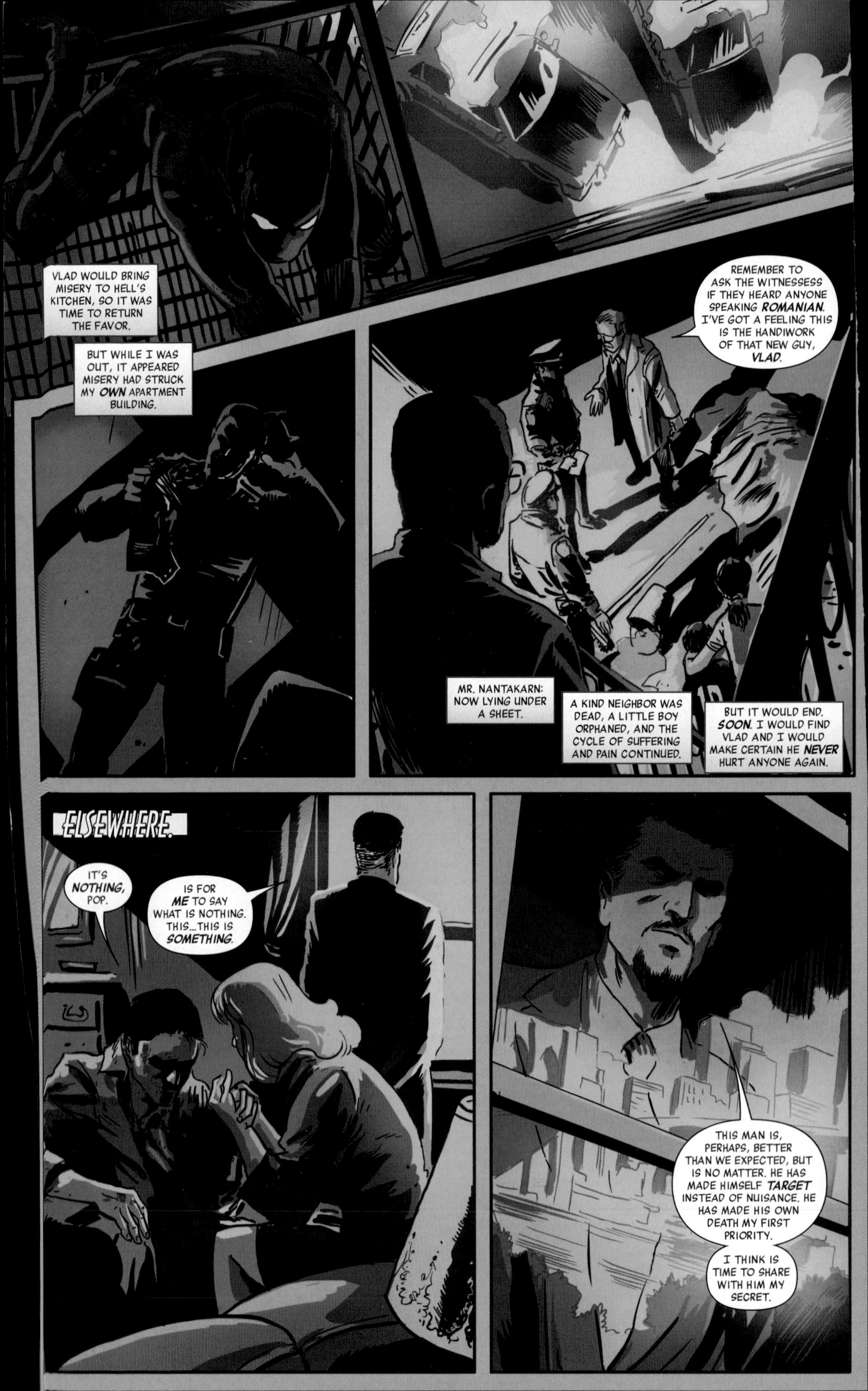
VLAD WOULD BRING MISERY TO HELL'S KITCHEN, SO IT WAS TIME TO RETURN THE FAVOR.
BUT WHILE I WAS OUT, IT APPEARED MISERY HAD STRUCK MY OWN APARTMENT BUILDING.
REMEMBER TO ASK THE WITNESSESS IF THEY HEARD ANYONE SPEAKING ROMANIAN. I'VE GOT A FEELING THIS IS THE HANDIWORK OF THAT NEW GUY, VLAD.
MR. NANTAKARN: NOW LYING UNDER A SHEET.
A KIND NEIGHBOR WAS DEAD, A LITTLE BOY ORPHANED, AND THE CYCLE OF SUFFERING AND PAIN CONTINUED.
BUT IT WOULD END. SOON. I WOULD FIND VLAD AND I WOULD MAKE CERTAIN HE NEVER HURT ANYONE AGAIN.
ELSEWHERE.
IT'S NOTHING, POP.
IS FOR ME TO SAY WHAT IS NOTHING. THIS...THIS IS SOMETHING.
THIS MAN IS, PERHAPS, BETTER THAN WE EXPECTED, BUT IS NO MATTER. HE HAS MADE HIMSELF TARGET INSTEAD OF NUISANCE. HE HAS MADE HIS OWN DEATH MY FIRST PRIORITY.
I THINK IS TIME TO SHARE WITH HIM MY SECRET.

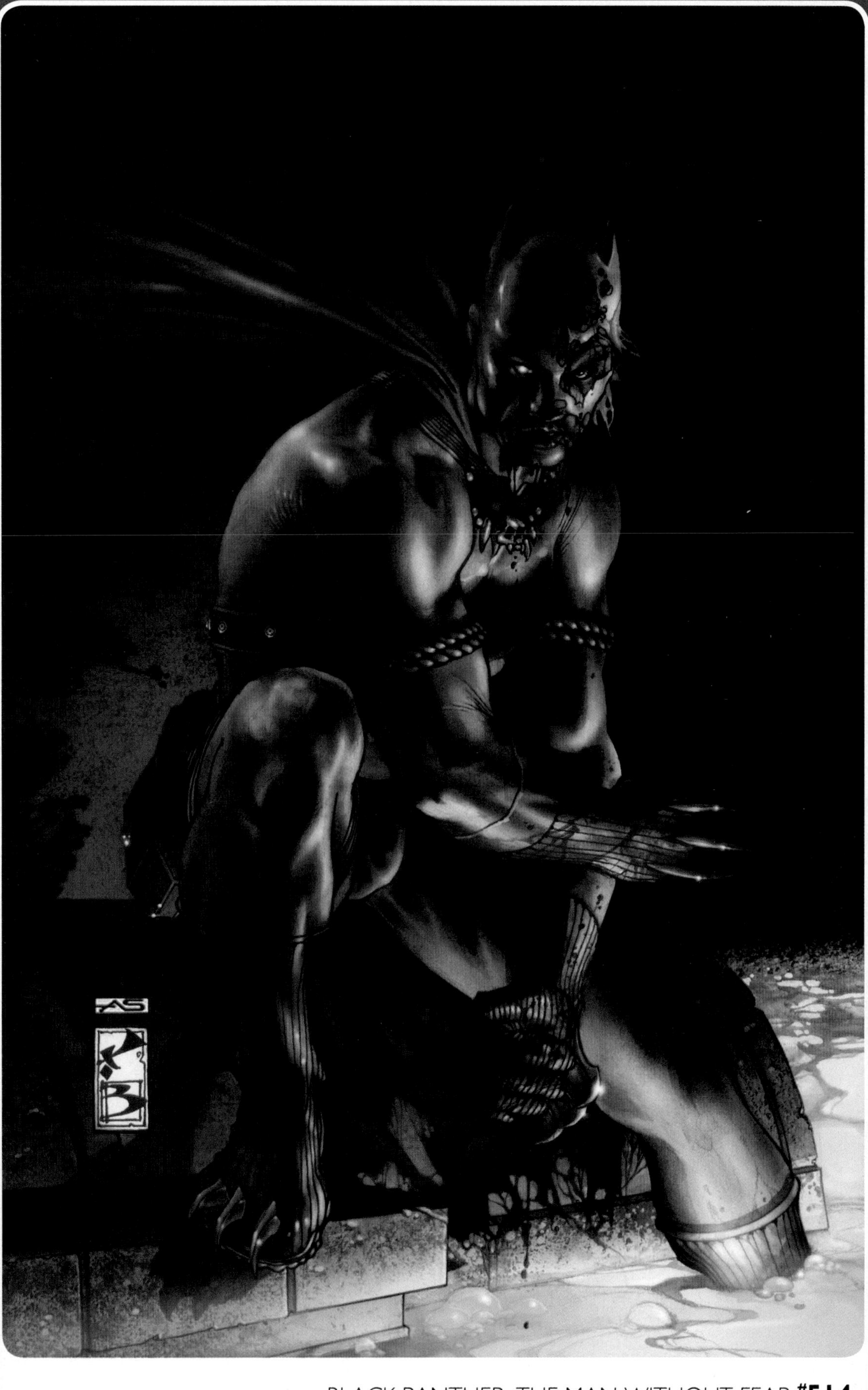

BLACK PANTHER: THE MAN WITHOUT FEAR #514

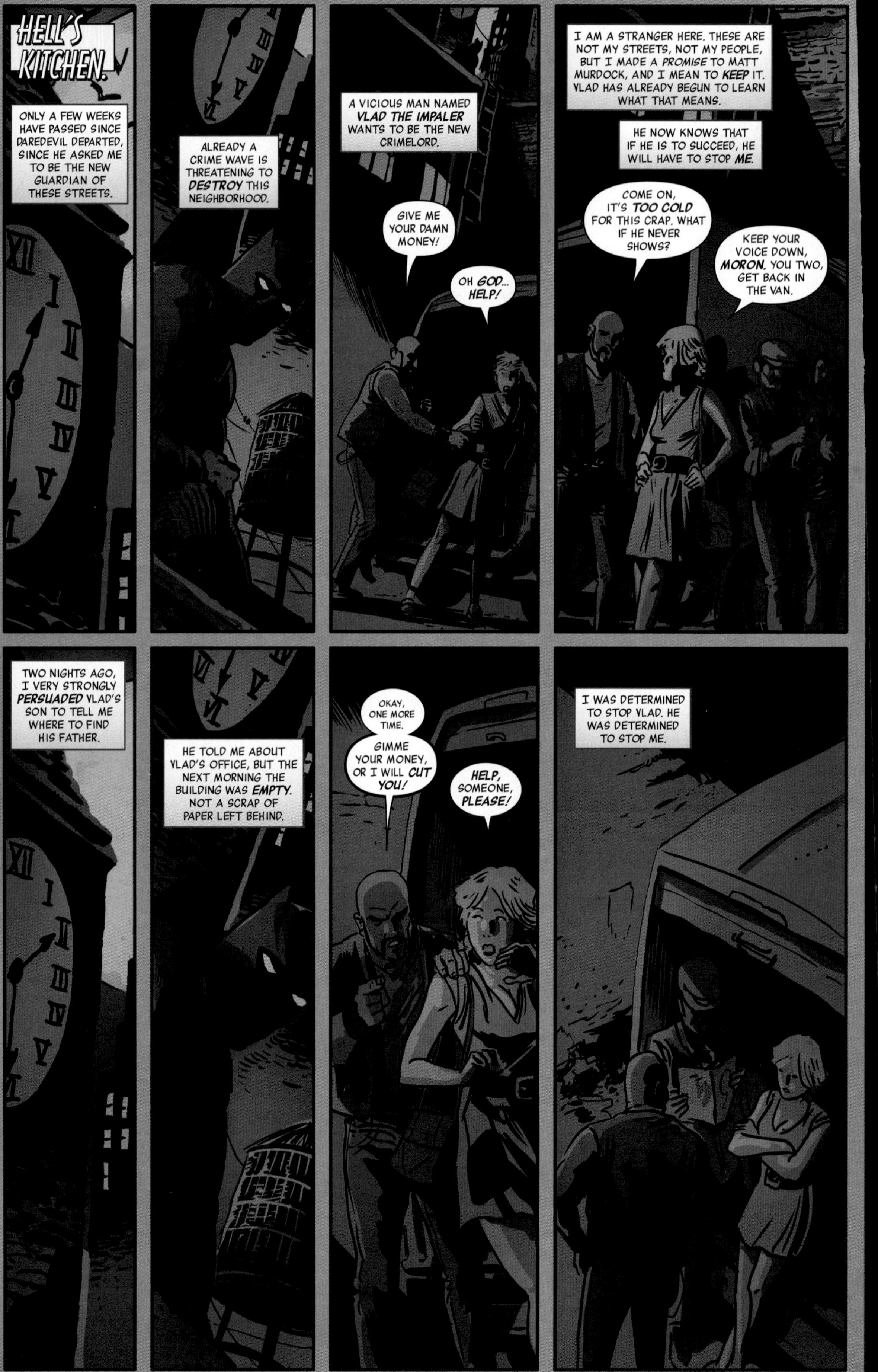

HELL'S KITCHEN.
ONLY A FEW WEEKS HAVE PASSED SINCE DAREDEVIL DEPARTED, SINCE HE ASKED ME TO BE THE NEW GUARDIAN OF THESE STREETS.
ALREADY A CRIME WAVE IS THREATENING TO DESTROY THIS NEIGHBORHOOD.
A VICIOUS MAN NAMED VLAD THE IMPALER WANTS TO BE THE NEW CRIMELORD.
GIVE ME YOUR DAMN MONEY!
OH GOD... HELP!
I AM A STRANGER HERE. THESE ARE NOT MY STREETS, NOT MY PEOPLE, BUT I MADE A PROMISE TO MATT MURDOCK, AND I MEAN TO KEEP IT. VLAD HAS ALREADY BEGUN TO LEARN WHAT THAT MEANS.
HE NOW KNOWS THAT IF HE IS TO SUCCEED, HE WILL HAVE TO STOP ME.
COME ON, IT'S TOO COLD FOR THIS CRAP. WHAT IF HE NEVER SHOWS?
KEEP YOUR VOICE DOWN, MORON. YOU TWO, GET BACK IN THE VAN.
TWO NIGHTS AGO, I VERY STRONGLY PERSUADED VLAD'S SON TO TELL ME WHERE TO FIND HIS FATHER.
HE TOLD ME ABOUT VLAD'S OFFICE, BUT THE NEXT MORNING THE BUILDING WAS EMPTY. NOT A SCRAP OF PAPER LEFT BEHIND.
OKAY, ONE MORE TIME.
GIMME YOUR MONEY, OR I WILL CUT YOU!
HELP, SOMEONE, PLEASE!
I WAS DETERMINED TO STOP VLAD. HE WAS DETERMINED TO STOP ME.

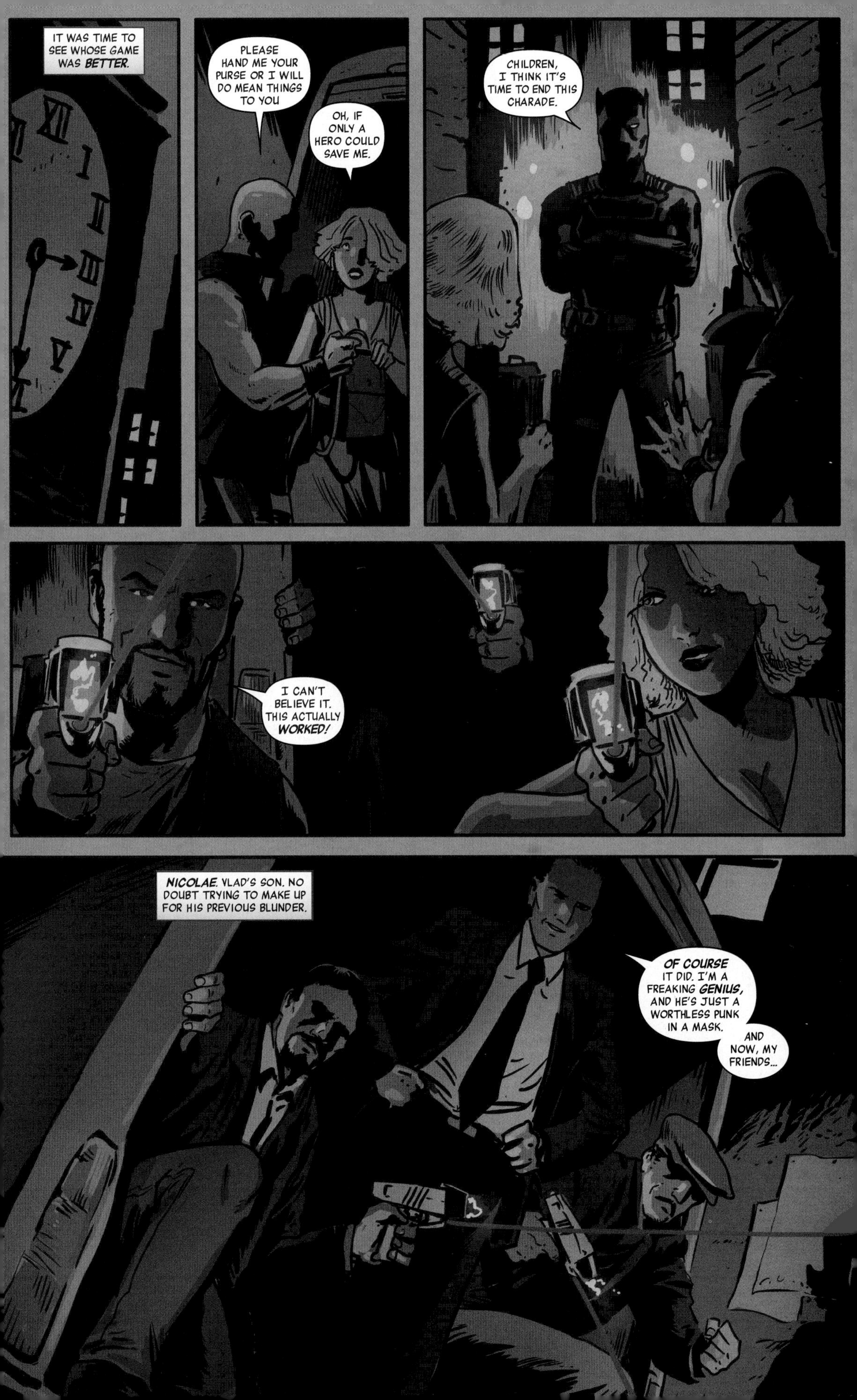
IT WAS TIME TO SEE WHOSE GAME WAS BETTER.
PLEASE HAND ME YOUR PURSE OR I WILL DO MEAN THINGS TO YOU
OH, IF ONLY A HERO COULD SAVE ME.
CHILDREN, I THINK IT'S TIME TO END THIS CHARADE.
I CAN'T BELIEVE IT. THIS ACTUALLY WORKED!
NICOLAE. VLAD'S SON. NO DOUBT TRYING TO MAKE UP FOR HIS PREVIOUS BLUNDER.
OF COURSE IT DID. I'M A FREAKING GENIUS, AND HE'S JUST A WORTHLESS PUNK IN A MASK.
AND NOW, MY FRIENDS...

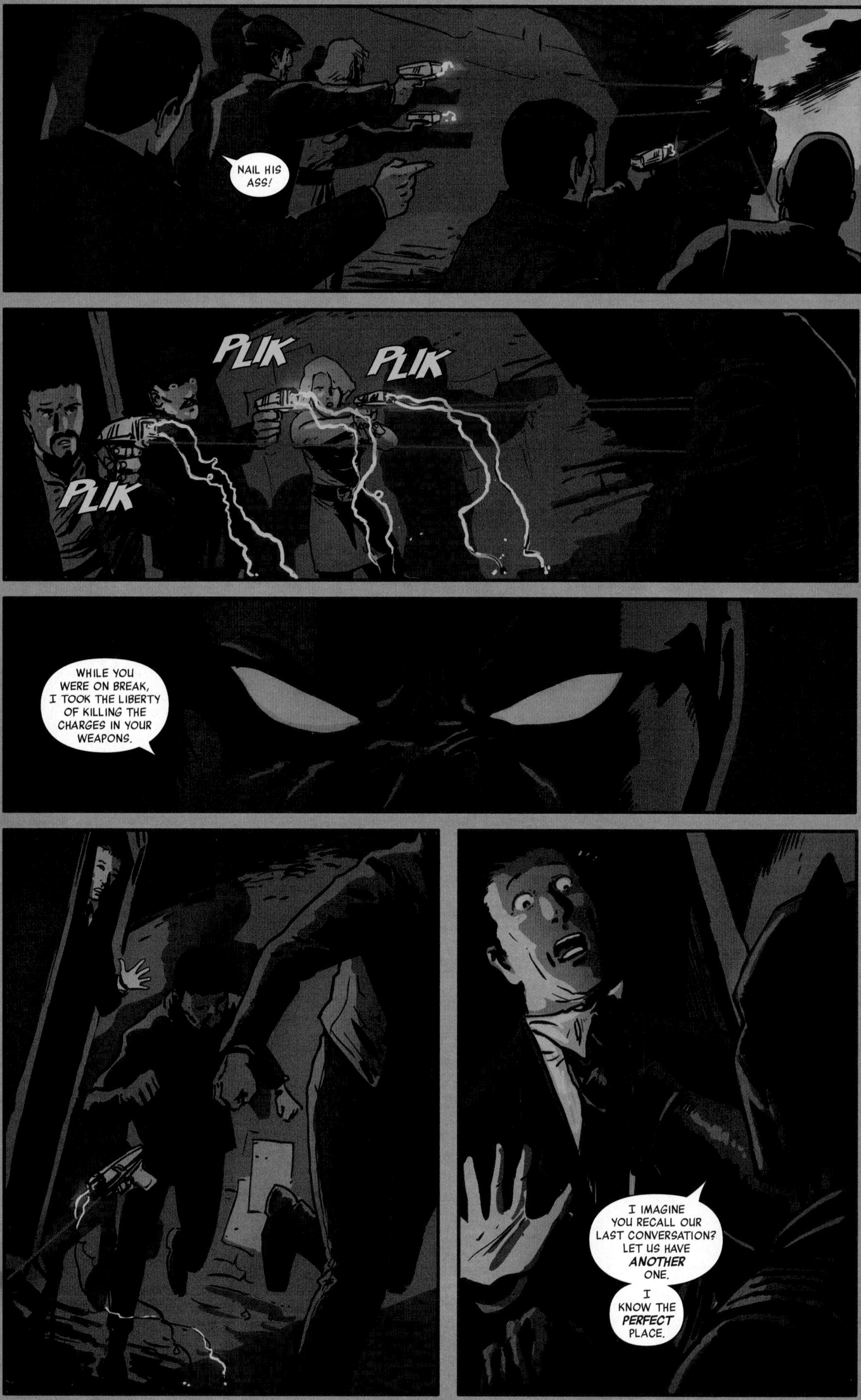
NAIL HIS ASS!
PLIK
PLIK
PLIK
WHILE YOU WERE ON BREAK, I TOOK THE LIBERTY OF KILLING THE CHARGES IN YOUR WEAPONS.
I IMAGINE YOU RECALL OUR LAST CONVERSATION? LET US HAVE ANOTHER ONE.
I KNOW THE PERFECT PLACE.

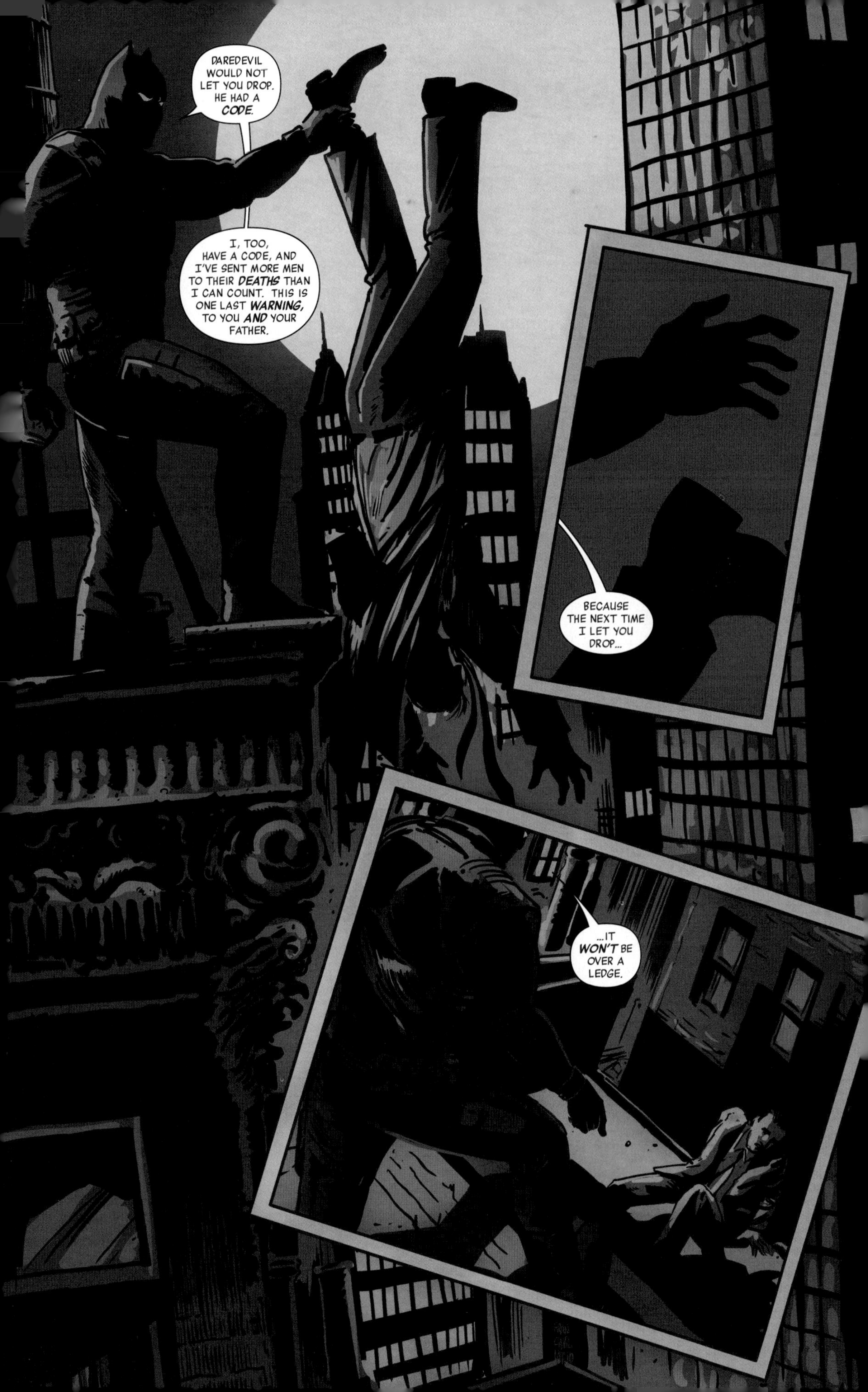
DAREDEVIL WOULD NOT LET YOU DROP. HE HAD A *CODE*.
I, TOO, HAVE A CODE, AND I'VE SENT MORE MEN TO THEIR *DEATHS* THAN I CAN COUNT. THIS IS ONE LAST *WARNING,* TO YOU *AND* YOUR FATHER.
BECAUSE THE NEXT TIME I LET YOU DROP...
...IT *WON'T* BE OVER A LEDGE.

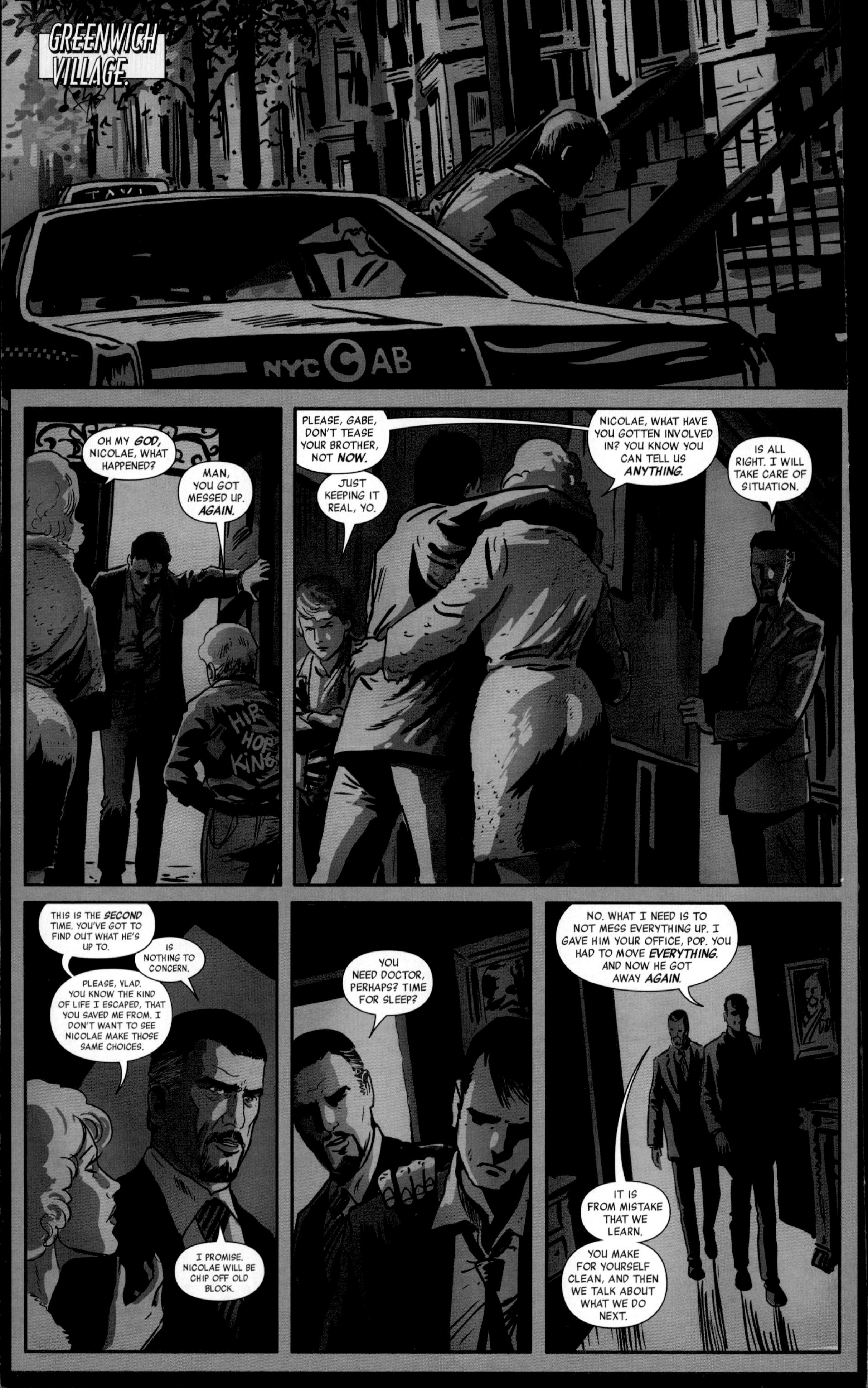
GREENWICH VILLAGE.
TAXI
NYC CAB
OH MY GOD, NICOLAE, WHAT HAPPENED?
MAN, YOU GOT MESSED UP. AGAIN.
HIP HOP KING
PLEASE, GABE, DON'T TEASE YOUR BROTHER, NOT NOW.
JUST KEEPING IT REAL, YO.
NICOLAE, WHAT HAVE YOU GOTTEN INVOLVED IN? YOU KNOW YOU CAN TELL US ANYTHING.
IS ALL RIGHT. I WILL TAKE CARE OF SITUATION.
THIS IS THE SECOND TIME. YOU'VE GOT TO FIND OUT WHAT HE'S UP TO.
IS NOTHING TO CONCERN.
PLEASE, VLAD. YOU KNOW THE KIND OF LIFE I ESCAPED, THAT YOU SAVED ME FROM. I DON'T WANT TO SEE NICOLAE MAKE THOSE SAME CHOICES.
I PROMISE. NICOLAE WILL BE CHIP OFF OLD BLOCK.
YOU NEED DOCTOR, PERHAPS? TIME FOR SLEEP?
NO. WHAT I NEED IS TO NOT MESS EVERYTHING UP. I GAVE HIM YOUR OFFICE, POP. YOU HAD TO MOVE EVERYTHING. AND NOW HE GOT AWAY AGAIN.
IT IS FROM MISTAKE THAT WE LEARN.
YOU MAKE FOR YOURSELF CLEAN, AND THEN WE TALK ABOUT WHAT WE DO NEXT.

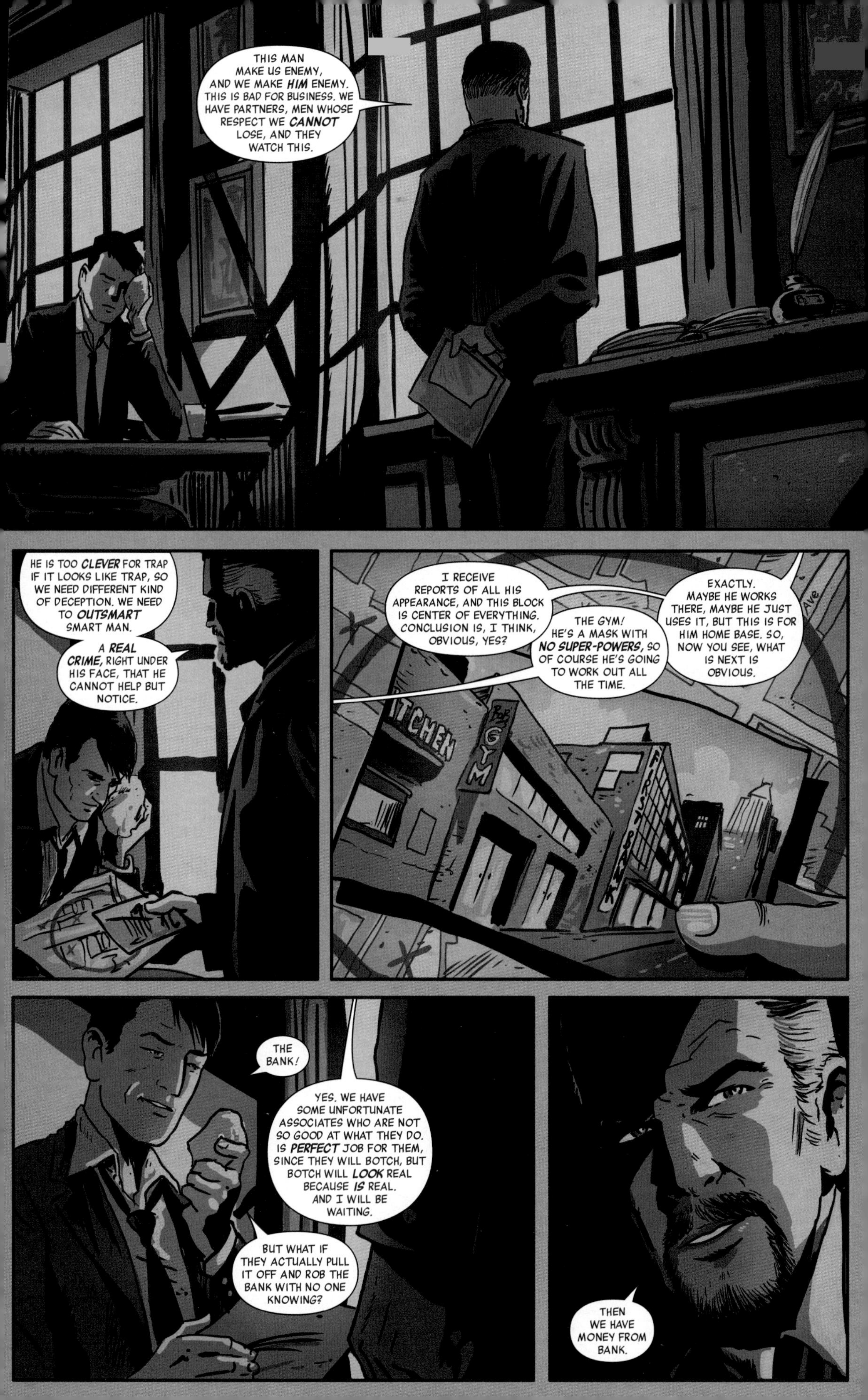
THIS MAN MAKE US ENEMY, AND WE MAKE HIM ENEMY. THIS IS BAD FOR BUSINESS. WE HAVE PARTNERS, MEN WHOSE RESPECT WE CANNOT LOSE, AND THEY WATCH THIS.
HE IS TOO CLEVER FOR TRAP IF IT LOOKS LIKE TRAP, SO WE NEED DIFFERENT KIND OF DECEPTION. WE NEED TO OUTSMART SMART MAN.
A REAL CRIME, RIGHT UNDER HIS FACE, THAT HE CANNOT HELP BUT NOTICE.
I RECEIVE REPORTS OF ALL HIS APPEARANCE, AND THIS BLOCK IS CENTER OF EVERYTHING. CONCLUSION IS, I THINK, OBVIOUS, YES?
THE GYM! HE'S A MASK WITH NO SUPER-POWERS, SO OF COURSE HE'S GOING TO WORK OUT ALL THE TIME.
EXACTLY. MAYBE HE WORKS THERE, MAYBE HE JUST USES IT, BUT THIS IS FOR HIM HOME BASE. SO, NOW YOU SEE, WHAT IS NEXT IS OBVIOUS.
Ave
ITCHEN
GYM
THE BANK!
YES. WE HAVE SOME UNFORTUNATE ASSOCIATES WHO ARE NOT SO GOOD AT WHAT THEY DO. IS PERFECT JOB FOR THEM, SINCE THEY WILL BOTCH, BUT BOTCH WILL LOOK REAL BECAUSE IS REAL. AND I WILL BE WAITING.
BUT WHAT IF THEY ACTUALLY PULL IT OFF AND ROB THE BANK WITH NO ONE KNOWING?
THEN WE HAVE MONEY FROM BANK.

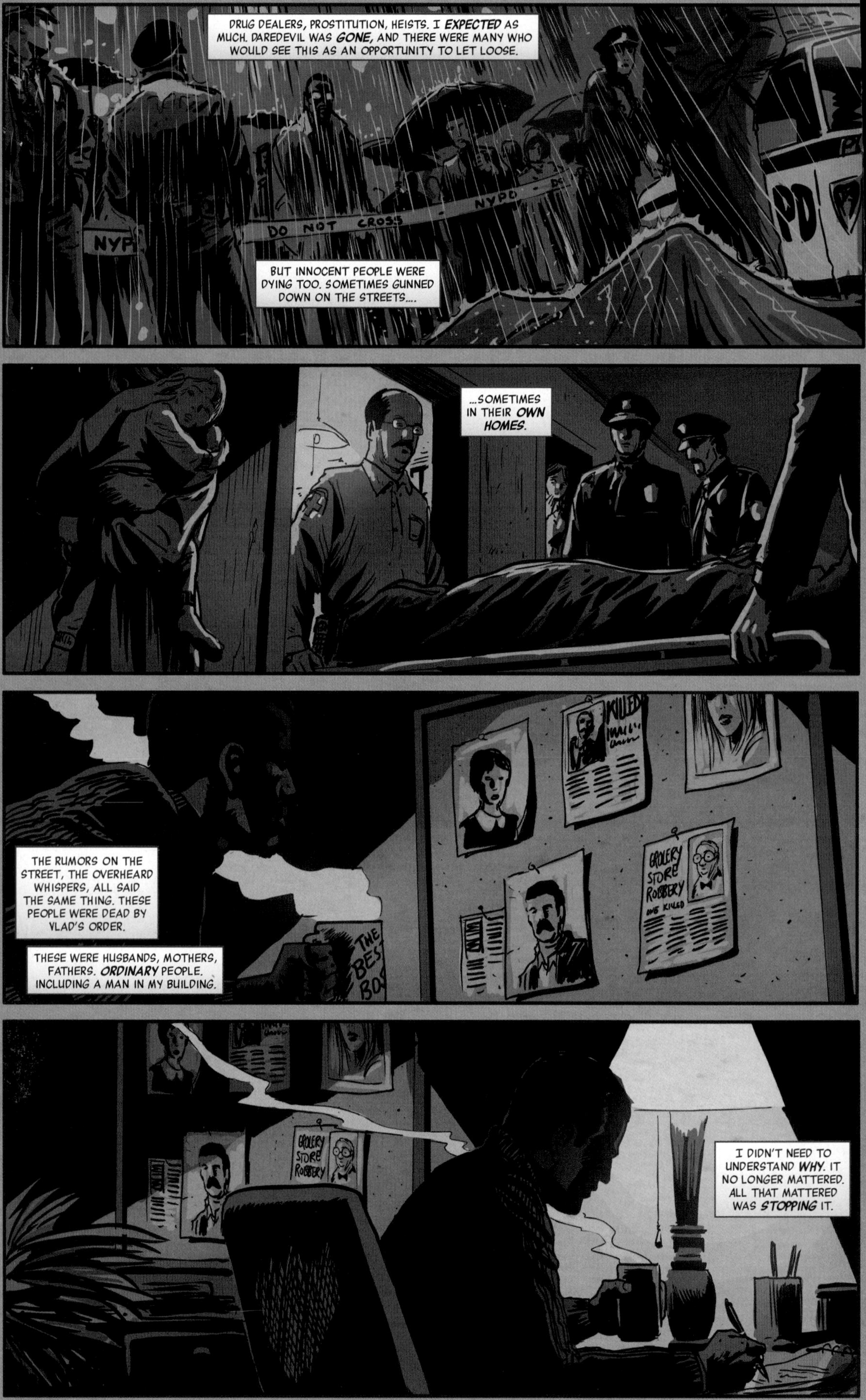

DRUG DEALERS, PROSTITUTION, HEISTS. I EXPECTED AS MUCH. DAREDEVIL WAS GONE, AND THERE WERE MANY WHO WOULD SEE THIS AS AN OPPORTUNITY TO LET LOOSE.
NYPD
DO NOT CROSS
BUT INNOCENT PEOPLE WERE DYING TOO. SOMETIMES GUNNED DOWN ON THE STREETS....
...SOMETIMES IN THEIR OWN HOMES.
KILLED
GROCERY STORE ROBBERY
ONE KILLED
THE RUMORS ON THE STREET, THE OVERHEARD WHISPERS, ALL SAID THE SAME THING. THESE PEOPLE WERE DEAD BY VLAD'S ORDER.
THESE WERE HUSBANDS, MOTHERS, FATHERS. ORDINARY PEOPLE. INCLUDING A MAN IN MY BUILDING.
I DIDN'T NEED TO UNDERSTAND WHY. IT NO LONGER MATTERED. ALL THAT MATTERED WAS STOPPING IT.

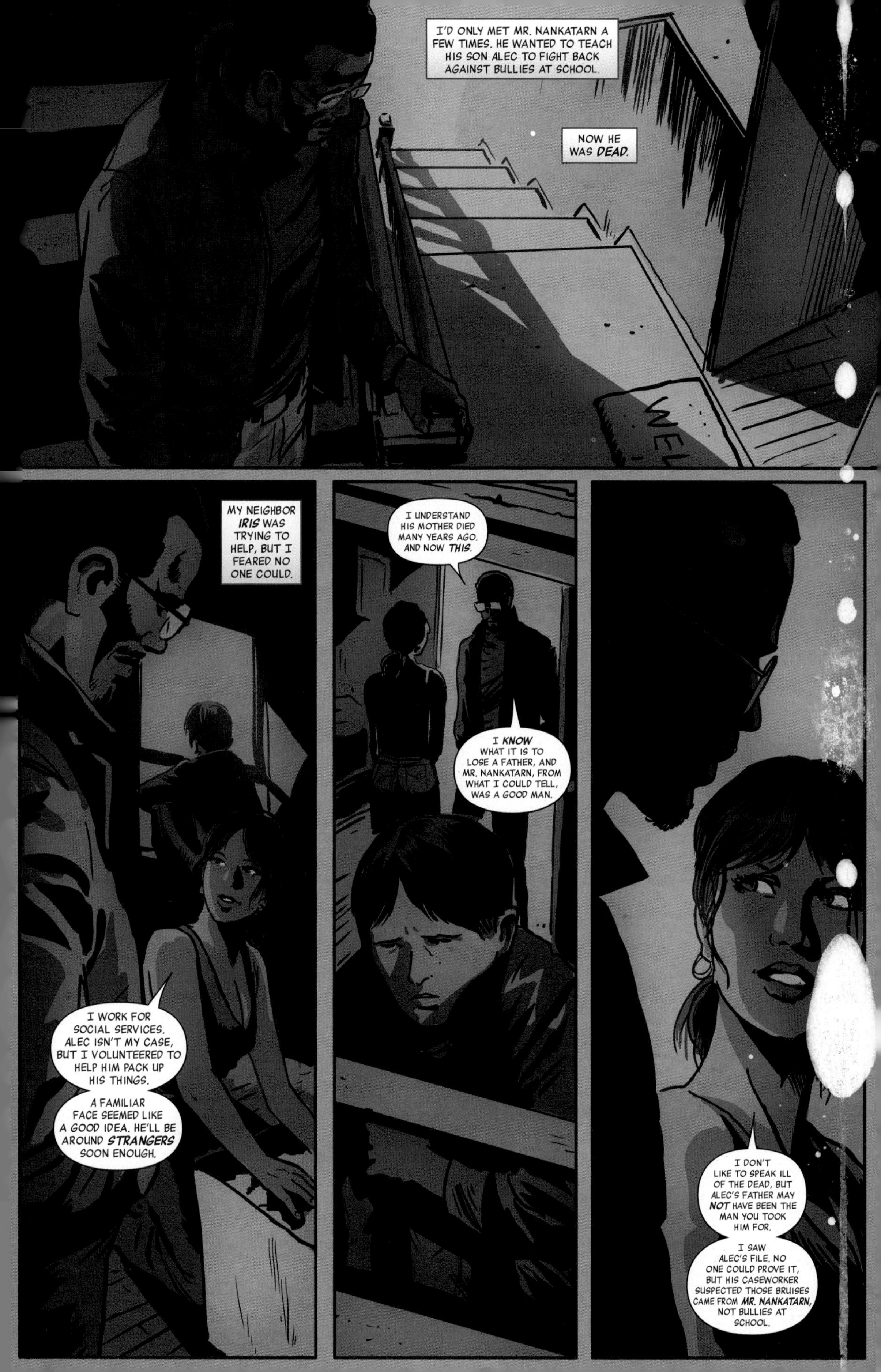
I'D ONLY MET MR. NANKATARN A FEW TIMES. HE WANTED TO TEACH HIS SON ALEC TO FIGHT BACK AGAINST BULLIES AT SCHOOL.
NOW HE WAS DEAD.
MY NEIGHBOR IRIS WAS TRYING TO HELP, BUT I FEARED NO ONE COULD.
I WORK FOR SOCIAL SERVICES. ALEC ISN'T MY CASE, BUT I VOLUNTEERED TO HELP HIM PACK UP HIS THINGS.
A FAMILIAR FACE SEEMED LIKE A GOOD IDEA. HE'LL BE AROUND STRANGERS SOON ENOUGH.
I UNDERSTAND HIS MOTHER DIED MANY YEARS AGO. AND NOW THIS.
I KNOW WHAT IT IS TO LOSE A FATHER, AND MR. NANKATARN, FROM WHAT I COULD TELL, WAS A GOOD MAN.
I DON'T LIKE TO SPEAK ILL OF THE DEAD, BUT ALEC'S FATHER MAY NOT HAVE BEEN THE MAN YOU TOOK HIM FOR.
I SAW ALEC'S FILE. NO ONE COULD PROVE IT, BUT HIS CASEWORKER SUSPECTED THOSE BRUISES CAME FROM MR. NANKATARN, NOT BULLIES AT SCHOOL.

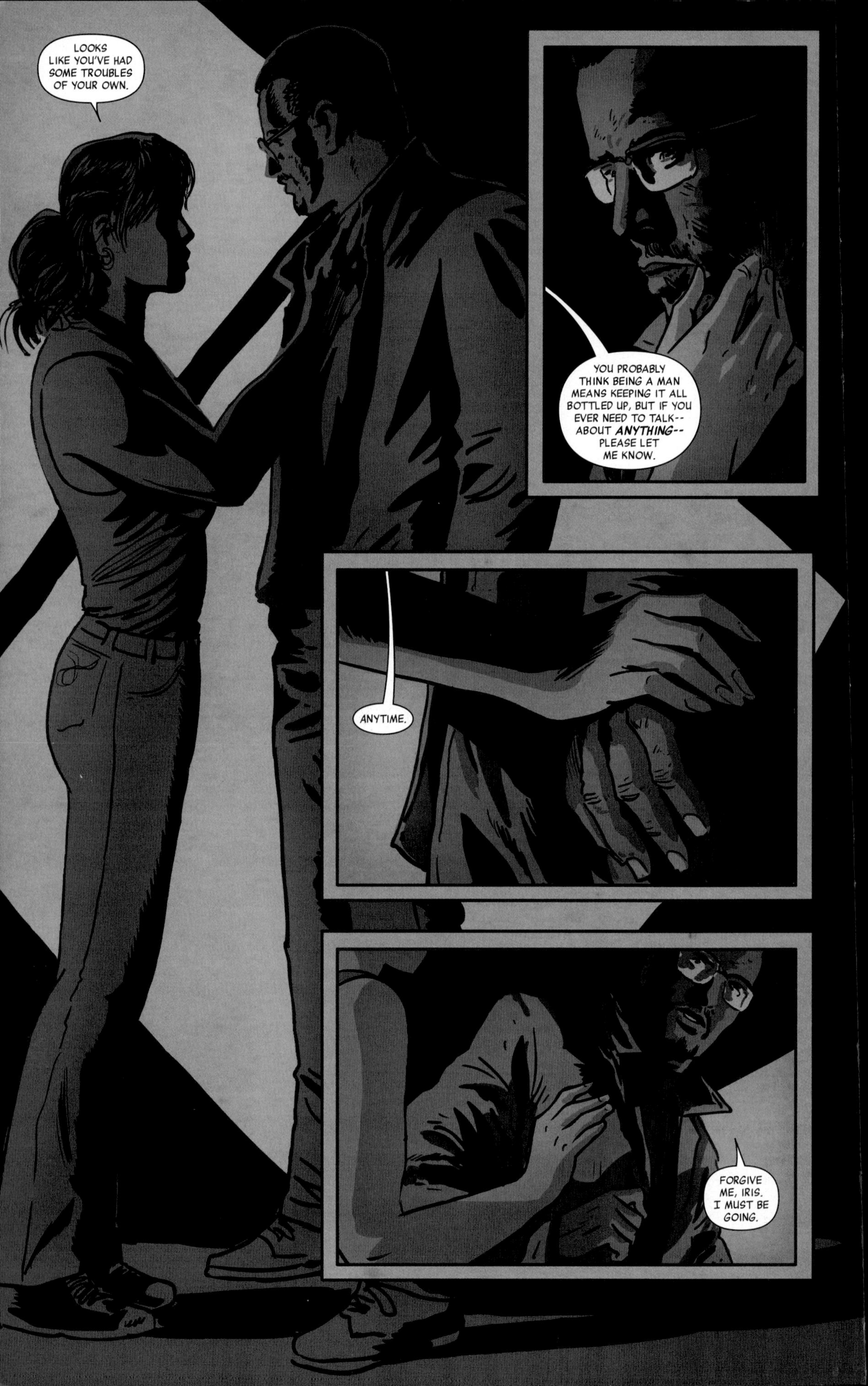
LOOKS LIKE YOU'VE HAD SOME TROUBLES OF YOUR OWN.
YOU PROBABLY THINK BEING A MAN MEANS KEEPING IT ALL BOTTLED UP, BUT IF YOU EVER NEED TO TALK-- ABOUT ANYTHING-- PLEASE LET ME KNOW.
ANYTIME.
FORGIVE ME, IRIS. I MUST BE GOING.

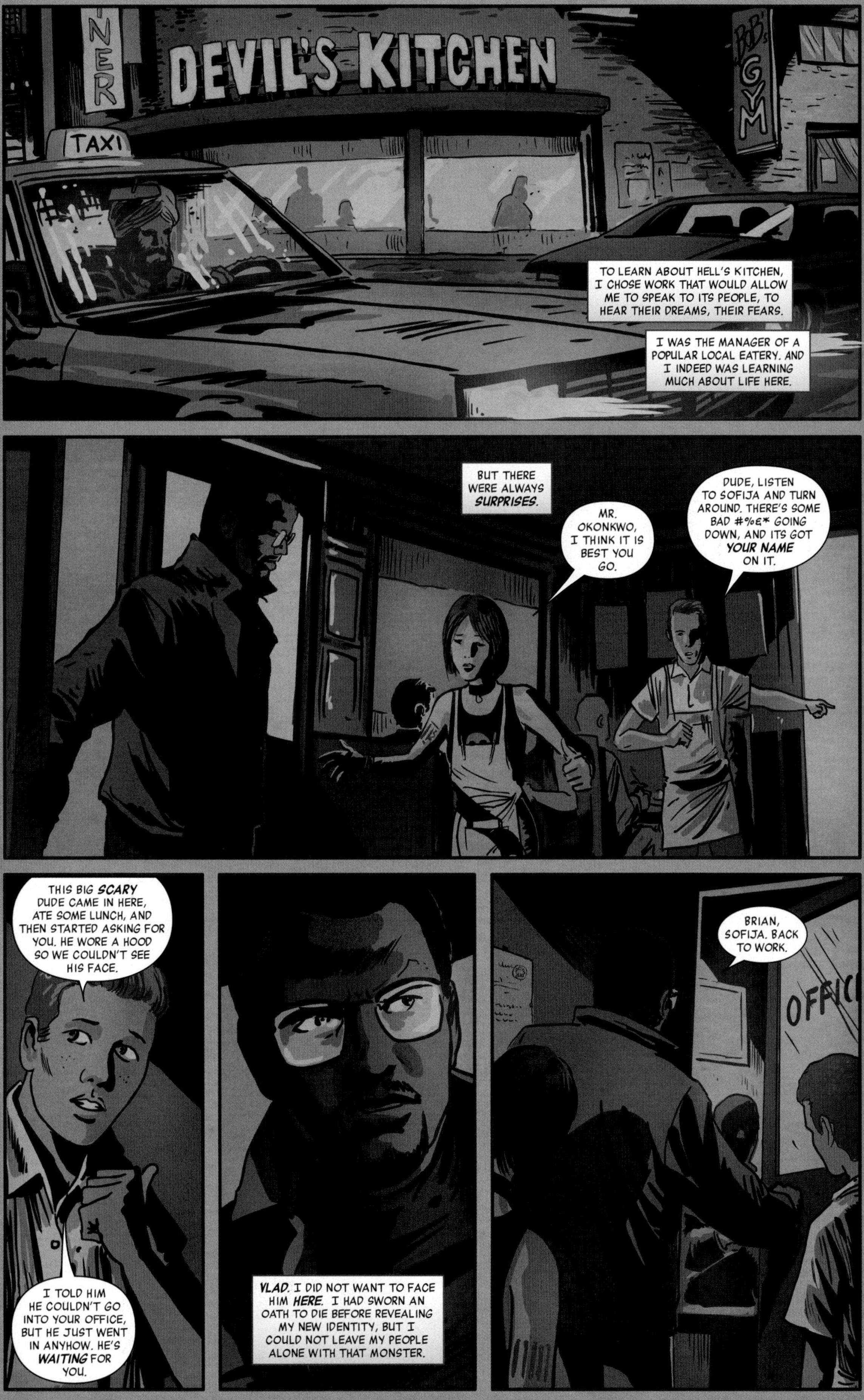
DINER
DEVIL'S KITCHEN
BOB'S GYM
TAXI
TO LEARN ABOUT HELL'S KITCHEN, I CHOSE WORK THAT WOULD ALLOW ME TO SPEAK TO ITS PEOPLE, TO HEAR THEIR DREAMS, THEIR FEARS.
I WAS THE MANAGER OF A POPULAR LOCAL EATERY. AND I INDEED WAS LEARNING MUCH ABOUT LIFE HERE.
BUT THERE WERE ALWAYS *SURPRISES*.
MR. OKONKWO, I THINK IT IS BEST YOU GO.
DUDE, LISTEN TO SOFIJA AND TURN AROUND. THERE'S SOME BAD #%£* GOING DOWN, AND ITS GOT **YOUR NAME** ON IT.
THIS BIG *SCARY* DUDE CAME IN HERE, ATE SOME LUNCH, AND THEN STARTED ASKING FOR YOU. HE WORE A HOOD SO WE COULDN'T SEE HIS FACE.
I TOLD HIM HE COULDN'T GO INTO YOUR OFFICE, BUT HE JUST WENT IN ANYHOW. HE'S *WAITING* FOR YOU.
VLAD. I DID NOT WANT TO FACE HIM *HERE*. I HAD SWORN AN OATH TO DIE BEFORE REVEALING MY NEW IDENTITY, BUT I COULD NOT LEAVE MY PEOPLE ALONE WITH THAT MONSTER.
BRIAN, SOFIJA. BACK TO WORK.
OFFIC

LUKE CAGE, A SELF-STYLED "HERO FOR FIRE" OF THE STREETS WHO HAD GRADUATED TO BECOME AN AVENGER.

HE ALSO ONCE ATTEMPTED TO ORGANIZE A BACHELOR PARTY FOR ME. IT WAS IN *VERY* POOR TASTE.

YOU ARE IN MY CHAIR.

T'CHALLA! *MY MAN!*

IT'S COOL. DIDN'T MEAN TO GET TOO FRIENDLY WITH YOUR *DINER-MANAGER CHAIR.*

HOW DID YOU KNOW WHERE TO FIND ME?

I KNEW YOU WERE AROUND HERE SOMEWHERE. BEING A GUY WHO CAN GET STEVE ROGERS ON THE PHONE ANY DAMN TIME I *WANT* MEANS I GET ACCESS TO ALL KINDS OF GOOD INTEL. THE C.I.A. IS *TRYING* TO FIND YOUR ASS, BUT I FOUND YOU *FIRST.*

WASN'T *EASY,* BUT WHAT'S WORTH DOING THAT IS?

AND WHAT DO YOU WANT?

WHAT DO I *WANT?* THAT'S *COLD.*

I GET THAT YOU'RE FILLING IN FOR MURDOCK WHILE HE'S OFF FIGURING OUT THE INSIDE OF HIS OWN HEAD. I GET YOU WENT THROUGH SOME HARD TIMES WITH DOOM AND YOU NEED TO FIGURE OUT YOUR *OWN* HEAD.

WHAT I *WANT* IS TO LET YOU KNOW I'VE GOT YOUR BACK. SAY THE WORD, AND I'LL GET MY *TEAM* ALL OVER IT. SOMEONE GIVING YOU GRIEF? WE'LL SICK BEN GRIMM ON HIM, AND I GUARANTEE YOU: NO MORE GRIEF.

NO THANK YOU.

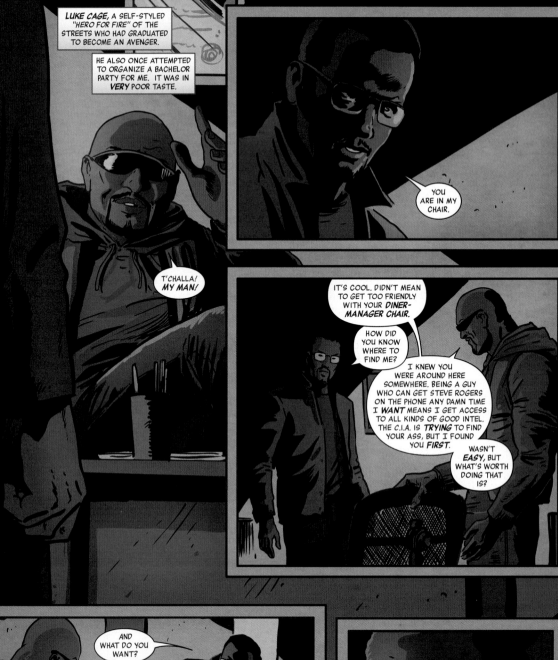

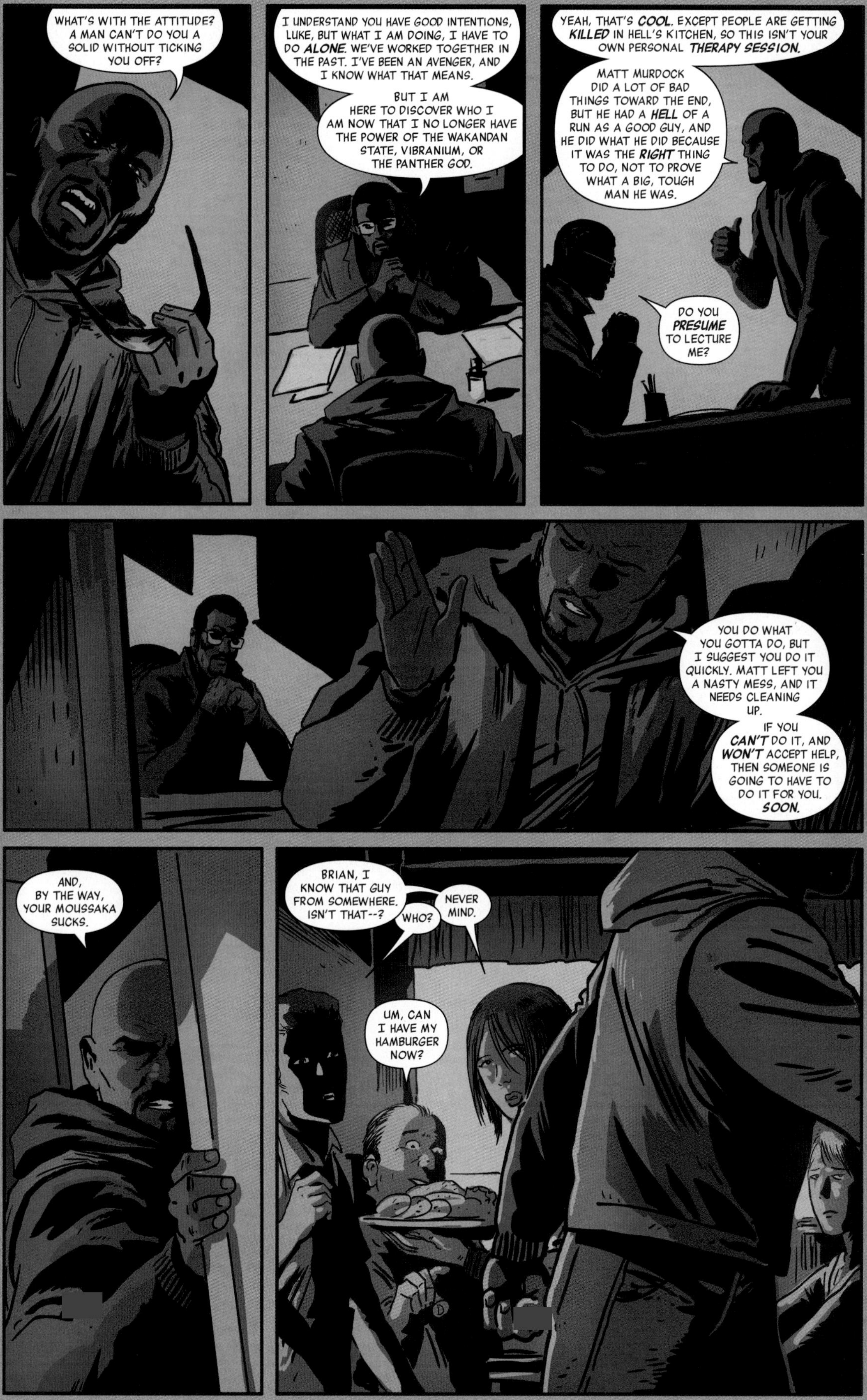
WHAT'S WITH THE ATTITUDE? A MAN CAN'T DO YOU A SOLID WITHOUT TICKING YOU OFF?
I UNDERSTAND YOU HAVE GOOD INTENTIONS, LUKE, BUT WHAT I AM DOING, I HAVE TO DO ALONE. WE'VE WORKED TOGETHER IN THE PAST. I'VE BEEN AN AVENGER, AND I KNOW WHAT THAT MEANS.
BUT I AM HERE TO DISCOVER WHO I AM NOW THAT I NO LONGER HAVE THE POWER OF THE WAKANDAN STATE, VIBRANIUM, OR THE PANTHER GOD.
YEAH, THAT'S COOL. EXCEPT PEOPLE ARE GETTING KILLED IN HELL'S KITCHEN, SO THIS ISN'T YOUR OWN PERSONAL THERAPY SESSION.
MATT MURDOCK DID A LOT OF BAD THINGS TOWARD THE END, BUT HE HAD A HELL OF A RUN AS A GOOD GUY, AND HE DID WHAT HE DID BECAUSE IT WAS THE RIGHT THING TO DO, NOT TO PROVE WHAT A BIG, TOUGH MAN HE WAS.
DO YOU PRESUME TO LECTURE ME?
YOU DO WHAT YOU GOTTA DO, BUT I SUGGEST YOU DO IT QUICKLY. MATT LEFT YOU A NASTY MESS, AND IT NEEDS CLEANING UP.
IF YOU CAN'T DO IT, AND WON'T ACCEPT HELP, THEN SOMEONE IS GOING TO HAVE TO DO IT FOR YOU. SOON.
AND, BY THE WAY, YOUR MOUSSAKA SUCKS.
BRIAN, I KNOW THAT GUY FROM SOMEWHERE. ISN'T THAT--?
WHO?
NEVER MIND.
UM, CAN I HAVE MY HAMBURGER NOW?

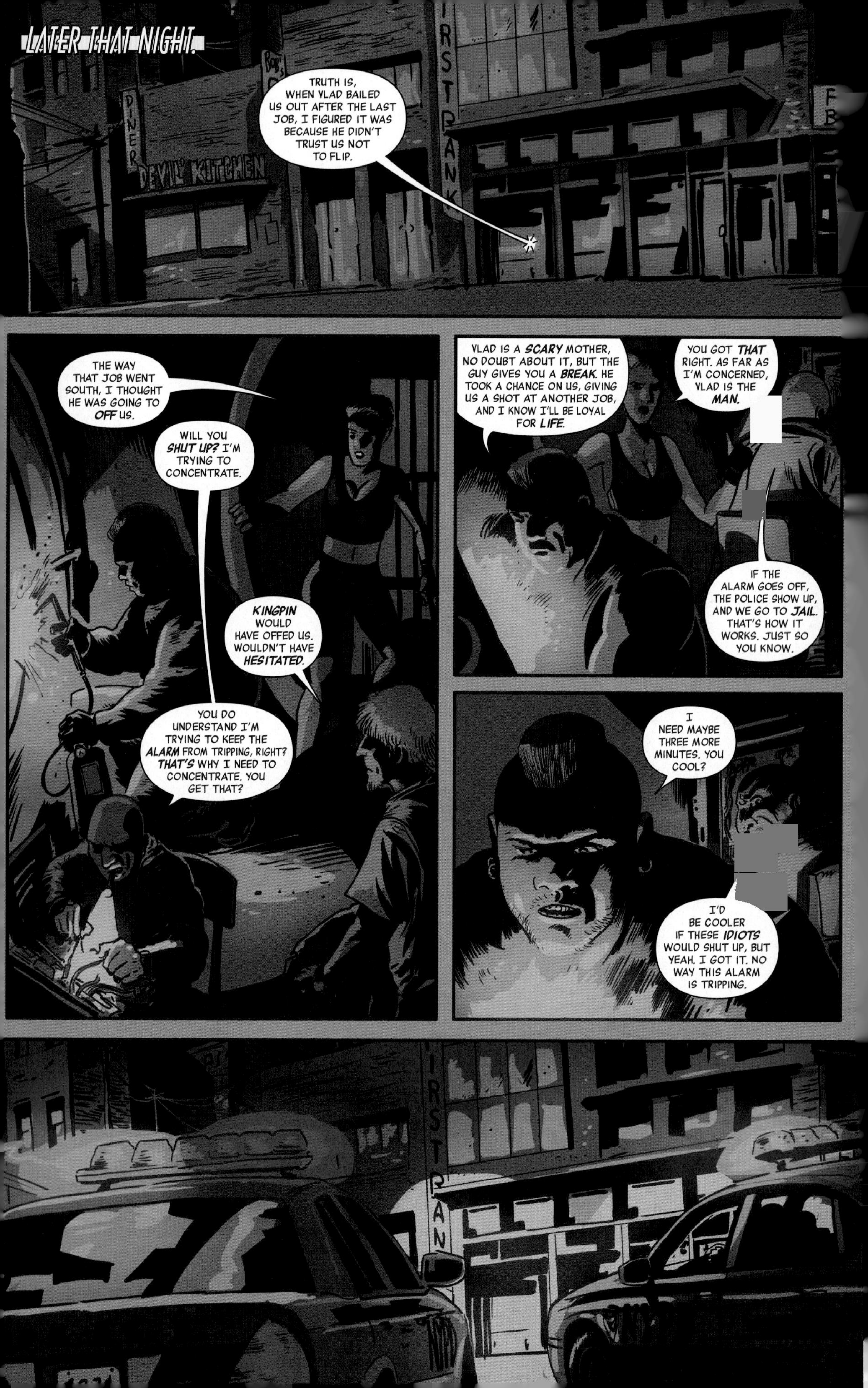
LATER THAT NIGHT.
DINER
DEVIL' KITCHEN
TRUTH IS, WHEN VLAD BAILED US OUT AFTER THE LAST JOB, I FIGURED IT WAS BECAUSE HE DIDN'T TRUST US NOT TO FLIP.
THE WAY THAT JOB WENT SOUTH, I THOUGHT HE WAS GOING TO OFF US.
WILL YOU SHUT UP? I'M TRYING TO CONCENTRATE.
KINGPIN WOULD HAVE OFFED US. WOULDN'T HAVE HESITATED.
YOU DO UNDERSTAND I'M TRYING TO KEEP THE ALARM FROM TRIPPING, RIGHT? THAT'S WHY I NEED TO CONCENTRATE. YOU GET THAT?
VLAD IS A SCARY MOTHER, NO DOUBT ABOUT IT, BUT THE GUY GIVES YOU A BREAK. HE TOOK A CHANCE ON US, GIVING US A SHOT AT ANOTHER JOB, AND I KNOW I'LL BE LOYAL FOR LIFE.
YOU GOT THAT RIGHT. AS FAR AS I'M CONCERNED, VLAD IS THE MAN.
IF THE ALARM GOES OFF, THE POLICE SHOW UP, AND WE GO TO JAIL. THAT'S HOW IT WORKS. JUST SO YOU KNOW.
I NEED MAYBE THREE MORE MINUTES. YOU COOL?
I'D BE COOLER IF THESE IDIOTS WOULD SHUT UP, BUT YEAH. I GOT IT. NO WAY THIS ALARM IS TRIPPING.

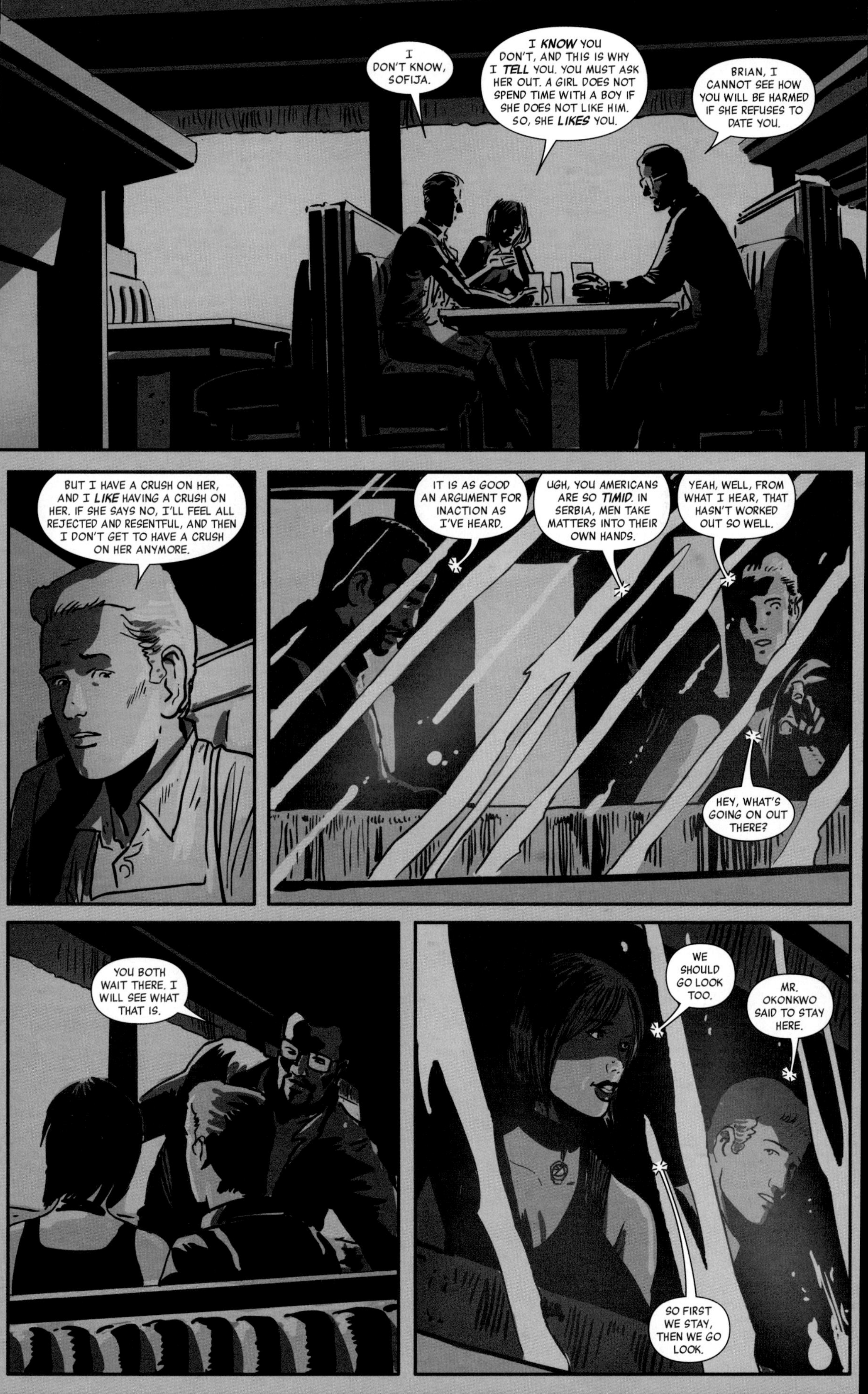
I DON'T KNOW, SOFIJA.
I KNOW YOU DON'T, AND THIS IS WHY I TELL YOU. YOU MUST ASK HER OUT. A GIRL DOES NOT SPEND TIME WITH A BOY IF SHE DOES NOT LIKE HIM. SO, SHE LIKES YOU.
BRIAN, I CANNOT SEE HOW YOU WILL BE HARMED IF SHE REFUSES TO DATE YOU.
BUT I HAVE A CRUSH ON HER, AND I LIKE HAVING A CRUSH ON HER. IF SHE SAYS NO, I'LL FEEL ALL REJECTED AND RESENTFUL, AND THEN I DON'T GET TO HAVE A CRUSH ON HER ANYMORE.
IT IS AS GOOD AN ARGUMENT FOR INACTION AS I'VE HEARD.
UGH, YOU AMERICANS ARE SO TIMID. IN SERBIA, MEN TAKE MATTERS INTO THEIR OWN HANDS.
YEAH, WELL, FROM WHAT I HEAR, THAT HASN'T WORKED OUT SO WELL.
HEY, WHAT'S GOING ON OUT THERE?
YOU BOTH WAIT THERE. I WILL SEE WHAT THAT IS.
WE SHOULD GO LOOK TOO.
MR. OKONKWO SAID TO STAY HERE.
SO FIRST WE STAY, THEN WE GO LOOK.

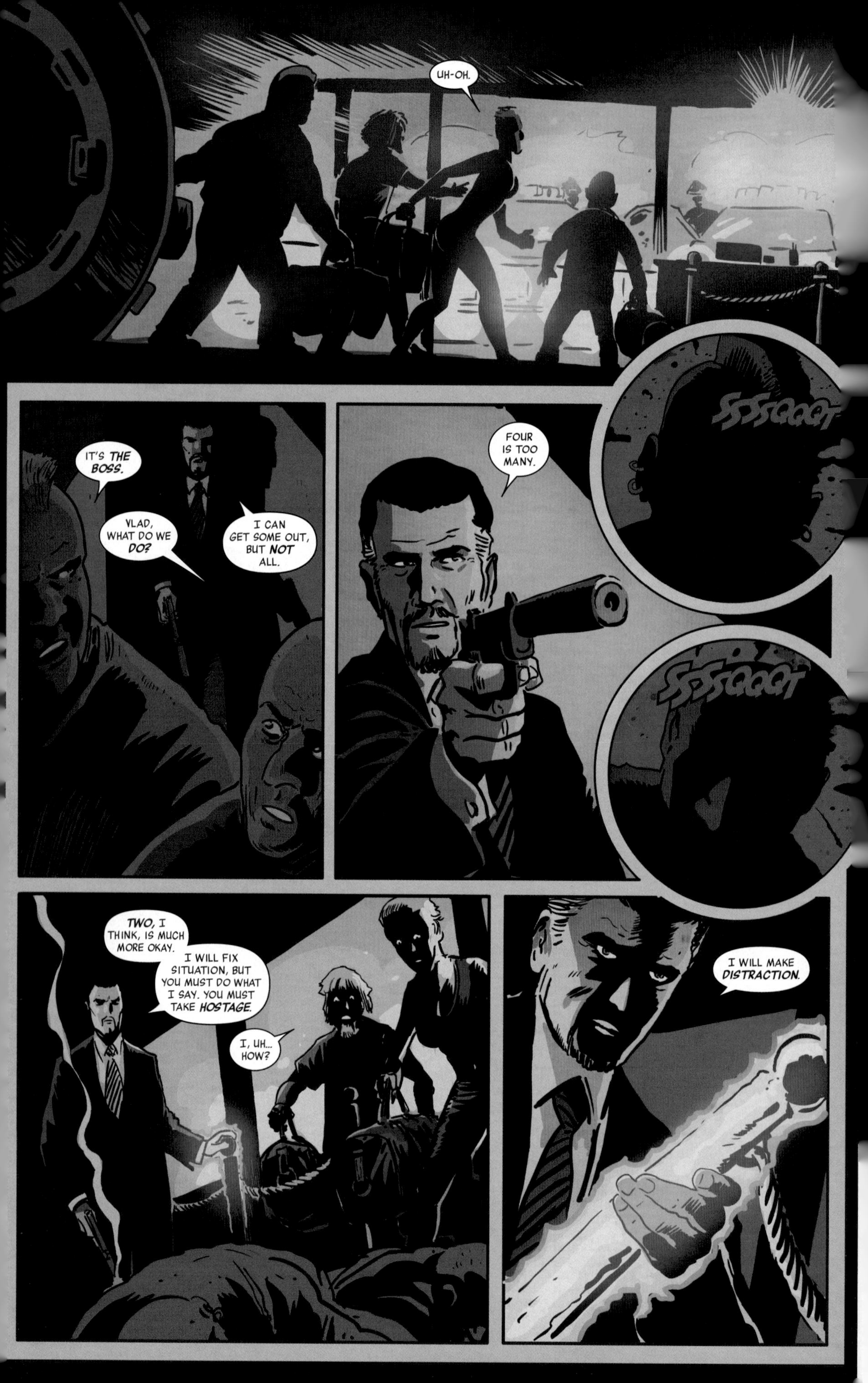
UH-OH.
IT'S THE BOSS.
VLAD, WHAT DO WE DO?
I CAN GET SOME OUT, BUT NOT ALL.
FOUR IS TOO MANY.
SSSQQQT
SSSQQQT
TWO, I THINK, IS MUCH MORE OKAY.
I WILL FIX SITUATION, BUT YOU MUST DO WHAT I SAY. YOU MUST TAKE HOSTAGE.
I, UH... HOW?
I WILL MAKE DISTRACTION.

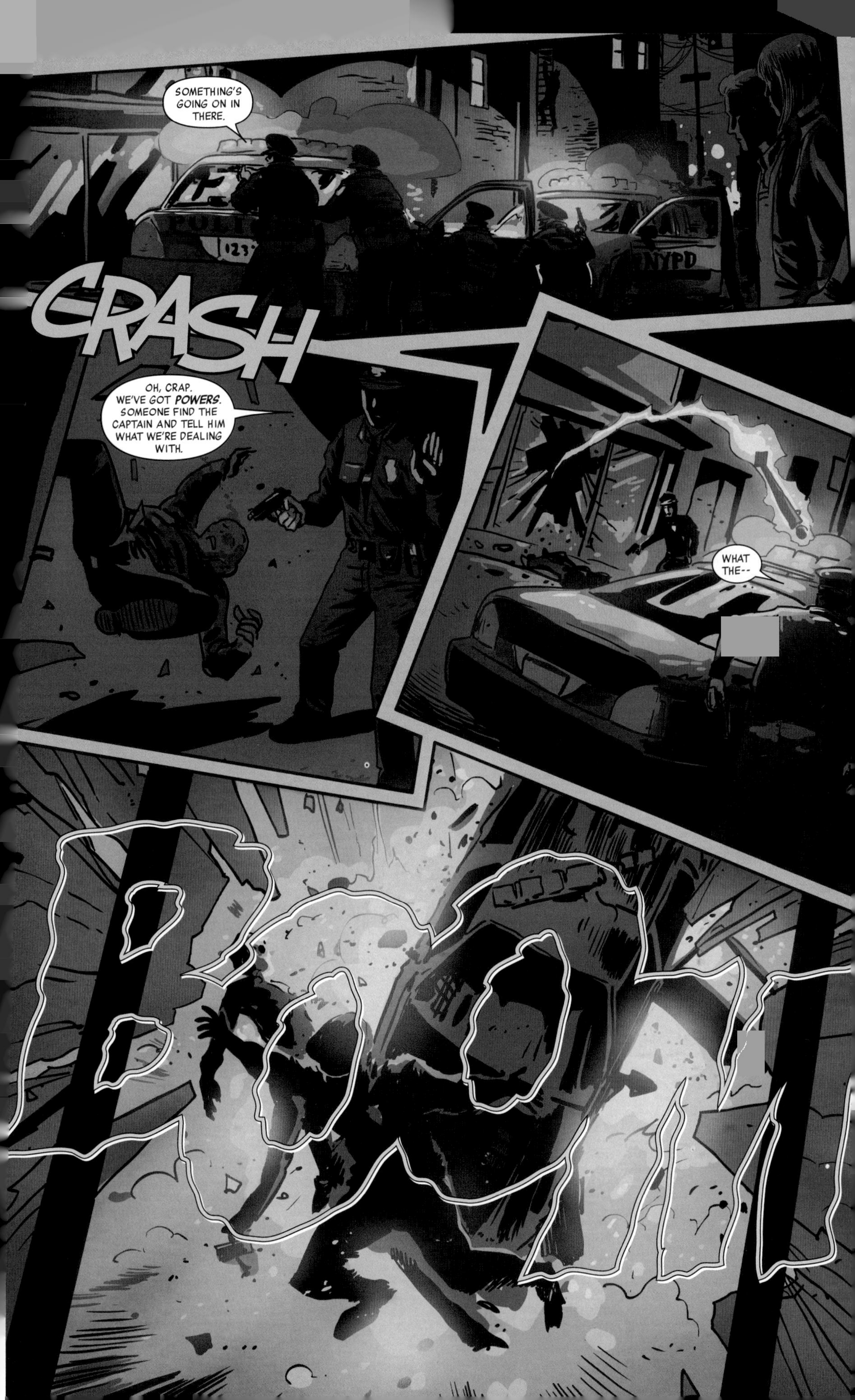
SOMETHING'S GOING ON IN THERE.
CRASH
OH, CRAP. WE'VE GOT POWERS. SOMEONE FIND THE CAPTAIN AND TELL HIM WHAT WE'RE DEALING WITH.
WHAT THE--
BOOM

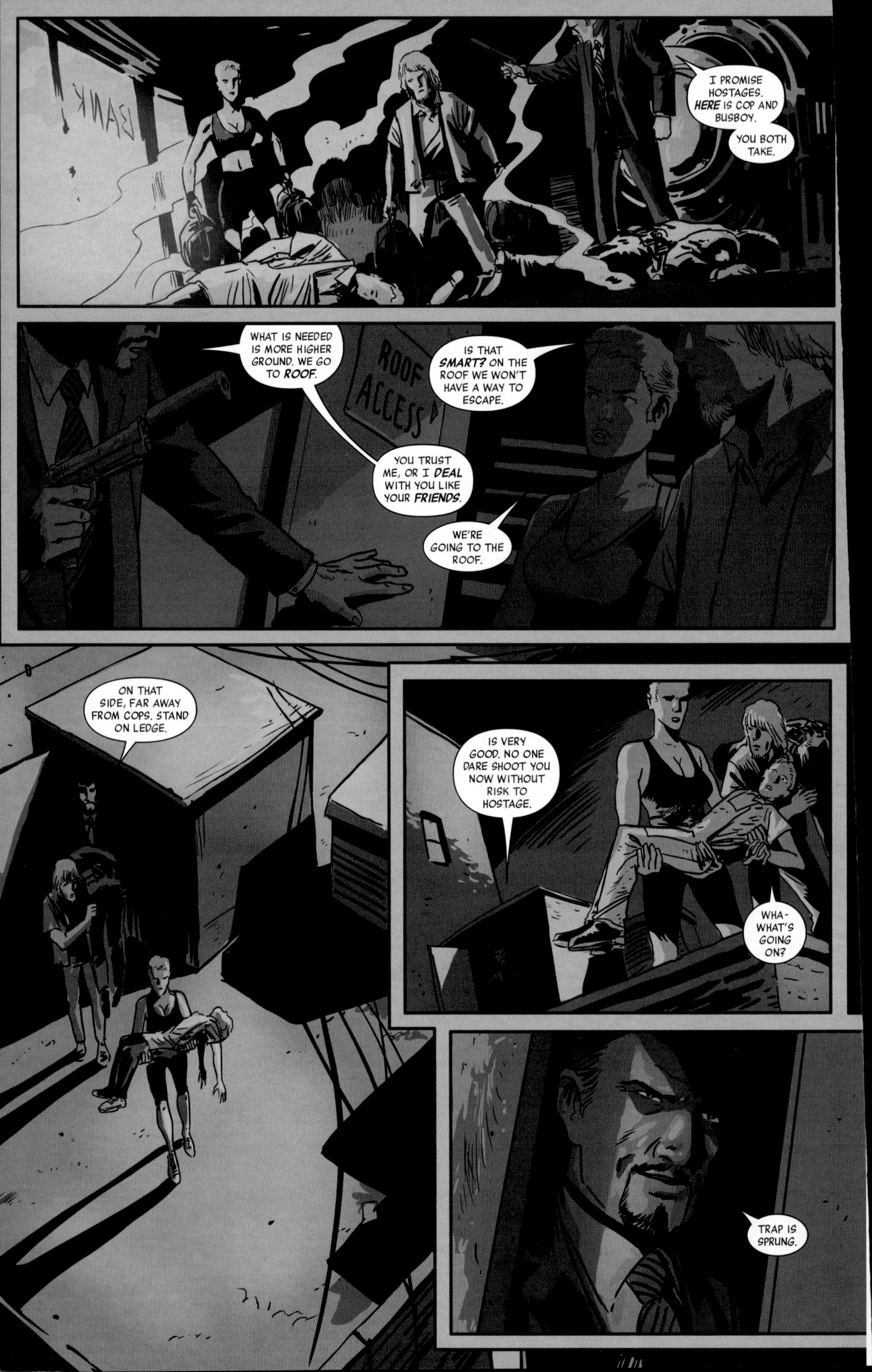
BANK
I PROMISE HOSTAGES. HERE IS COP AND BUSBOY.
YOU BOTH TAKE.
WHAT IS NEEDED IS MORE HIGHER GROUND. WE GO TO ROOF.
ROOF ACCESS
IS THAT SMART? ON THE ROOF WE WON'T HAVE A WAY TO ESCAPE.
YOU TRUST ME, OR I DEAL WITH YOU LIKE YOUR FRIENDS.
WE'RE GOING TO THE ROOF.
ON THAT SIDE, FAR AWAY FROM COPS. STAND ON LEDGE.
IS VERY GOOD. NO ONE DARE SHOOT YOU NOW WITHOUT RISK TO HOSTAGE.
WHA- WHAT'S GOING ON?
TRAP IS SPRUNG.

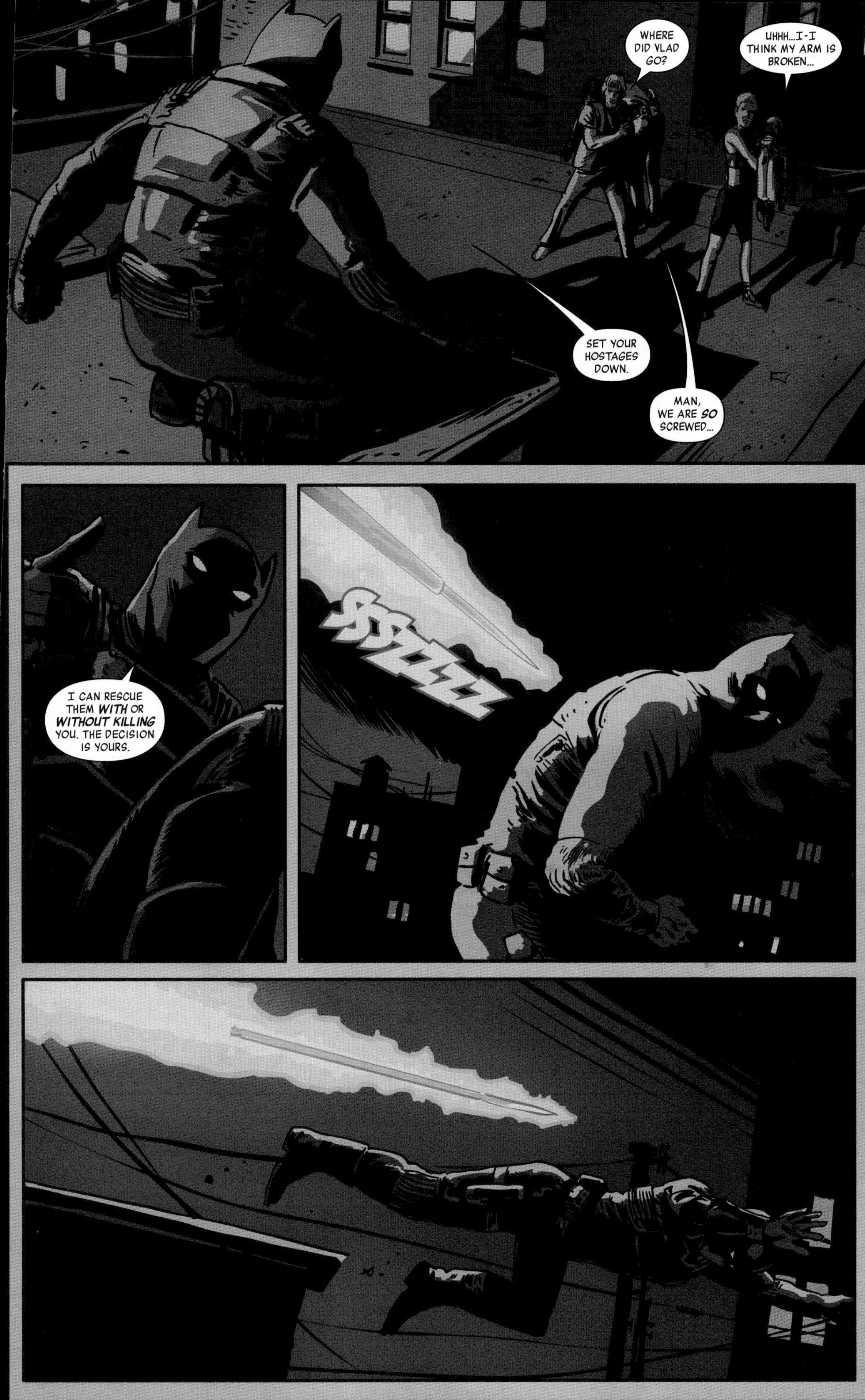
WHERE DID VLAD GO?
UHHH...I-I THINK MY ARM IS BROKEN...
SET YOUR HOSTAGES DOWN.
MAN, WE ARE SO SCREWED...
I CAN RESCUE THEM WITH OR WITHOUT KILLING YOU. THE DECISION IS YOURS.
SSZZZ

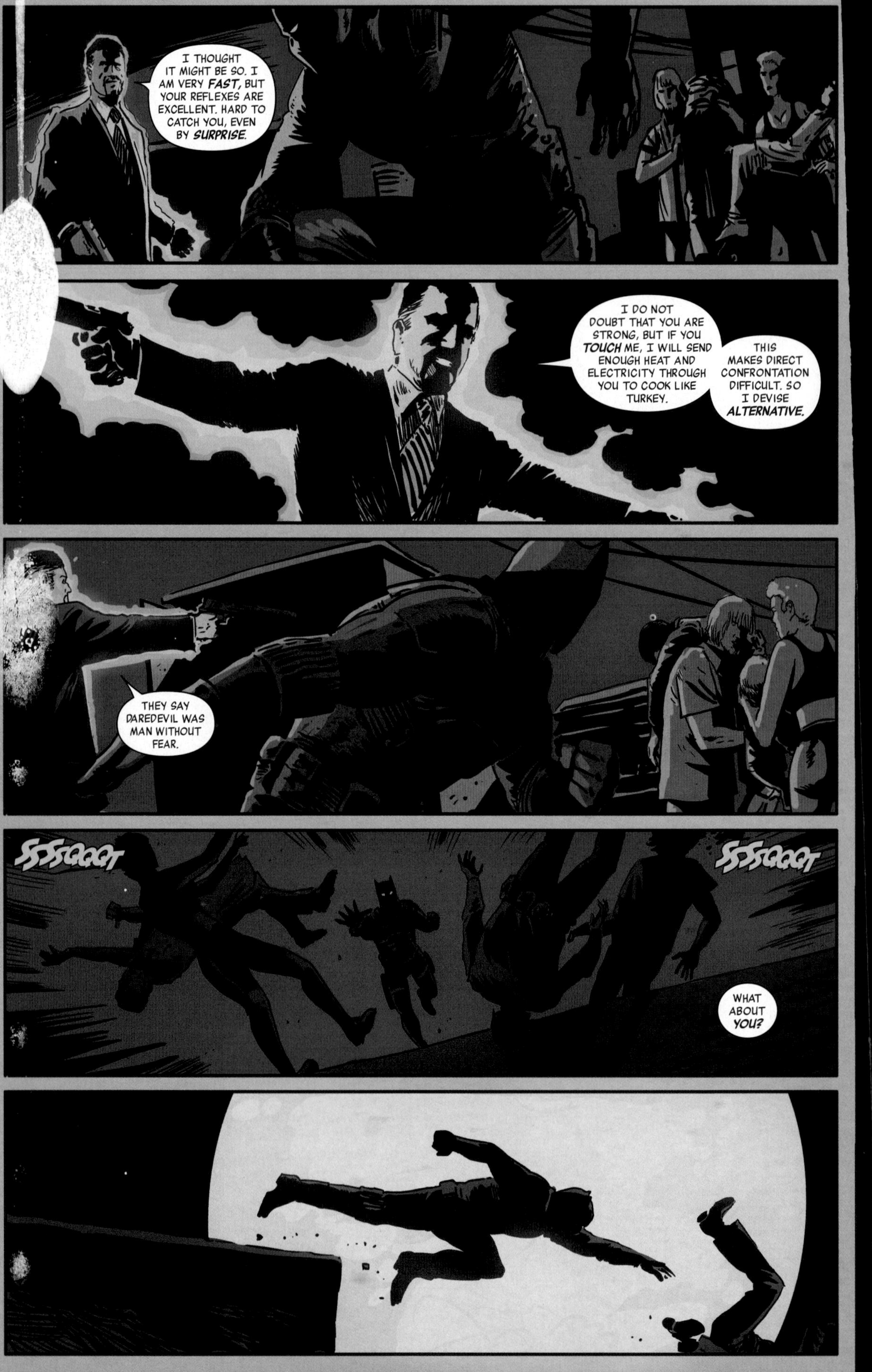
I THOUGHT IT MIGHT BE SO. I AM VERY FAST, BUT YOUR REFLEXES ARE EXCELLENT. HARD TO CATCH YOU, EVEN BY SURPRISE.
I DO NOT DOUBT THAT YOU ARE STRONG, BUT IF YOU TOUCH ME, I WILL SEND ENOUGH HEAT AND ELECTRICITY THROUGH YOU TO COOK LIKE TURKEY.
THIS MAKES DIRECT CONFRONTATION DIFFICULT. SO I DEVISE ALTERNATIVE.
THEY SAY DAREDEVIL WAS MAN WITHOUT FEAR.
SSSSQQQT
SSSSQQQT
WHAT ABOUT YOU?

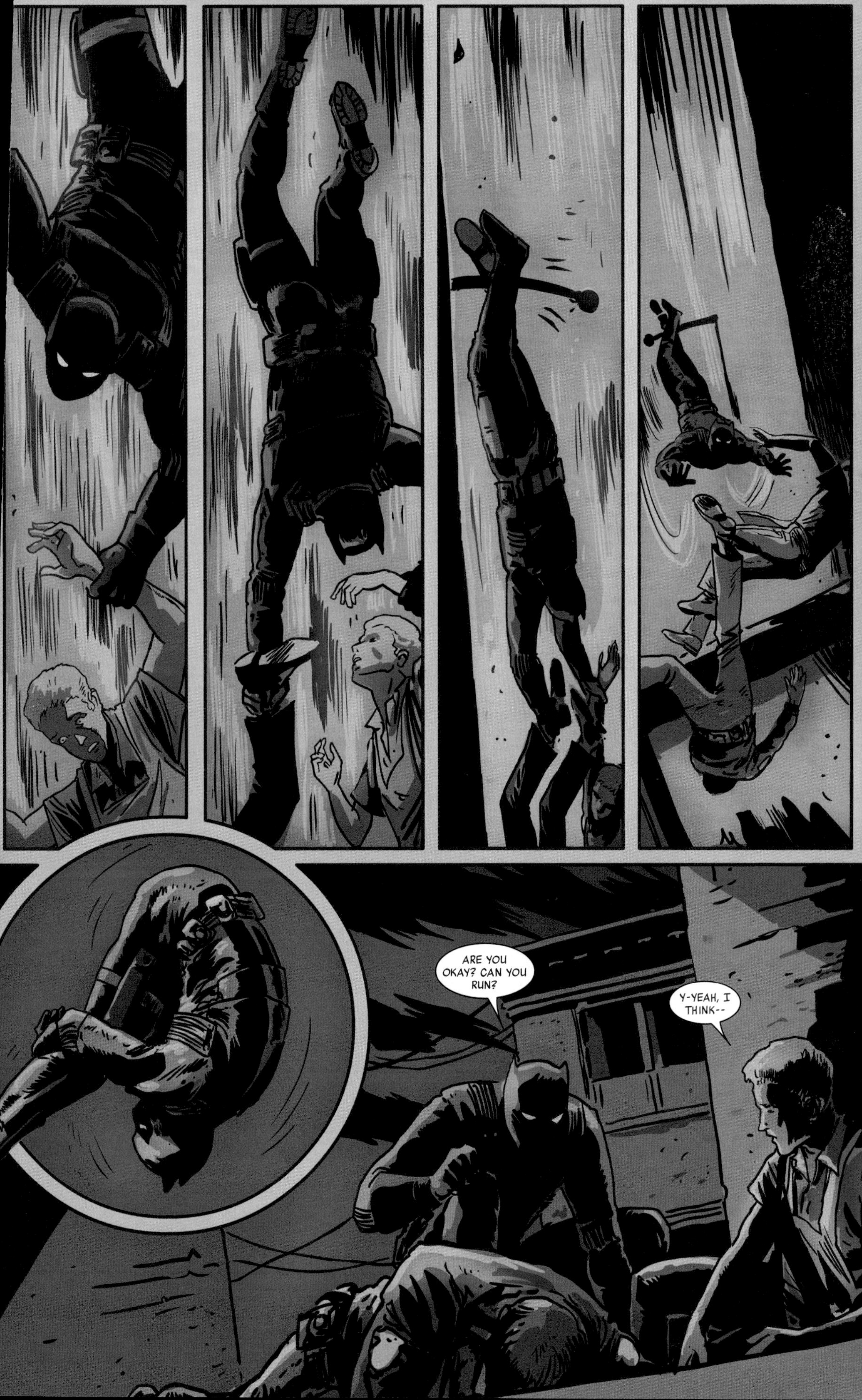
ARE YOU OKAY? CAN YOU RUN?
Y-YEAH, I THINK--

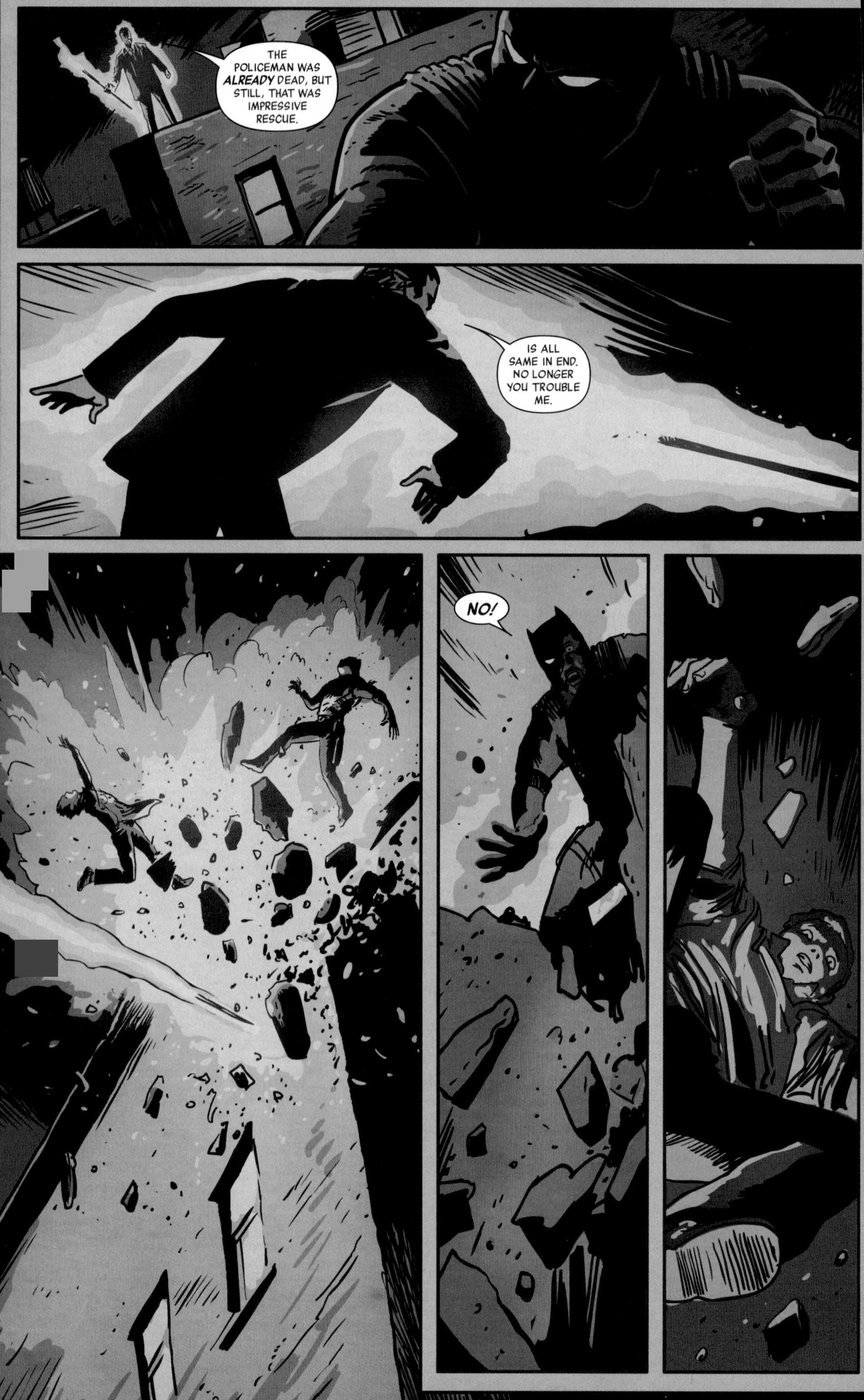
THE POLICEMAN WAS ALREADY DEAD, BUT STILL, THAT WAS IMPRESSIVE RESCUE.
IS ALL SAME IN END. NO LONGER YOU TROUBLE ME.
NO!

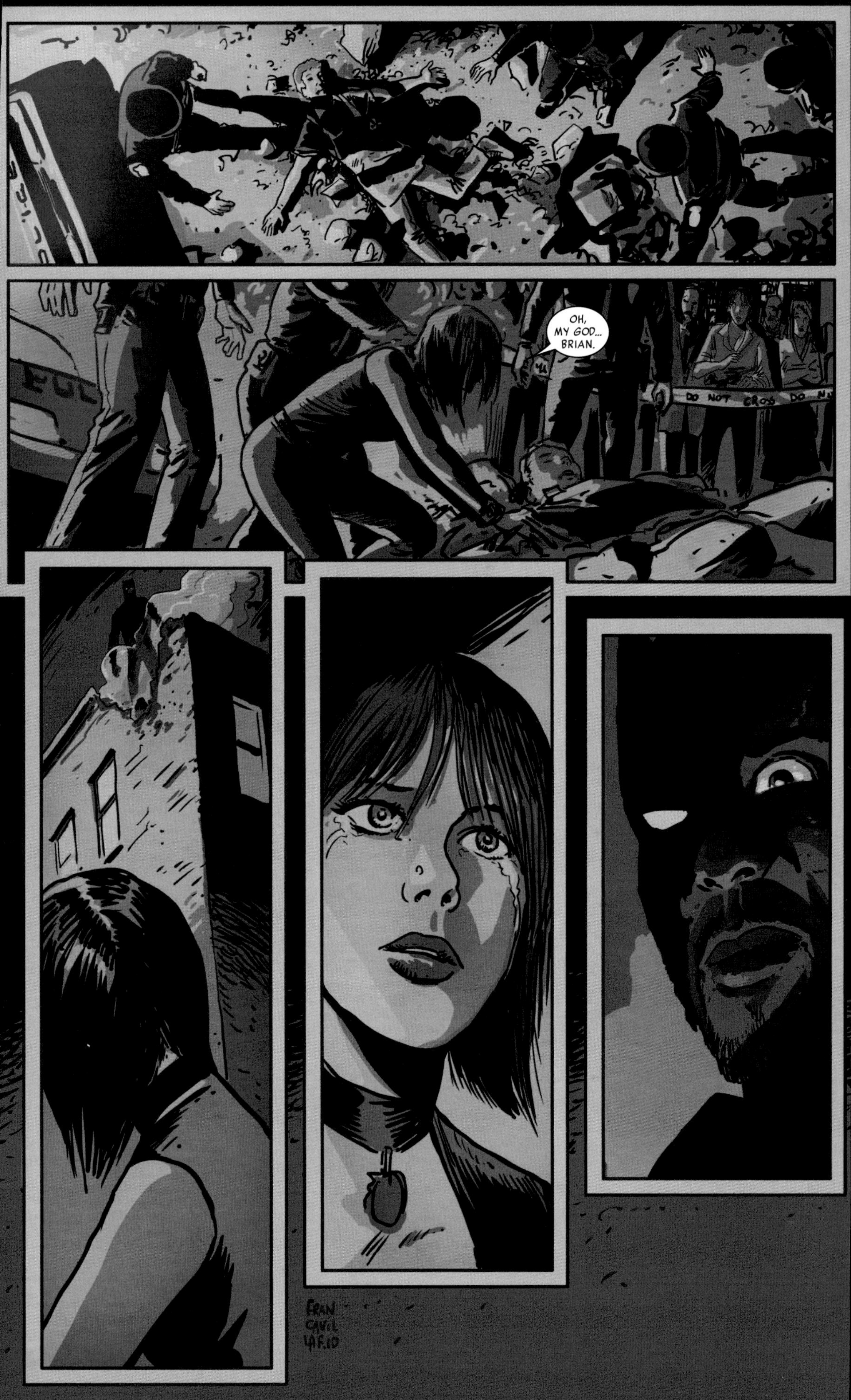
OH, MY GOD... BRIAN.
DO NOT CROSS DO N
FRAN CAVIL LAF.10

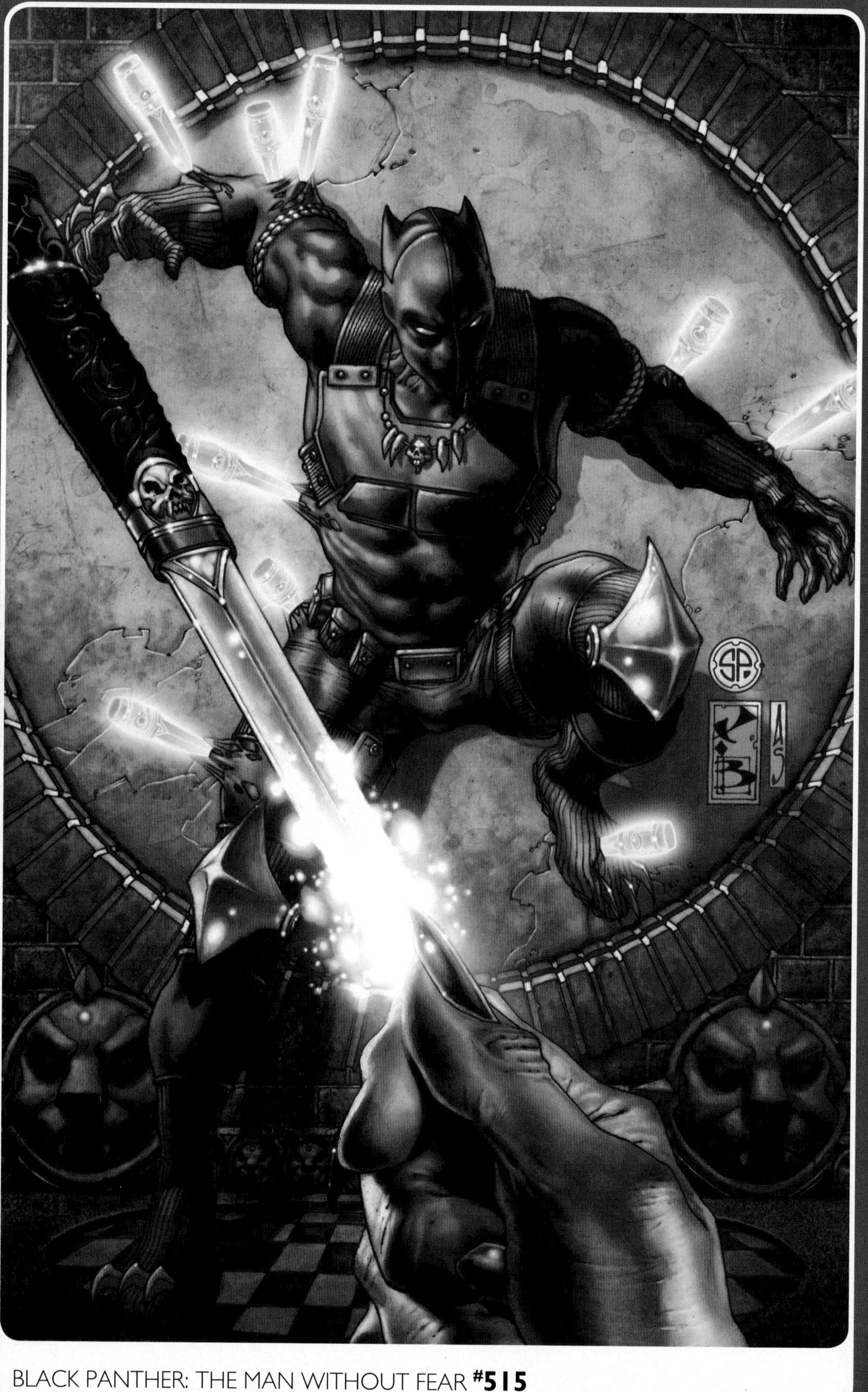

BLACK PANTHER: THE MAN WITHOUT FEAR #515

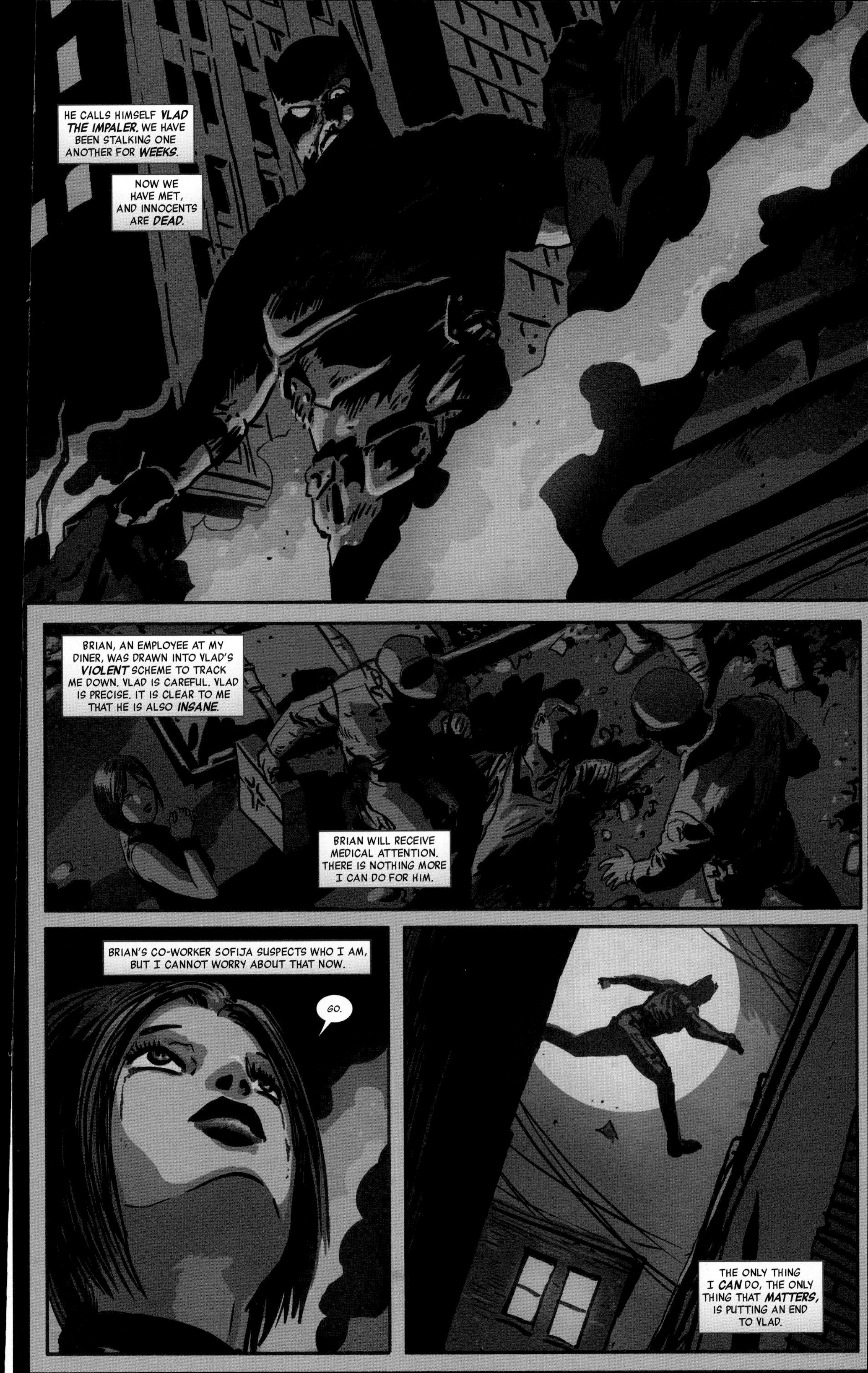
HE CALLS HIMSELF VLAD THE IMPALER. WE HAVE BEEN STALKING ONE ANOTHER FOR WEEKS.
NOW WE HAVE MET, AND INNOCENTS ARE DEAD.
BRIAN, AN EMPLOYEE AT MY DINER, WAS DRAWN INTO VLAD'S VIOLENT SCHEME TO TRACK ME DOWN. VLAD IS CAREFUL. VLAD IS PRECISE. IT IS CLEAR TO ME THAT HE IS ALSO INSANE.
BRIAN WILL RECEIVE MEDICAL ATTENTION. THERE IS NOTHING MORE I CAN DO FOR HIM.
BRIAN'S CO-WORKER SOFIJA SUSPECTS WHO I AM, BUT I CANNOT WORRY ABOUT THAT NOW.
GO.
THE ONLY THING I CAN DO, THE ONLY THING THAT MATTERS, IS PUTTING AN END TO VLAD.

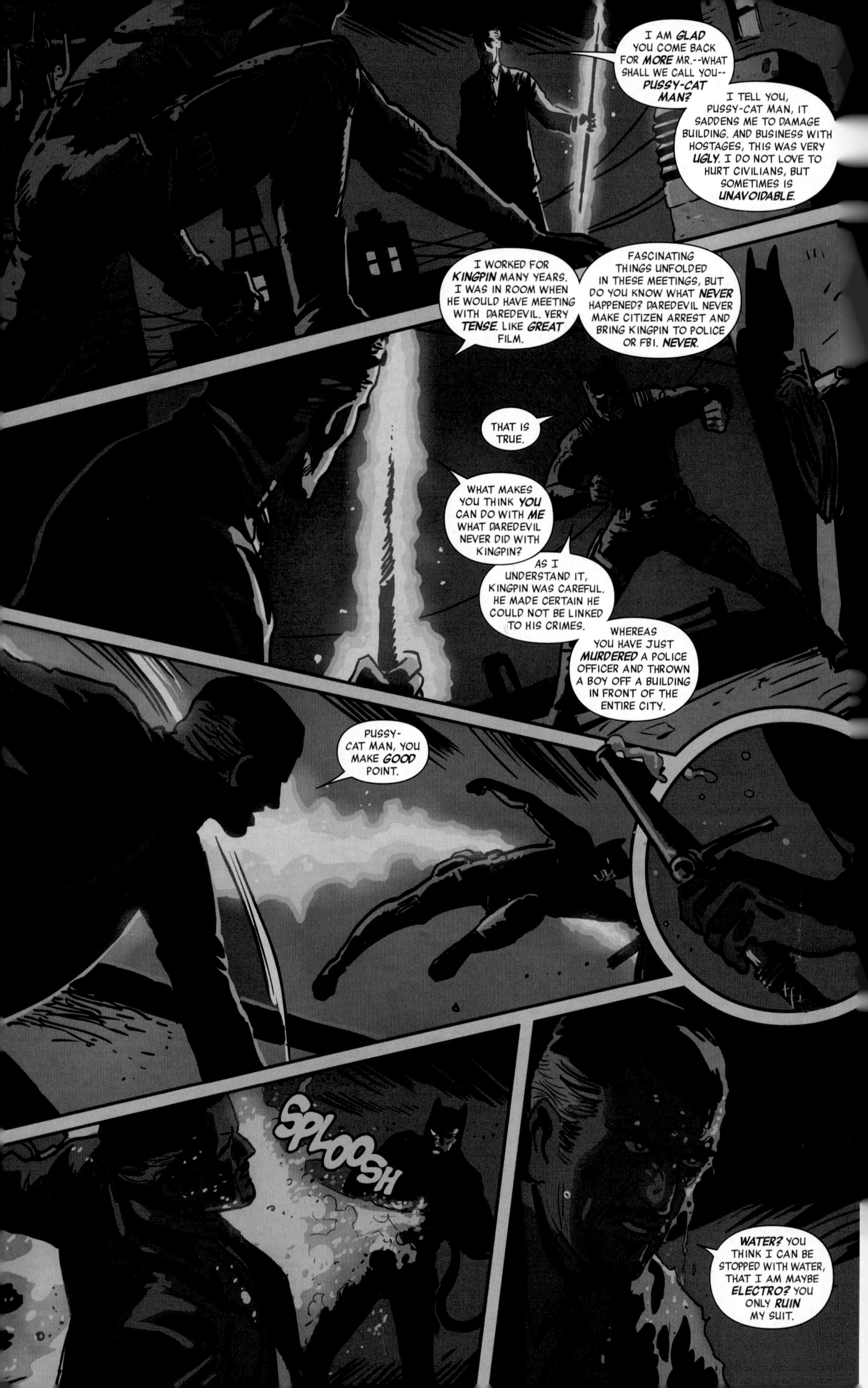
I AM GLAD YOU COME BACK FOR MORE MR.--WHAT SHALL WE CALL YOU-- PUSSY-CAT MAN?
I TELL YOU, PUSSY-CAT MAN, IT SADDENS ME TO DAMAGE BUILDING. AND BUSINESS WITH HOSTAGES, THIS WAS VERY UGLY. I DO NOT LOVE TO HURT CIVILIANS, BUT SOMETIMES IS UNAVOIDABLE.
I WORKED FOR KINGPIN MANY YEARS. I WAS IN ROOM WHEN HE WOULD HAVE MEETING WITH DAREDEVIL. VERY TENSE. LIKE GREAT FILM.
FASCINATING THINGS UNFOLDED IN THESE MEETINGS, BUT DO YOU KNOW WHAT NEVER HAPPENED? DAREDEVIL NEVER MAKE CITIZEN ARREST AND BRING KINGPIN TO POLICE OR FBI. NEVER.
THAT IS TRUE.
WHAT MAKES YOU THINK YOU CAN DO WITH ME WHAT DAREDEVIL NEVER DID WITH KINGPIN?
AS I UNDERSTAND IT, KINGPIN WAS CAREFUL. HE MADE CERTAIN HE COULD NOT BE LINKED TO HIS CRIMES.
WHEREAS YOU HAVE JUST MURDERED A POLICE OFFICER AND THROWN A BOY OFF A BUILDING IN FRONT OF THE ENTIRE CITY.
PUSSY-CAT MAN, YOU MAKE GOOD POINT.
SPLOOSH
WATER? YOU THINK I CAN BE STOPPED WITH WATER, THAT I AM MAYBE ELECTRO? YOU ONLY RUIN MY SUIT.

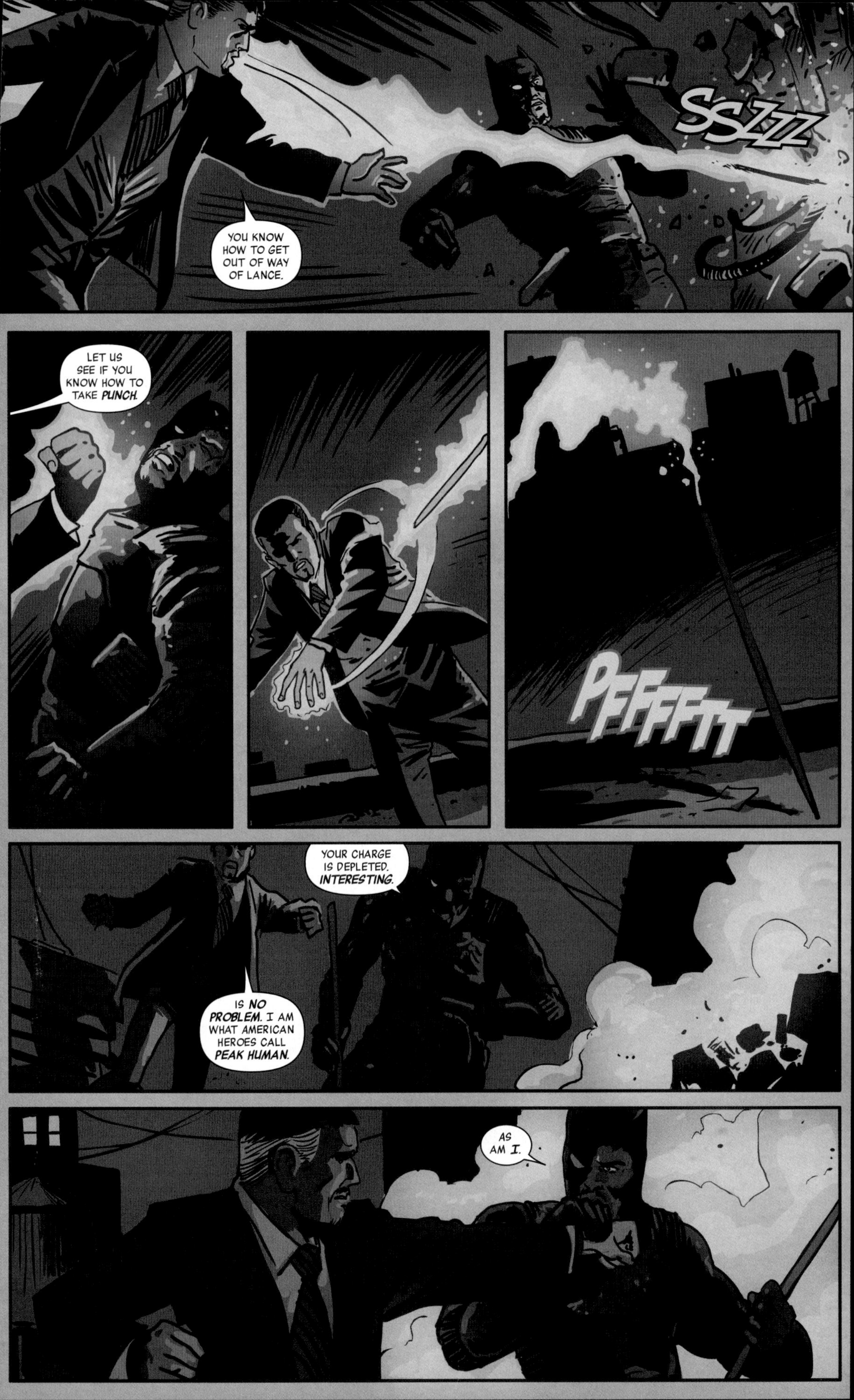
SSZZZ
YOU KNOW HOW TO GET OUT OF WAY OF LANCE.
LET US SEE IF YOU KNOW HOW TO TAKE PUNCH.
PFFFFTT
YOUR CHARGE IS DEPLETED. INTERESTING.
IS NO PROBLEM. I AM WHAT AMERICAN HEROES CALL PEAK HUMAN.
AS AM I.

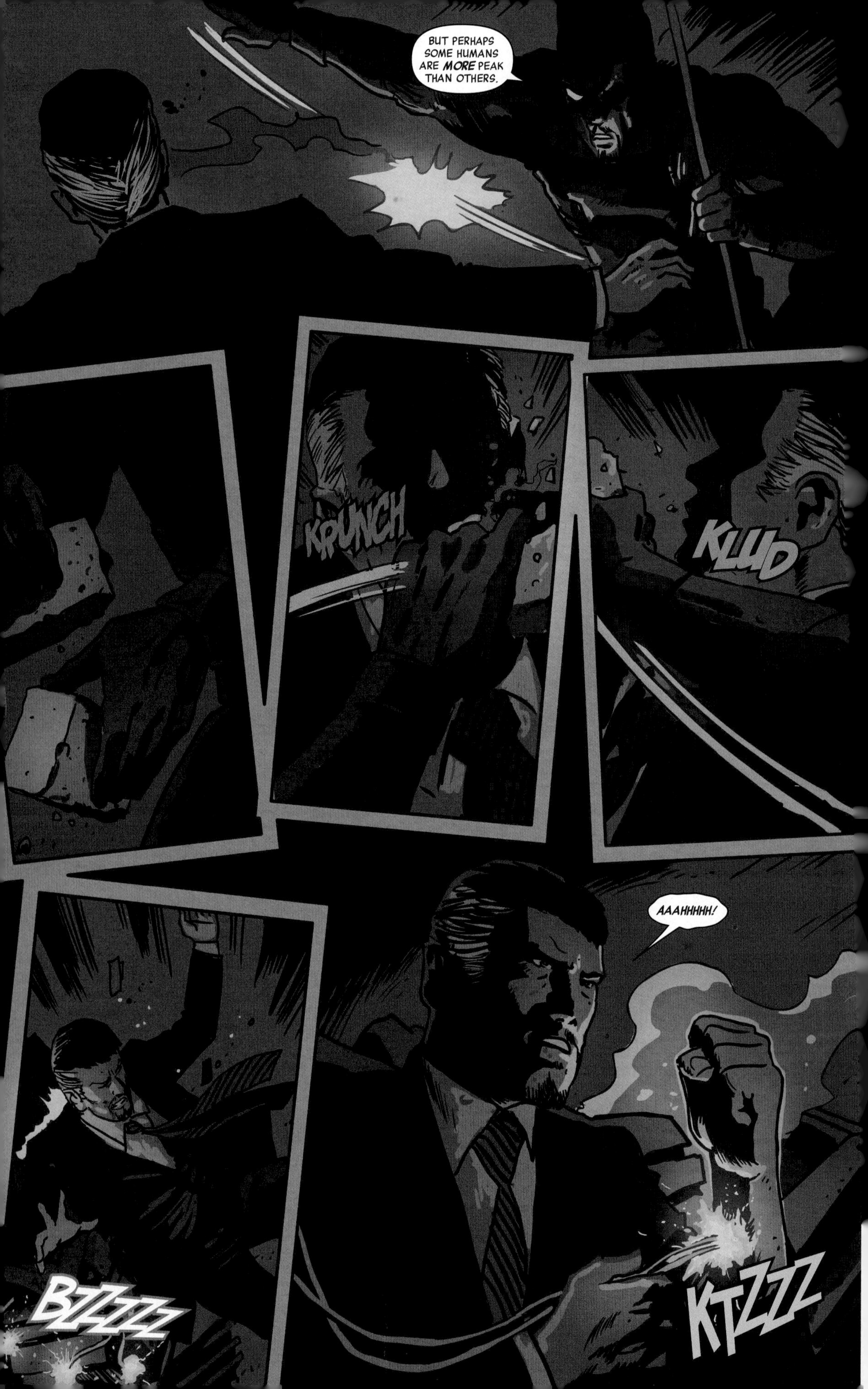
BUT PERHAPS SOME HUMANS ARE MORE PEAK THAN OTHERS.
KRUNCH
KLUD
AAAHHHHH!
BZZZZZ
KTZZZ

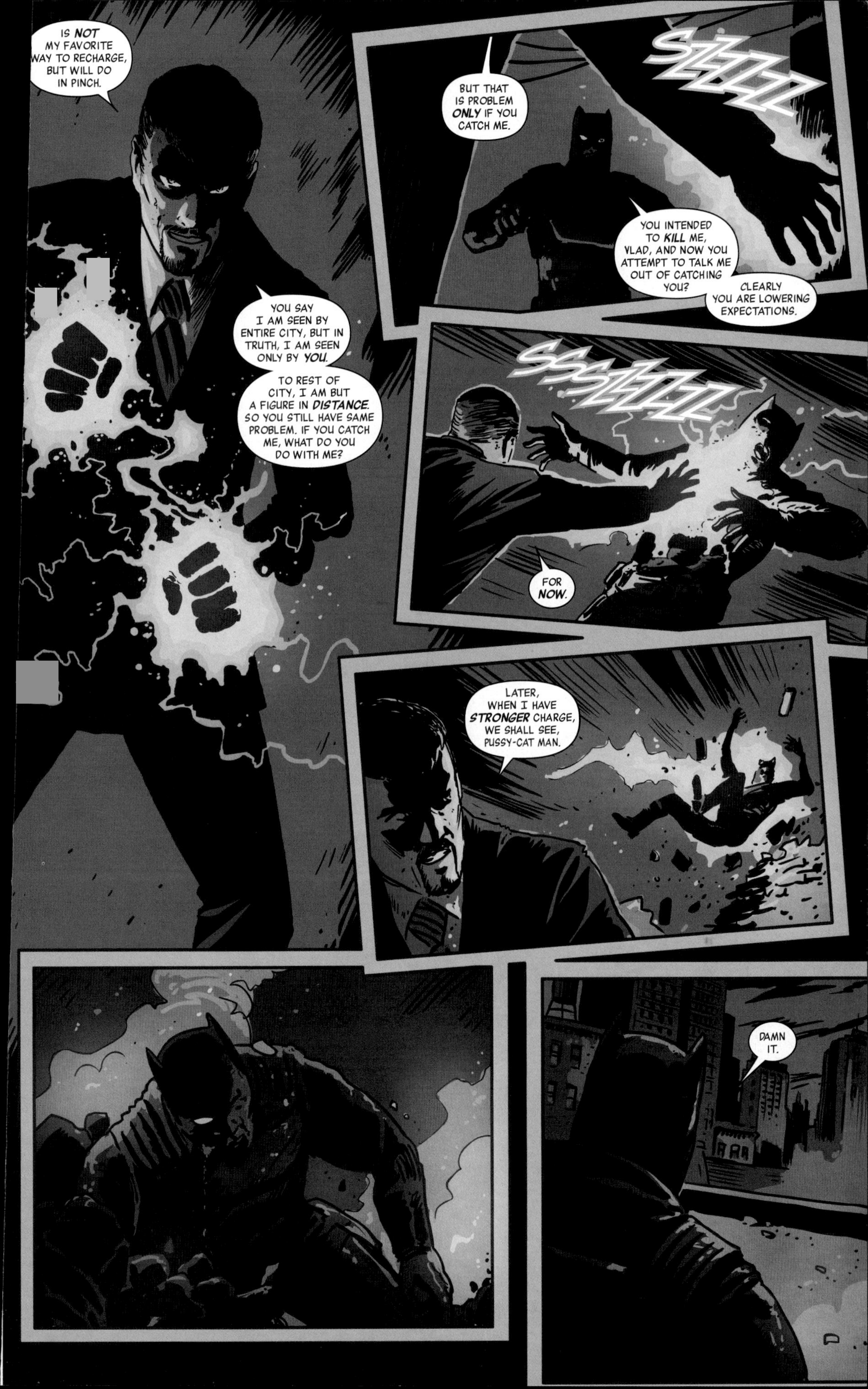
IS NOT MY FAVORITE WAY TO RECHARGE, BUT WILL DO IN PINCH.
YOU SAY I AM SEEN BY ENTIRE CITY, BUT IN TRUTH, I AM SEEN ONLY BY YOU.
TO REST OF CITY, I AM BUT A FIGURE IN DISTANCE. SO YOU STILL HAVE SAME PROBLEM. IF YOU CATCH ME, WHAT DO YOU DO WITH ME?
SZZZZZ
BUT THAT IS PROBLEM ONLY IF YOU CATCH ME.
YOU INTENDED TO KILL ME, VLAD, AND NOW YOU ATTEMPT TO TALK ME OUT OF CATCHING YOU?
CLEARLY YOU ARE LOWERING EXPECTATIONS.
SSSZZZZZ
FOR NOW.
LATER, WHEN I HAVE STRONGER CHARGE, WE SHALL SEE, PUSSY-CAT MAN.
DAMN IT.

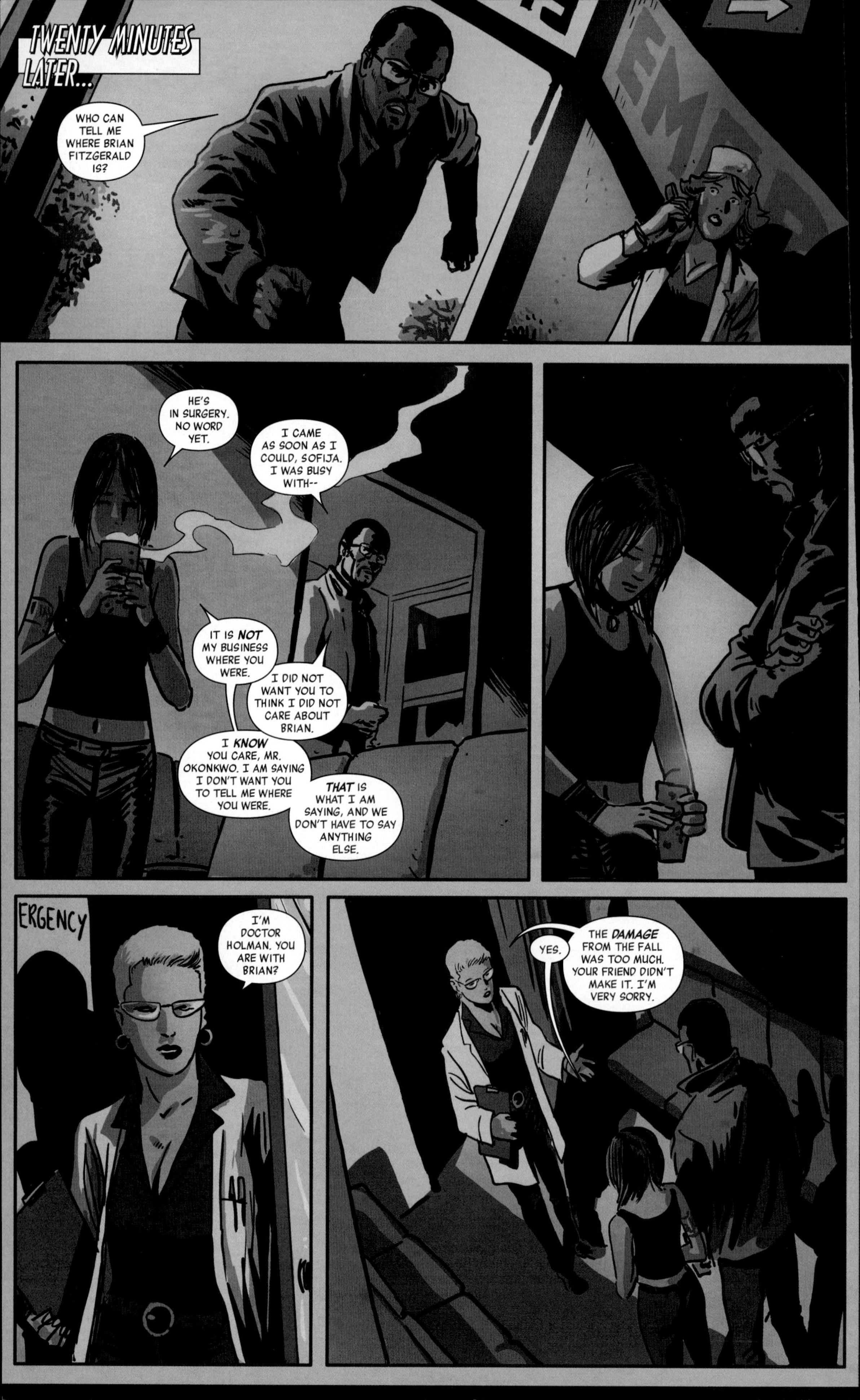
TWENTY MINUTES LATER...
WHO CAN TELL ME WHERE BRIAN FITZGERALD IS?
HE'S IN SURGERY. NO WORD YET.
I CAME AS SOON AS I COULD, SOFIJA. I WAS BUSY WITH--
IT IS NOT MY BUSINESS WHERE YOU WERE.
I DID NOT WANT YOU TO THINK I DID NOT CARE ABOUT BRIAN.
I KNOW YOU CARE, MR. OKONKWO. I AM SAYING I DON'T WANT YOU TO TELL ME WHERE YOU WERE.
THAT IS WHAT I AM SAYING, AND WE DON'T HAVE TO SAY ANYTHING ELSE.
ERGENCY
I'M DOCTOR HOLMAN. YOU ARE WITH BRIAN?
YES.
THE DAMAGE FROM THE FALL WAS TOO MUCH. YOUR FRIEND DIDN'T MAKE IT. I'M VERY SORRY.

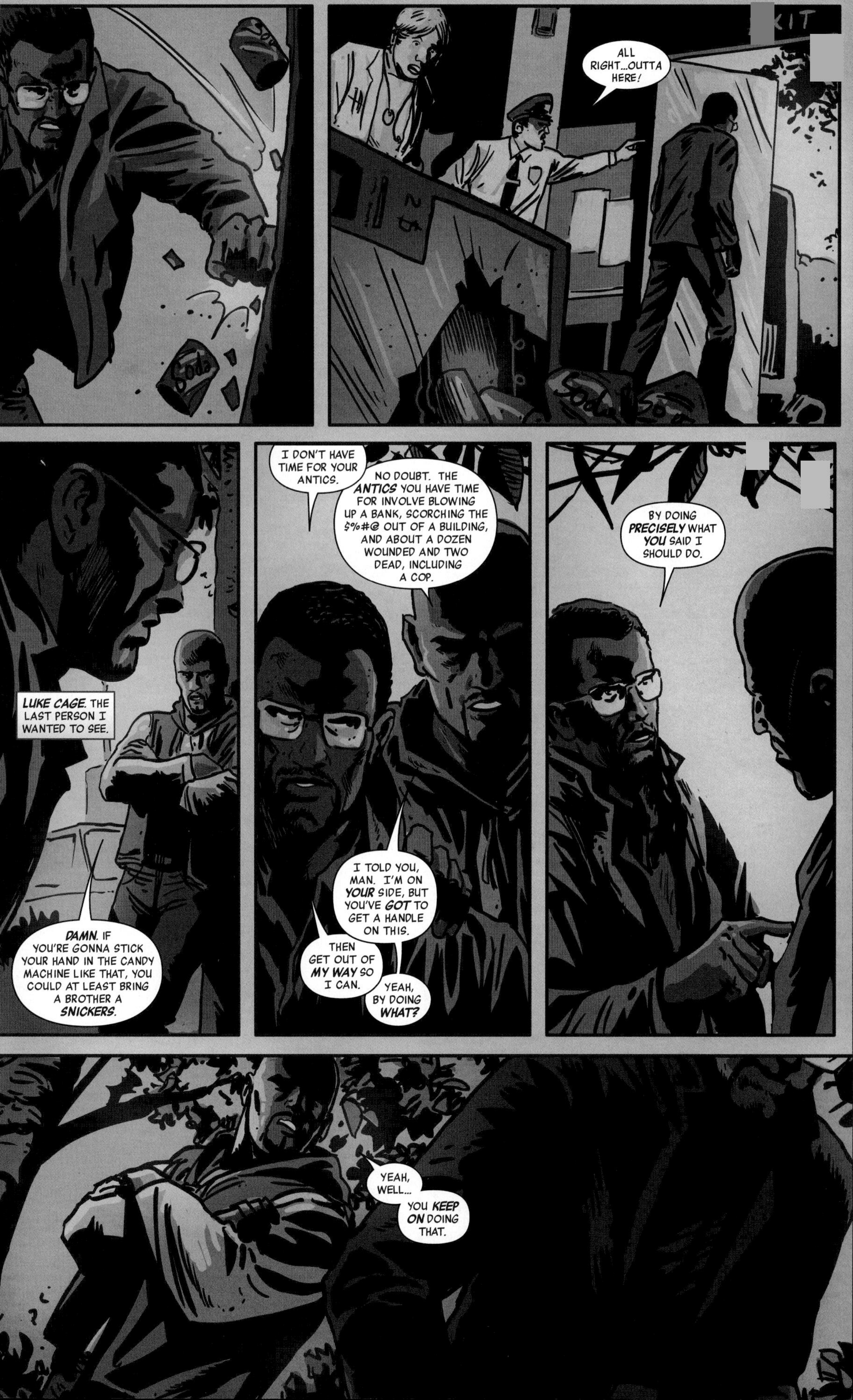

ALL RIGHT...OUTTA HERE!
LUKE CAGE. THE LAST PERSON I WANTED TO SEE.
DAMN. IF YOU'RE GONNA STICK YOUR HAND IN THE CANDY MACHINE LIKE THAT, YOU COULD AT LEAST BRING A BROTHER A SNICKERS.
I DON'T HAVE TIME FOR YOUR ANTICS.
NO DOUBT. THE ANTICS YOU HAVE TIME FOR INVOLVE BLOWING UP A BANK, SCORCHING THE $%#@ OUT OF A BUILDING, AND ABOUT A DOZEN WOUNDED AND TWO DEAD, INCLUDING A COP.
I TOLD YOU, MAN. I'M ON YOUR SIDE, BUT YOU'VE GOT TO GET A HANDLE ON THIS.
THEN GET OUT OF MY WAY SO I CAN.
YEAH, BY DOING WHAT?
BY DOING PRECISELY WHAT YOU SAID I SHOULD DO.
YEAH, WELL...
YOU KEEP ON DOING THAT.

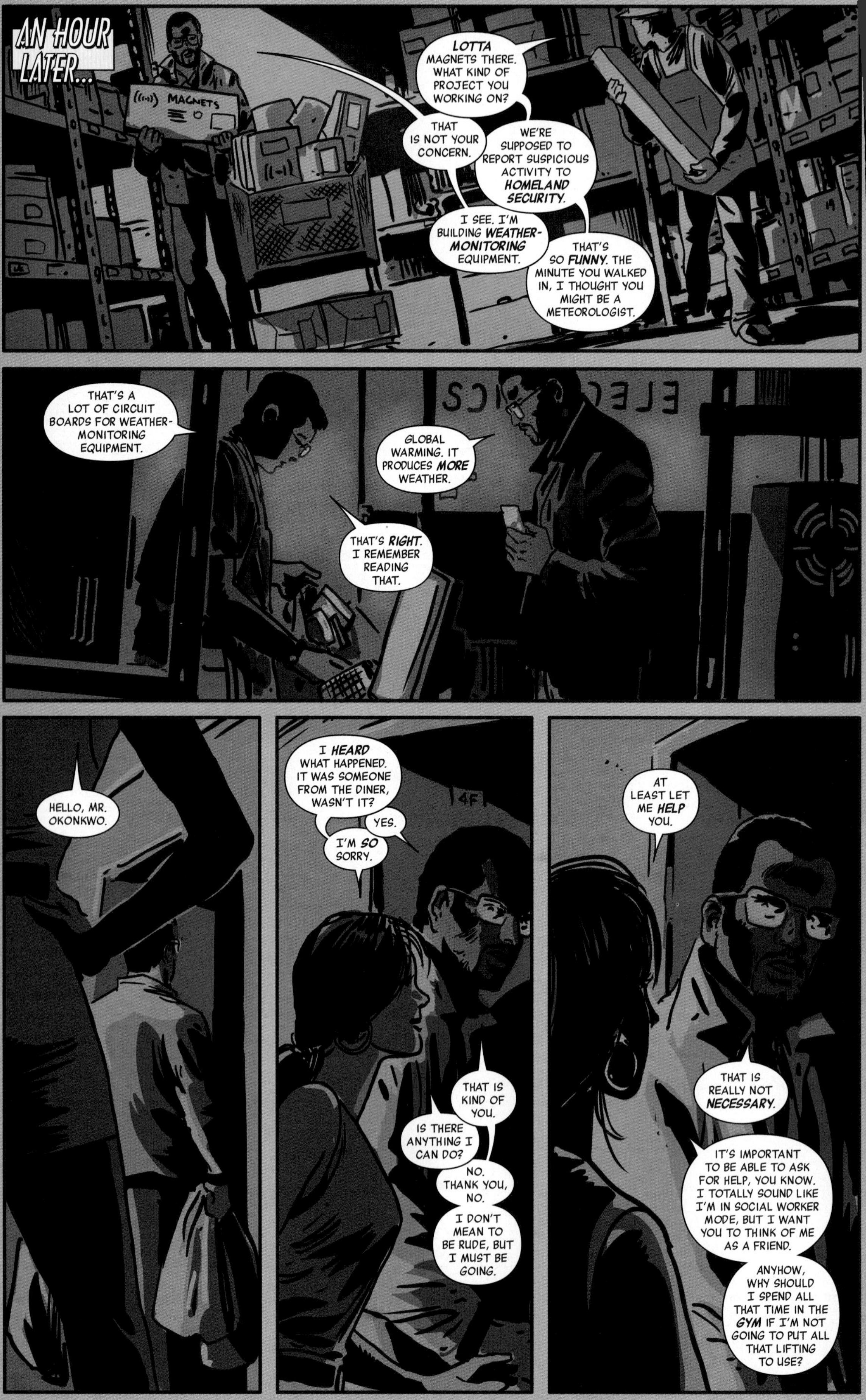
AN HOUR LATER...
MAGNETS
LOTTA MAGNETS THERE. WHAT KIND OF PROJECT YOU WORKING ON?
THAT IS NOT YOUR CONCERN.
WE'RE SUPPOSED TO REPORT SUSPICIOUS ACTIVITY TO HOMELAND SECURITY.
I SEE. I'M BUILDING WEATHER-MONITORING EQUIPMENT.
THAT'S SO FUNNY. THE MINUTE YOU WALKED IN, I THOUGHT YOU MIGHT BE A METEOROLOGIST.
THAT'S A LOT OF CIRCUIT BOARDS FOR WEATHER-MONITORING EQUIPMENT.
GLOBAL WARMING. IT PRODUCES MORE WEATHER.
THAT'S RIGHT. I REMEMBER READING THAT.
HELLO, MR. OKONKWO.
I HEARD WHAT HAPPENED. IT WAS SOMEONE FROM THE DINER, WASN'T IT?
YES.
I'M SO SORRY.
THAT IS KIND OF YOU.
IS THERE ANYTHING I CAN DO?
NO. THANK YOU, NO.
I DON'T MEAN TO BE RUDE, BUT I MUST BE GOING.
AT LEAST LET ME HELP YOU.
THAT IS REALLY NOT NECESSARY.
IT'S IMPORTANT TO BE ABLE TO ASK FOR HELP, YOU KNOW. I TOTALLY SOUND LIKE I'M IN SOCIAL WORKER MODE, BUT I WANT YOU TO THINK OF ME AS A FRIEND.
ANYHOW, WHY SHOULD I SPEND ALL THAT TIME IN THE GYM IF I'M NOT GOING TO PUT ALL THAT LIFTING TO USE?

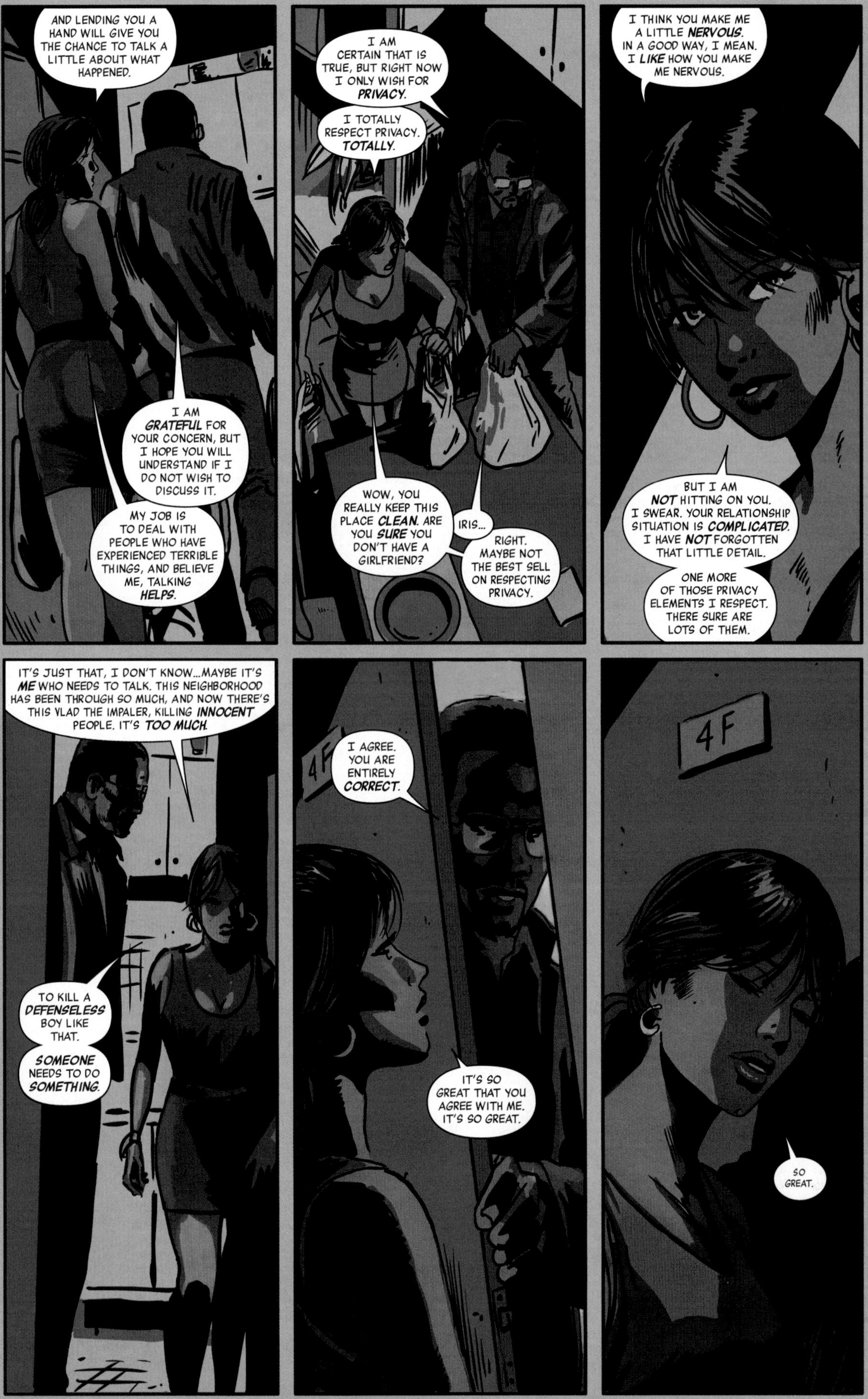
AND LENDING YOU A HAND WILL GIVE YOU THE CHANCE TO TALK A LITTLE ABOUT WHAT HAPPENED.
I AM GRATEFUL FOR YOUR CONCERN, BUT I HOPE YOU WILL UNDERSTAND IF I DO NOT WISH TO DISCUSS IT.
MY JOB IS TO DEAL WITH PEOPLE WHO HAVE EXPERIENCED TERRIBLE THINGS, AND BELIEVE ME, TALKING HELPS.
I AM CERTAIN THAT IS TRUE, BUT RIGHT NOW I ONLY WISH FOR PRIVACY.
I TOTALLY RESPECT PRIVACY. TOTALLY.
WOW, YOU REALLY KEEP THIS PLACE CLEAN. ARE YOU SURE YOU DON'T HAVE A GIRLFRIEND?
IRIS...
RIGHT. MAYBE NOT THE BEST SELL ON RESPECTING PRIVACY.
I THINK YOU MAKE ME A LITTLE NERVOUS. IN A GOOD WAY, I MEAN. I LIKE HOW YOU MAKE ME NERVOUS.
BUT I AM NOT HITTING ON YOU. I SWEAR. YOUR RELATIONSHIP SITUATION IS COMPLICATED. I HAVE NOT FORGOTTEN THAT LITTLE DETAIL.
ONE MORE OF THOSE PRIVACY ELEMENTS I RESPECT. THERE SURE ARE LOTS OF THEM.
IT'S JUST THAT, I DON'T KNOW...MAYBE IT'S ME WHO NEEDS TO TALK. THIS NEIGHBORHOOD HAS BEEN THROUGH SO MUCH, AND NOW THERE'S THIS VLAD THE IMPALER, KILLING INNOCENT PEOPLE. IT'S TOO MUCH.
TO KILL A DEFENSELESS BOY LIKE THAT.
SOMEONE NEEDS TO DO SOMETHING.
4F
I AGREE. YOU ARE ENTIRELY CORRECT.
IT'S SO GREAT THAT YOU AGREE WITH ME. IT'S SO GREAT.
4F
SO GREAT.

BRIAN WAS DEAD, AND THINGS COULD NOT BE MORE *CLEAR*.

IT WAS TIME TO ACCEPT I AM *NOT* WHO I *WAS*.

WHEN *LUKE CAGE* FIRST CAME TO SEE ME, I DID NOT WISH TO LISTEN.

THOUGH HE IRRITATED ME, I CANNOT *DENY* THE WISDOM OF HIS WORDS. I AM NO LONGER THE BLACK PANTHER, I NO LONGER HAVE THE TECHNOLOGY OF A WAKANDAN KING.

AND, BY MY OWN CHOICE, I AM *ALONE*.

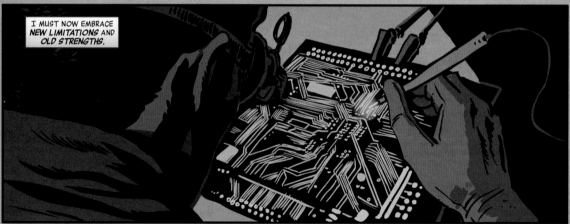

I MUST NOW EMBRACE *NEW LIMITATIONS* AND *OLD STRENGTHS*.

VLAD HAS SHOWN HIMSELF STRONG, RESOURCEFUL, AND DANGEROUS.

NOW IT IS TIME TO SHOW HIM WHAT *I* AM.

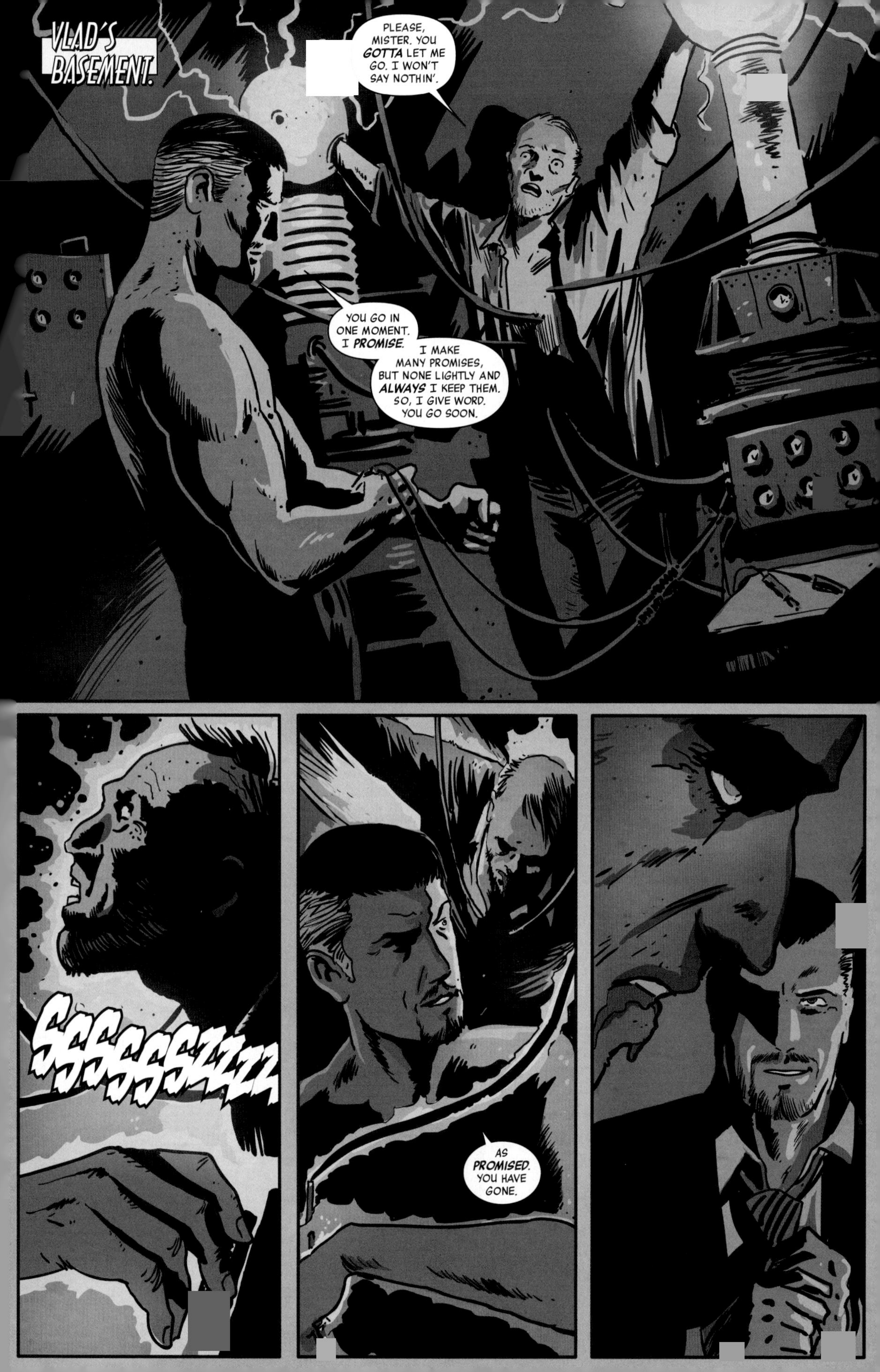
VLAD'S BASEMENT.
PLEASE, MISTER. YOU GOTTA LET ME GO. I WON'T SAY NOTHIN'.
YOU GO IN ONE MOMENT. I PROMISE.
I MAKE MANY PROMISES, BUT NONE LIGHTLY AND ALWAYS I KEEP THEM. SO, I GIVE WORD. YOU GO SOON.
SSSSSSZZZZZ
AS PROMISED. YOU HAVE GONE.

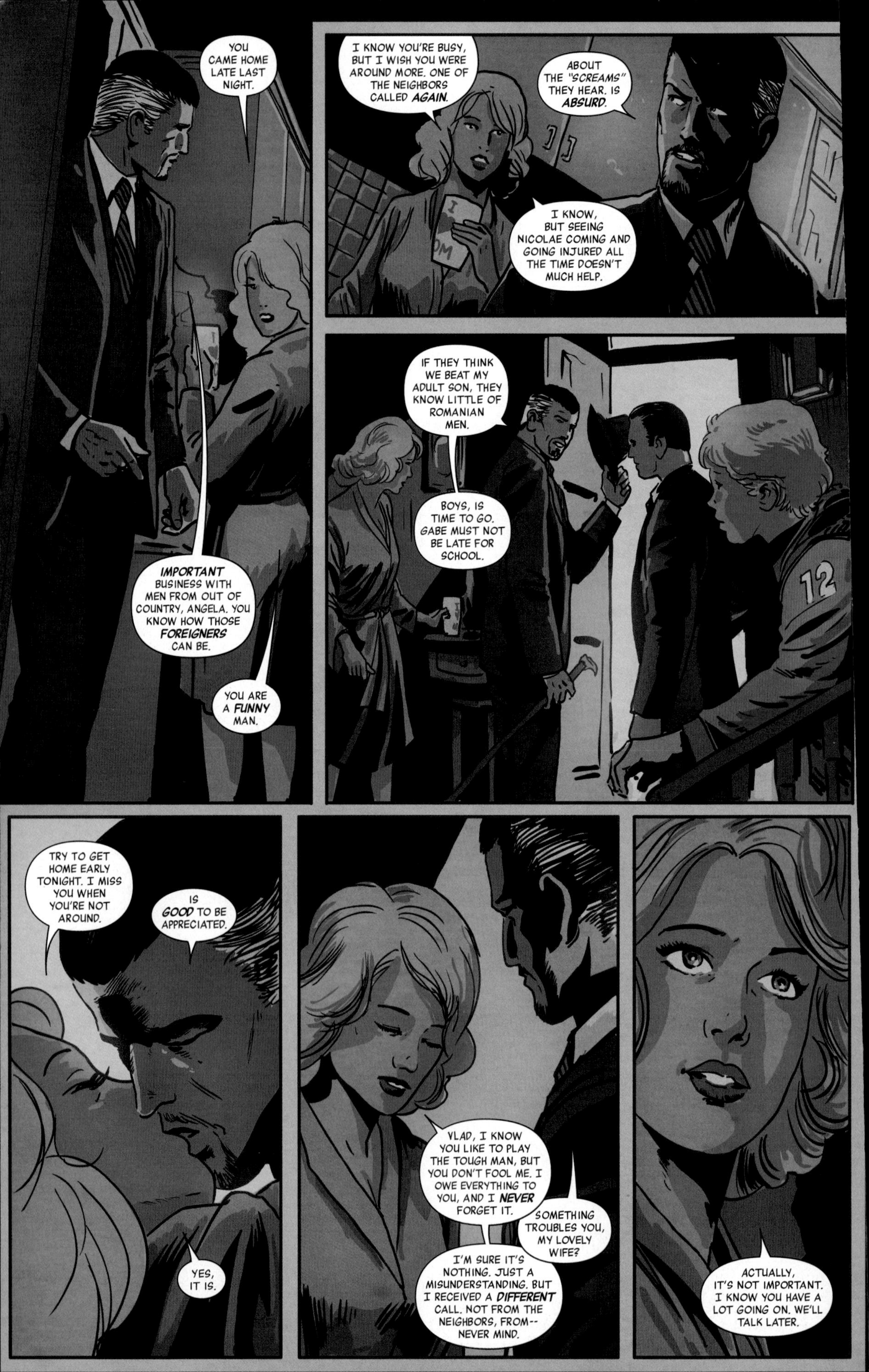
YOU CAME HOME LATE LAST NIGHT.
IMPORTANT BUSINESS WITH MEN FROM OUT OF COUNTRY, ANGELA. YOU KNOW HOW THOSE FOREIGNERS CAN BE.
YOU ARE A FUNNY MAN.
I KNOW YOU'RE BUSY, BUT I WISH YOU WERE AROUND MORE. ONE OF THE NEIGHBORS CALLED AGAIN.
ABOUT THE "SCREAMS" THEY HEAR. IS ABSURD.
I KNOW, BUT SEEING NICOLAE COMING AND GOING INJURED ALL THE TIME DOESN'T MUCH HELP.
IF THEY THINK WE BEAT MY ADULT SON, THEY KNOW LITTLE OF ROMANIAN MEN.
BOYS, IS TIME TO GO. GABE MUST NOT BE LATE FOR SCHOOL.
12
TRY TO GET HOME EARLY TONIGHT. I MISS YOU WHEN YOU'RE NOT AROUND.
IS GOOD TO BE APPRECIATED.
YES, IT IS.
VLAD, I KNOW YOU LIKE TO PLAY THE TOUGH MAN, BUT YOU DON'T FOOL ME. I OWE EVERYTHING TO YOU, AND I NEVER FORGET IT.
SOMETHING TROUBLES YOU, MY LOVELY WIFE?
I'M SURE IT'S NOTHING. JUST A MISUNDERSTANDING. BUT I RECEIVED A DIFFERENT CALL. NOT FROM THE NEIGHBORS, FROM-- NEVER MIND.
ACTUALLY, IT'S NOT IMPORTANT. I KNOW YOU HAVE A LOT GOING ON. WE'LL TALK LATER.

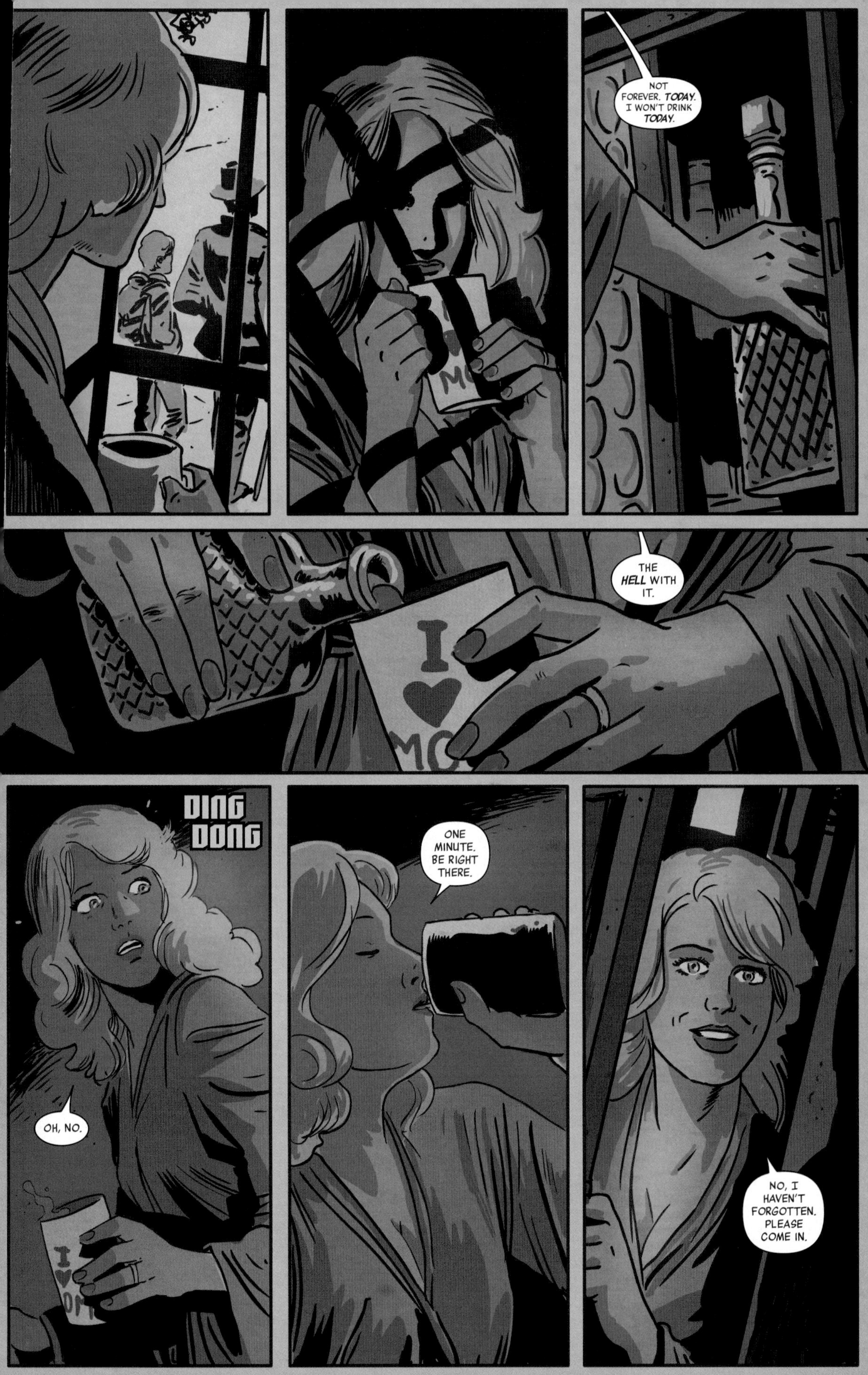
NOT FOREVER. TODAY. I WON'T DRINK TODAY.
THE HELL WITH IT.
DING DONG
OH, NO.
ONE MINUTE. BE RIGHT THERE.
NO, I HAVEN'T FORGOTTEN. PLEASE COME IN.

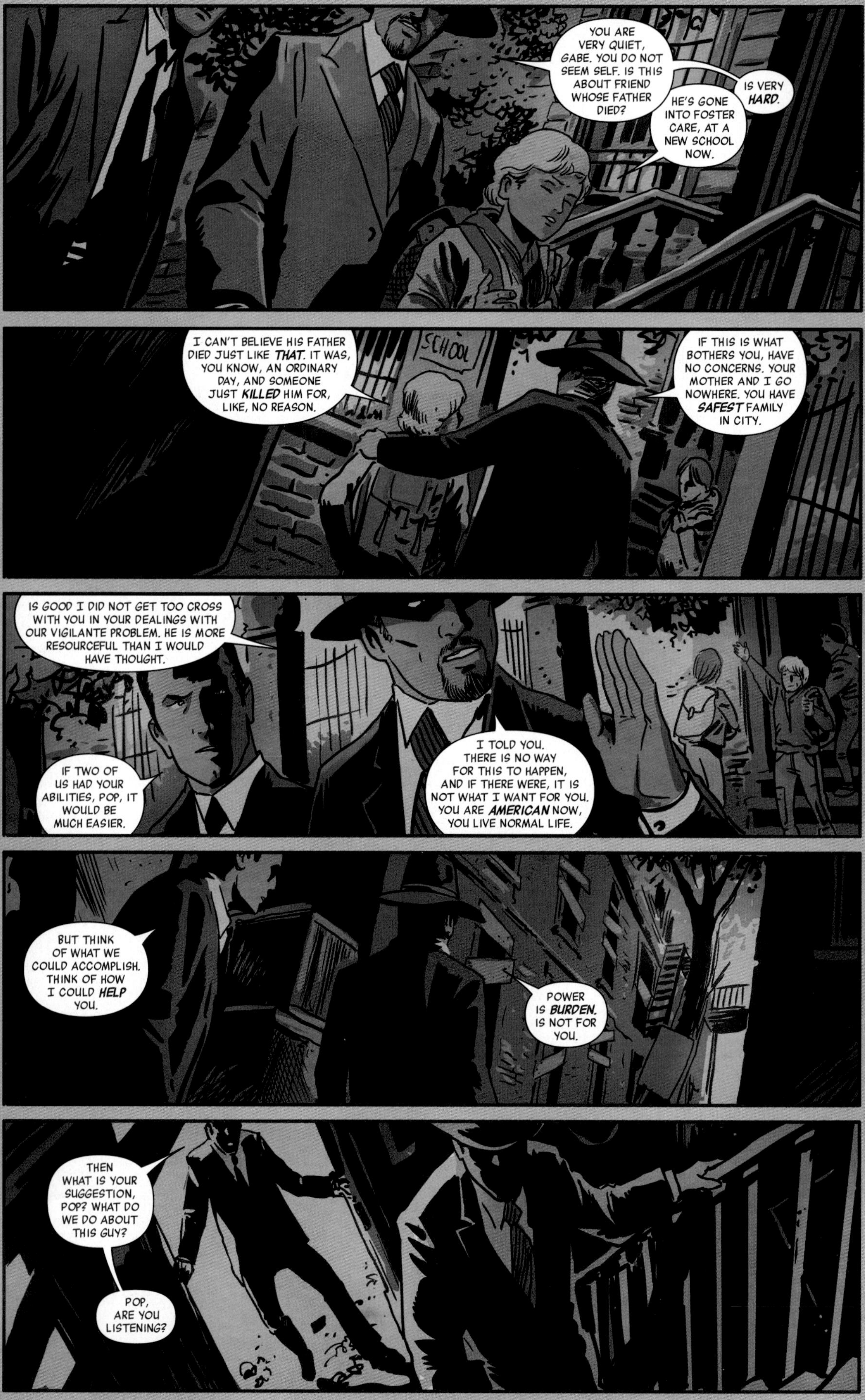
YOU ARE VERY QUIET, GABE. YOU DO NOT SEEM SELF. IS THIS ABOUT FRIEND WHOSE FATHER DIED?
IS VERY HARD.
HE'S GONE INTO FOSTER CARE, AT A NEW SCHOOL NOW.
SCHOOL
I CAN'T BELIEVE HIS FATHER DIED JUST LIKE THAT. IT WAS, YOU KNOW, AN ORDINARY DAY, AND SOMEONE JUST KILLED HIM FOR, LIKE, NO REASON.
IF THIS IS WHAT BOTHERS YOU, HAVE NO CONCERNS. YOUR MOTHER AND I GO NOWHERE. YOU HAVE SAFEST FAMILY IN CITY.
IS GOOD I DID NOT GET TOO CROSS WITH YOU IN YOUR DEALINGS WITH OUR VIGILANTE PROBLEM. HE IS MORE RESOURCEFUL THAN I WOULD HAVE THOUGHT.
IF TWO OF US HAD YOUR ABILITIES, POP, IT WOULD BE MUCH EASIER.
I TOLD YOU. THERE IS NO WAY FOR THIS TO HAPPEN, AND IF THERE WERE, IT IS NOT WHAT I WANT FOR YOU. YOU ARE AMERICAN NOW, YOU LIVE NORMAL LIFE.
BUT THINK OF WHAT WE COULD ACCOMPLISH. THINK OF HOW I COULD HELP YOU.
POWER IS BURDEN. IS NOT FOR YOU.
THEN WHAT IS YOUR SUGGESTION, POP? WHAT DO WE DO ABOUT THIS GUY?
POP, ARE YOU LISTENING?

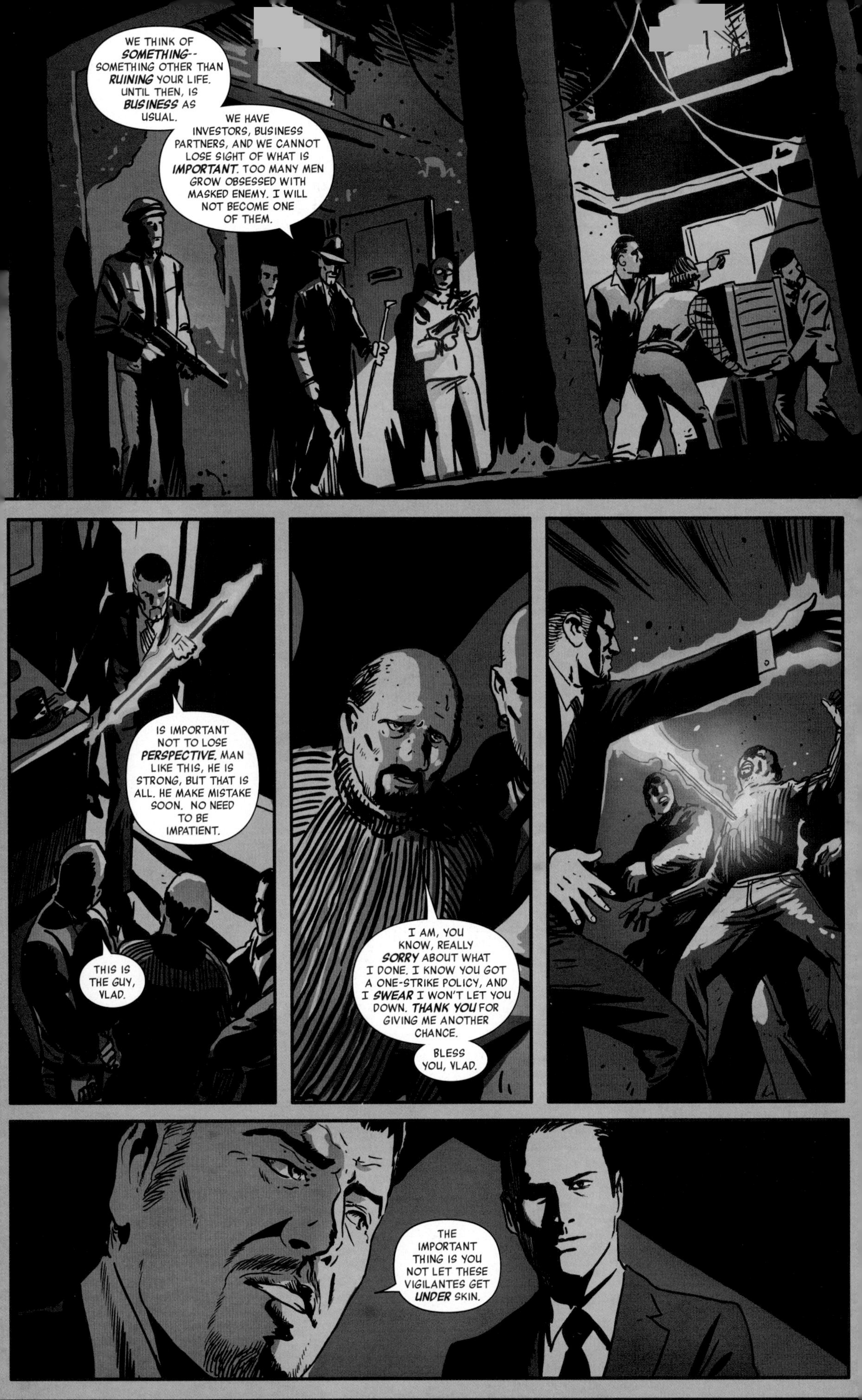
WE THINK OF SOMETHING-- SOMETHING OTHER THAN RUINING YOUR LIFE. UNTIL THEN, IS BUSINESS AS USUAL.
WE HAVE INVESTORS, BUSINESS PARTNERS, AND WE CANNOT LOSE SIGHT OF WHAT IS IMPORTANT. TOO MANY MEN GROW OBSESSED WITH MASKED ENEMY. I WILL NOT BECOME ONE OF THEM.
IS IMPORTANT NOT TO LOSE PERSPECTIVE. MAN LIKE THIS, HE IS STRONG, BUT THAT IS ALL. HE MAKE MISTAKE SOON. NO NEED TO BE IMPATIENT.
THIS IS THE GUY, VLAD.
I AM, YOU KNOW, REALLY SORRY ABOUT WHAT I DONE. I KNOW YOU GOT A ONE-STRIKE POLICY, AND I SWEAR I WON'T LET YOU DOWN. THANK YOU FOR GIVING ME ANOTHER CHANCE.
BLESS YOU, VLAD.
THE IMPORTANT THING IS YOU NOT LET THESE VIGILANTES GET UNDER SKIN.

Rush Medical Office Building

Registration/ Admissions

Visitor/Patient Parking

Emergency Entrance

"I THINK YOU'LL BE VERY PLEASED. EVERYTHING HAS GONE SMOOTHLY."

SUBBASEMENT E.

THE SUBJECT'S ONLY FAMILY IS HIS UNCLE, A VERY *UNENTHUSIASTIC* GUARDIAN, WHO WAS ONLY TOO HAPPY TO BUY OUR STORY ABOUT THE SUBJECT NOT SURVIVING. HE ONLY WANTED TO KNOW WHO HE COULD *SUE*.

SO, NICOLAE, THE WORLD THINKS THE SUBJECT IS DEAD, AND HE'S *OURS* TO DO WITH AS WE PLEASE.

THEN WE CAN FINALLY MOVE FORWARD, DR. HOLMAN. SEVEN MONTHS AND MORE MONEY THAN I WANT TO THINK ABOUT, AND NOW WE'RE READY.

WE *FINALLY* HAVE A LIVING SPECIMEN--SOMEONE WHO HAS ABSORBED A PORTION OF MY FATHER'S ENERGY AND *SURVIVED*.

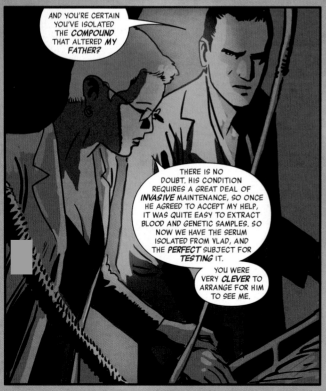

AND YOU'RE CERTAIN YOU'VE ISOLATED THE *COMPOUND* THAT ALTERED *MY FATHER?*

THERE IS NO DOUBT. HIS CONDITION REQUIRES A GREAT DEAL OF *INVASIVE* MAINTENANCE, SO ONCE HE AGREED TO ACCEPT MY HELP, IT WAS QUITE EASY TO EXTRACT BLOOD AND GENETIC SAMPLES. SO NOW WE HAVE THE SERUM ISOLATED FROM VLAD, AND THE *PERFECT* SUBJECT FOR *TESTING* IT.

YOU WERE VERY *CLEVER* TO ARRANGE FOR HIM TO SEE ME.

I HOPE HE DOESN'T *FIND OUT* WHAT YOU'RE UP TO. MY GUESS IS HE WOULD *NOT* BE HAPPY, AND HE STRIKES ME AS A MAN WITH A *TEMPER*.

YEAH. SOMETIMES. BUT HE HAS NO REASON TO SUSPECT, AND I'VE BEEN *VERY* CLEVER.

HE'S A SMART MAN, BUT IT TURNS OUT HIS SON IS A LITTLE BIT *SMARTER*.

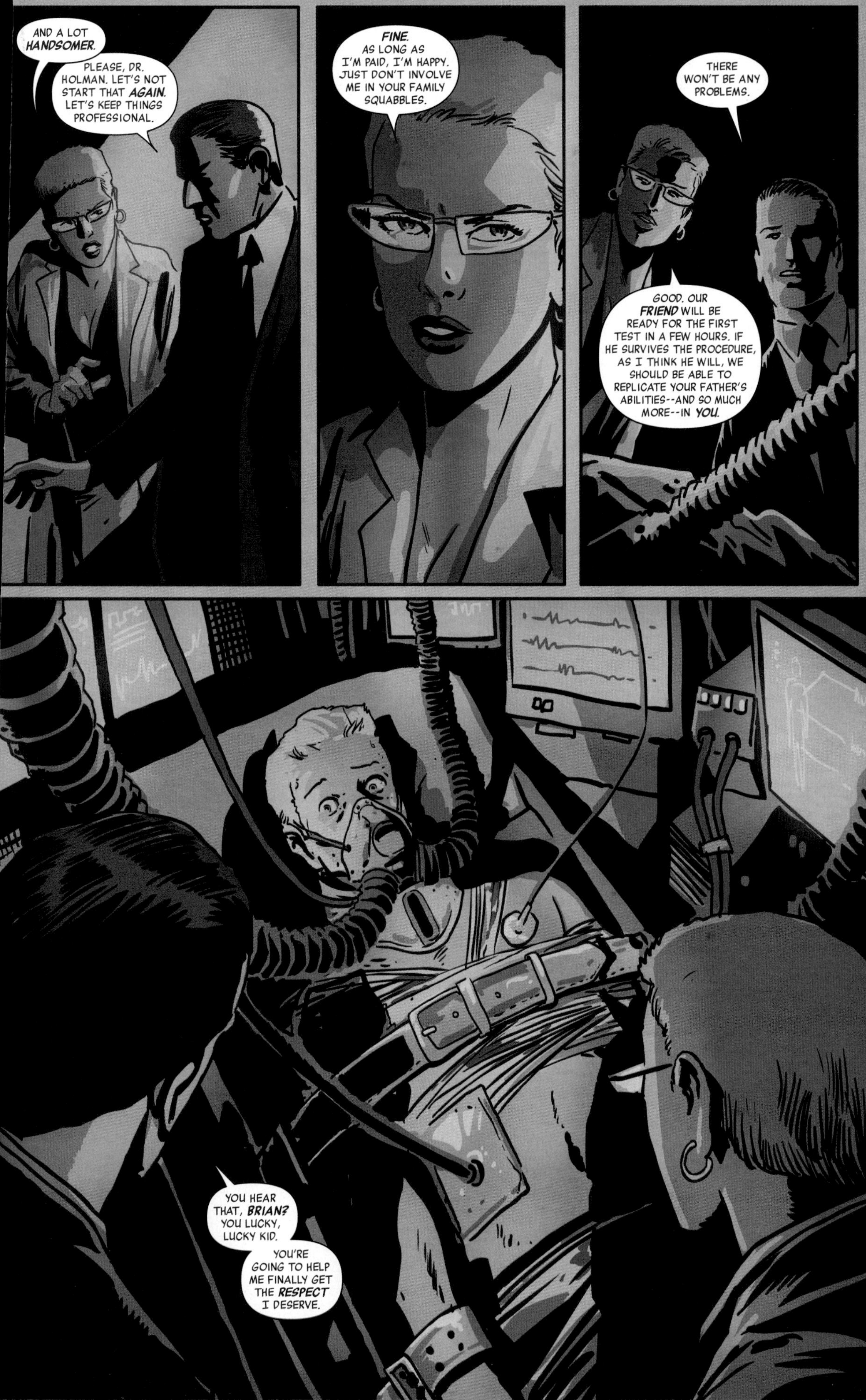
AND A LOT HANDSOMER.
PLEASE, DR. HOLMAN. LET'S NOT START THAT AGAIN. LET'S KEEP THINGS PROFESSIONAL.
FINE. AS LONG AS I'M PAID, I'M HAPPY. JUST DON'T INVOLVE ME IN YOUR FAMILY SQUABBLES.
THERE WON'T BE ANY PROBLEMS.
GOOD. OUR FRIEND WILL BE READY FOR THE FIRST TEST IN A FEW HOURS. IF HE SURVIVES THE PROCEDURE, AS I THINK HE WILL, WE SHOULD BE ABLE TO REPLICATE YOUR FATHER'S ABILITIES--AND SO MUCH MORE--IN YOU.
YOU HEAR THAT, BRIAN? YOU LUCKY, LUCKY KID.
YOU'RE GOING TO HELP ME FINALLY GET THE RESPECT I DESERVE.

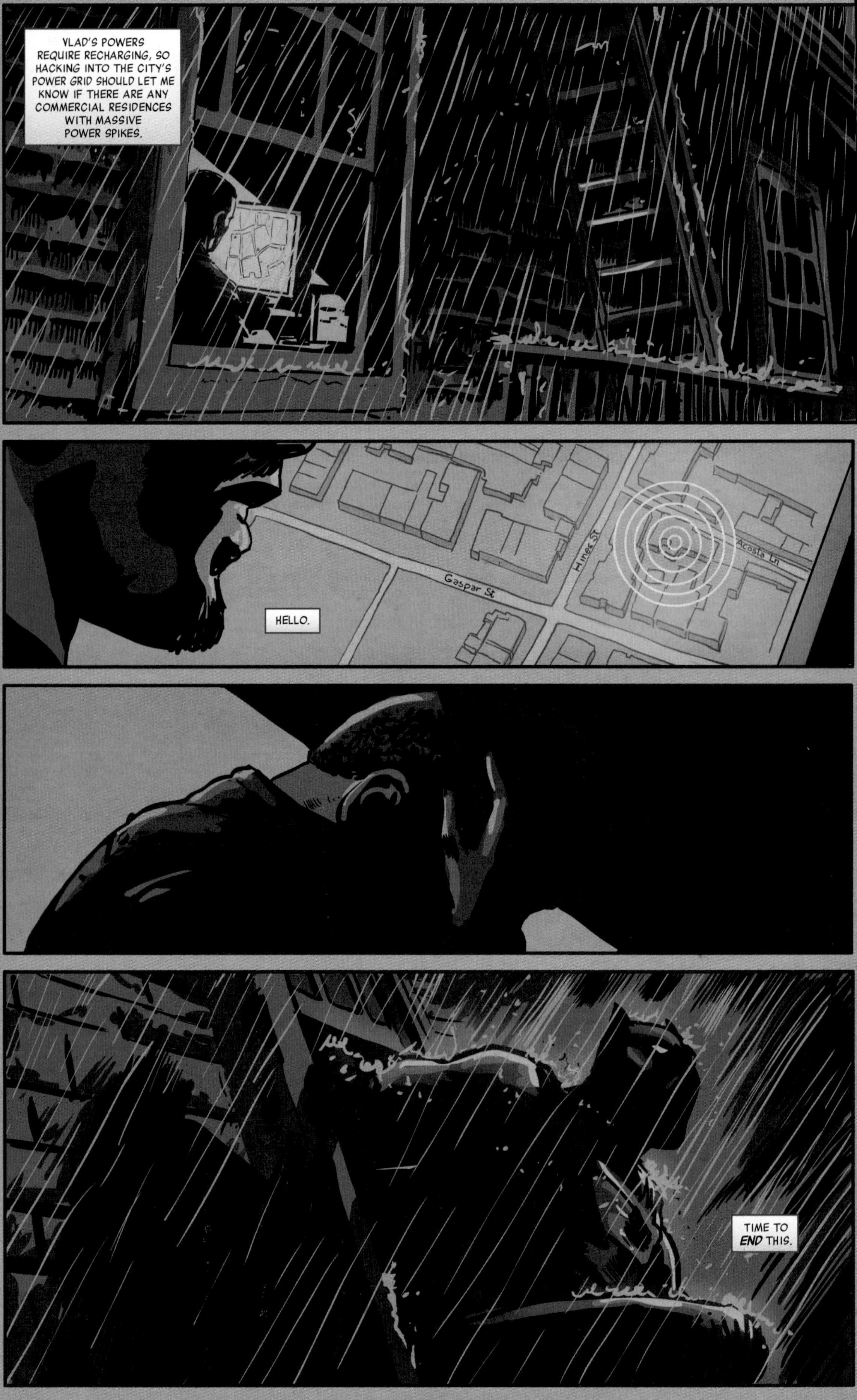
VLAD'S POWERS REQUIRE RECHARGING, SO HACKING INTO THE CITY'S POWER GRID SHOULD LET ME KNOW IF THERE ARE ANY COMMERCIAL RESIDENCES WITH MASSIVE POWER SPIKES.
Hines St
Acosta Ln
Gaspar St
HELLO.
TIME TO END THIS.

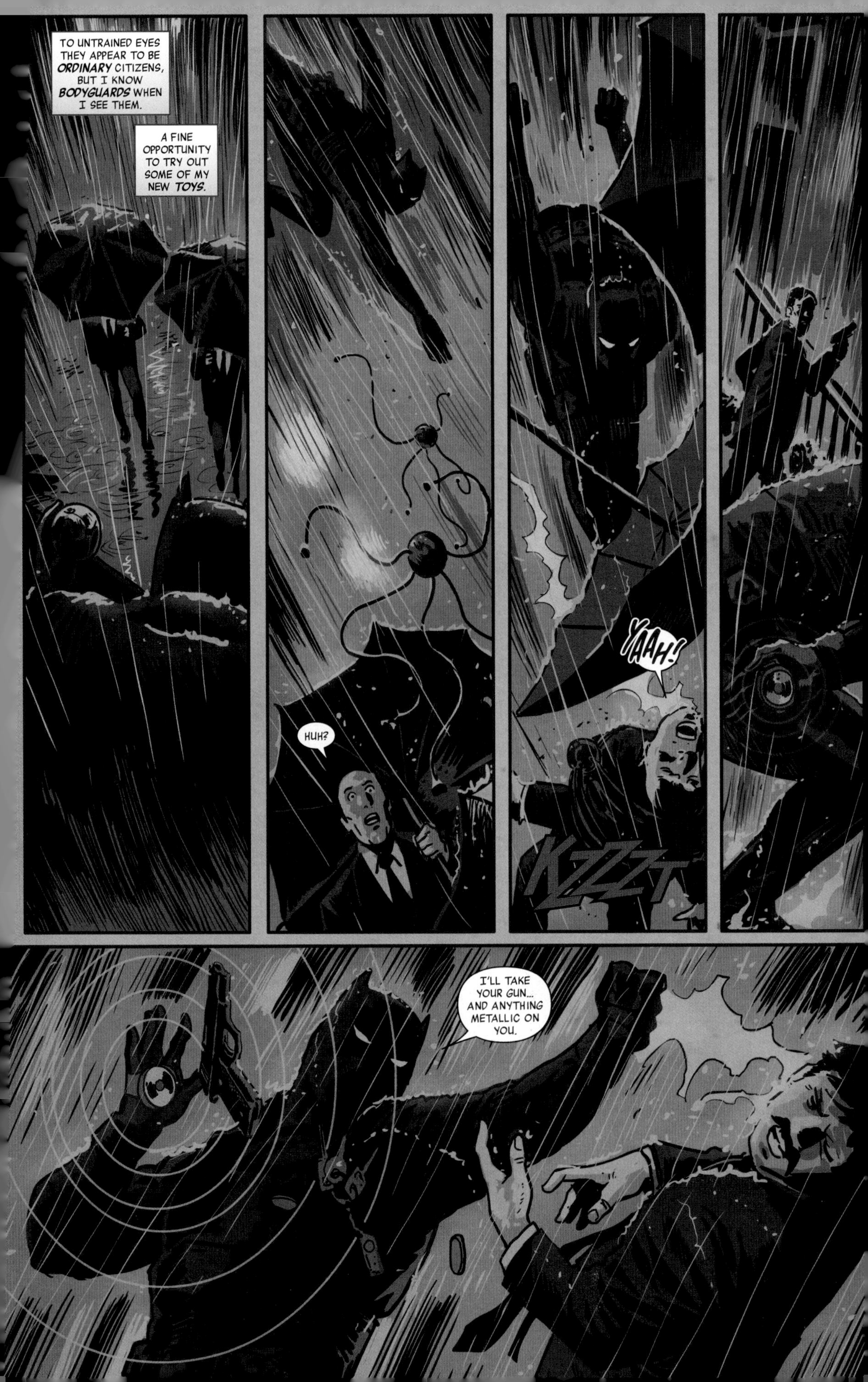
TO UNTRAINED EYES THEY APPEAR TO BE ORDINARY CITIZENS, BUT I KNOW BODYGUARDS WHEN I SEE THEM.
A FINE OPPORTUNITY TO TRY OUT SOME OF MY NEW TOYS.
HUH?
YAAAH!
KZZZT
I'LL TAKE YOUR GUN... AND ANYTHING METALLIC ON YOU.

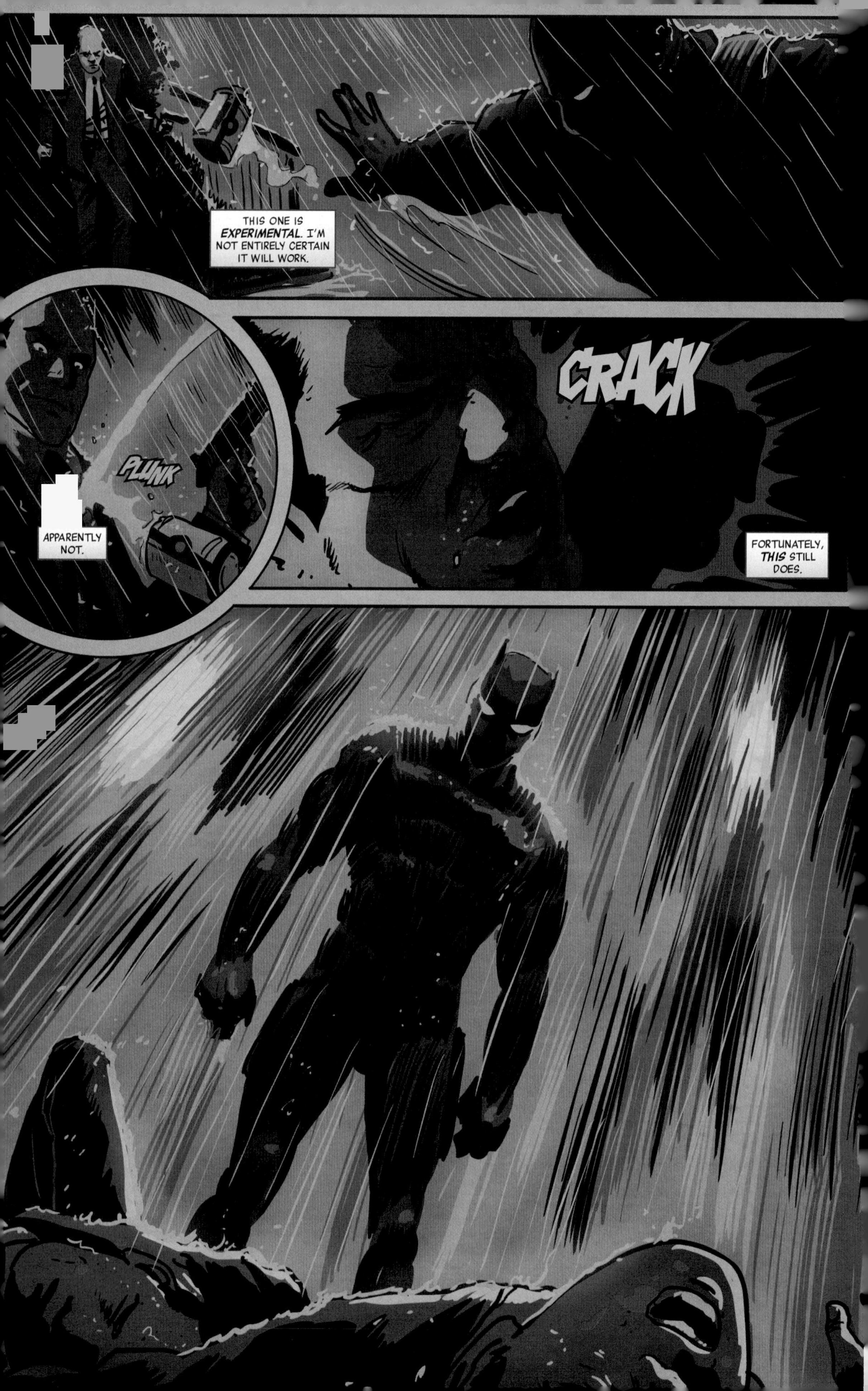
THIS ONE IS EXPERIMENTAL. I'M NOT ENTIRELY CERTAIN IT WILL WORK.
PLUNK
APPARENTLY NOT.
CRACK
FORTUNATELY, THIS STILL DOES.

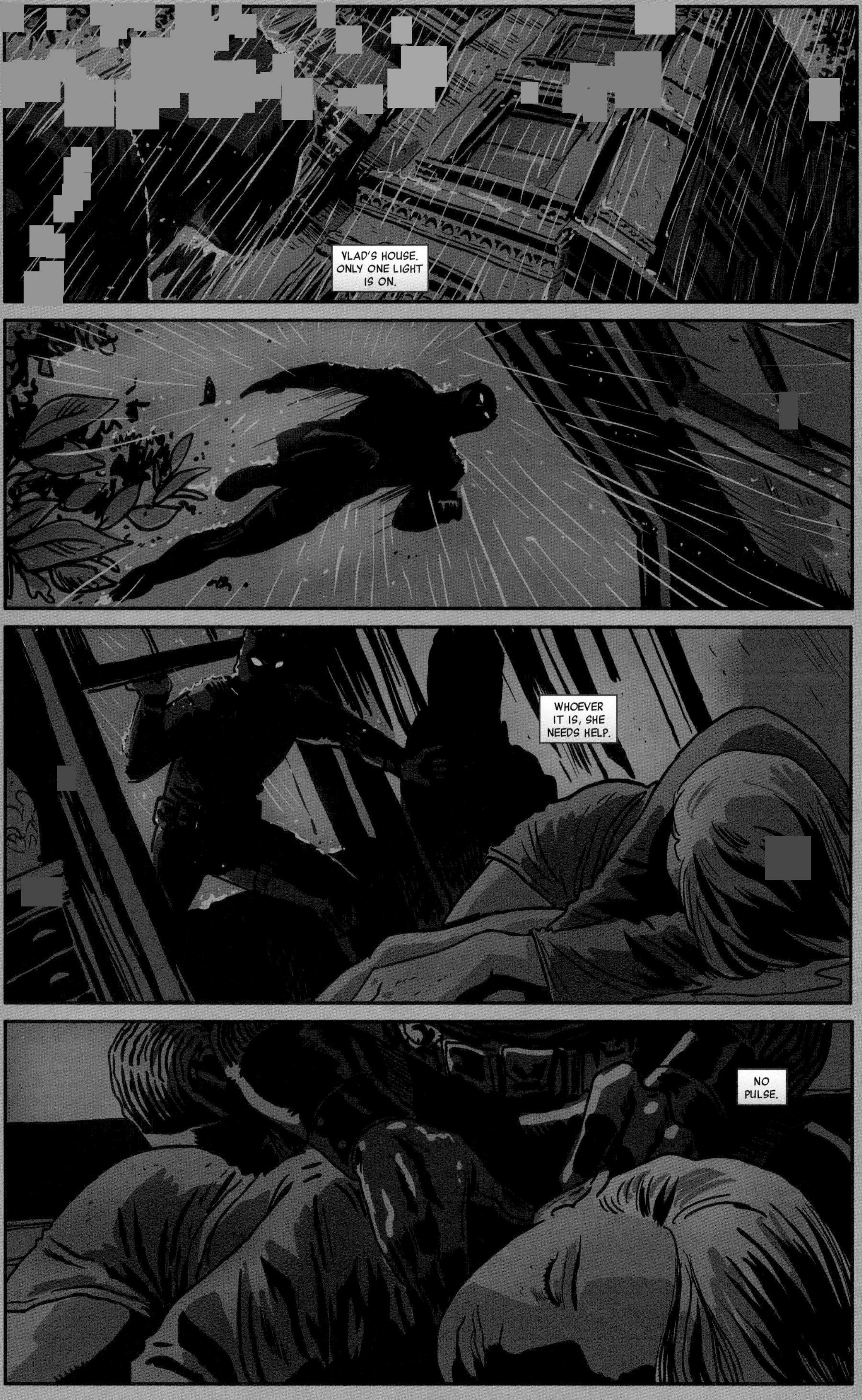
VLAD'S HOUSE. ONLY ONE LIGHT IS ON.
WHOEVER IT IS, SHE NEEDS HELP.
NO PULSE.

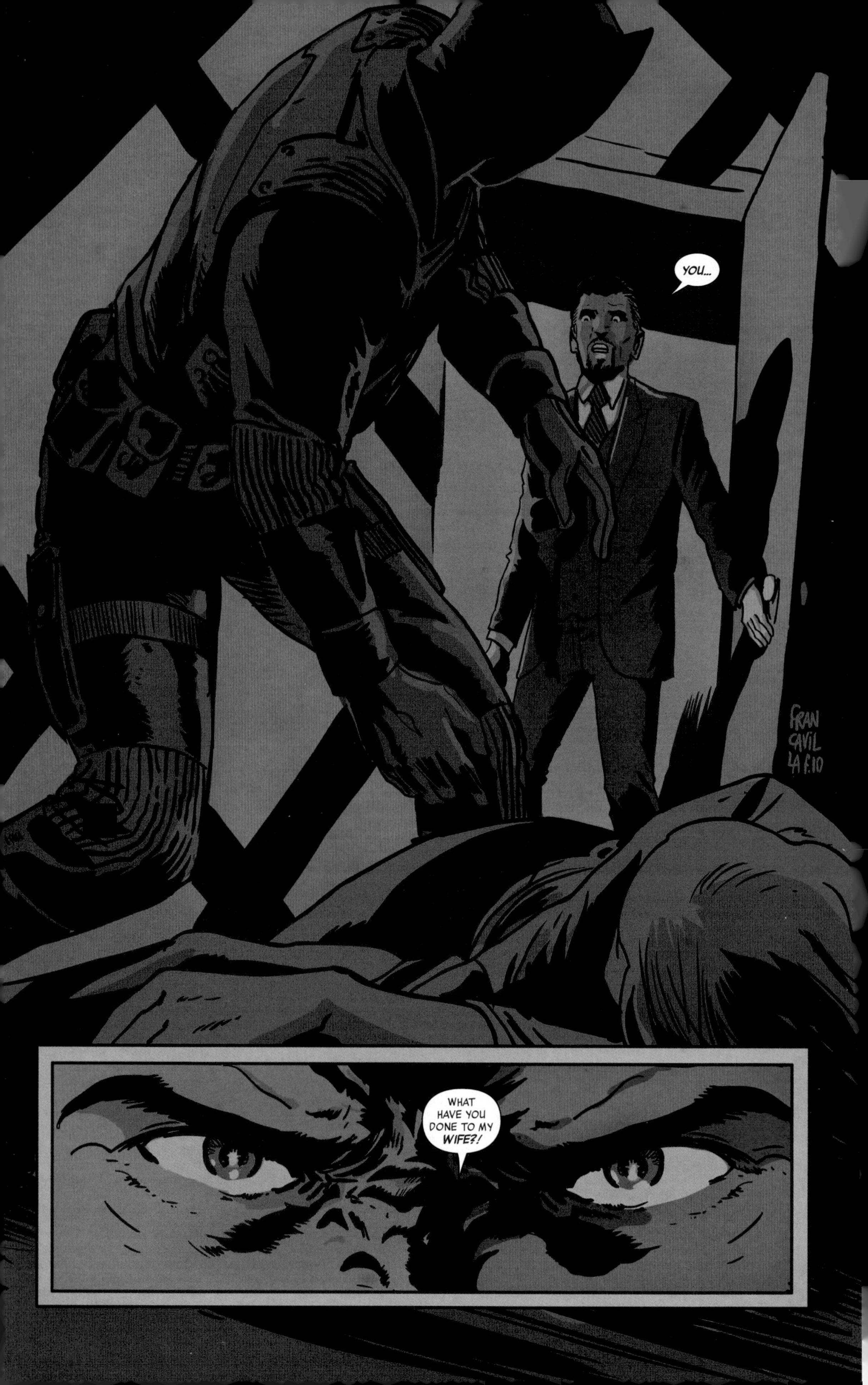
YOU...
FRAN CAVIL LA f.10
WHAT HAVE YOU DONE TO MY WIFE?!

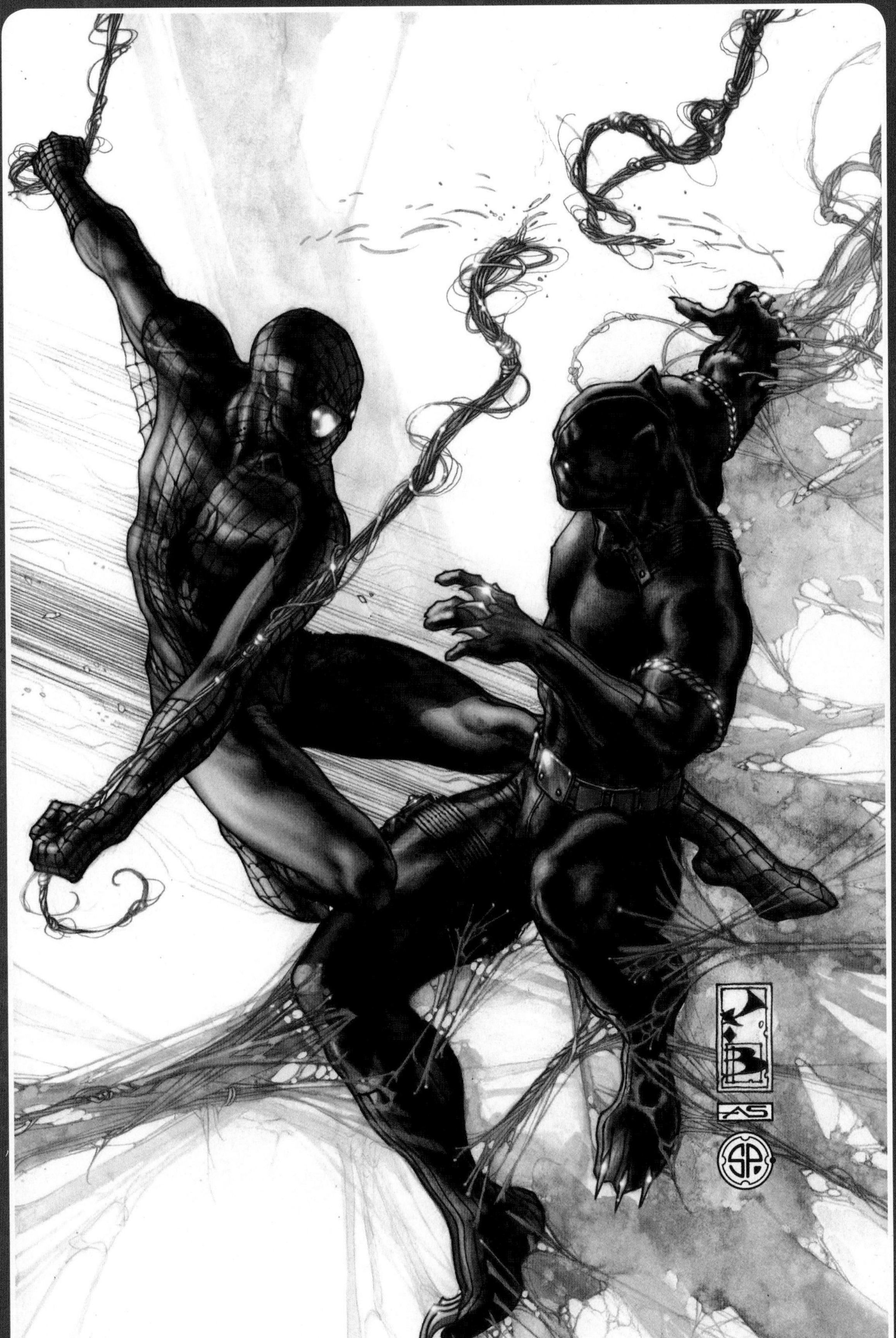

BLACK PANTHER: THE MAN WITHOUT FEAR #516

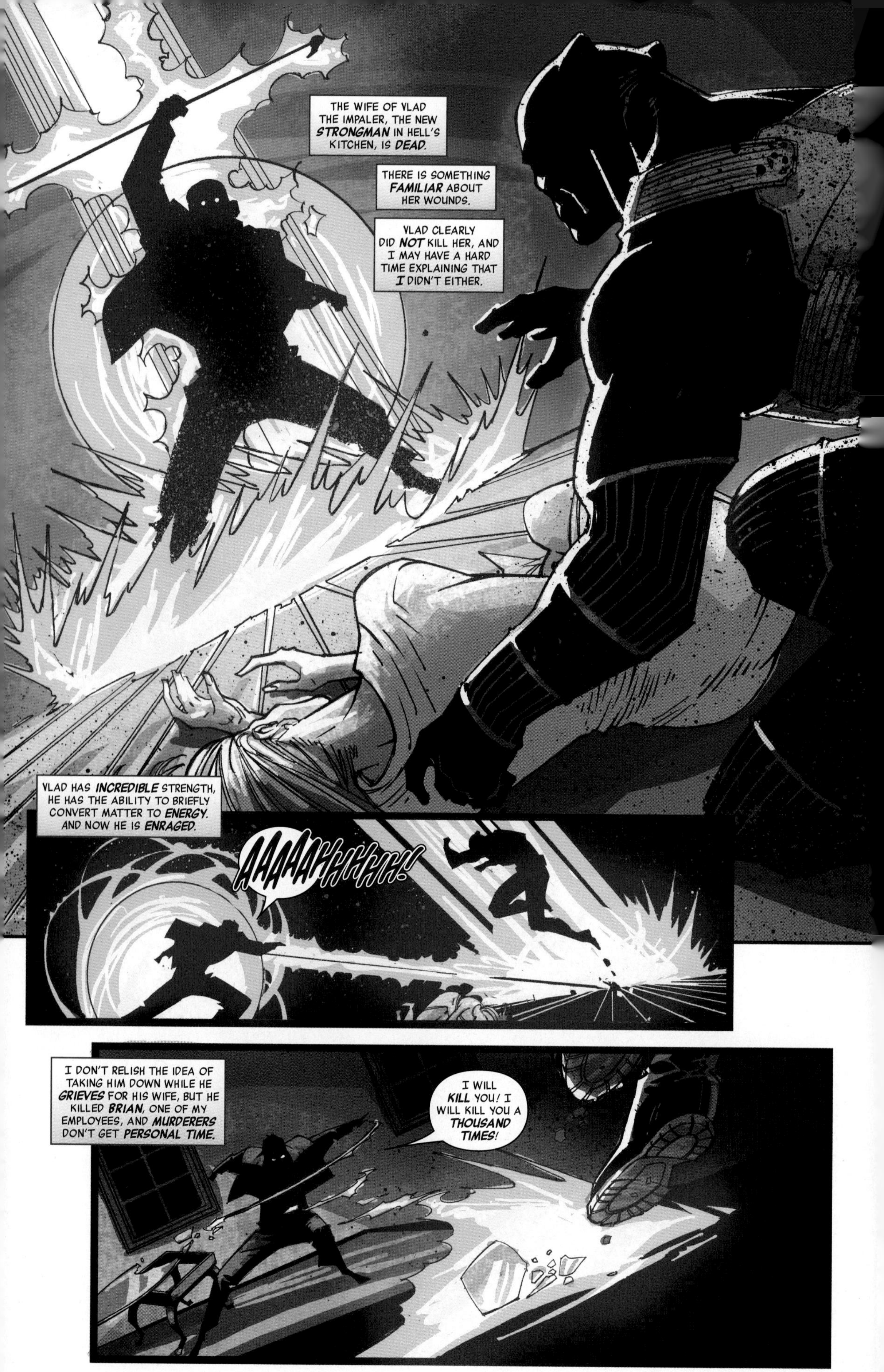
THE WIFE OF VLAD THE IMPALER, THE NEW STRONGMAN IN HELL'S KITCHEN, IS DEAD.
THERE IS SOMETHING FAMILIAR ABOUT HER WOUNDS.
VLAD CLEARLY DID NOT KILL HER, AND I MAY HAVE A HARD TIME EXPLAINING THAT I DIDN'T EITHER.
VLAD HAS INCREDIBLE STRENGTH, HE HAS THE ABILITY TO BRIEFLY CONVERT MATTER TO ENERGY. AND NOW HE IS ENRAGED.
AAAAAHHHHHH!
I DON'T RELISH THE IDEA OF TAKING HIM DOWN WHILE HE GRIEVES FOR HIS WIFE, BUT HE KILLED BRIAN, ONE OF MY EMPLOYEES, AND MURDERERS DON'T GET PERSONAL TIME.
I WILL KILL YOU! I WILL KILL YOU A THOUSAND TIMES!

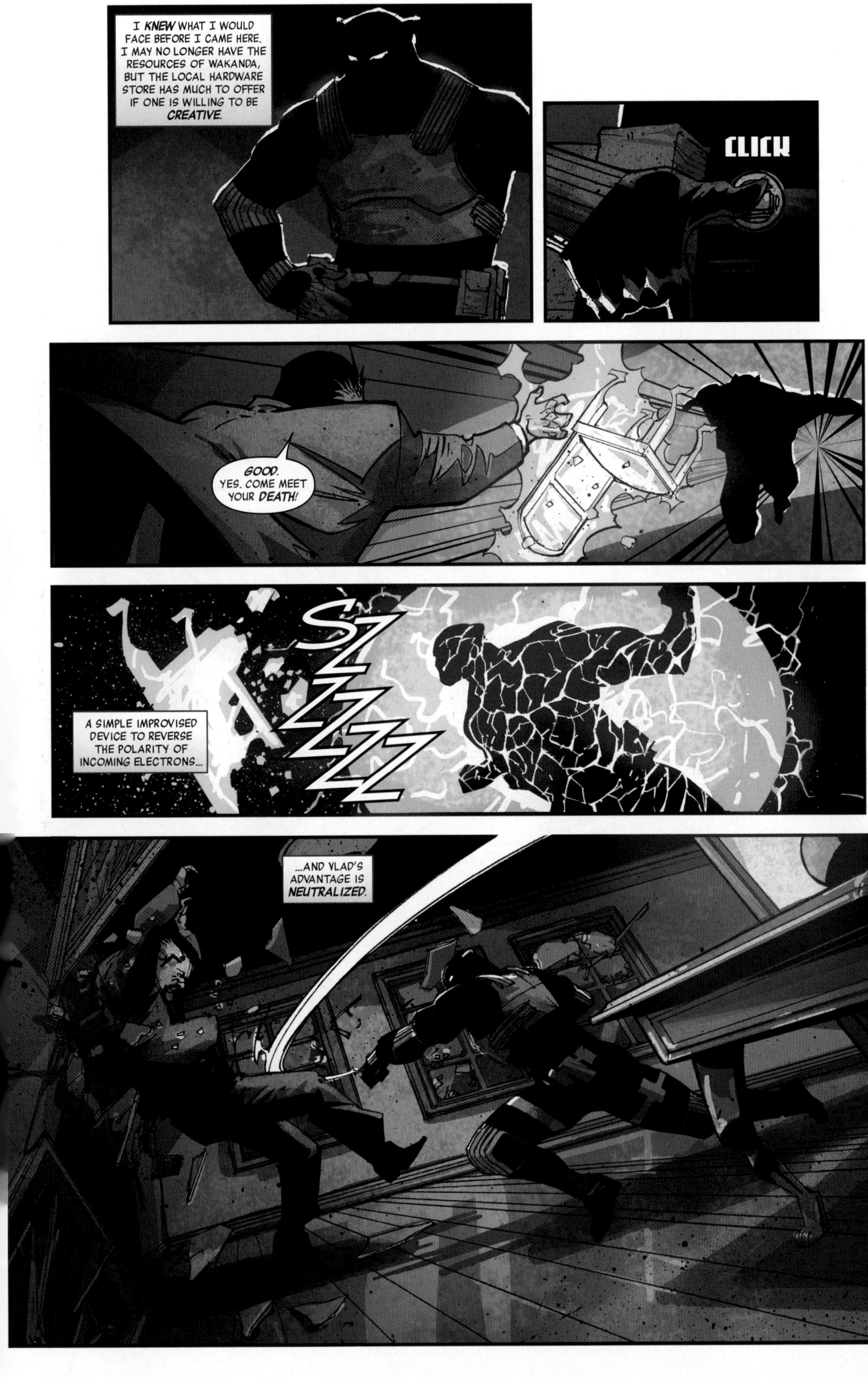
I KNEW WHAT I WOULD FACE BEFORE I CAME HERE. I MAY NO LONGER HAVE THE RESOURCES OF WAKANDA, BUT THE LOCAL HARDWARE STORE HAS MUCH TO OFFER IF ONE IS WILLING TO BE CREATIVE.
CLICK
GOOD. YES. COME MEET YOUR DEATH!
SZZZZZ
A SIMPLE IMPROVISED DEVICE TO REVERSE THE POLARITY OF INCOMING ELECTRONS...
...AND VLAD'S ADVANTAGE IS NEUTRALIZED.

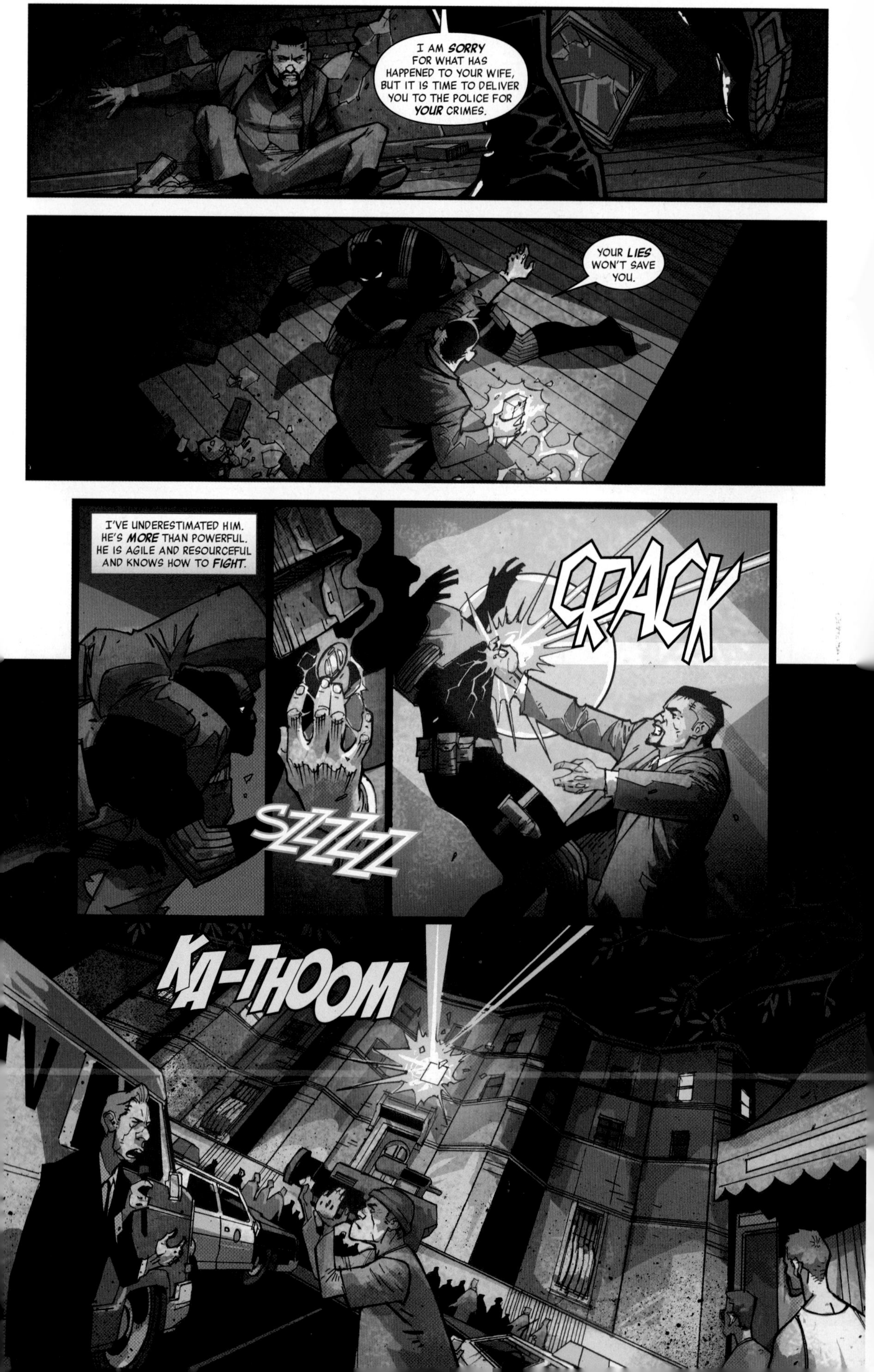
I AM SORRY FOR WHAT HAS HAPPENED TO YOUR WIFE, BUT IT IS TIME TO DELIVER YOU TO THE POLICE FOR YOUR CRIMES.
YOUR LIES WON'T SAVE YOU.
I'VE UNDERESTIMATED HIM. HE'S MORE THAN POWERFUL. HE IS AGILE AND RESOURCEFUL AND KNOWS HOW TO FIGHT.
SZZZZZ
CRACK
KA-THOOM

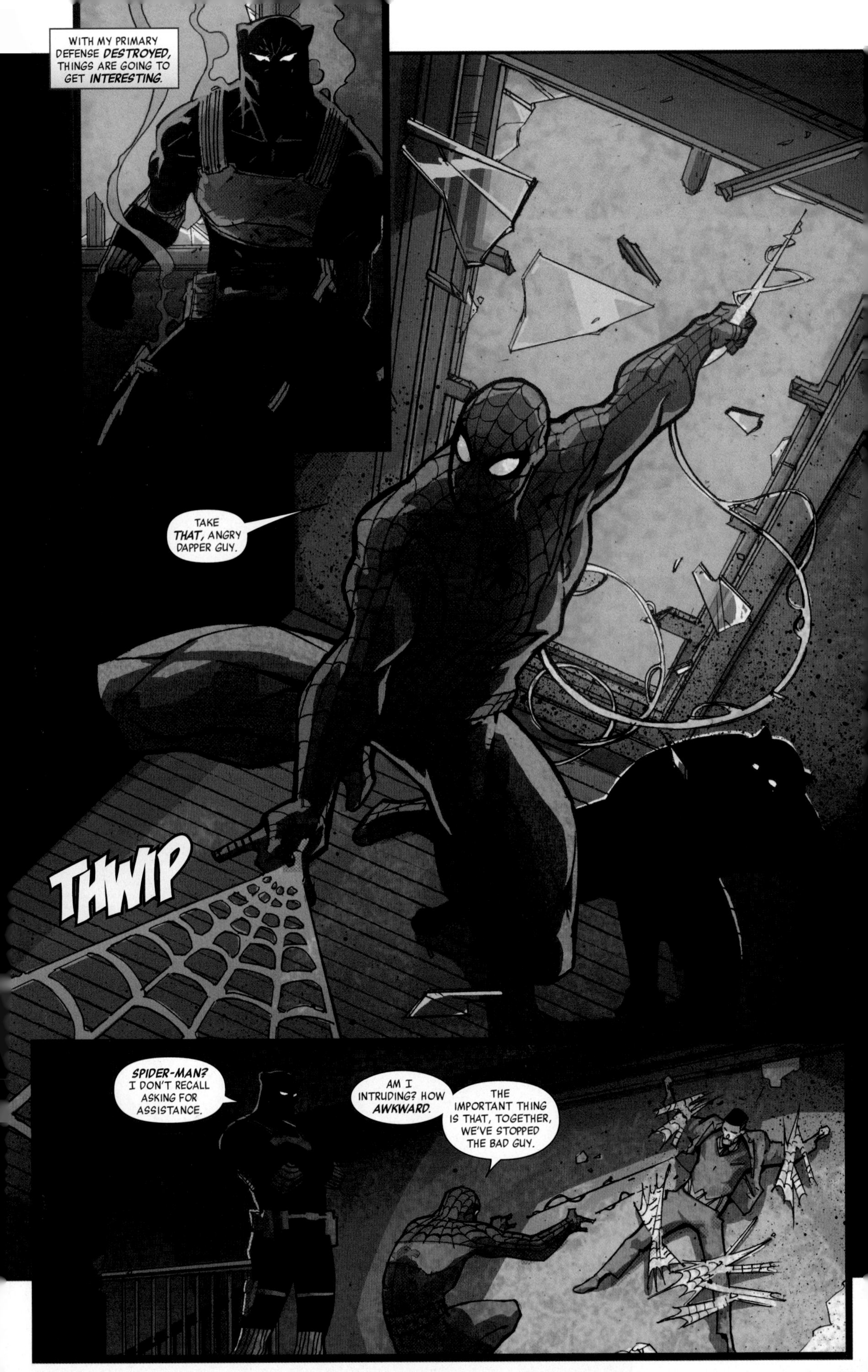
WITH MY PRIMARY DEFENSE DESTROYED, THINGS ARE GOING TO GET INTERESTING.
TAKE THAT, ANGRY DAPPER GUY.
THWIP
SPIDER-MAN? I DON'T RECALL ASKING FOR ASSISTANCE.
AM I INTRUDING? HOW AWKWARD.
THE IMPORTANT THING IS THAT, TOGETHER, WE'VE STOPPED THE BAD GUY.

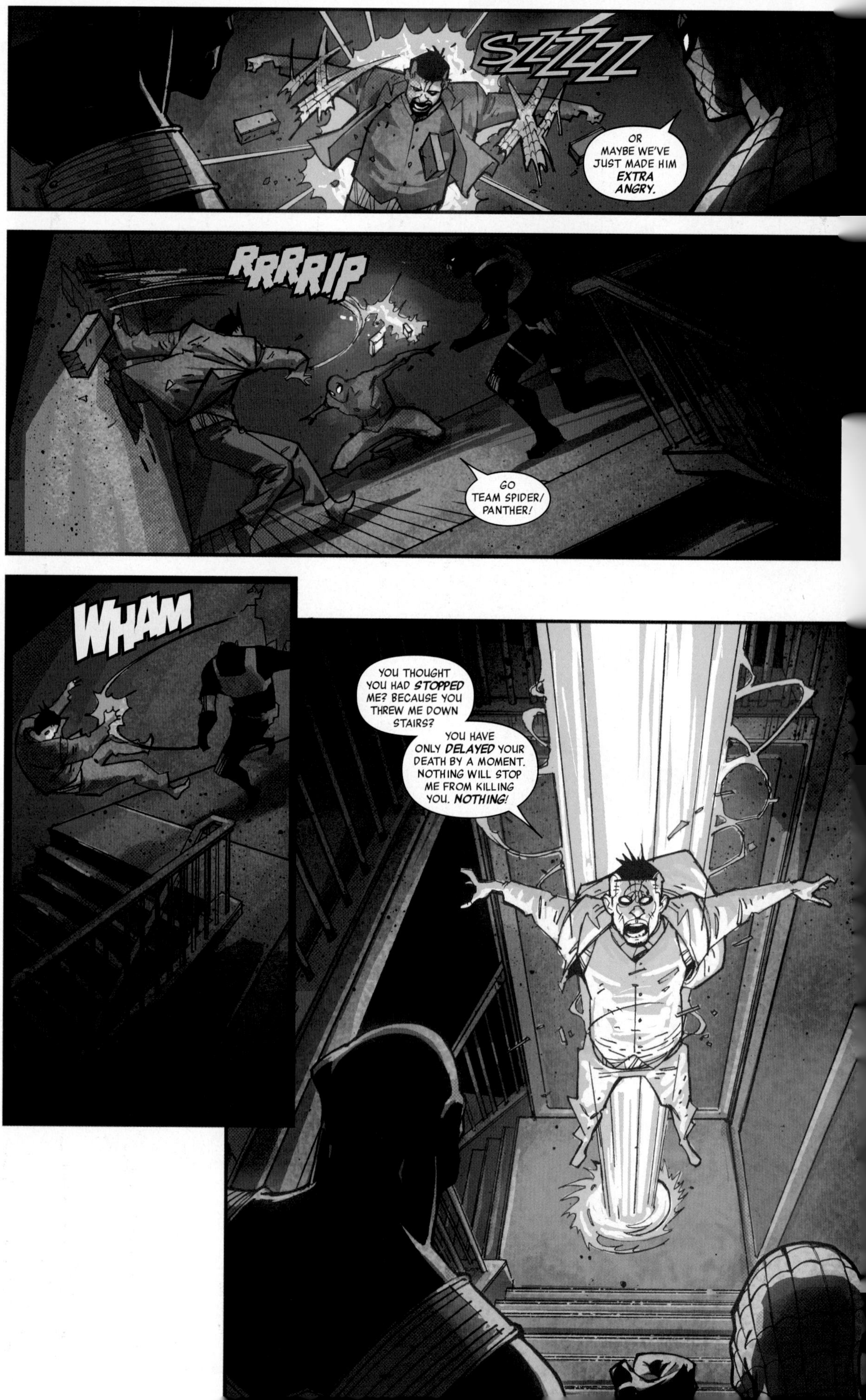
SZZZZ
OR MAYBE WE'VE JUST MADE HIM EXTRA ANGRY.
RRRRIP
GO TEAM SPIDER/ PANTHER!
WHAM
YOU THOUGHT YOU HAD STOPPED ME? BECAUSE YOU THREW ME DOWN STAIRS?
YOU HAVE ONLY DELAYED YOUR DEATH BY A MOMENT. NOTHING WILL STOP ME FROM KILLING YOU. NOTHING!

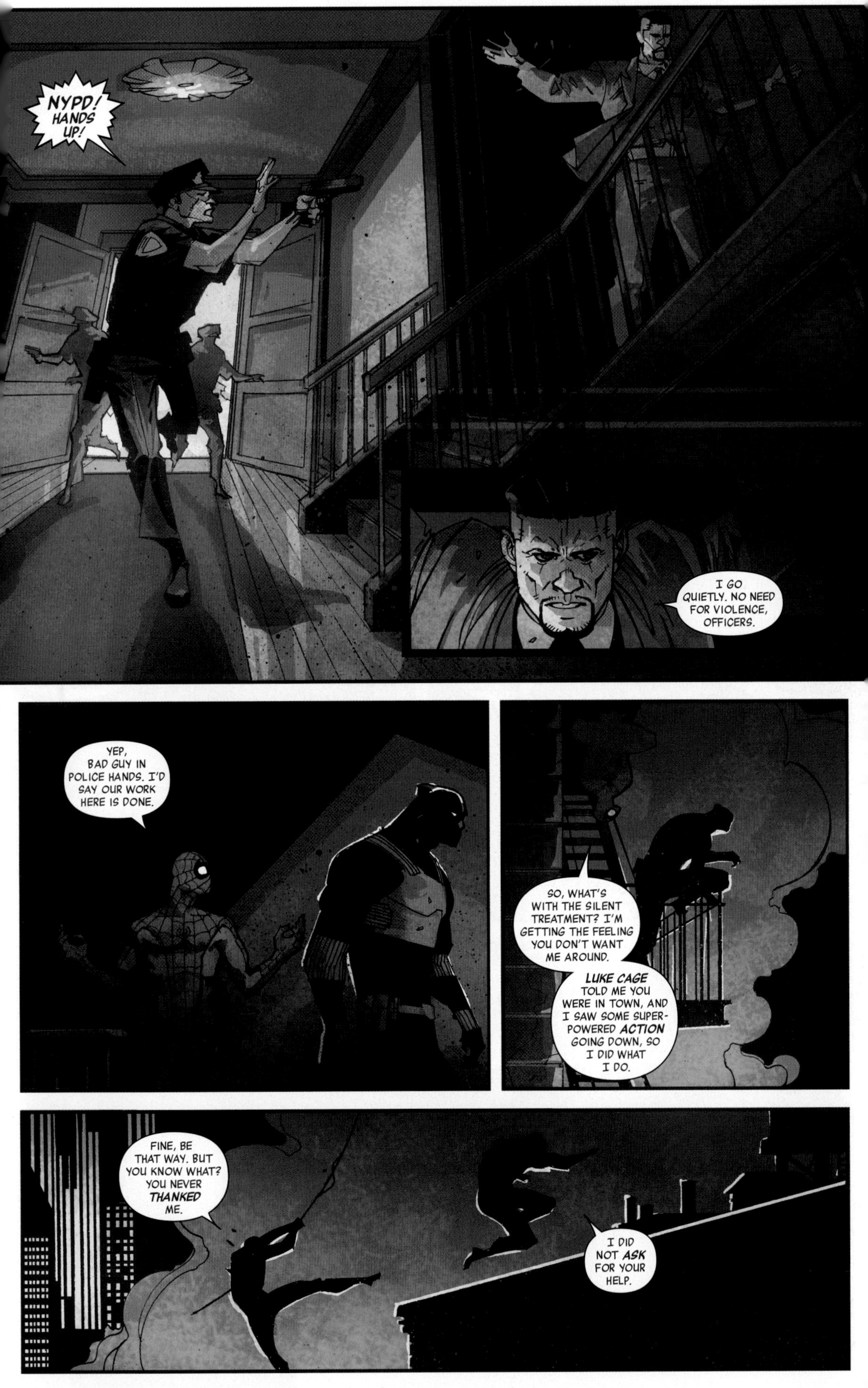
NYPD! HANDS UP!
I GO QUIETLY. NO NEED FOR VIOLENCE, OFFICERS.
YEP, BAD GUY IN POLICE HANDS. I'D SAY OUR WORK HERE IS DONE.
SO, WHAT'S WITH THE SILENT TREATMENT? I'M GETTING THE FEELING YOU DON'T WANT ME AROUND.
LUKE CAGE TOLD ME YOU WERE IN TOWN, AND I SAW SOME SUPER-POWERED ACTION GOING DOWN, SO I DID WHAT I DO.
FINE, BE THAT WAY. BUT YOU KNOW WHAT? YOU NEVER THANKED ME.
I DID NOT ASK FOR YOUR HELP.

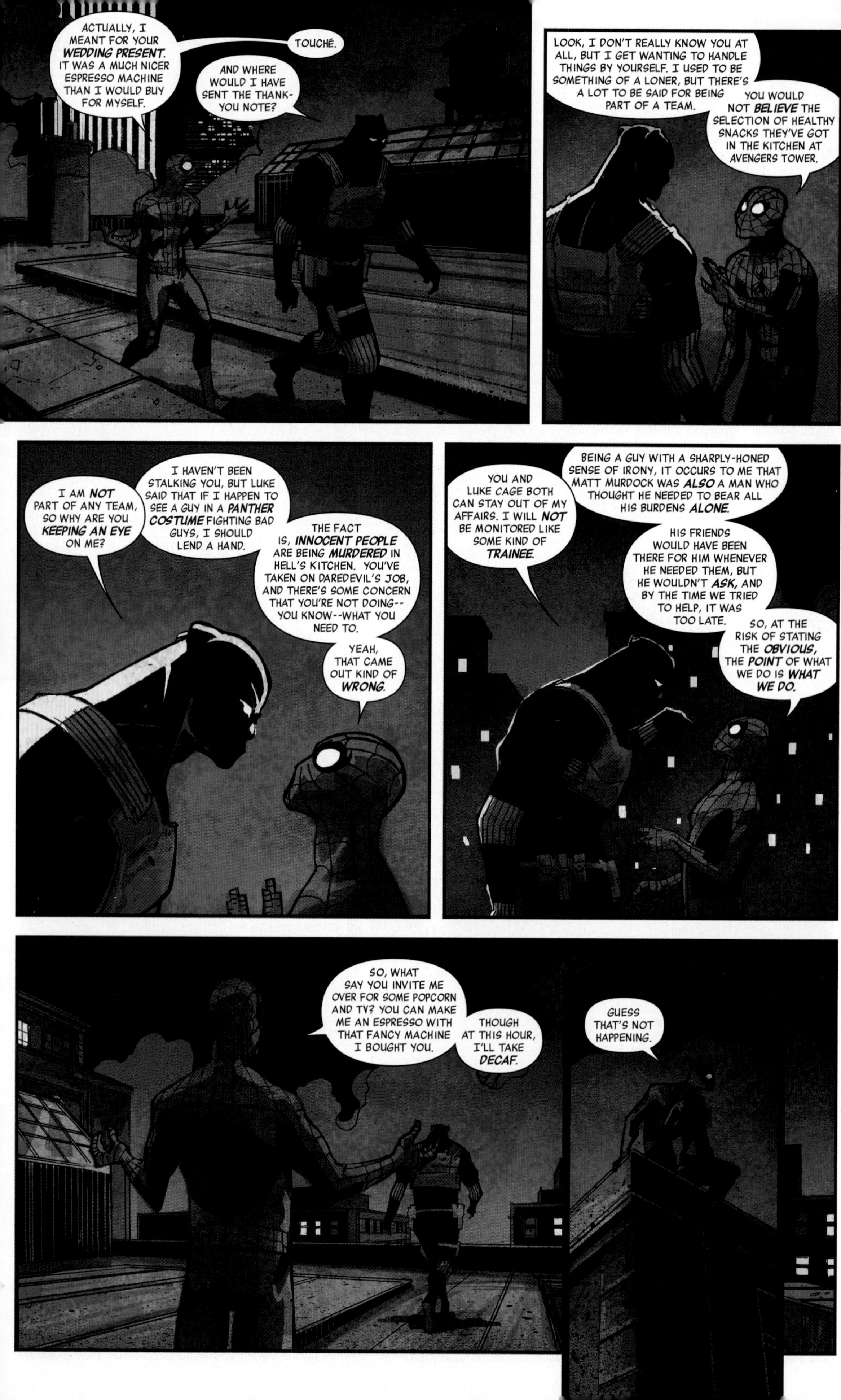
ACTUALLY, I MEANT FOR YOUR WEDDING PRESENT. IT WAS A MUCH NICER ESPRESSO MACHINE THAN I WOULD BUY FOR MYSELF.
TOUCHÉ.
AND WHERE WOULD I HAVE SENT THE THANK-YOU NOTE?
LOOK, I DON'T REALLY KNOW YOU AT ALL, BUT I GET WANTING TO HANDLE THINGS BY YOURSELF. I USED TO BE SOMETHING OF A LONER, BUT THERE'S A LOT TO BE SAID FOR BEING PART OF A TEAM.
YOU WOULD NOT BELIEVE THE SELECTION OF HEALTHY SNACKS THEY'VE GOT IN THE KITCHEN AT AVENGERS TOWER.
I AM NOT PART OF ANY TEAM, SO WHY ARE YOU KEEPING AN EYE ON ME?
I HAVEN'T BEEN STALKING YOU, BUT LUKE SAID THAT IF I HAPPEN TO SEE A GUY IN A PANTHER COSTUME FIGHTING BAD GUYS, I SHOULD LEND A HAND.
THE FACT IS, INNOCENT PEOPLE ARE BEING MURDERED IN HELL'S KITCHEN. YOU'VE TAKEN ON DAREDEVIL'S JOB, AND THERE'S SOME CONCERN THAT YOU'RE NOT DOING--YOU KNOW--WHAT YOU NEED TO.
YEAH, THAT CAME OUT KIND OF WRONG.
YOU AND LUKE CAGE BOTH CAN STAY OUT OF MY AFFAIRS. I WILL NOT BE MONITORED LIKE SOME KIND OF TRAINEE.
BEING A GUY WITH A SHARPLY-HONED SENSE OF IRONY, IT OCCURS TO ME THAT MATT MURDOCK WAS ALSO A MAN WHO THOUGHT HE NEEDED TO BEAR ALL HIS BURDENS ALONE.
HIS FRIENDS WOULD HAVE BEEN THERE FOR HIM WHENEVER HE NEEDED THEM, BUT HE WOULDN'T ASK, AND BY THE TIME WE TRIED TO HELP, IT WAS TOO LATE.
SO, AT THE RISK OF STATING THE OBVIOUS, THE POINT OF WHAT WE DO IS WHAT WE DO.
SO, WHAT SAY YOU INVITE ME OVER FOR SOME POPCORN AND TV? YOU CAN MAKE ME AN ESPRESSO WITH THAT FANCY MACHINE I BOUGHT YOU.
THOUGH AT THIS HOUR, I'LL TAKE DECAF.
GUESS THAT'S NOT HAPPENING.

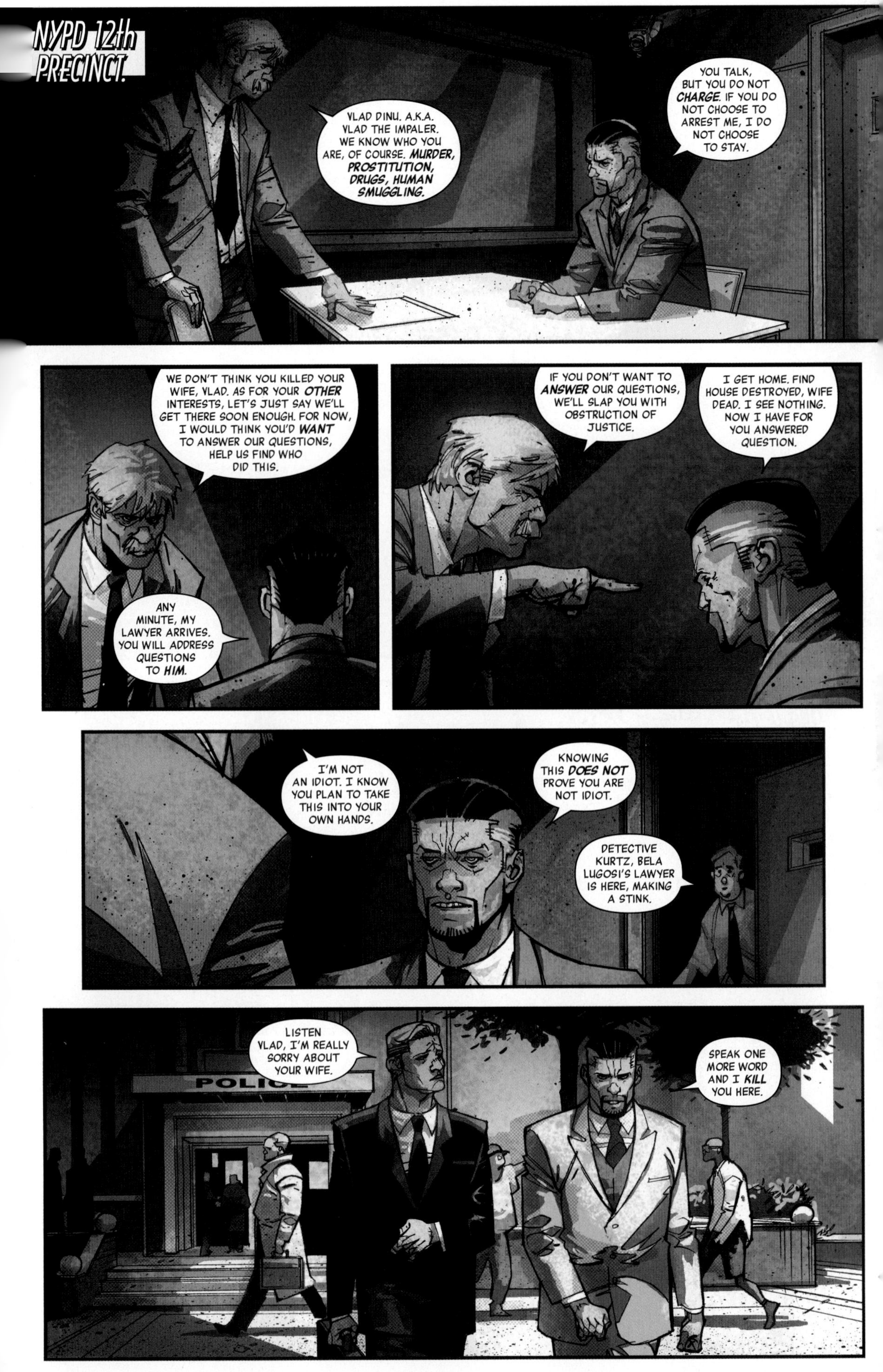
NYPD 12th PRECINCT.
VLAD DINU. A.K.A. VLAD THE IMPALER. WE KNOW WHO YOU ARE, OF COURSE. MURDER, PROSTITUTION, DRUGS, HUMAN SMUGGLING.
YOU TALK, BUT YOU DO NOT CHARGE. IF YOU DO NOT CHOOSE TO ARREST ME, I DO NOT CHOOSE TO STAY.
WE DON'T THINK YOU KILLED YOUR WIFE, VLAD. AS FOR YOUR OTHER INTERESTS, LET'S JUST SAY WE'LL GET THERE SOON ENOUGH. FOR NOW, I WOULD THINK YOU'D WANT TO ANSWER OUR QUESTIONS, HELP US FIND WHO DID THIS.
ANY MINUTE, MY LAWYER ARRIVES. YOU WILL ADDRESS QUESTIONS TO HIM.
IF YOU DON'T WANT TO ANSWER OUR QUESTIONS, WE'LL SLAP YOU WITH OBSTRUCTION OF JUSTICE.
I GET HOME. FIND HOUSE DESTROYED, WIFE DEAD. I SEE NOTHING. NOW I HAVE FOR YOU ANSWERED QUESTION.
I'M NOT AN IDIOT. I KNOW YOU PLAN TO TAKE THIS INTO YOUR OWN HANDS.
KNOWING THIS DOES NOT PROVE YOU ARE NOT IDIOT.
DETECTIVE KURTZ, BELA LUGOSI'S LAWYER IS HERE, MAKING A STINK.
LISTEN VLAD, I'M REALLY SORRY ABOUT YOUR WIFE.
POLICE
SPEAK ONE MORE WORD AND I KILL YOU HERE.

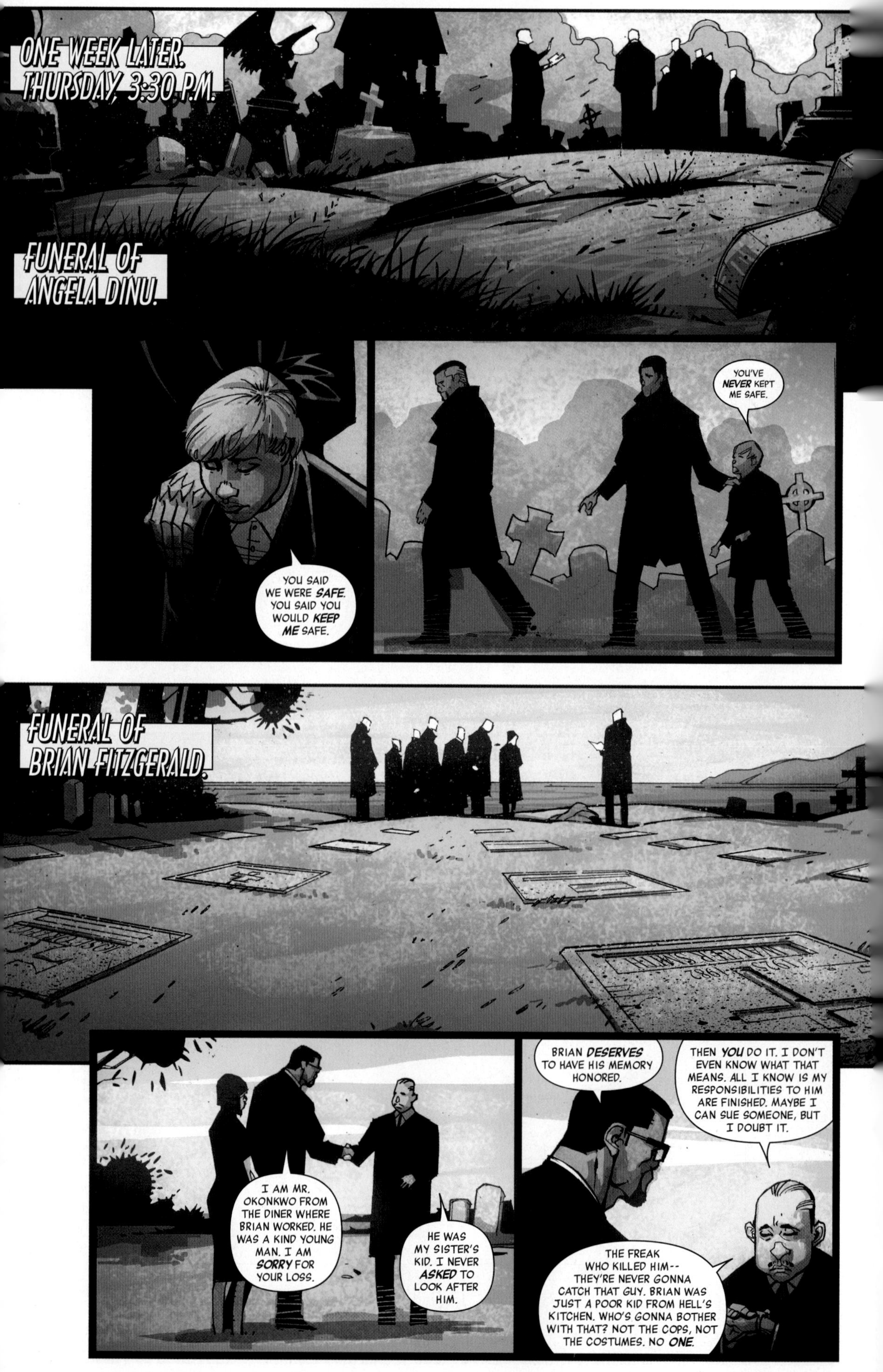
ONE WEEK LATER. THURSDAY, 3:30 P.M.
FUNERAL OF ANGELA DINU.
YOU SAID WE WERE SAFE. YOU SAID YOU WOULD KEEP ME SAFE.
YOU'VE NEVER KEPT ME SAFE.
FUNERAL OF BRIAN FITZGERALD.
I AM MR. OKONKWO FROM THE DINER WHERE BRIAN WORKED. HE WAS A KIND YOUNG MAN. I AM SORRY FOR YOUR LOSS.
HE WAS MY SISTER'S KID. I NEVER ASKED TO LOOK AFTER HIM.
BRIAN DESERVES TO HAVE HIS MEMORY HONORED.
THEN YOU DO IT. I DON'T EVEN KNOW WHAT THAT MEANS. ALL I KNOW IS MY RESPONSIBILITIES TO HIM ARE FINISHED. MAYBE I CAN SUE SOMEONE, BUT I DOUBT IT.
THE FREAK WHO KILLED HIM-- THEY'RE NEVER GONNA CATCH THAT GUY. BRIAN WAS JUST A POOR KID FROM HELL'S KITCHEN. WHO'S GONNA BOTHER WITH THAT? NOT THE COPS, NOT THE COSTUMES. NO ONE.

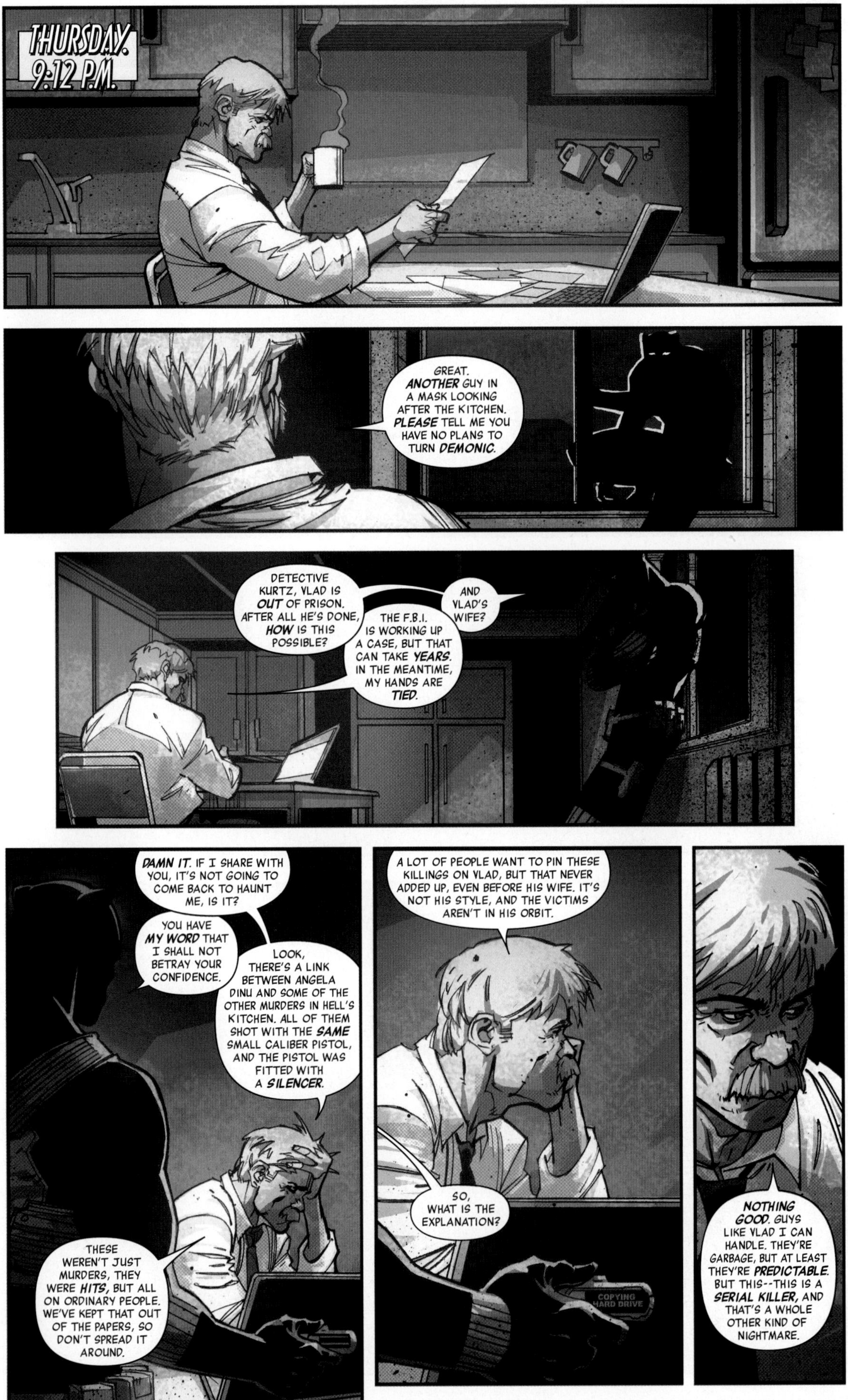
THURSDAY. 9:12 P.M.
GREAT. ANOTHER GUY IN A MASK LOOKING AFTER THE KITCHEN. PLEASE TELL ME YOU HAVE NO PLANS TO TURN DEMONIC.
DETECTIVE KURTZ, VLAD IS OUT OF PRISON. AFTER ALL HE'S DONE, HOW IS THIS POSSIBLE?
THE F.B.I. IS WORKING UP A CASE, BUT THAT CAN TAKE YEARS. IN THE MEANTIME, MY HANDS ARE TIED.
AND VLAD'S WIFE?
DAMN IT. IF I SHARE WITH YOU, IT'S NOT GOING TO COME BACK TO HAUNT ME, IS IT?
YOU HAVE MY WORD THAT I SHALL NOT BETRAY YOUR CONFIDENCE.
LOOK, THERE'S A LINK BETWEEN ANGELA DINU AND SOME OF THE OTHER MURDERS IN HELL'S KITCHEN. ALL OF THEM SHOT WITH THE SAME SMALL CALIBER PISTOL, AND THE PISTOL WAS FITTED WITH A SILENCER.
THESE WEREN'T JUST MURDERS, THEY WERE HITS, BUT ALL ON ORDINARY PEOPLE. WE'VE KEPT THAT OUT OF THE PAPERS, SO DON'T SPREAD IT AROUND.
A LOT OF PEOPLE WANT TO PIN THESE KILLINGS ON VLAD, BUT THAT NEVER ADDED UP, EVEN BEFORE HIS WIFE. IT'S NOT HIS STYLE, AND THE VICTIMS AREN'T IN HIS ORBIT.
SO, WHAT IS THE EXPLANATION?
COPYING HARD DRIVE
NOTHING GOOD. GUYS LIKE VLAD I CAN HANDLE. THEY'RE GARBAGE, BUT AT LEAST THEY'RE PREDICTABLE. BUT THIS--THIS IS A SERIAL KILLER, AND THAT'S A WHOLE OTHER KIND OF NIGHTMARE.

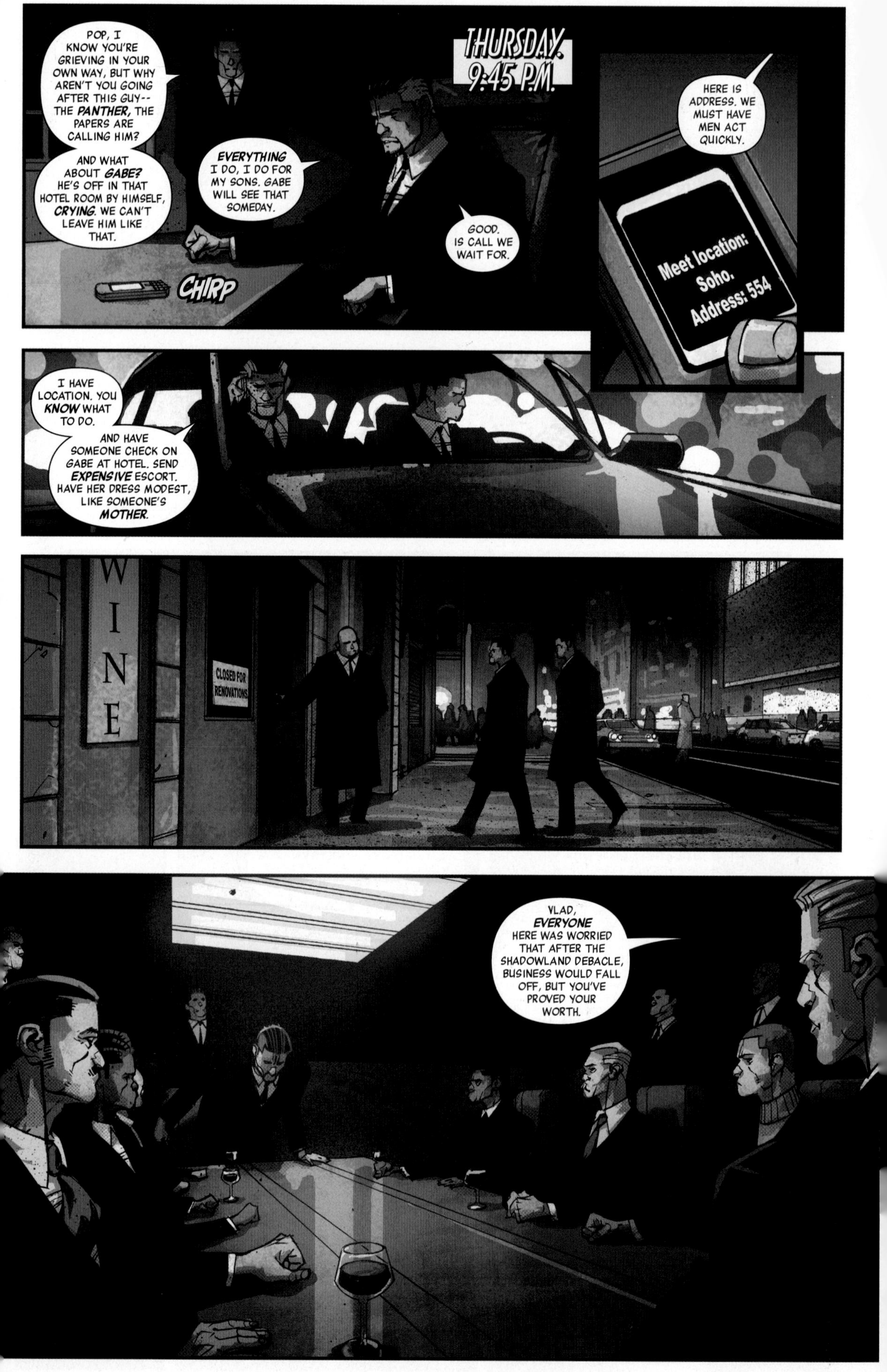
THURSDAY. 9:45 P.M.
POP, I KNOW YOU'RE GRIEVING IN YOUR OWN WAY, BUT WHY AREN'T YOU GOING AFTER THIS GUY-- THE PANTHER, THE PAPERS ARE CALLING HIM?
AND WHAT ABOUT GABE? HE'S OFF IN THAT HOTEL ROOM BY HIMSELF, CRYING. WE CAN'T LEAVE HIM LIKE THAT.
EVERYTHING I DO, I DO FOR MY SONS. GABE WILL SEE THAT SOMEDAY.
CHIRP
GOOD. IS CALL WE WAIT FOR.
HERE IS ADDRESS. WE MUST HAVE MEN ACT QUICKLY.
Meet location: Soho. Address: 554
I HAVE LOCATION. YOU KNOW WHAT TO DO.
AND HAVE SOMEONE CHECK ON GABE AT HOTEL. SEND EXPENSIVE ESCORT. HAVE HER DRESS MODEST, LIKE SOMEONE'S MOTHER.
WINE
CLOSED FOR RENOVATIONS
VLAD, EVERYONE HERE WAS WORRIED THAT AFTER THE SHADOWLAND DEBACLE, BUSINESS WOULD FALL OFF, BUT YOU'VE PROVED YOUR WORTH.

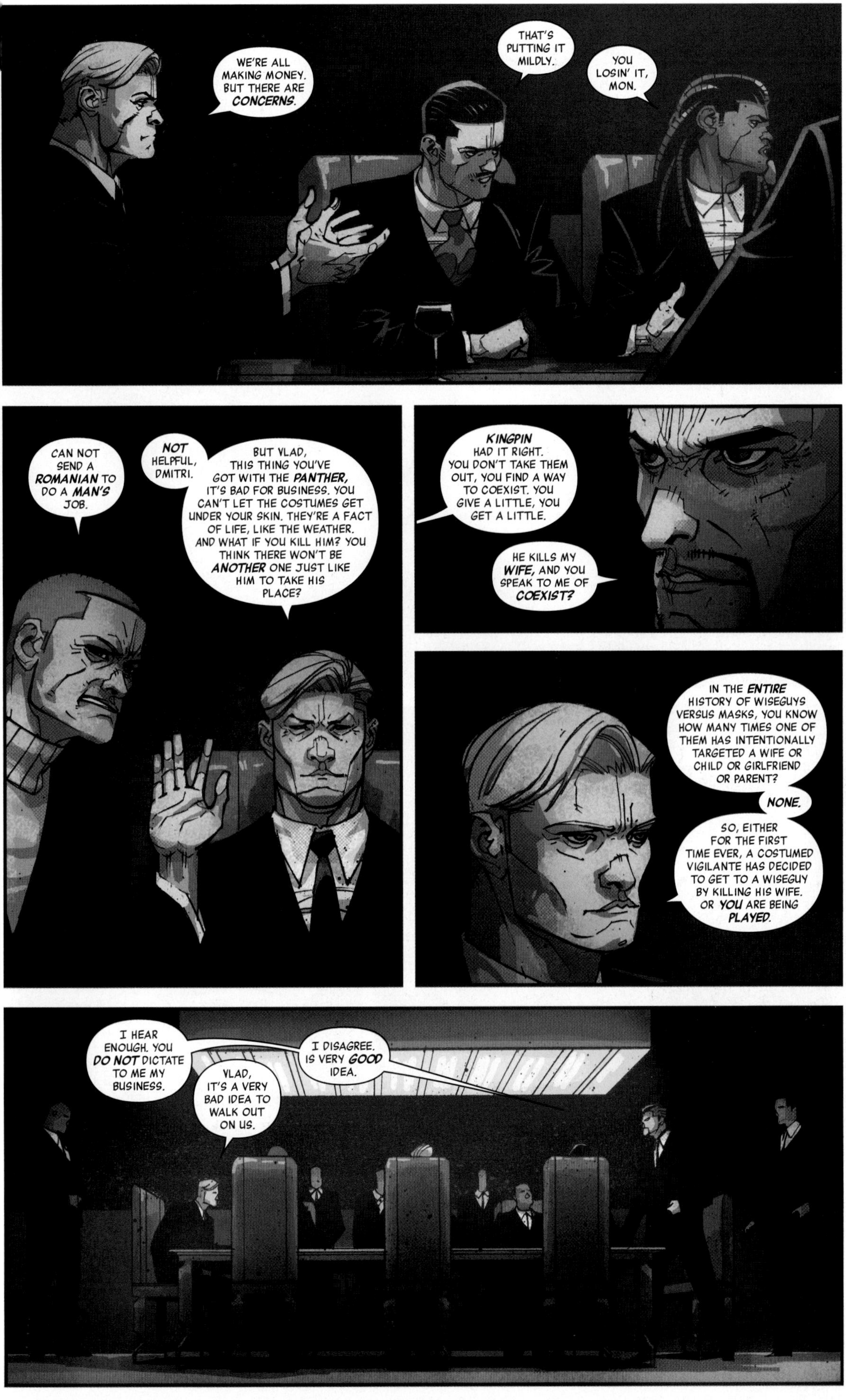

WE'RE ALL MAKING MONEY. BUT THERE ARE CONCERNS.
THAT'S PUTTING IT MILDLY.
YOU LOSIN' IT, MON.
CAN NOT SEND A ROMANIAN TO DO A MAN'S JOB.
NOT HELPFUL, DMITRI.
BUT VLAD, THIS THING YOU'VE GOT WITH THE PANTHER, IT'S BAD FOR BUSINESS. YOU CAN'T LET THE COSTUMES GET UNDER YOUR SKIN. THEY'RE A FACT OF LIFE, LIKE THE WEATHER. AND WHAT IF YOU KILL HIM? YOU THINK THERE WON'T BE ANOTHER ONE JUST LIKE HIM TO TAKE HIS PLACE?
KINGPIN HAD IT RIGHT. YOU DON'T TAKE THEM OUT, YOU FIND A WAY TO COEXIST. YOU GIVE A LITTLE, YOU GET A LITTLE.
HE KILLS MY WIFE, AND YOU SPEAK TO ME OF COEXIST?
IN THE ENTIRE HISTORY OF WISEGUYS VERSUS MASKS, YOU KNOW HOW MANY TIMES ONE OF THEM HAS INTENTIONALLY TARGETED A WIFE OR CHILD OR GIRLFRIEND OR PARENT?
NONE.
SO, EITHER FOR THE FIRST TIME EVER, A COSTUMED VIGILANTE HAS DECIDED TO GET TO A WISEGUY BY KILLING HIS WIFE. OR YOU ARE BEING PLAYED.
I HEAR ENOUGH. YOU DO NOT DICTATE TO ME MY BUSINESS.
VLAD, IT'S A VERY BAD IDEA TO WALK OUT ON US.
I DISAGREE. IS VERY GOOD IDEA.

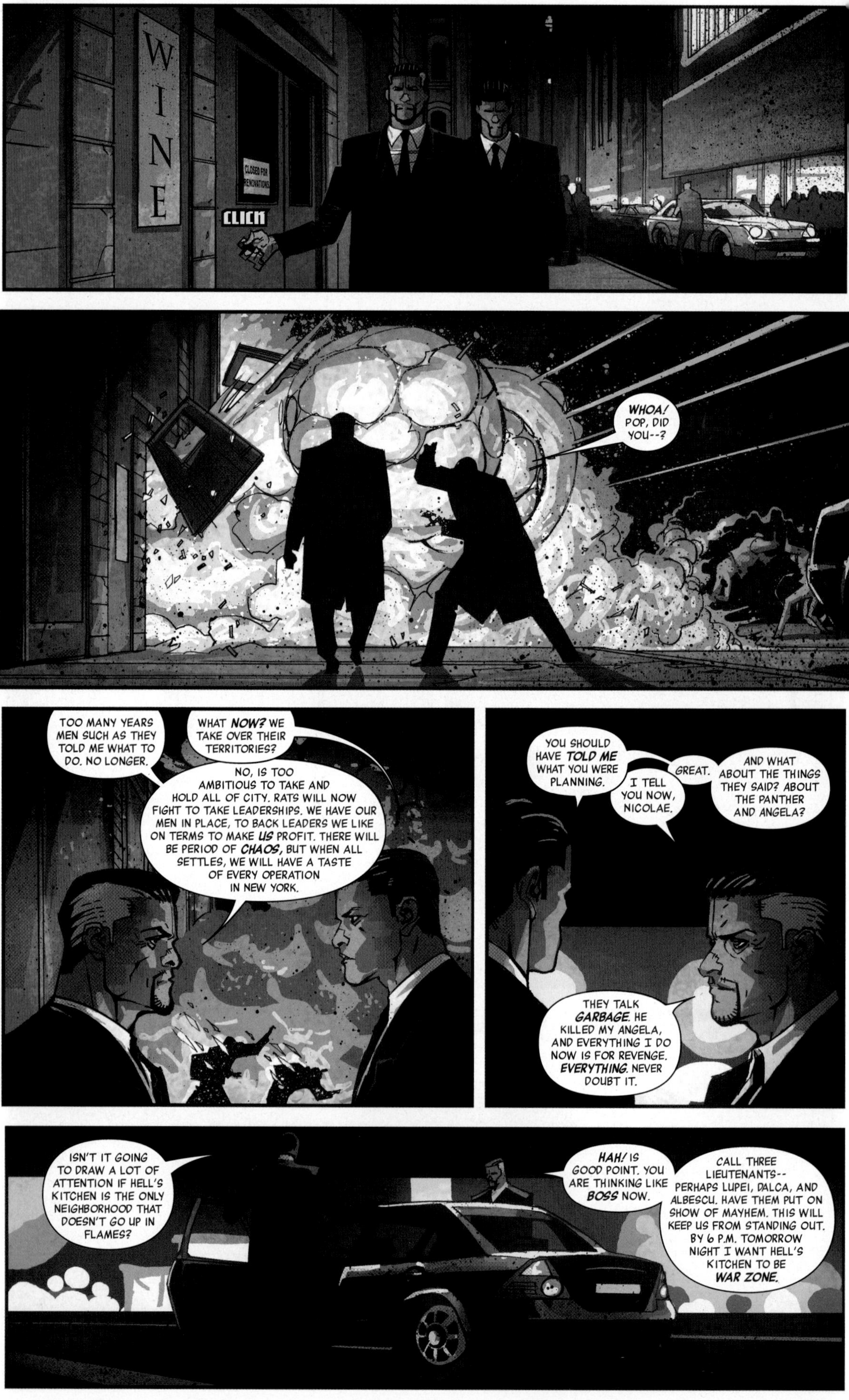
WINE
CLOSED FOR RENOVATIONS
CLICK
WHOA! POP, DID YOU--?
TOO MANY YEARS MEN SUCH AS THEY TOLD ME WHAT TO DO. NO LONGER.
WHAT NOW? WE TAKE OVER THEIR TERRITORIES?
NO, IS TOO AMBITIOUS TO TAKE AND HOLD ALL OF CITY. RATS WILL NOW FIGHT TO TAKE LEADERSHIPS. WE HAVE OUR MEN IN PLACE, TO BACK LEADERS WE LIKE ON TERMS TO MAKE US PROFIT. THERE WILL BE PERIOD OF CHAOS, BUT WHEN ALL SETTLES, WE WILL HAVE A TASTE OF EVERY OPERATION IN NEW YORK.
YOU SHOULD HAVE TOLD ME WHAT YOU WERE PLANNING.
I TELL YOU NOW, NICOLAE.
GREAT.
AND WHAT ABOUT THE THINGS THEY SAID? ABOUT THE PANTHER AND ANGELA?
THEY TALK GARBAGE. HE KILLED MY ANGELA, AND EVERYTHING I DO NOW IS FOR REVENGE. EVERYTHING. NEVER DOUBT IT.
ISN'T IT GOING TO DRAW A LOT OF ATTENTION IF HELL'S KITCHEN IS THE ONLY NEIGHBORHOOD THAT DOESN'T GO UP IN FLAMES?
HAH! IS GOOD POINT. YOU ARE THINKING LIKE BOSS NOW.
CALL THREE LIEUTENANTS-- PERHAPS LUPEI, DALCA, AND ALBESCU. HAVE THEM PUT ON SHOW OF MAYHEM. THIS WILL KEEP US FROM STANDING OUT. BY 6 P.M. TOMORROW NIGHT I WANT HELL'S KITCHEN TO BE WAR ZONE.

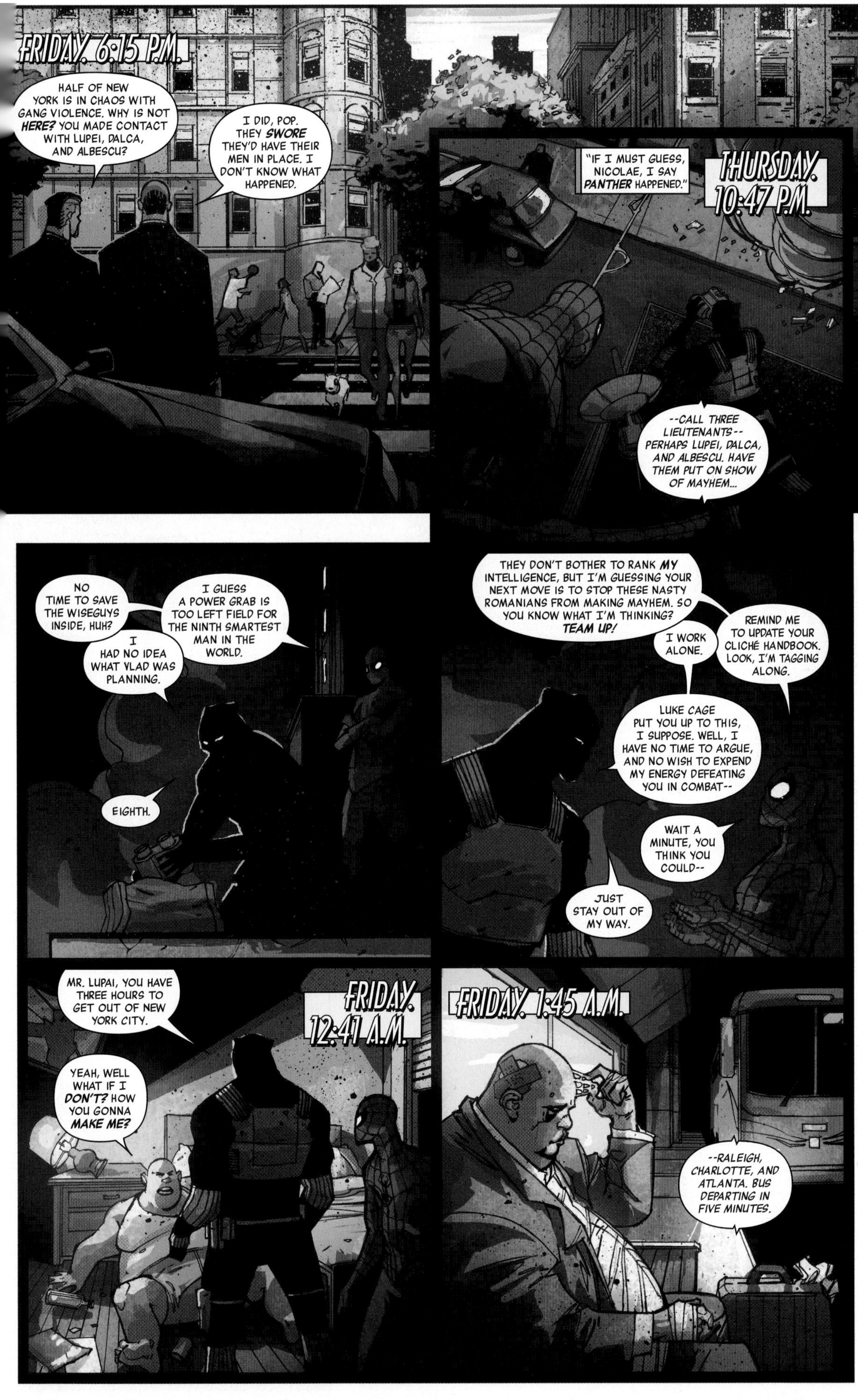
FRIDAY. 6:15 P.M.
HALF OF NEW YORK IS IN CHAOS WITH GANG VIOLENCE. WHY IS NOT HERE? YOU MADE CONTACT WITH LUPEI, DALCA, AND ALBESCU?
I DID, POP. THEY SWORE THEY'D HAVE THEIR MEN IN PLACE. I DON'T KNOW WHAT HAPPENED.
"IF I MUST GUESS, NICOLAE, I SAY PANTHER HAPPENED."
THURSDAY. 10:47 P.M.
--CALL THREE LIEUTENANTS-- PERHAPS LUPEI, DALCA, AND ALBESCU. HAVE THEM PUT ON SHOW OF MAYHEM...
NO TIME TO SAVE THE WISEGUYS INSIDE, HUH?
I GUESS A POWER GRAB IS TOO LEFT FIELD FOR THE NINTH SMARTEST MAN IN THE WORLD.
I HAD NO IDEA WHAT VLAD WAS PLANNING.
EIGHTH.
THEY DON'T BOTHER TO RANK MY INTELLIGENCE, BUT I'M GUESSING YOUR NEXT MOVE IS TO STOP THESE NASTY ROMANIANS FROM MAKING MAYHEM. SO YOU KNOW WHAT I'M THINKING? TEAM UP!
I WORK ALONE.
REMIND ME TO UPDATE YOUR CLICHÉ HANDBOOK. LOOK, I'M TAGGING ALONG.
LUKE CAGE PUT YOU UP TO THIS, I SUPPOSE. WELL, I HAVE NO TIME TO ARGUE, AND NO WISH TO EXPEND MY ENERGY DEFEATING YOU IN COMBAT--
WAIT A MINUTE, YOU THINK YOU COULD--
JUST STAY OUT OF MY WAY.
MR. LUPAI, YOU HAVE THREE HOURS TO GET OUT OF NEW YORK CITY.
FRIDAY. 12:41 A.M.
YEAH, WELL WHAT IF I DON'T? HOW YOU GONNA MAKE ME?
FRIDAY. 1:45 A.M.
--RALEIGH, CHARLOTTE, AND ATLANTA. BUS DEPARTING IN FIVE MINUTES.

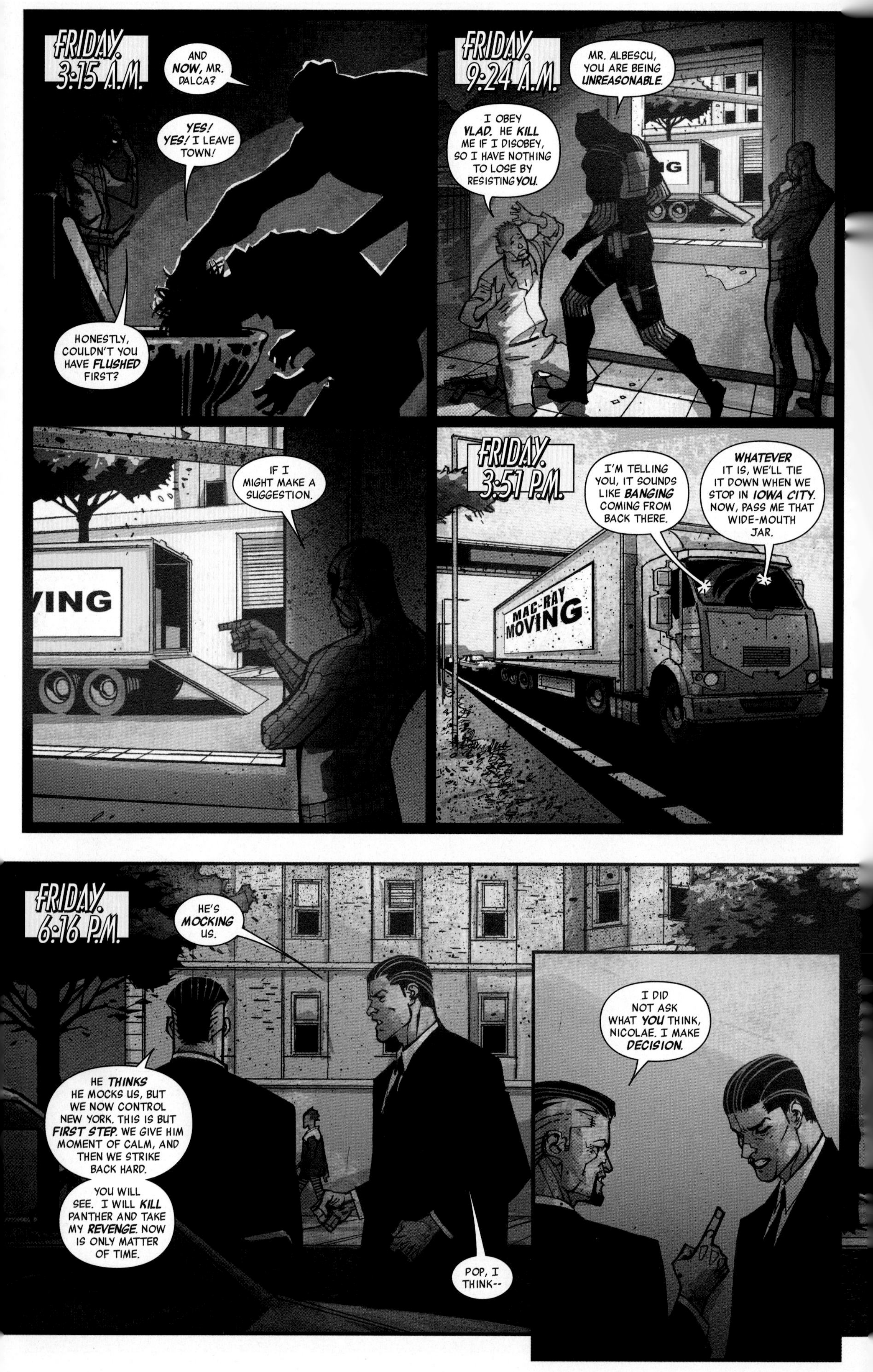
FRIDAY. 3:15 A.M.
AND NOW, MR. DALCA?
YES! YES! I LEAVE TOWN!
HONESTLY, COULDN'T YOU HAVE FLUSHED FIRST?
FRIDAY. 9:24 A.M.
MR. ALBESCU, YOU ARE BEING UNREASONABLE.
I OBEY VLAD. HE KILL ME IF I DISOBEY, SO I HAVE NOTHING TO LOSE BY RESISTING YOU.
IF I MIGHT MAKE A SUGGESTION.
VING
FRIDAY. 3:51 P.M.
I'M TELLING YOU, IT SOUNDS LIKE BANGING COMING FROM BACK THERE.
WHATEVER IT IS, WE'LL TIE IT DOWN WHEN WE STOP IN IOWA CITY. NOW, PASS ME THAT WIDE-MOUTH JAR.
MAC-RAY MOVING
FRIDAY. 6:16 P.M.
HE'S MOCKING US.
HE THINKS HE MOCKS US, BUT WE NOW CONTROL NEW YORK. THIS IS BUT FIRST STEP. WE GIVE HIM MOMENT OF CALM, AND THEN WE STRIKE BACK HARD.
YOU WILL SEE. I WILL KILL PANTHER AND TAKE MY REVENGE. NOW IS ONLY MATTER OF TIME.
POP, I THINK--
I DID NOT ASK WHAT YOU THINK, NICOLAE. I MAKE DECISION.

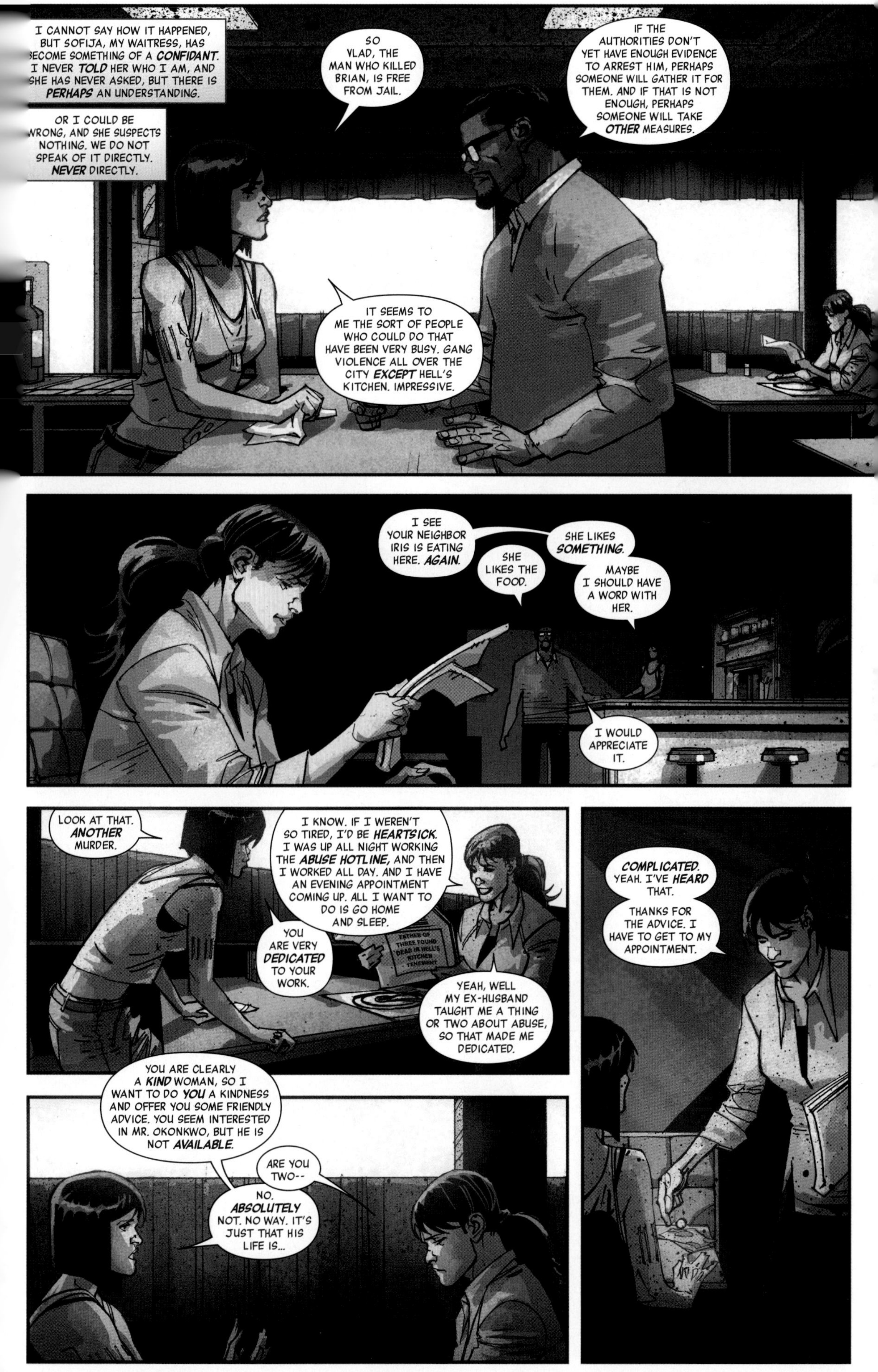
I CANNOT SAY HOW IT HAPPENED, BUT SOFIJA, MY WAITRESS, HAS BECOME SOMETHING OF A CONFIDANT. I NEVER TOLD HER WHO I AM, AND SHE HAS NEVER ASKED, BUT THERE IS PERHAPS AN UNDERSTANDING.
OR I COULD BE WRONG, AND SHE SUSPECTS NOTHING. WE DO NOT SPEAK OF IT DIRECTLY. NEVER DIRECTLY.
SO VLAD, THE MAN WHO KILLED BRIAN, IS FREE FROM JAIL.
IF THE AUTHORITIES DON'T YET HAVE ENOUGH EVIDENCE TO ARREST HIM, PERHAPS SOMEONE WILL GATHER IT FOR THEM. AND IF THAT IS NOT ENOUGH, PERHAPS SOMEONE WILL TAKE OTHER MEASURES.
IT SEEMS TO ME THE SORT OF PEOPLE WHO COULD DO THAT HAVE BEEN VERY BUSY. GANG VIOLENCE ALL OVER THE CITY EXCEPT HELL'S KITCHEN. IMPRESSIVE.
I SEE YOUR NEIGHBOR IRIS IS EATING HERE. AGAIN.
SHE LIKES THE FOOD.
SHE LIKES SOMETHING.
MAYBE I SHOULD HAVE A WORD WITH HER.
I WOULD APPRECIATE IT.
LOOK AT THAT. ANOTHER MURDER.
I KNOW. IF I WEREN'T SO TIRED, I'D BE HEARTSICK. I WAS UP ALL NIGHT WORKING THE ABUSE HOTLINE, AND THEN I WORKED ALL DAY. AND I HAVE AN EVENING APPOINTMENT COMING UP. ALL I WANT TO DO IS GO HOME AND SLEEP.
FATHER OF THREE FOUND DEAD IN HELL'S KITCHEN TENEMENT
YOU ARE VERY DEDICATED TO YOUR WORK.
YEAH, WELL MY EX-HUSBAND TAUGHT ME A THING OR TWO ABOUT ABUSE, SO THAT MADE ME DEDICATED.
YOU ARE CLEARLY A KIND WOMAN, SO I WANT TO DO YOU A KINDNESS AND OFFER YOU SOME FRIENDLY ADVICE. YOU SEEM INTERESTED IN MR. OKONKWO, BUT HE IS NOT AVAILABLE.
ARE YOU TWO--
NO. ABSOLUTELY NOT. NO WAY. IT'S JUST THAT HIS LIFE IS...
COMPLICATED. YEAH. I'VE HEARD THAT.
THANKS FOR THE ADVICE. I HAVE TO GET TO MY APPOINTMENT.

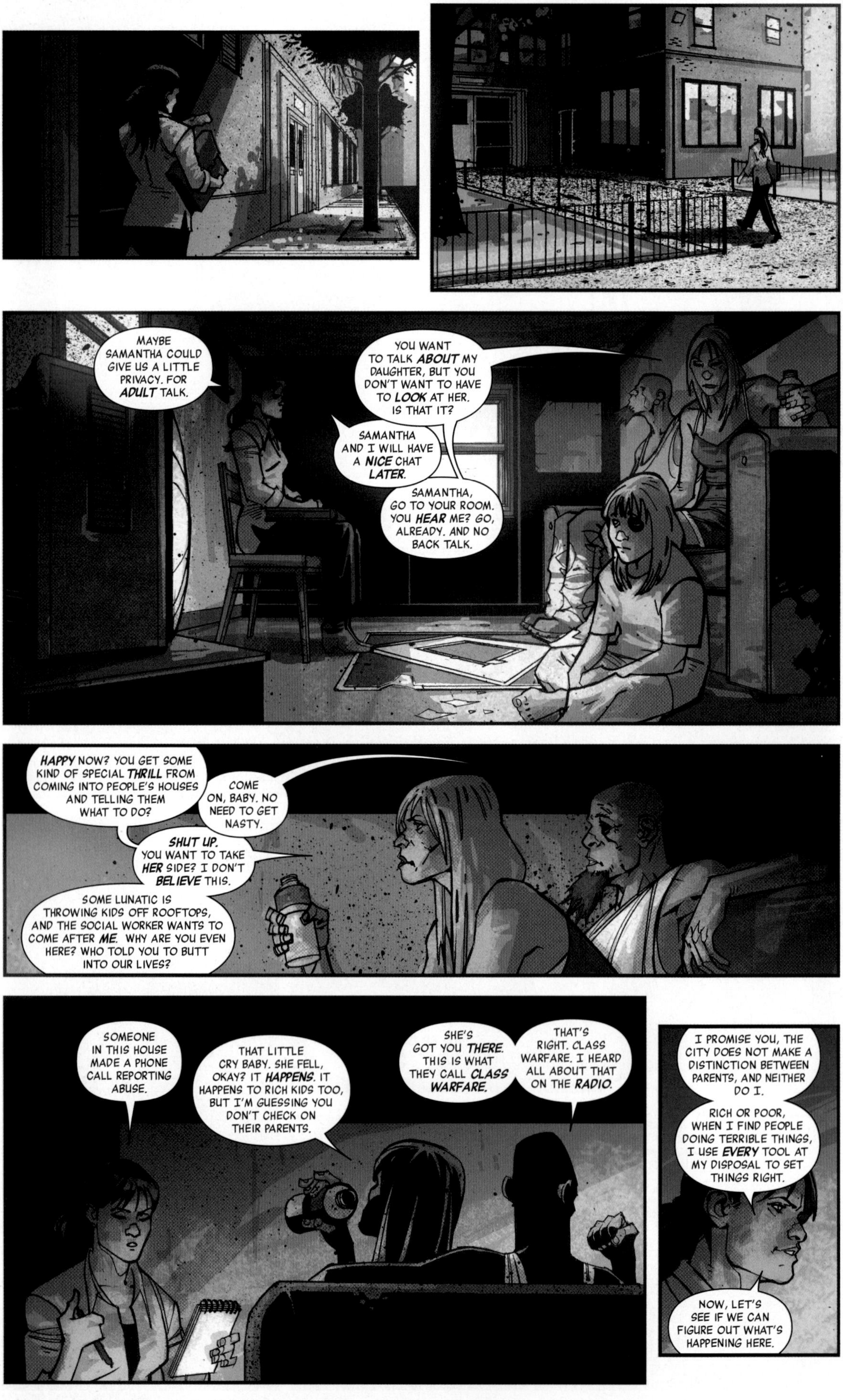
MAYBE SAMANTHA COULD GIVE US A LITTLE PRIVACY. FOR ADULT TALK.
YOU WANT TO TALK ABOUT MY DAUGHTER, BUT YOU DON'T WANT TO HAVE TO LOOK AT HER. IS THAT IT?
SAMANTHA AND I WILL HAVE A NICE CHAT LATER.
SAMANTHA, GO TO YOUR ROOM. YOU HEAR ME? GO, ALREADY. AND NO BACK TALK.
HAPPY NOW? YOU GET SOME KIND OF SPECIAL THRILL FROM COMING INTO PEOPLE'S HOUSES AND TELLING THEM WHAT TO DO?
COME ON, BABY. NO NEED TO GET NASTY.
SHUT UP. YOU WANT TO TAKE HER SIDE? I DON'T BELIEVE THIS.
SOME LUNATIC IS THROWING KIDS OFF ROOFTOPS, AND THE SOCIAL WORKER WANTS TO COME AFTER ME. WHY ARE YOU EVEN HERE? WHO TOLD YOU TO BUTT INTO OUR LIVES?
SOMEONE IN THIS HOUSE MADE A PHONE CALL REPORTING ABUSE.
THAT LITTLE CRY BABY. SHE FELL, OKAY? IT HAPPENS. IT HAPPENS TO RICH KIDS TOO, BUT I'M GUESSING YOU DON'T CHECK ON THEIR PARENTS.
SHE'S GOT YOU THERE. THIS IS WHAT THEY CALL CLASS WARFARE.
THAT'S RIGHT. CLASS WARFARE. I HEARD ALL ABOUT THAT ON THE RADIO.
I PROMISE YOU, THE CITY DOES NOT MAKE A DISTINCTION BETWEEN PARENTS, AND NEITHER DO I.
RICH OR POOR, WHEN I FIND PEOPLE DOING TERRIBLE THINGS, I USE EVERY TOOL AT MY DISPOSAL TO SET THINGS RIGHT.
NOW, LET'S SEE IF WE CAN FIGURE OUT WHAT'S HAPPENING HERE.

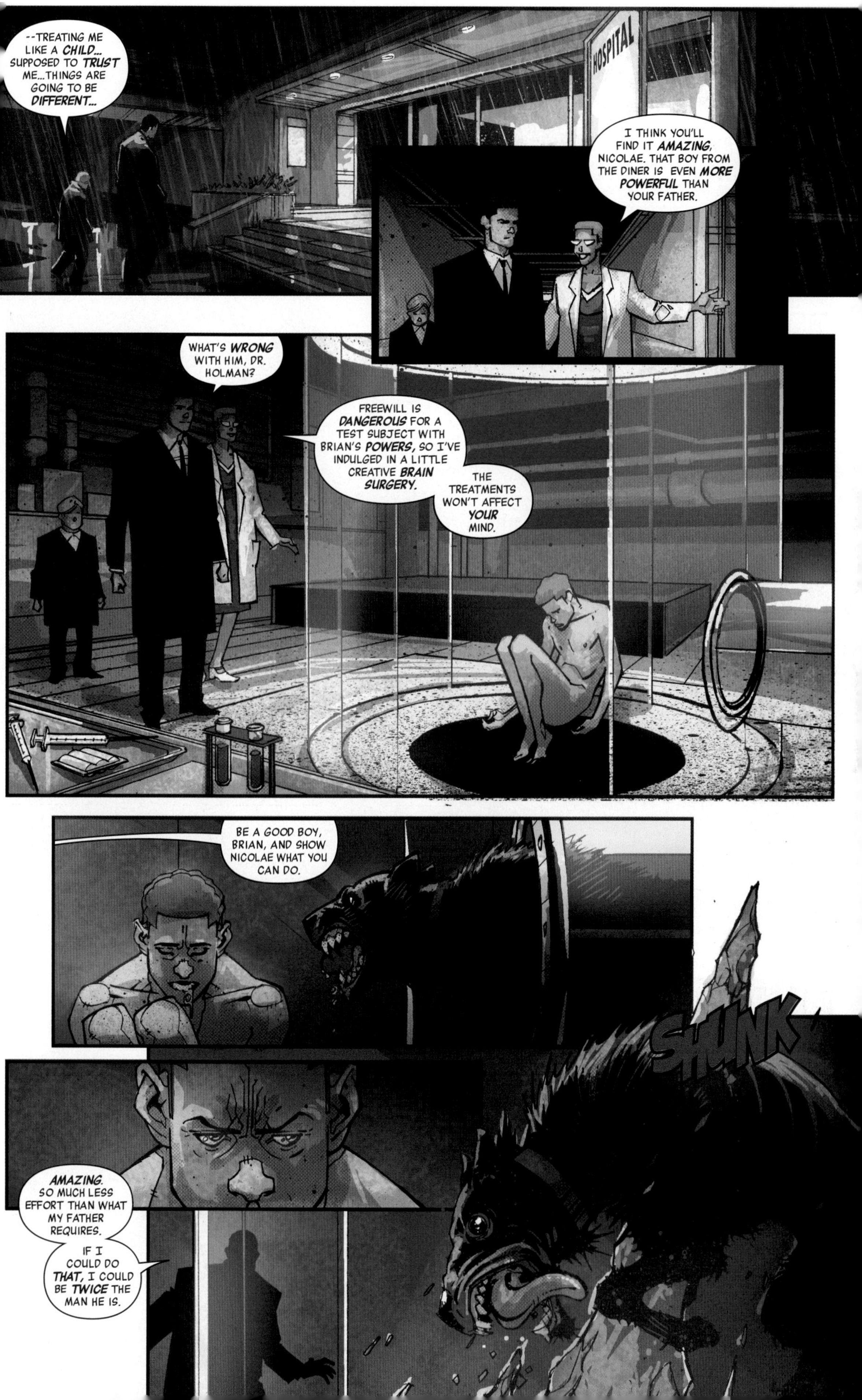
--TREATING ME LIKE A CHILD... SUPPOSED TO TRUST ME...THINGS ARE GOING TO BE DIFFERENT...
HOSPITAL
I THINK YOU'LL FIND IT AMAZING, NICOLAE. THAT BOY FROM THE DINER IS EVEN MORE POWERFUL THAN YOUR FATHER.
WHAT'S WRONG WITH HIM, DR. HOLMAN?
FREEWILL IS DANGEROUS FOR A TEST SUBJECT WITH BRIAN'S POWERS, SO I'VE INDULGED IN A LITTLE CREATIVE BRAIN SURGERY.
THE TREATMENTS WON'T AFFECT YOUR MIND.
BE A GOOD BOY, BRIAN, AND SHOW NICOLAE WHAT YOU CAN DO.
SHUNK
AMAZING. SO MUCH LESS EFFORT THAN WHAT MY FATHER REQUIRES.
IF I COULD DO THAT, I COULD BE TWICE THE MAN HE IS.

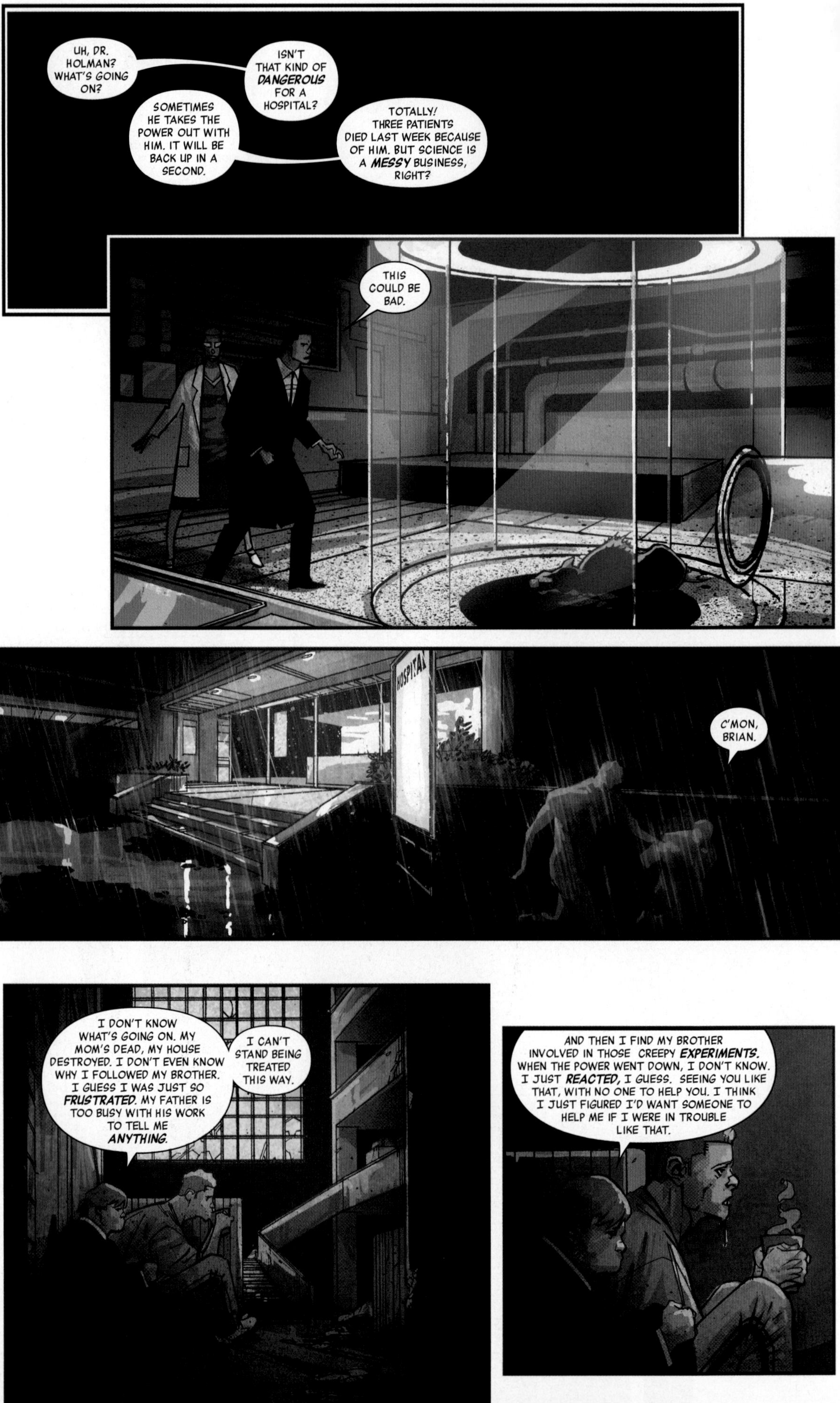
UH, DR. HOLMAN? WHAT'S GOING ON?
ISN'T THAT KIND OF DANGEROUS FOR A HOSPITAL?
SOMETIMES HE TAKES THE POWER OUT WITH HIM. IT WILL BE BACK UP IN A SECOND.
TOTALLY! THREE PATIENTS DIED LAST WEEK BECAUSE OF HIM. BUT SCIENCE IS A MESSY BUSINESS, RIGHT?
THIS COULD BE BAD.
HOSPITAL
C'MON, BRIAN.
I DON'T KNOW WHAT'S GOING ON. MY MOM'S DEAD, MY HOUSE DESTROYED. I DON'T EVEN KNOW WHY I FOLLOWED MY BROTHER. I GUESS I WAS JUST SO FRUSTRATED. MY FATHER IS TOO BUSY WITH HIS WORK TO TELL ME ANYTHING.
I CAN'T STAND BEING TREATED THIS WAY.
AND THEN I FIND MY BROTHER INVOLVED IN THOSE CREEPY EXPERIMENTS. WHEN THE POWER WENT DOWN, I DON'T KNOW. I JUST REACTED, I GUESS. SEEING YOU LIKE THAT, WITH NO ONE TO HELP YOU. I THINK I JUST FIGURED I'D WANT SOMEONE TO HELP ME IF I WERE IN TROUBLE LIKE THAT.

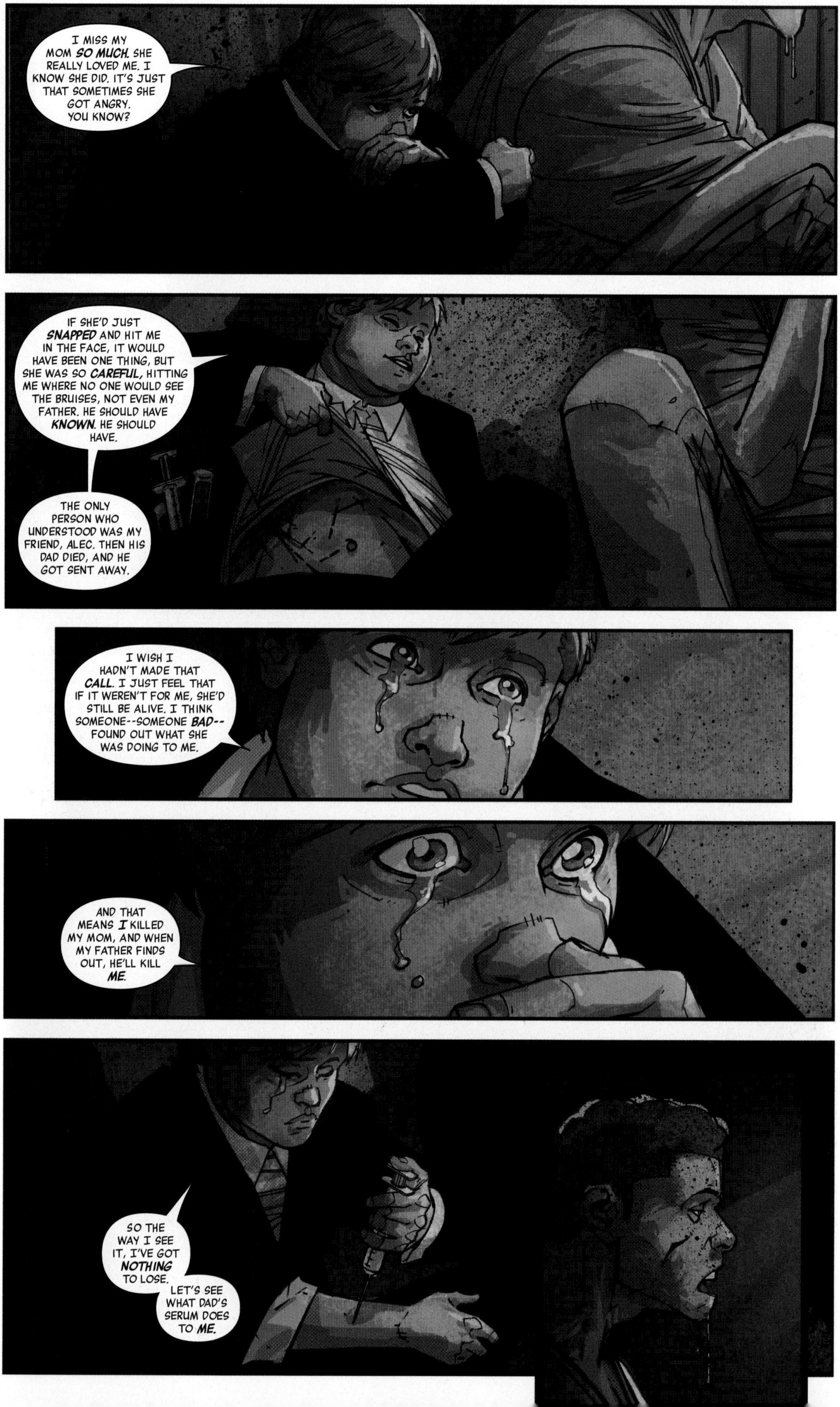
I MISS MY MOM SO MUCH. SHE REALLY LOVED ME. I KNOW SHE DID. IT'S JUST THAT SOMETIMES SHE GOT ANGRY. YOU KNOW?
IF SHE'D JUST SNAPPED AND HIT ME IN THE FACE, IT WOULD HAVE BEEN ONE THING, BUT SHE WAS SO CAREFUL, HITTING ME WHERE NO ONE WOULD SEE THE BRUISES, NOT EVEN MY FATHER. HE SHOULD HAVE KNOWN. HE SHOULD HAVE.
THE ONLY PERSON WHO UNDERSTOOD WAS MY FRIEND, ALEC. THEN HIS DAD DIED, AND HE GOT SENT AWAY.
I WISH I HADN'T MADE THAT CALL. I JUST FEEL THAT IF IT WEREN'T FOR ME, SHE'D STILL BE ALIVE. I THINK SOMEONE--SOMEONE BAD--FOUND OUT WHAT SHE WAS DOING TO ME.
AND THAT MEANS I KILLED MY MOM, AND WHEN MY FATHER FINDS OUT, HE'LL KILL ME.
SO THE WAY I SEE IT, I'VE GOT NOTHING TO LOSE.
LET'S SEE WHAT DAD'S SERUM DOES TO ME.

ORDINARY PEOPLE GUNNED DOWN--ASSASSINATED--IN THEIR OWN HOMES. AND IT'S ESCALATING.

OFFICIAL NYPD DOCUMENT

THERE'S GOT TO BE A **CONNECTION.** I AM CERTAIN DETECTIVE KURTZ HAS GONE OVER THESE FILES THOROUGHLY. I HEAR HE IS A GOOD MAN, BUT HE MUST BE **MISSING** SOMETHING.

ONE MOMENT...

Angela Dinu

Nankatarn
Phone

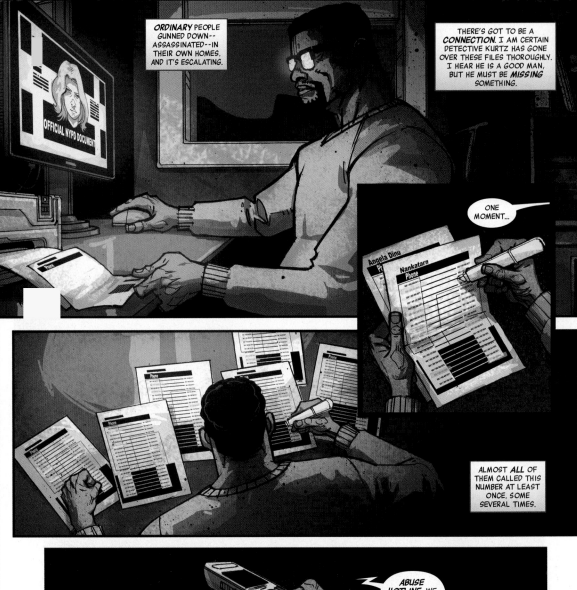

ALMOST **ALL** OF THEM CALLED THIS NUMBER AT LEAST ONCE. SOME SEVERAL TIMES.

ABUSE HOTLINE. WE UNDERSTAND, AND WE CAN HELP.

THIS IS **IRIS** SPEAKING.

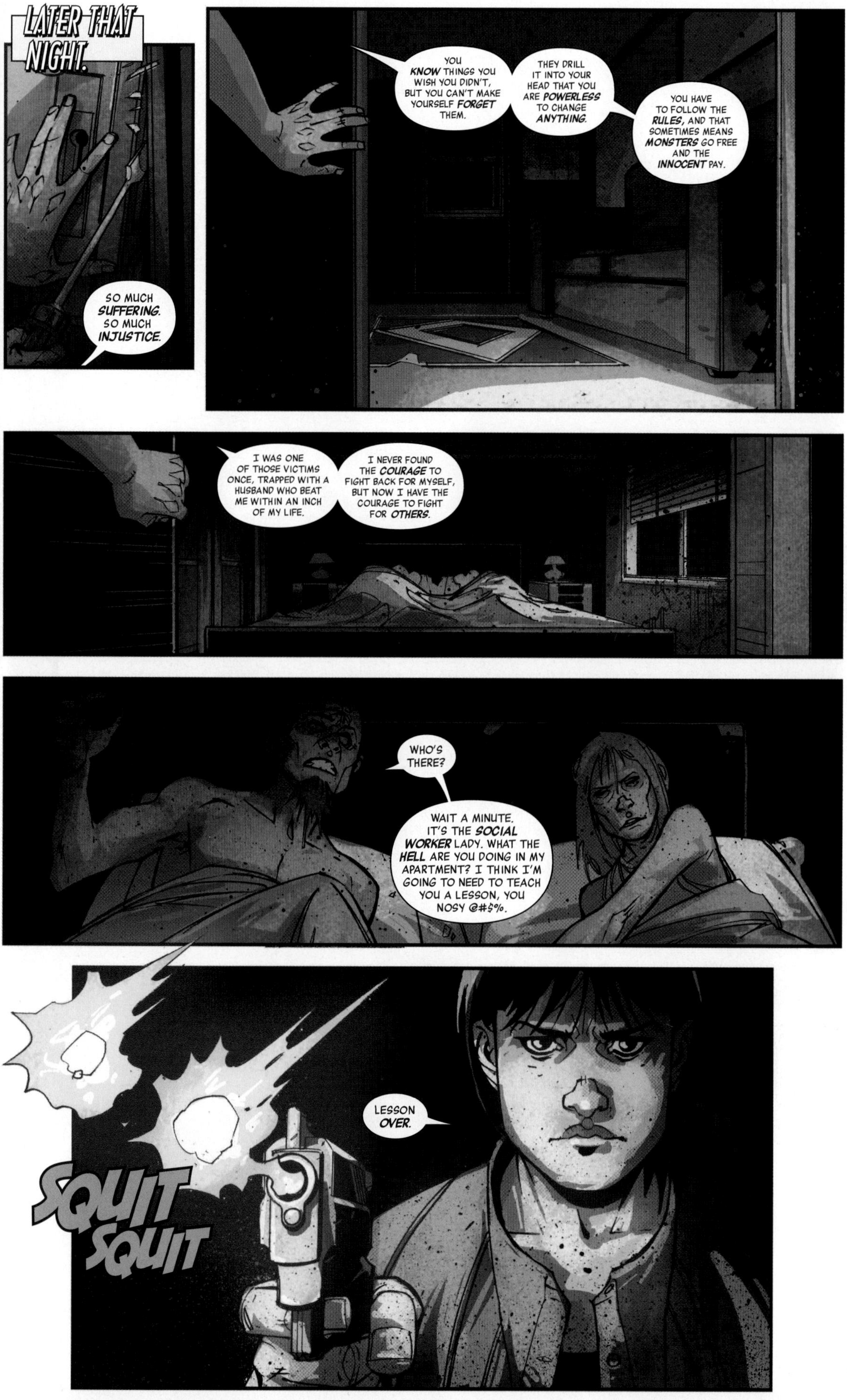
LATER THAT NIGHT.
SO MUCH SUFFERING. SO MUCH INJUSTICE.
YOU KNOW THINGS YOU WISH YOU DIDN'T, BUT YOU CAN'T MAKE YOURSELF FORGET THEM.
THEY DRILL IT INTO YOUR HEAD THAT YOU ARE POWERLESS TO CHANGE ANYTHING.
YOU HAVE TO FOLLOW THE RULES, AND THAT SOMETIMES MEANS MONSTERS GO FREE AND THE INNOCENT PAY.
I WAS ONE OF THOSE VICTIMS ONCE, TRAPPED WITH A HUSBAND WHO BEAT ME WITHIN AN INCH OF MY LIFE.
I NEVER FOUND THE COURAGE TO FIGHT BACK FOR MYSELF, BUT NOW I HAVE THE COURAGE TO FIGHT FOR OTHERS.
WHO'S THERE?
WAIT A MINUTE. IT'S THE SOCIAL WORKER LADY. WHAT THE HELL ARE YOU DOING IN MY APARTMENT? I THINK I'M GOING TO NEED TO TEACH YOU A LESSON, YOU NOSY @#$%.
SQUIT SQUIT
LESSON OVER.

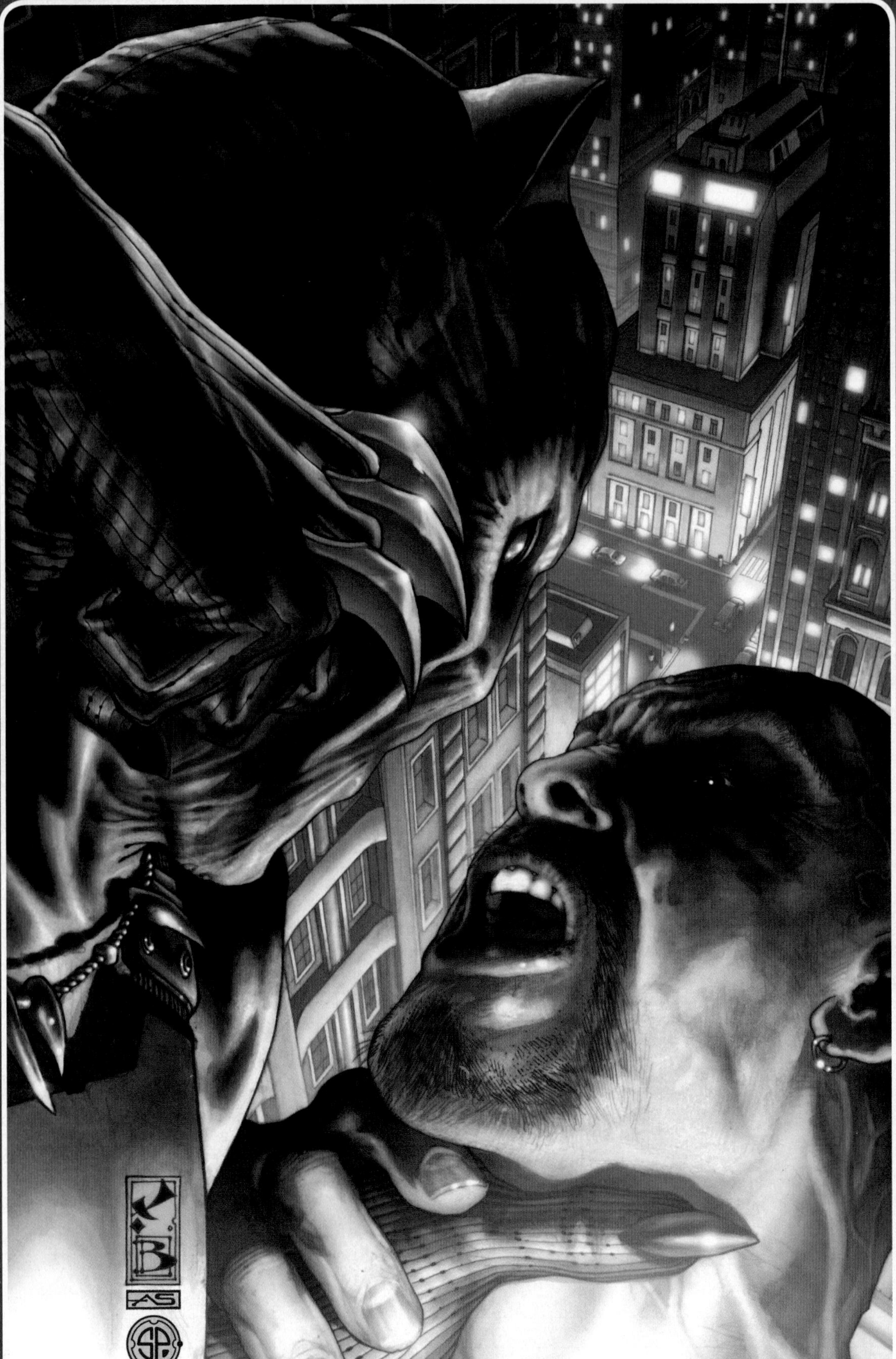

BLACK PANTHER: THE MAN WITHOUT FEAR #517

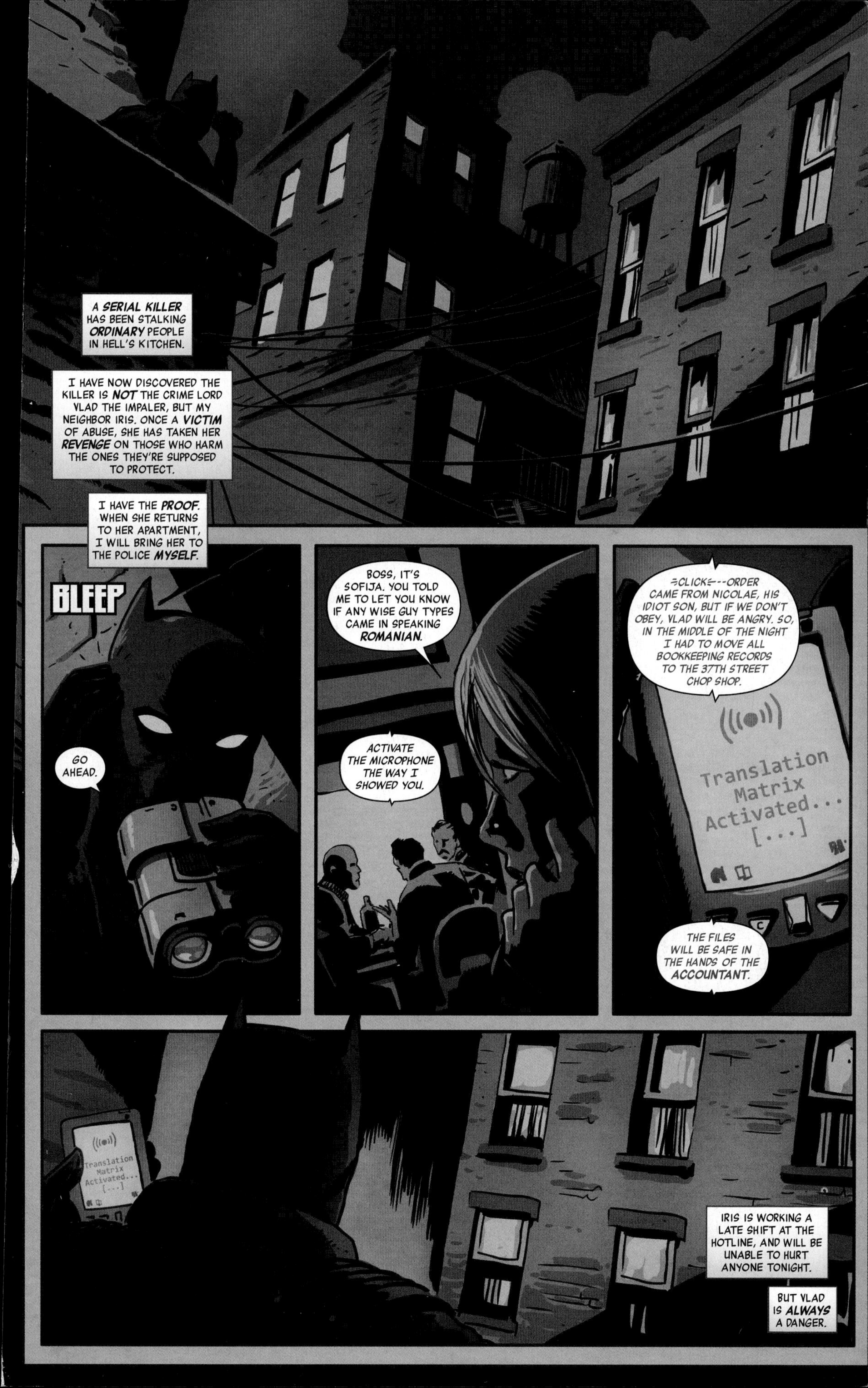
A SERIAL KILLER HAS BEEN STALKING ORDINARY PEOPLE IN HELL'S KITCHEN.
I HAVE NOW DISCOVERED THE KILLER IS NOT THE CRIME LORD VLAD THE IMPALER, BUT MY NEIGHBOR IRIS. ONCE A VICTIM OF ABUSE, SHE HAS TAKEN HER REVENGE ON THOSE WHO HARM THE ONES THEY'RE SUPPOSED TO PROTECT.
I HAVE THE PROOF. WHEN SHE RETURNS TO HER APARTMENT, I WILL BRING HER TO THE POLICE MYSELF.
BLEEP
GO AHEAD.
BOSS, IT'S SOFIJA. YOU TOLD ME TO LET YOU KNOW IF ANY WISE GUY TYPES CAME IN SPEAKING ROMANIAN.
ACTIVATE THE MICROPHONE THE WAY I SHOWED YOU.
=CLICK=--ORDER CAME FROM NICOLAE, HIS IDIOT SON, BUT IF WE DON'T OBEY, VLAD WILL BE ANGRY. SO, IN THE MIDDLE OF THE NIGHT I HAD TO MOVE ALL BOOKKEEPING RECORDS TO THE 37TH STREET CHOP SHOP.
Translation Matrix Activated... [...]
THE FILES WILL BE SAFE IN THE HANDS OF THE ACCOUNTANT.
Translation Matrix Activated... [...]
IRIS IS WORKING A LATE SHIFT AT THE HOTLINE, AND WILL BE UNABLE TO HURT ANYONE TONIGHT.
BUT VLAD IS ALWAYS A DANGER.

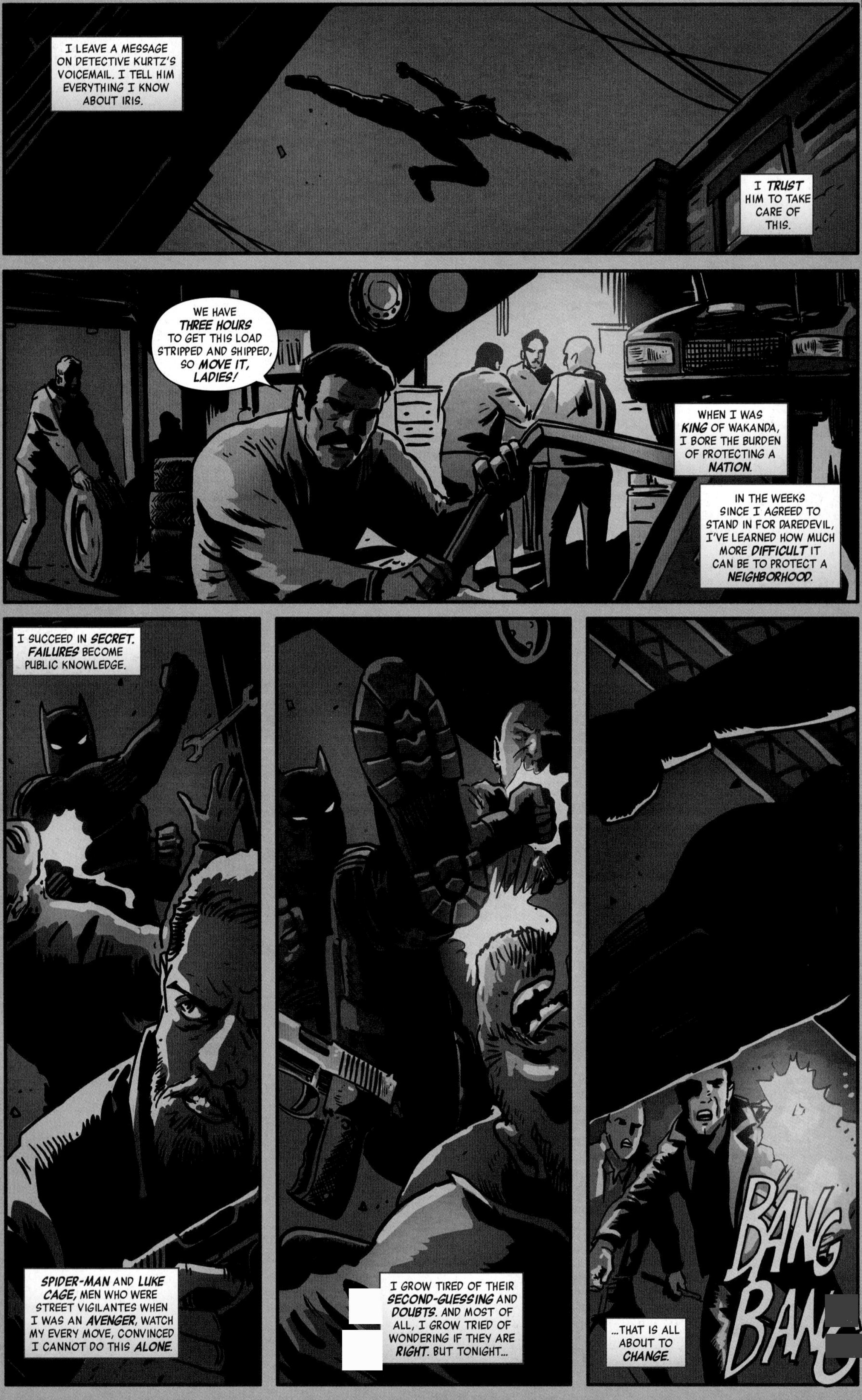

I LEAVE A MESSAGE ON DETECTIVE KURTZ'S VOICEMAIL. I TELL HIM EVERYTHING I KNOW ABOUT IRIS.
I TRUST HIM TO TAKE CARE OF THIS.
WE HAVE THREE HOURS TO GET THIS LOAD STRIPPED AND SHIPPED, SO MOVE IT, LADIES!
WHEN I WAS KING OF WAKANDA, I BORE THE BURDEN OF PROTECTING A NATION.
IN THE WEEKS SINCE I AGREED TO STAND IN FOR DAREDEVIL, I'VE LEARNED HOW MUCH MORE DIFFICULT IT CAN BE TO PROTECT A NEIGHBORHOOD.
I SUCCEED IN SECRET. FAILURES BECOME PUBLIC KNOWLEDGE.
SPIDER-MAN AND LUKE CAGE, MEN WHO WERE STREET VIGILANTES WHEN I WAS AN AVENGER, WATCH MY EVERY MOVE, CONVINCED I CANNOT DO THIS ALONE.
I GROW TIRED OF THEIR SECOND-GUESSING AND DOUBTS. AND MOST OF ALL, I GROW TIRED OF WONDERING IF THEY ARE RIGHT. BUT TONIGHT...
...THAT IS ALL ABOUT TO CHANGE.
BANG
BAN

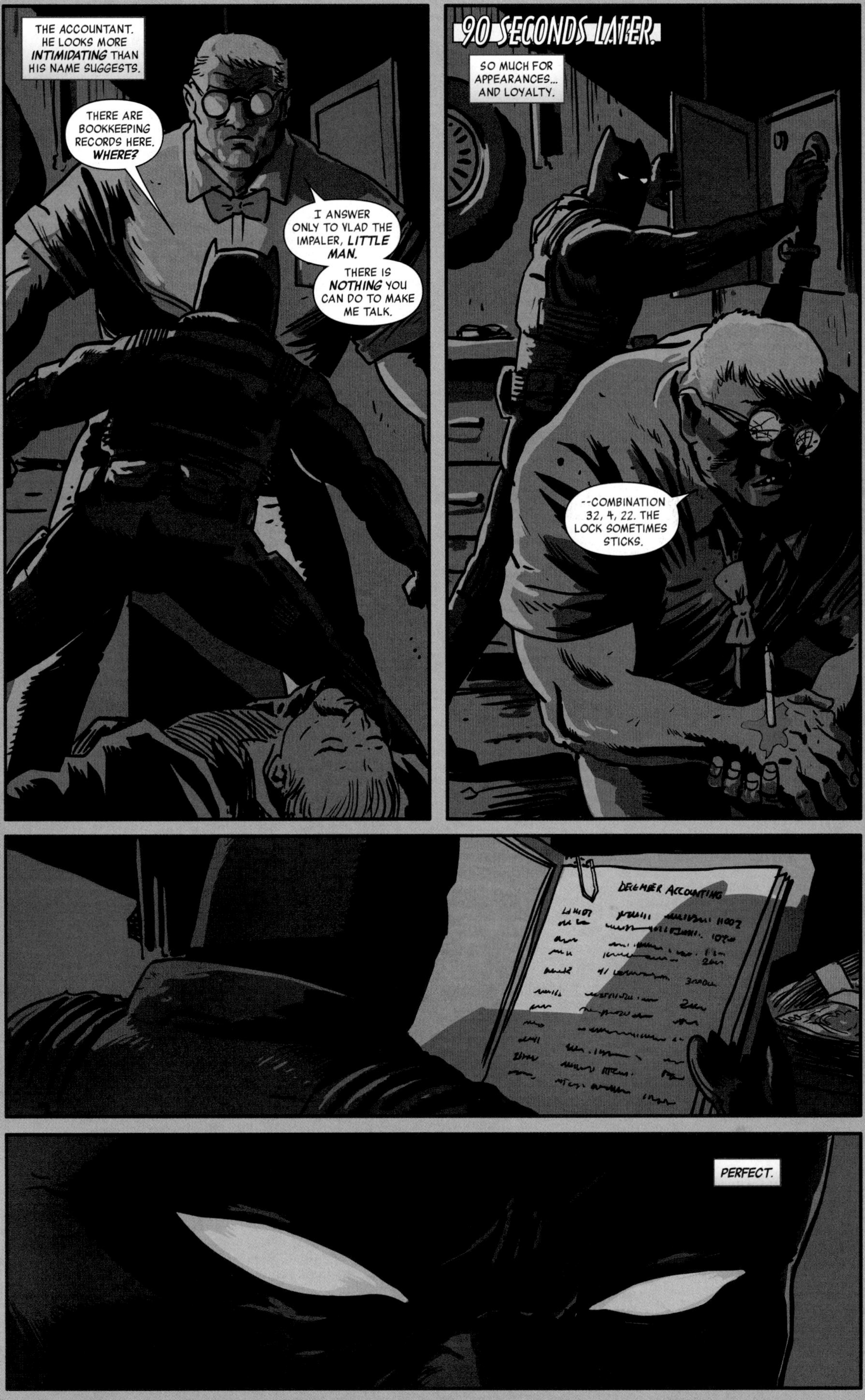
THE ACCOUNTANT. HE LOOKS MORE INTIMIDATING THAN HIS NAME SUGGESTS.
THERE ARE BOOKKEEPING RECORDS HERE. WHERE?
I ANSWER ONLY TO VLAD THE IMPALER, LITTLE MAN.
THERE IS NOTHING YOU CAN DO TO MAKE ME TALK.
90 SECONDS LATER.
SO MUCH FOR APPEARANCES... AND LOYALTY.
--COMBINATION 32, 4, 22. THE LOCK SOMETIMES STICKS.
DECEMBER ACCOUNTING
PERFECT.

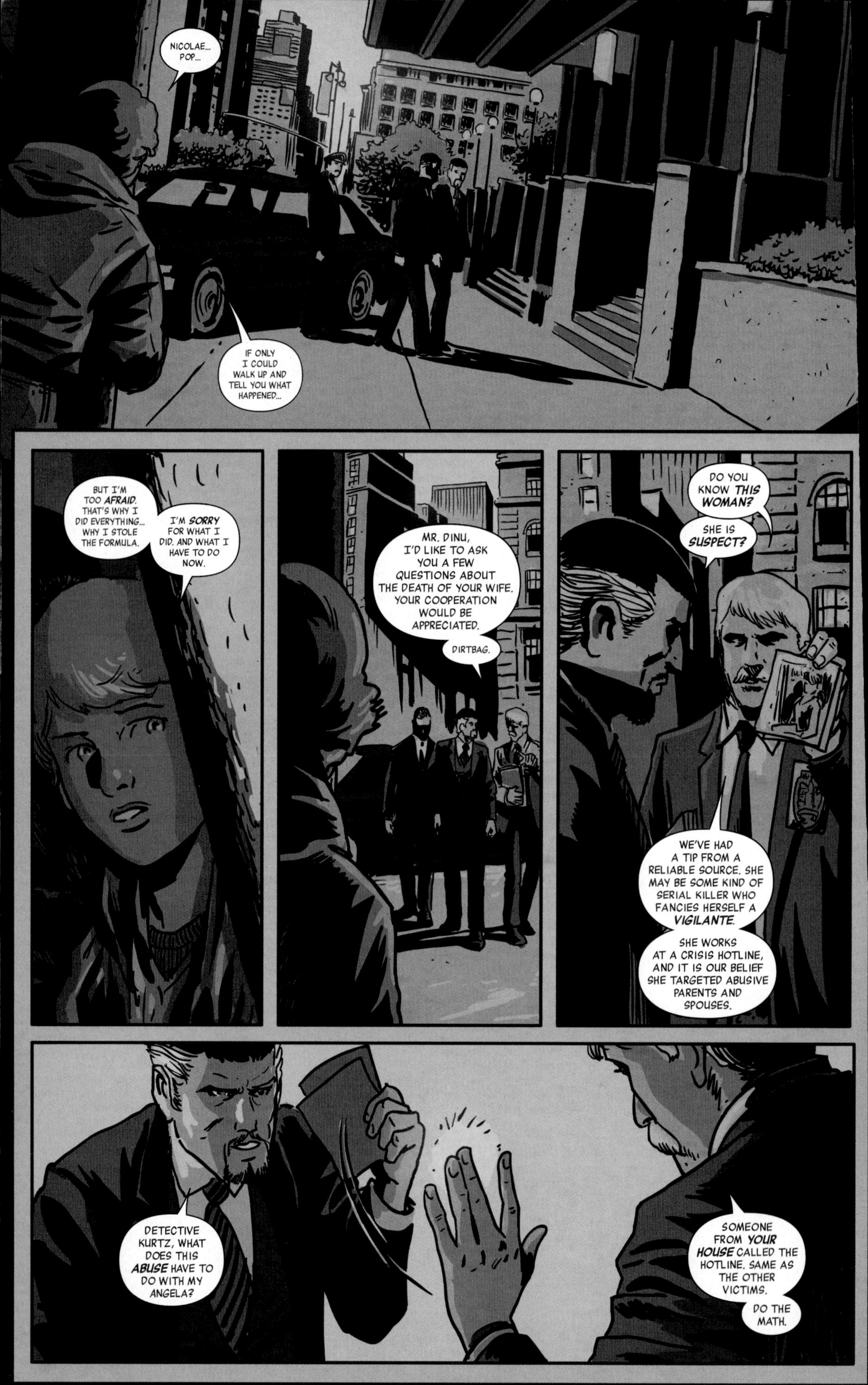
NICOLAE... POP...
IF ONLY I COULD WALK UP AND TELL YOU WHAT HAPPENED...
BUT I'M TOO AFRAID. THAT'S WHY I DID EVERYTHING... WHY I STOLE THE FORMULA.
I'M SORRY FOR WHAT I DID. AND WHAT I HAVE TO DO NOW.
MR. DINU, I'D LIKE TO ASK YOU A FEW QUESTIONS ABOUT THE DEATH OF YOUR WIFE. YOUR COOPERATION WOULD BE APPRECIATED.
DIRTBAG.
DO YOU KNOW THIS WOMAN?
SHE IS SUSPECT?
WE'VE HAD A TIP FROM A RELIABLE SOURCE. SHE MAY BE SOME KIND OF SERIAL KILLER WHO FANCIES HERSELF A VIGILANTE.
SHE WORKS AT A CRISIS HOTLINE, AND IT IS OUR BELIEF SHE TARGETED ABUSIVE PARENTS AND SPOUSES.
DETECTIVE KURTZ, WHAT DOES THIS ABUSE HAVE TO DO WITH MY ANGELA?
SOMEONE FROM YOUR HOUSE CALLED THE HOTLINE. SAME AS THE OTHER VICTIMS.
DO THE MATH.

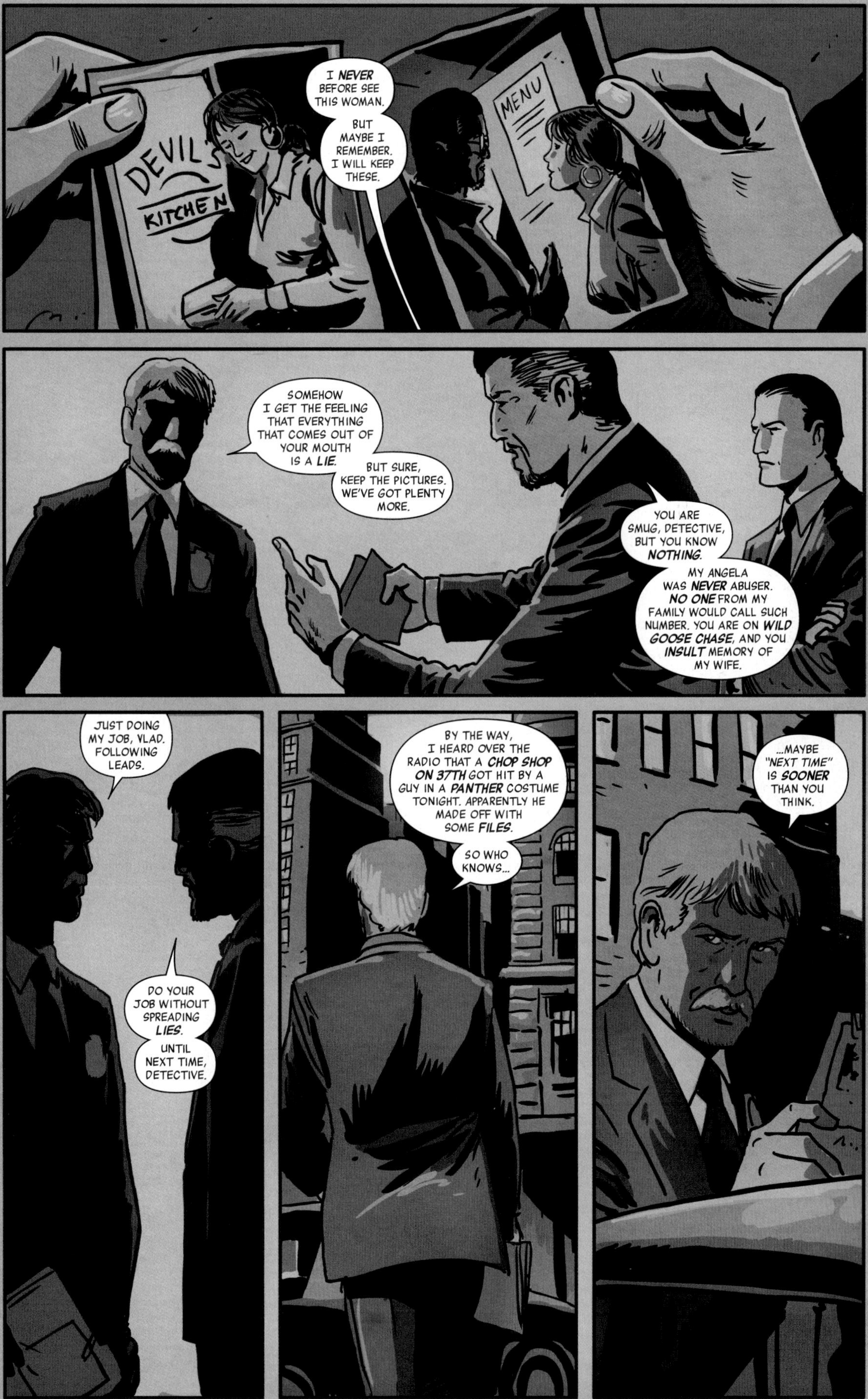

I NEVER BEFORE SEE THIS WOMAN.
BUT MAYBE I REMEMBER. I WILL KEEP THESE.
DEVIL'S KITCHEN
MENU
SOMEHOW I GET THE FEELING THAT EVERYTHING THAT COMES OUT OF YOUR MOUTH IS A LIE.
BUT SURE, KEEP THE PICTURES. WE'VE GOT PLENTY MORE.
YOU ARE SMUG, DETECTIVE, BUT YOU KNOW NOTHING.
MY ANGELA WAS NEVER ABUSER. NO ONE FROM MY FAMILY WOULD CALL SUCH NUMBER. YOU ARE ON WILD GOOSE CHASE, AND YOU INSULT MEMORY OF MY WIFE.
JUST DOING MY JOB, VLAD. FOLLOWING LEADS.
DO YOUR JOB WITHOUT SPREADING LIES.
UNTIL NEXT TIME, DETECTIVE.
BY THE WAY, I HEARD OVER THE RADIO THAT A CHOP SHOP ON 37TH GOT HIT BY A GUY IN A PANTHER COSTUME TONIGHT. APPARENTLY HE MADE OFF WITH SOME FILES.
SO WHO KNOWS...
...MAYBE "NEXT TIME" IS SOONER THAN YOU THINK.

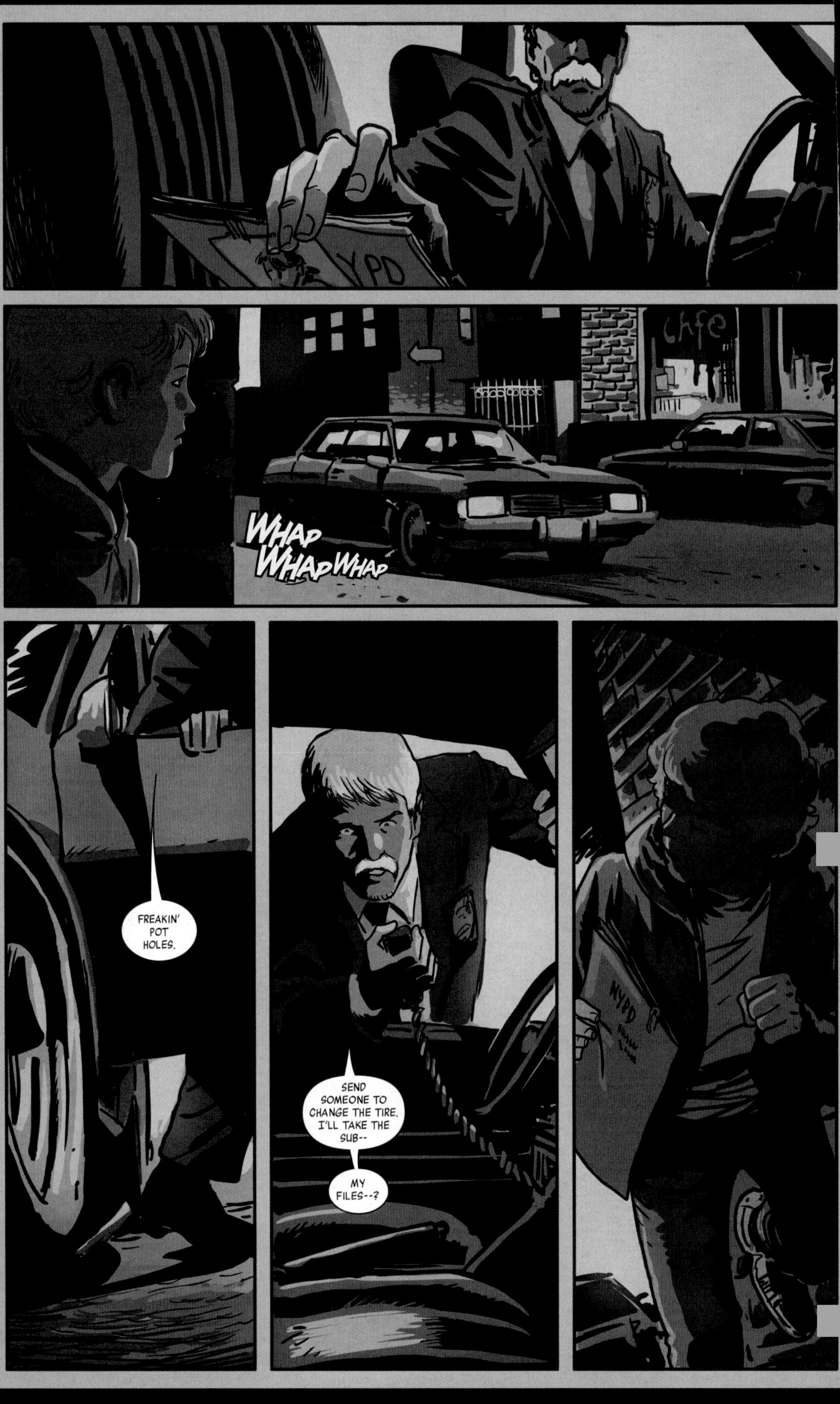
NYPD
WHAP
WHAP WHAP
FREAKIN' POT HOLES.
SEND SOMEONE TO CHANGE THE TIRE. I'LL TAKE THE SUB--
MY FILES--?
NYPD

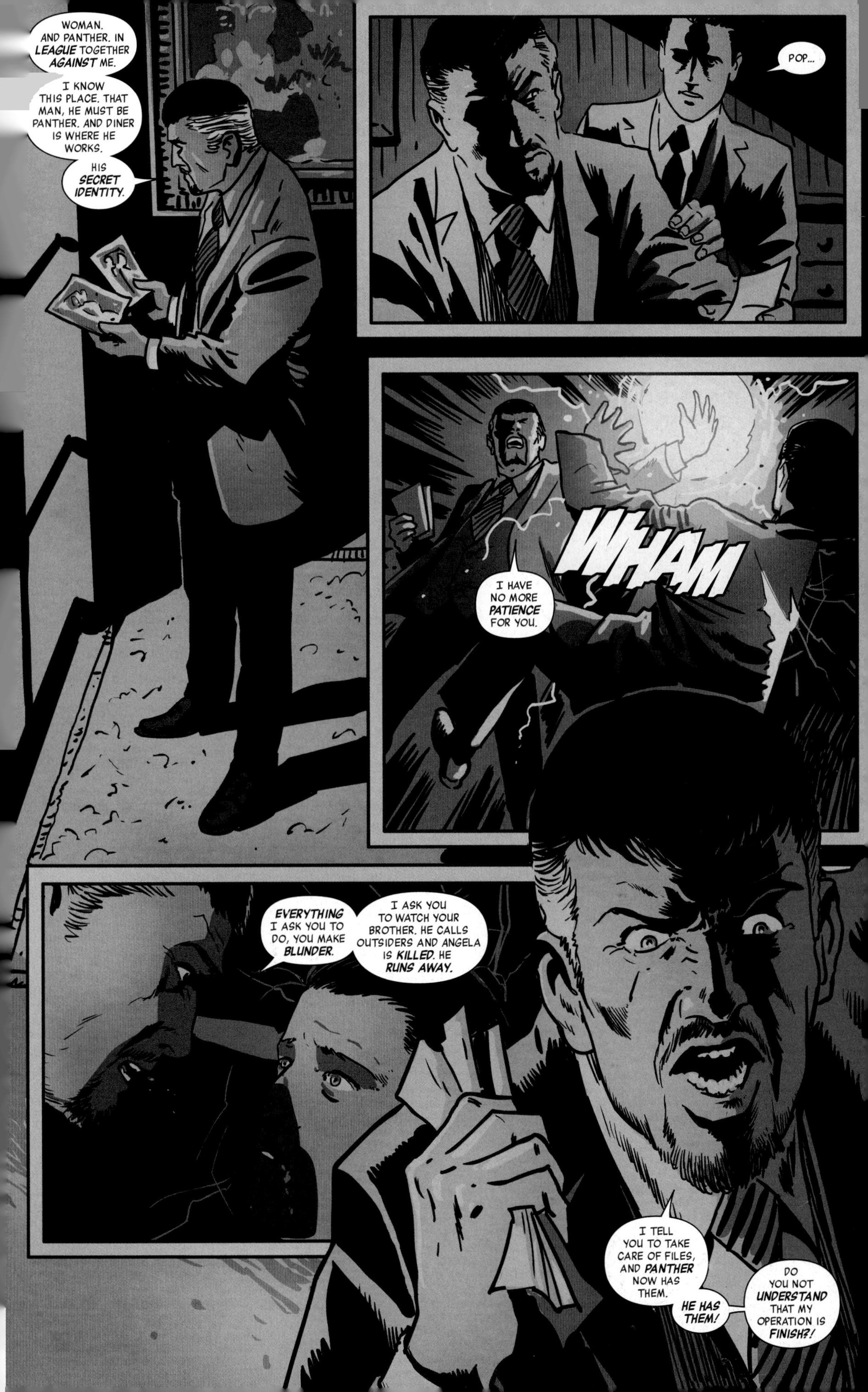
WOMAN. AND PANTHER. IN LEAGUE TOGETHER AGAINST ME.
I KNOW THIS PLACE. THAT MAN, HE MUST BE PANTHER. AND DINER IS WHERE HE WORKS.
HIS SECRET IDENTITY.
POP...
WHAM
I HAVE NO MORE PATIENCE FOR YOU.
EVERYTHING I ASK YOU TO DO, YOU MAKE BLUNDER.
I ASK YOU TO WATCH YOUR BROTHER. HE CALLS OUTSIDERS AND ANGELA IS KILLED. HE RUNS AWAY.
I TELL YOU TO TAKE CARE OF FILES, AND PANTHER NOW HAS THEM.
HE HAS THEM!
DO YOU NOT UNDERSTAND THAT MY OPERATION IS FINISH?!

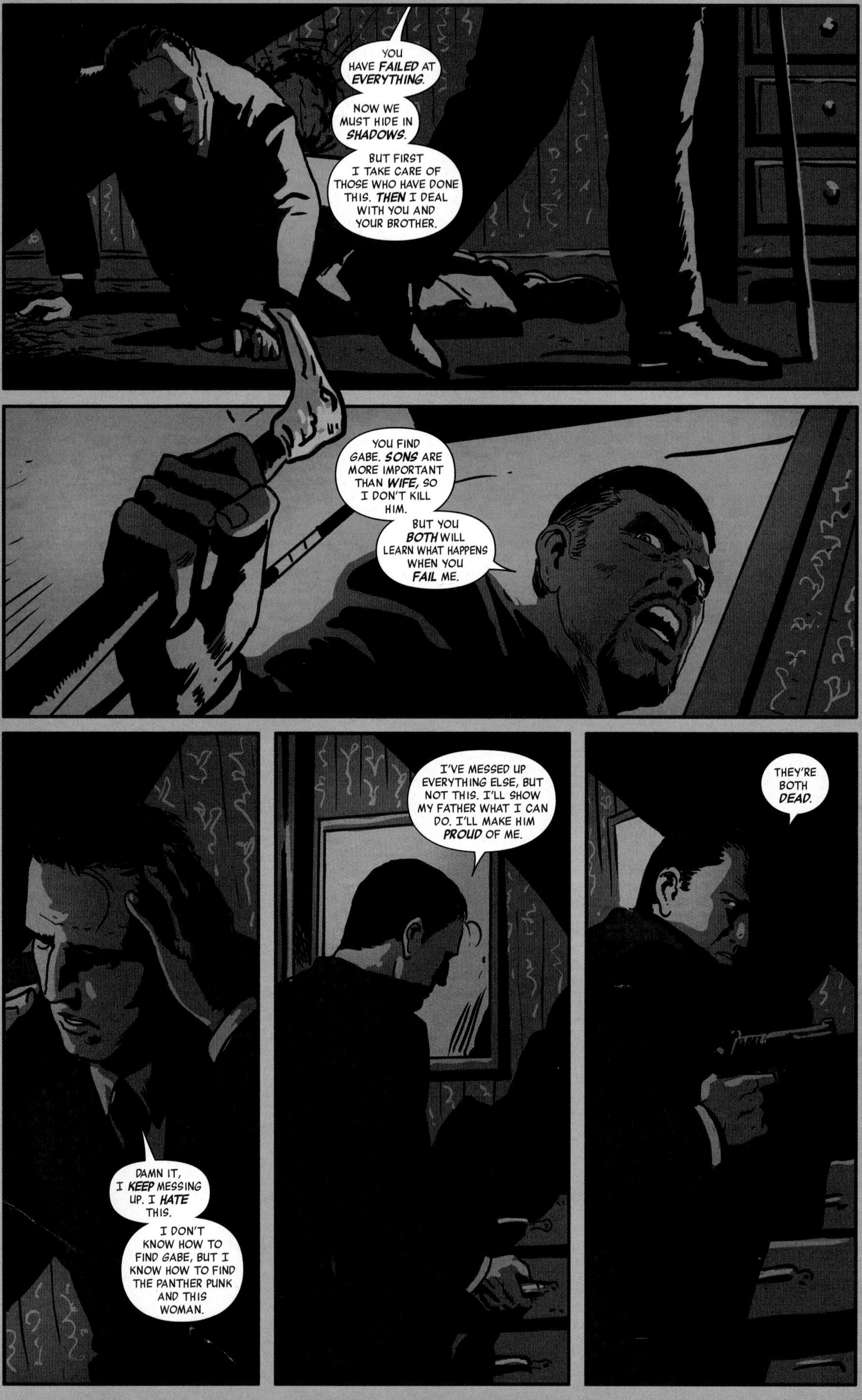

YOU HAVE FAILED AT EVERYTHING.
NOW WE MUST HIDE IN SHADOWS.
BUT FIRST I TAKE CARE OF THOSE WHO HAVE DONE THIS. THEN I DEAL WITH YOU AND YOUR BROTHER.
YOU FIND GABE. SONS ARE MORE IMPORTANT THAN WIFE, SO I DON'T KILL HIM.
BUT YOU BOTH WILL LEARN WHAT HAPPENS WHEN YOU FAIL ME.
DAMN IT, I KEEP MESSING UP. I HATE THIS.
I DON'T KNOW HOW TO FIND GABE, BUT I KNOW HOW TO FIND THE PANTHER PUNK AND THIS WOMAN.
I'VE MESSED UP EVERYTHING ELSE, BUT NOT THIS. I'LL SHOW MY FATHER WHAT I CAN DO. I'LL MAKE HIM PROUD OF ME.
THEY'RE BOTH DEAD.

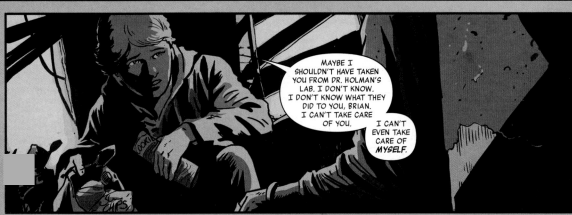

MAYBE I SHOULDN'T HAVE TAKEN YOU FROM DR. HOLMAN'S LAB. I DON'T KNOW. I DON'T KNOW WHAT THEY DID TO YOU, BRIAN. I CAN'T TAKE CARE OF YOU.

I CAN'T EVEN TAKE CARE OF *MYSELF.*

I CALLED THIS WOMAN BECAUSE MY MOTHER WAS *HURTING* ME. NOW MY MOTHER IS DEAD, AND MY FATHER IS GOING TO *KILL* ME.

SO, THE *CRAZY* THING IS, SHE MURDERED MY MOTHER, BUT SHE DID IT BECAUSE SHE WANTS TO *HELP* PEOPLE.

MAYBE SHE CAN HELP ME FIX THINGS.

YOU'LL BE OKAY BY YOURSELF FOR A WHILE.

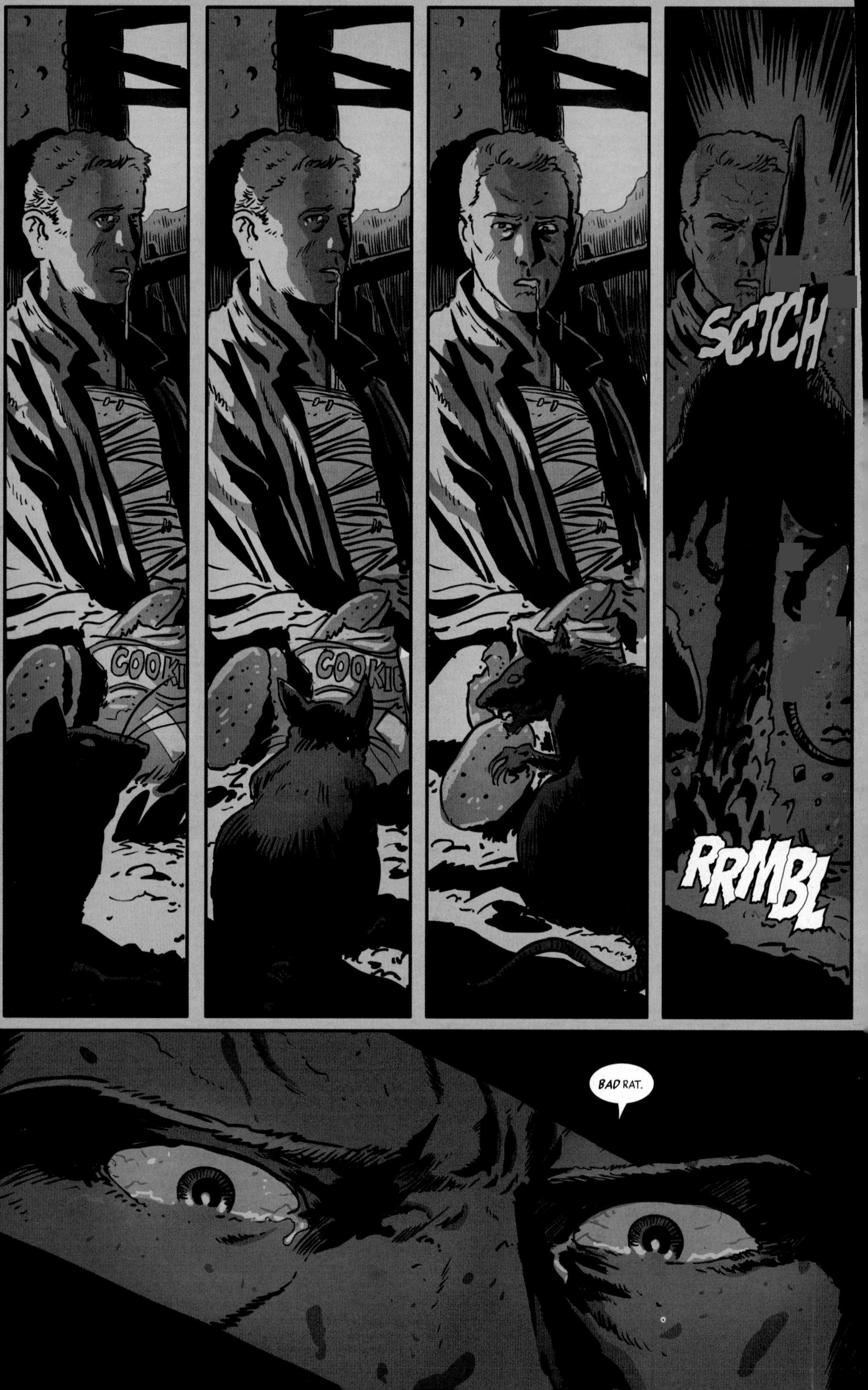
COOKI
COOKI
SCTCH
RRMBL
BAD RAT.

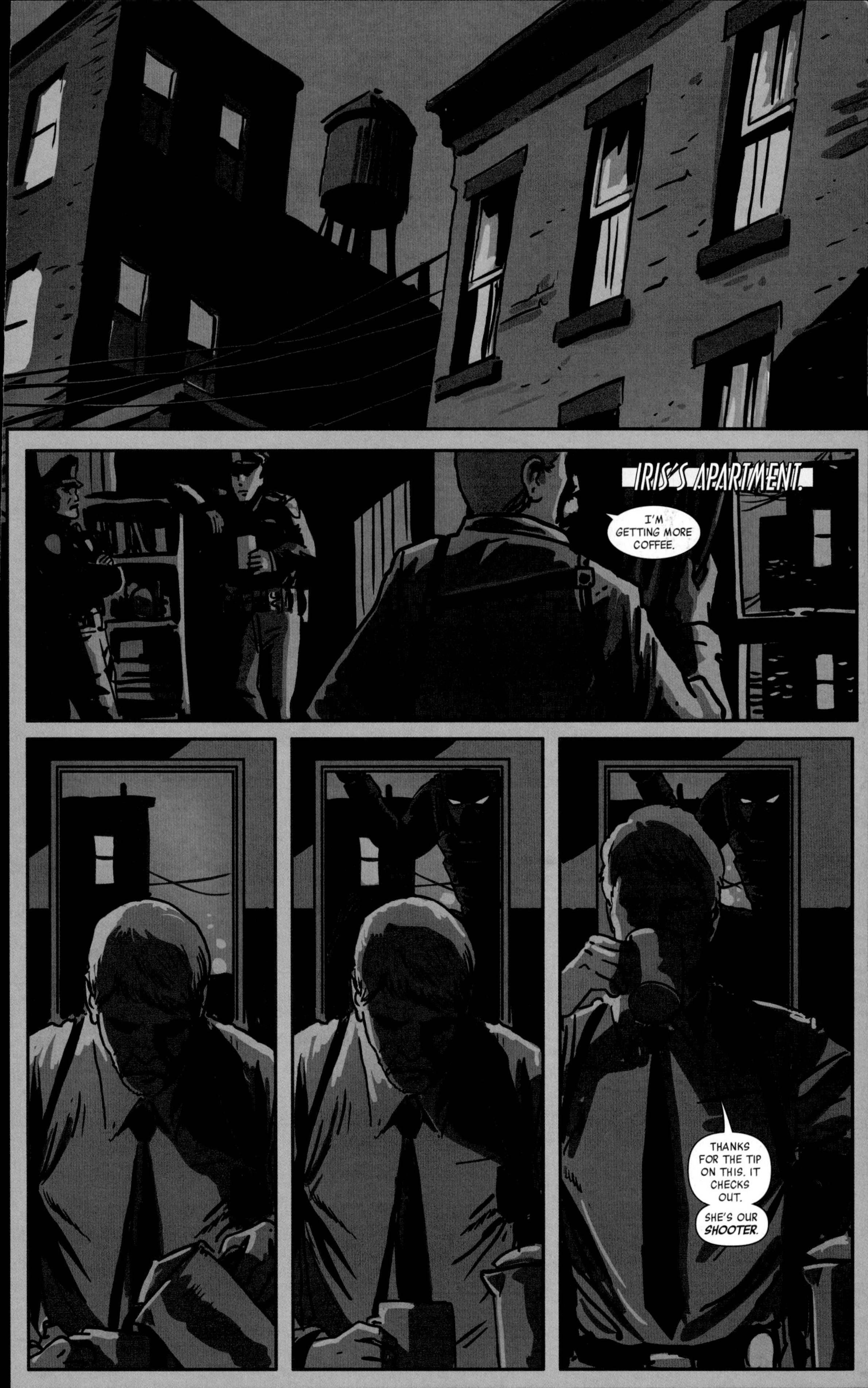
IRIS'S APARTMENT.
I'M GETTING MORE COFFEE.
THANKS FOR THE TIP ON THIS. IT CHECKS OUT.
SHE'S OUR *SHOOTER*.

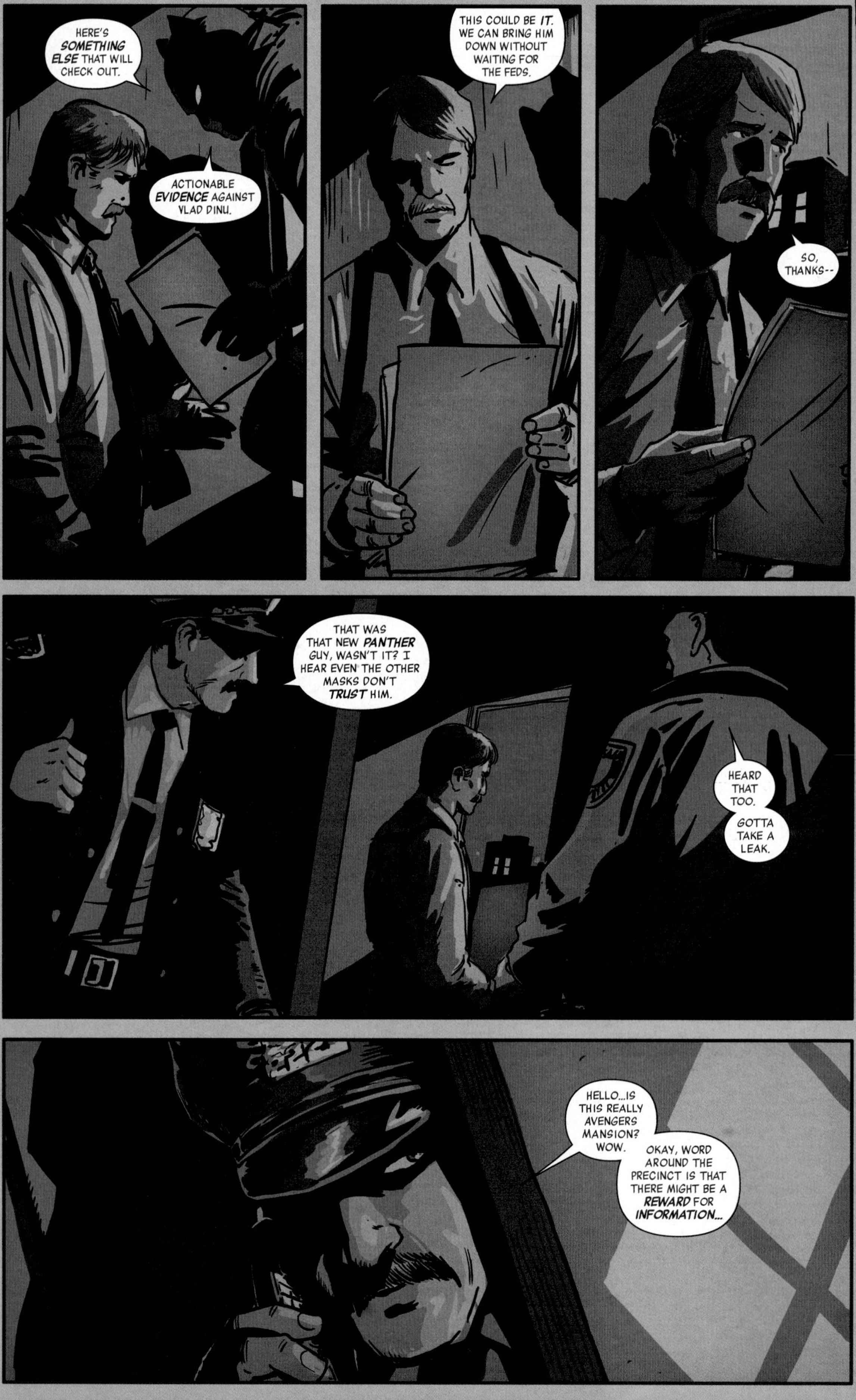
HERE'S SOMETHING ELSE THAT WILL CHECK OUT.
ACTIONABLE EVIDENCE AGAINST VLAD DINU.
THIS COULD BE IT. WE CAN BRING HIM DOWN WITHOUT WAITING FOR THE FEDS.
SO, THANKS--
THAT WAS THAT NEW PANTHER GUY, WASN'T IT? I HEAR EVEN THE OTHER MASKS DON'T TRUST HIM.
HEARD THAT TOO.
GOTTA TAKE A LEAK.
HELLO...IS THIS REALLY AVENGERS MANSION? WOW.
OKAY, WORD AROUND THE PRECINCT IS THAT THERE MIGHT BE A REWARD FOR INFORMATION...

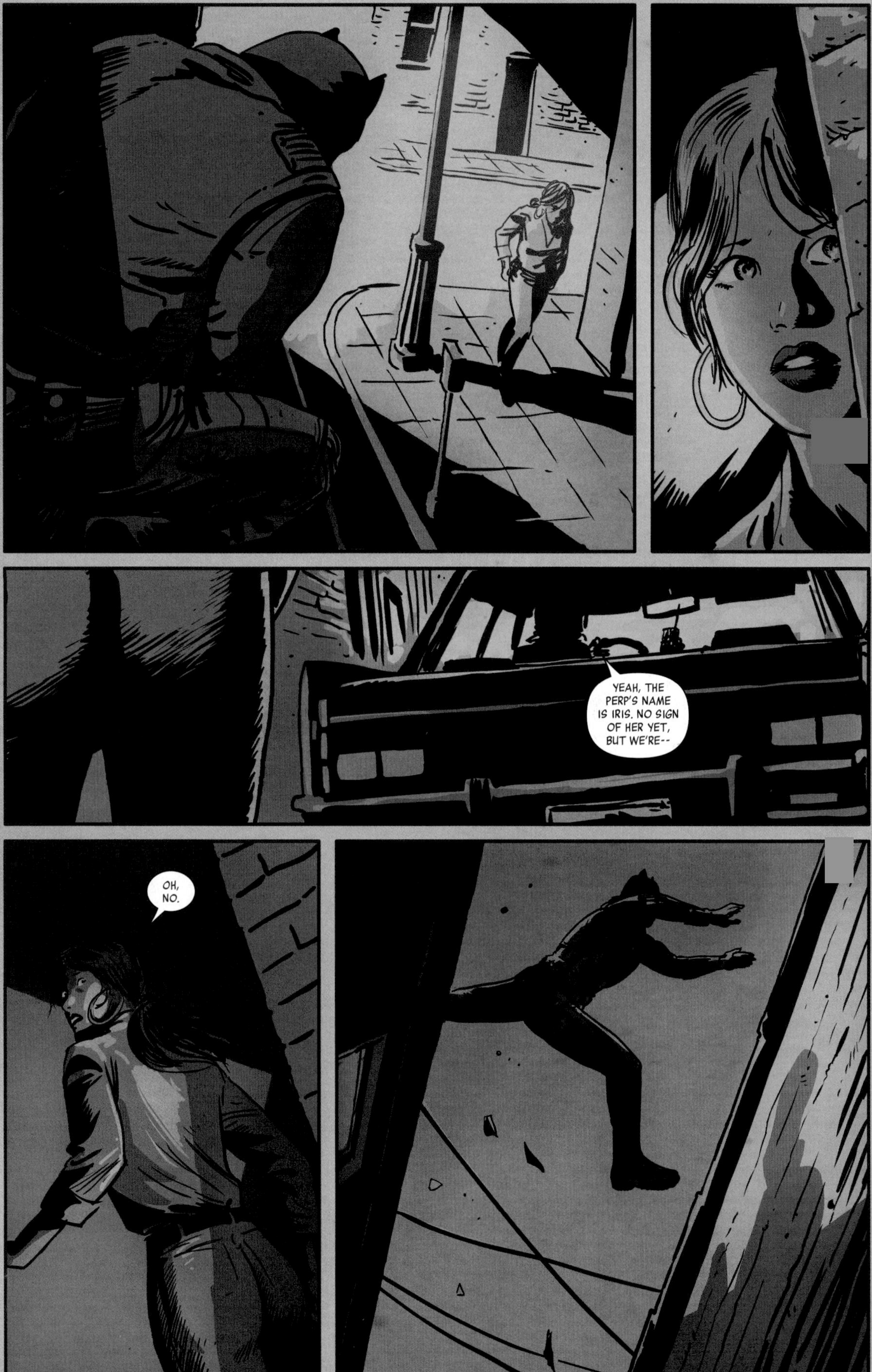
YEAH, THE PERP'S NAME IS IRIS. NO SIGN OF HER YET, BUT WE'RE--
OH, NO.

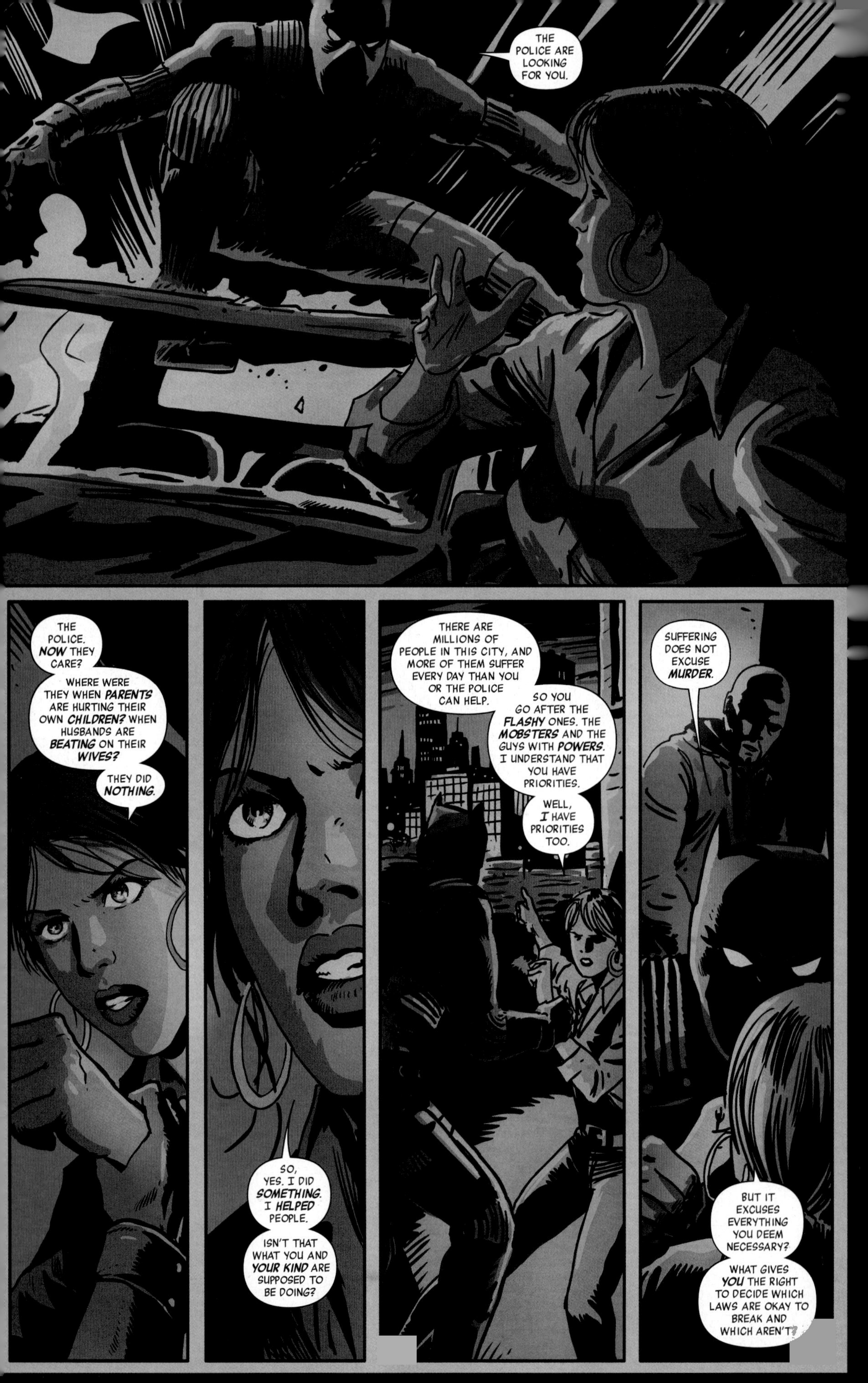
THE POLICE ARE LOOKING FOR YOU.
THE POLICE. NOW THEY CARE?
WHERE WERE THEY WHEN PARENTS ARE HURTING THEIR OWN CHILDREN? WHEN HUSBANDS ARE BEATING ON THEIR WIVES?
THEY DID NOTHING.
SO, YES. I DID SOMETHING. I HELPED PEOPLE.
ISN'T THAT WHAT YOU AND YOUR KIND ARE SUPPOSED TO BE DOING?
THERE ARE MILLIONS OF PEOPLE IN THIS CITY, AND MORE OF THEM SUFFER EVERY DAY THAN YOU OR THE POLICE CAN HELP.
SO YOU GO AFTER THE FLASHY ONES. THE MOBSTERS AND THE GUYS WITH POWERS. I UNDERSTAND THAT YOU HAVE PRIORITIES.
WELL, I HAVE PRIORITIES TOO.
SUFFERING DOES NOT EXCUSE MURDER.
BUT IT EXCUSES EVERYTHING YOU DEEM NECESSARY?
WHAT GIVES YOU THE RIGHT TO DECIDE WHICH LAWS ARE OKAY TO BREAK AND WHICH AREN'T?

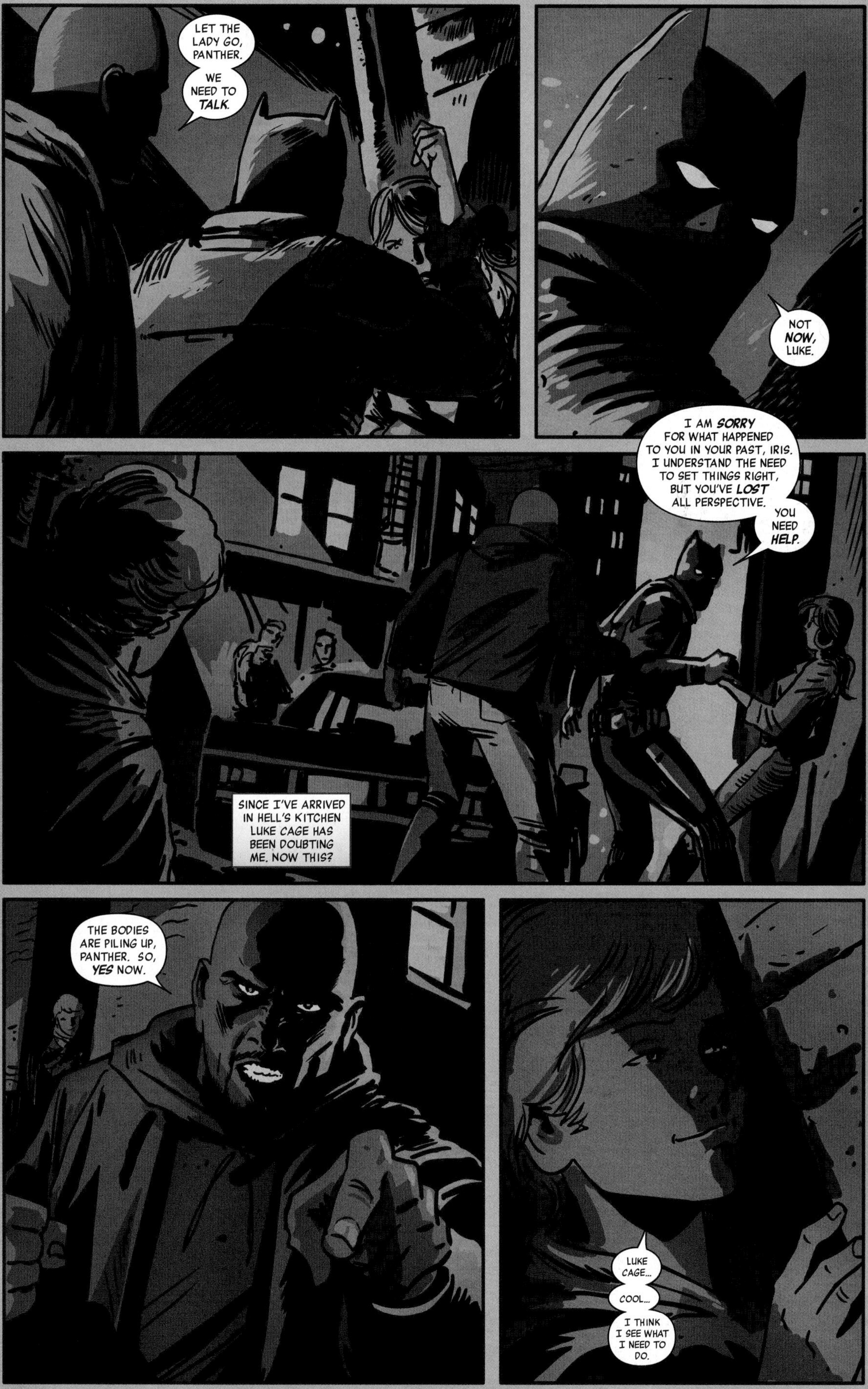
LET THE LADY GO, PANTHER.
WE NEED TO TALK.
NOT NOW, LUKE.
I AM SORRY FOR WHAT HAPPENED TO YOU IN YOUR PAST, IRIS. I UNDERSTAND THE NEED TO SET THINGS RIGHT, BUT YOU'VE LOST ALL PERSPECTIVE.
YOU NEED HELP.
SINCE I'VE ARRIVED IN HELL'S KITCHEN LUKE CAGE HAS BEEN DOUBTING ME. NOW THIS?
THE BODIES ARE PILING UP, PANTHER. SO, YES NOW.
LUKE CAGE...
COOL...
I THINK I SEE WHAT I NEED TO DO.

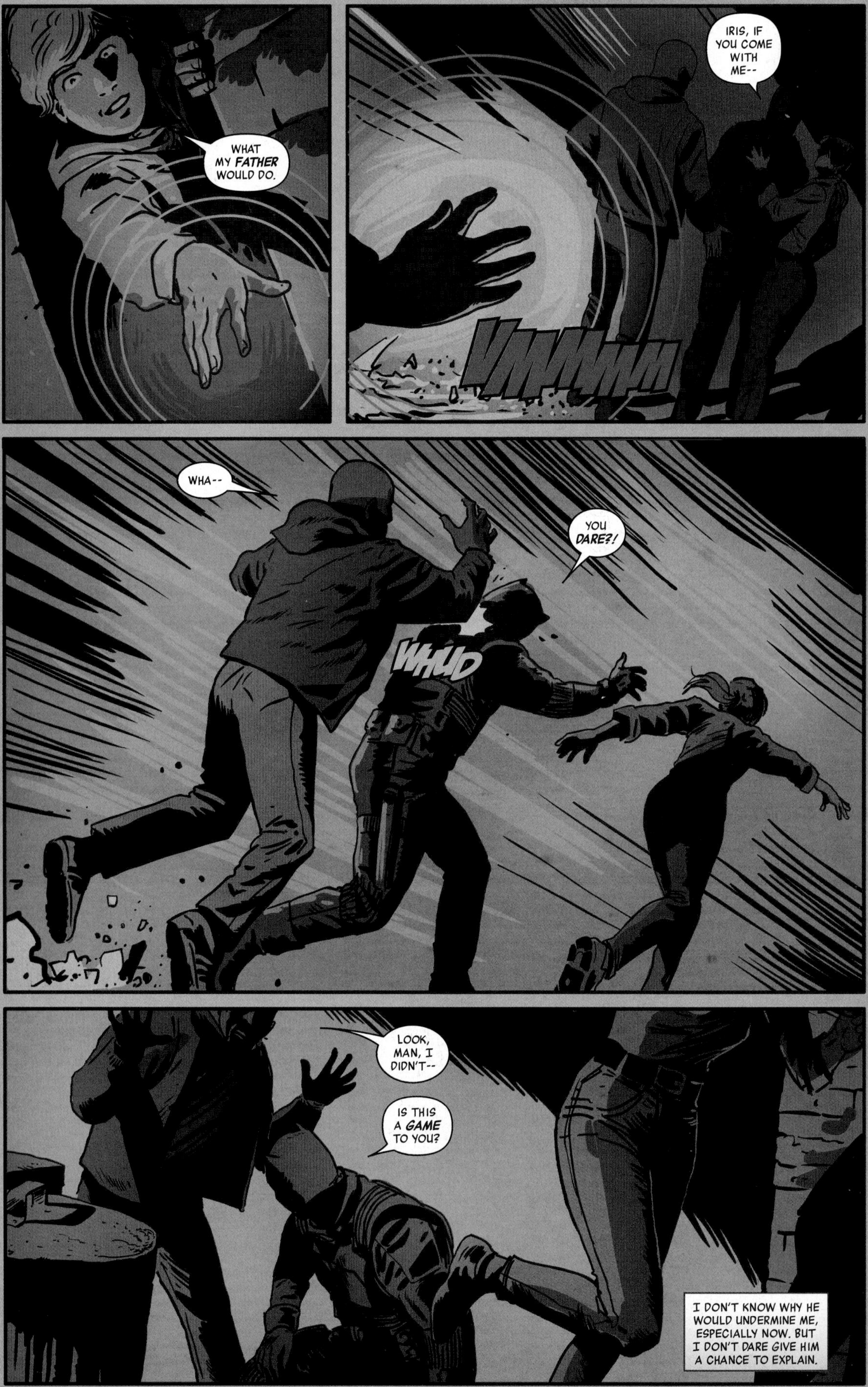
WHAT MY **FATHER** WOULD DO.
IRIS, IF YOU COME WITH ME--
VMMMMM
WHA--
YOU **DARE?!**
WHUD
LOOK, MAN, I DIDN'T--
IS THIS A **GAME** TO YOU?
I DON'T KNOW WHY HE WOULD UNDERMINE ME, ESPECIALLY NOW. BUT I DON'T DARE GIVE HIM A CHANCE TO EXPLAIN.

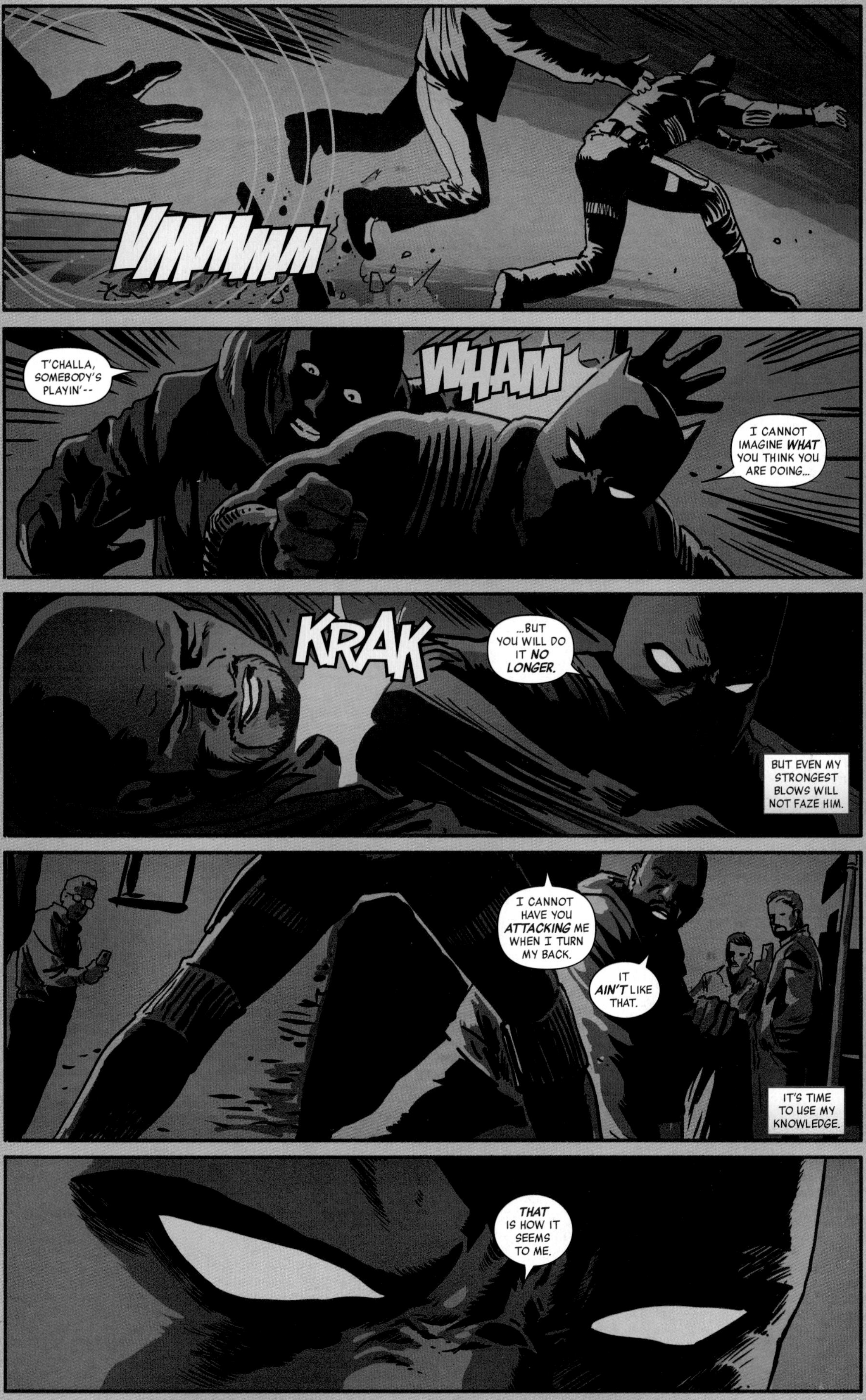
VMMMMM
T'CHALLA, SOMEBODY'S PLAYIN'--
WHAM
I CANNOT IMAGINE WHAT YOU THINK YOU ARE DOING...
KRAK
...BUT YOU WILL DO IT NO LONGER.
BUT EVEN MY STRONGEST BLOWS WILL NOT FAZE HIM.
I CANNOT HAVE YOU ATTACKING ME WHEN I TURN MY BACK.
IT AIN'T LIKE THAT.
IT'S TIME TO USE MY KNOWLEDGE.
THAT IS HOW IT SEEMS TO ME.

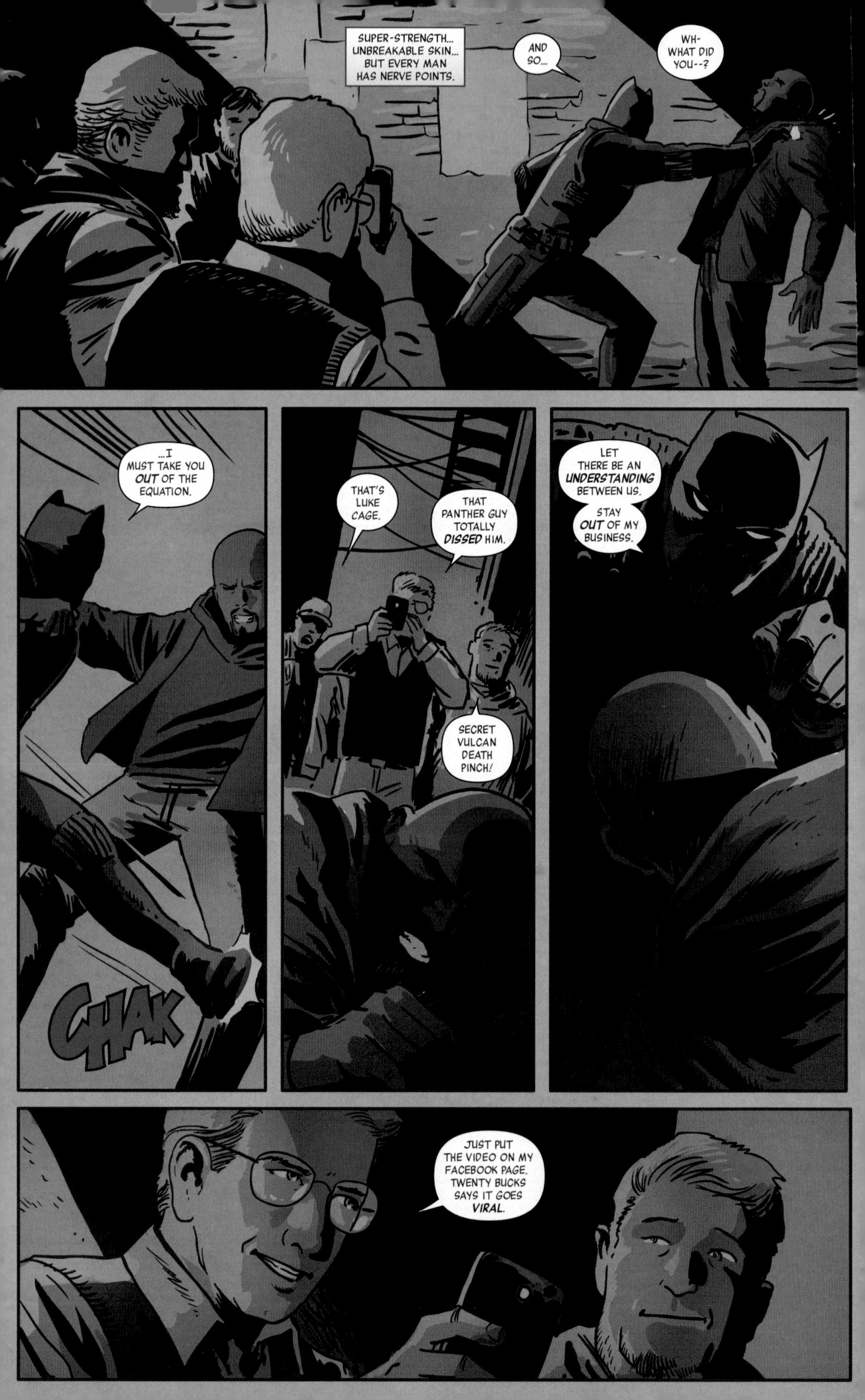
SUPER-STRENGTH... UNBREAKABLE SKIN... BUT EVERY MAN HAS NERVE POINTS.
AND SO...
WH- WHAT DID YOU--?
...I MUST TAKE YOU *OUT* OF THE EQUATION.
CHAK
THAT'S LUKE CAGE.
THAT PANTHER GUY TOTALLY *DISSED* HIM.
SECRET VULCAN DEATH PINCH!
LET THERE BE AN *UNDERSTANDING* BETWEEN US.
STAY *OUT* OF MY BUSINESS.
JUST PUT THE VIDEO ON MY FACEBOOK PAGE. TWENTY BUCKS SAYS IT GOES *VIRAL*.

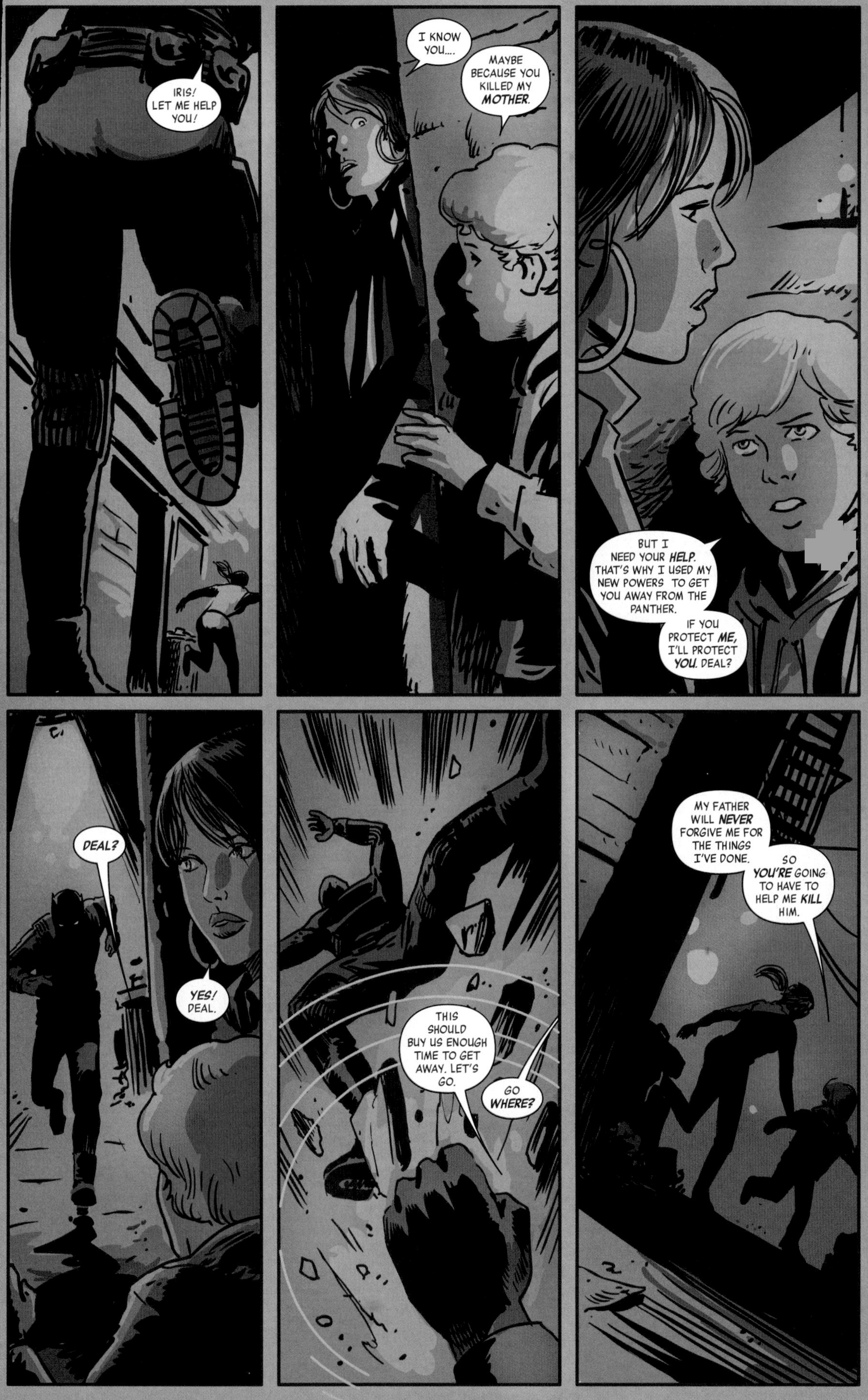
IRIS! LET ME HELP YOU!
I KNOW YOU....
MAYBE BECAUSE YOU KILLED MY MOTHER.
BUT I NEED YOUR HELP. THAT'S WHY I USED MY NEW POWERS TO GET YOU AWAY FROM THE PANTHER.
IF YOU PROTECT ME, I'LL PROTECT YOU. DEAL?
DEAL?
YES! DEAL.
THIS SHOULD BUY US ENOUGH TIME TO GET AWAY. LET'S GO.
GO WHERE?
MY FATHER WILL NEVER FORGIVE ME FOR THE THINGS I'VE DONE.
SO YOU'RE GOING TO HAVE TO HELP ME KILL HIM.

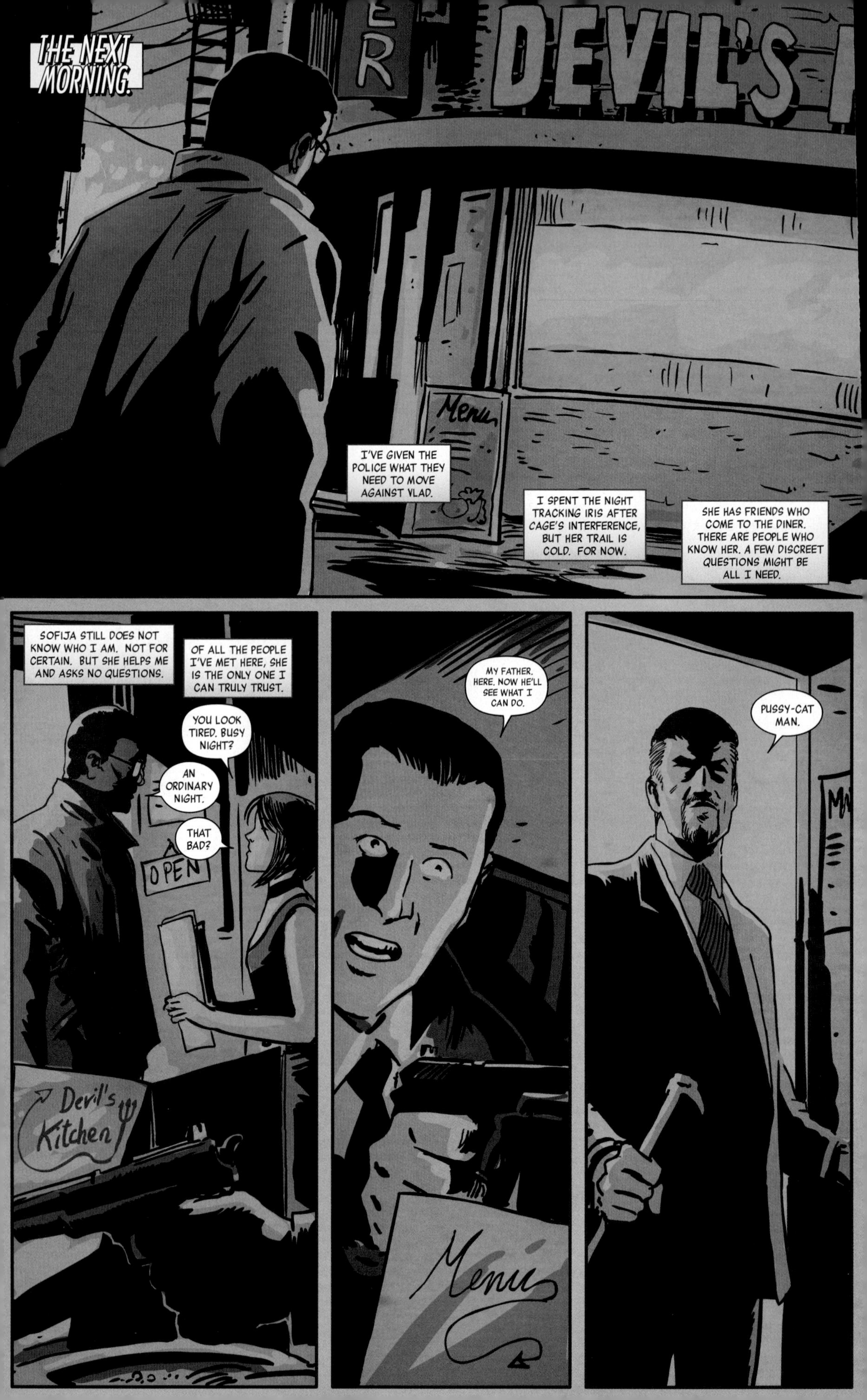
THE NEXT MORNING.
DEVIL'S
I'VE GIVEN THE POLICE WHAT THEY NEED TO MOVE AGAINST VLAD.
I SPENT THE NIGHT TRACKING IRIS AFTER CAGE'S INTERFERENCE, BUT HER TRAIL IS COLD. FOR NOW.
SHE HAS FRIENDS WHO COME TO THE DINER. THERE ARE PEOPLE WHO KNOW HER. A FEW DISCREET QUESTIONS MIGHT BE ALL I NEED.
SOFIJA STILL DOES NOT KNOW WHO I AM. NOT FOR CERTAIN. BUT SHE HELPS ME AND ASKS NO QUESTIONS.
OF ALL THE PEOPLE I'VE MET HERE, SHE IS THE ONLY ONE I CAN TRULY TRUST.
YOU LOOK TIRED. BUSY NIGHT?
AN ORDINARY NIGHT.
THAT BAD?
OPEN
Devil's Kitchen
MY FATHER. HERE. NOW HE'LL SEE WHAT I CAN DO.
Menu
PUSSY-CAT MAN.

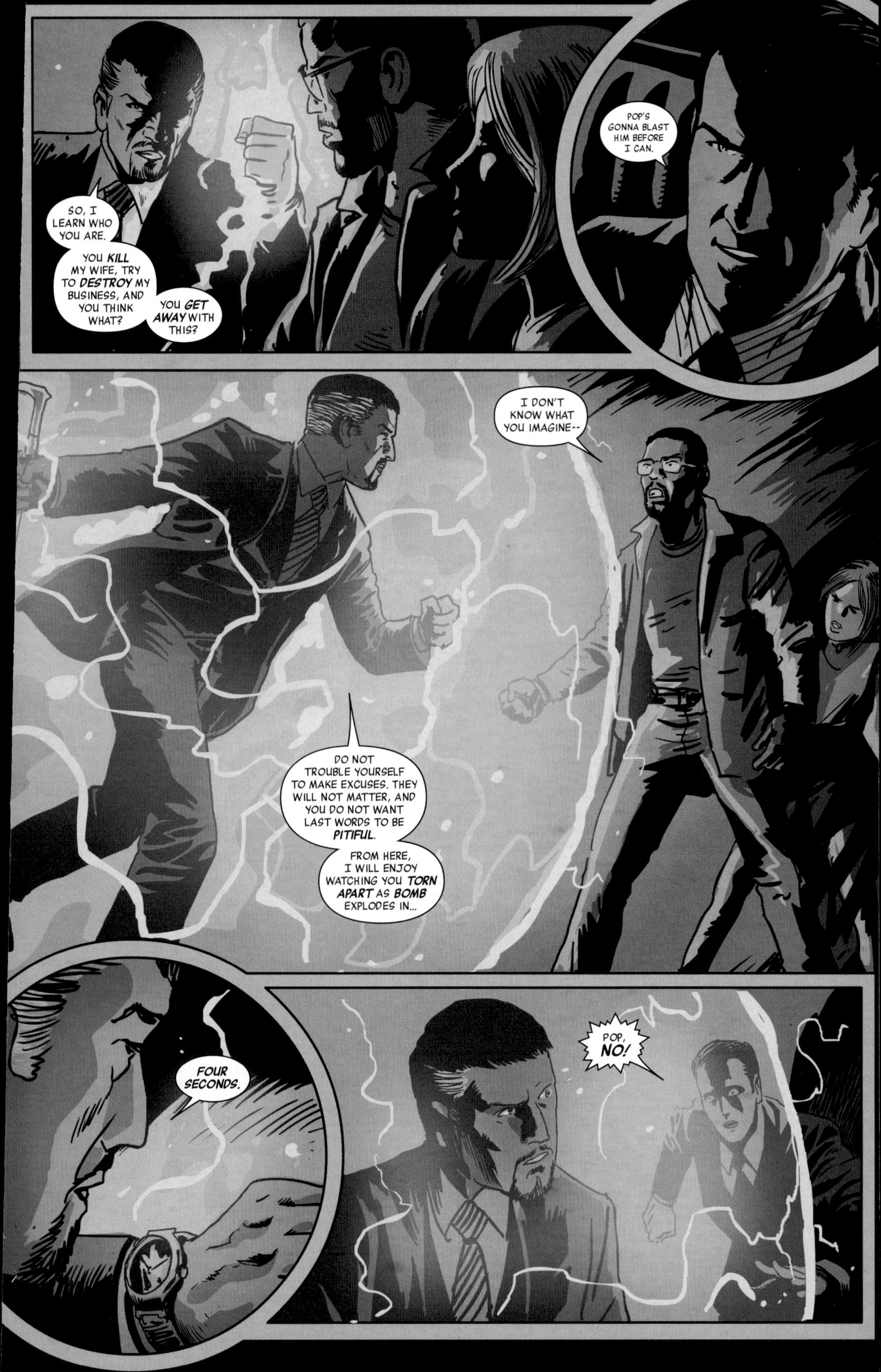
SO, I LEARN WHO YOU ARE.
YOU KILL MY WIFE, TRY TO DESTROY MY BUSINESS, AND YOU THINK WHAT?
YOU GET AWAY WITH THIS?
POP'S GONNA BLAST HIM BEFORE I CAN.
I DON'T KNOW WHAT YOU IMAGINE--
DO NOT TROUBLE YOURSELF TO MAKE EXCUSES. THEY WILL NOT MATTER, AND YOU DO NOT WANT LAST WORDS TO BE PITIFUL.
FROM HERE, I WILL ENJOY WATCHING YOU TORN APART AS BOMB EXPLODES IN...
FOUR SECONDS.
POP, NO!

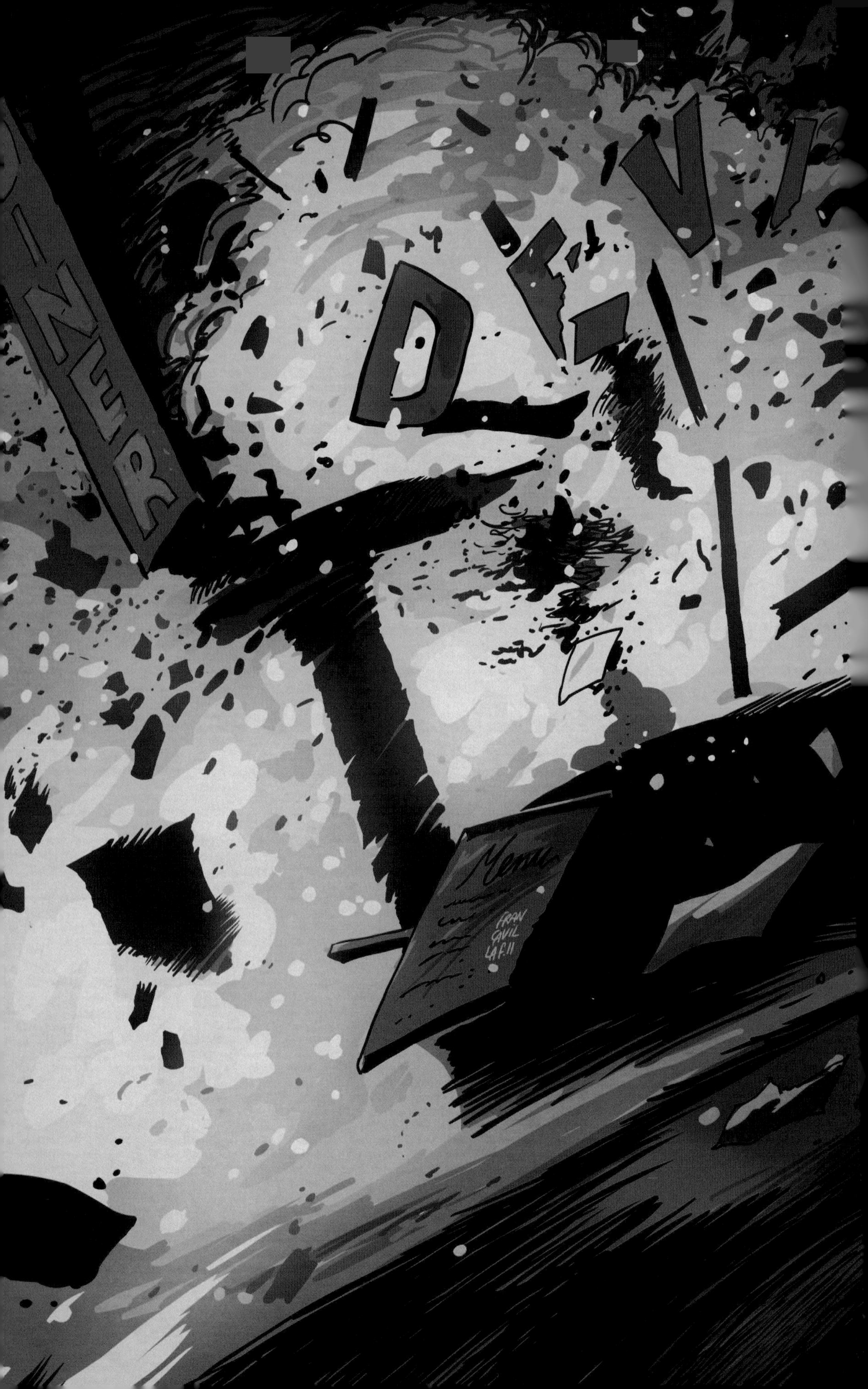
Menu

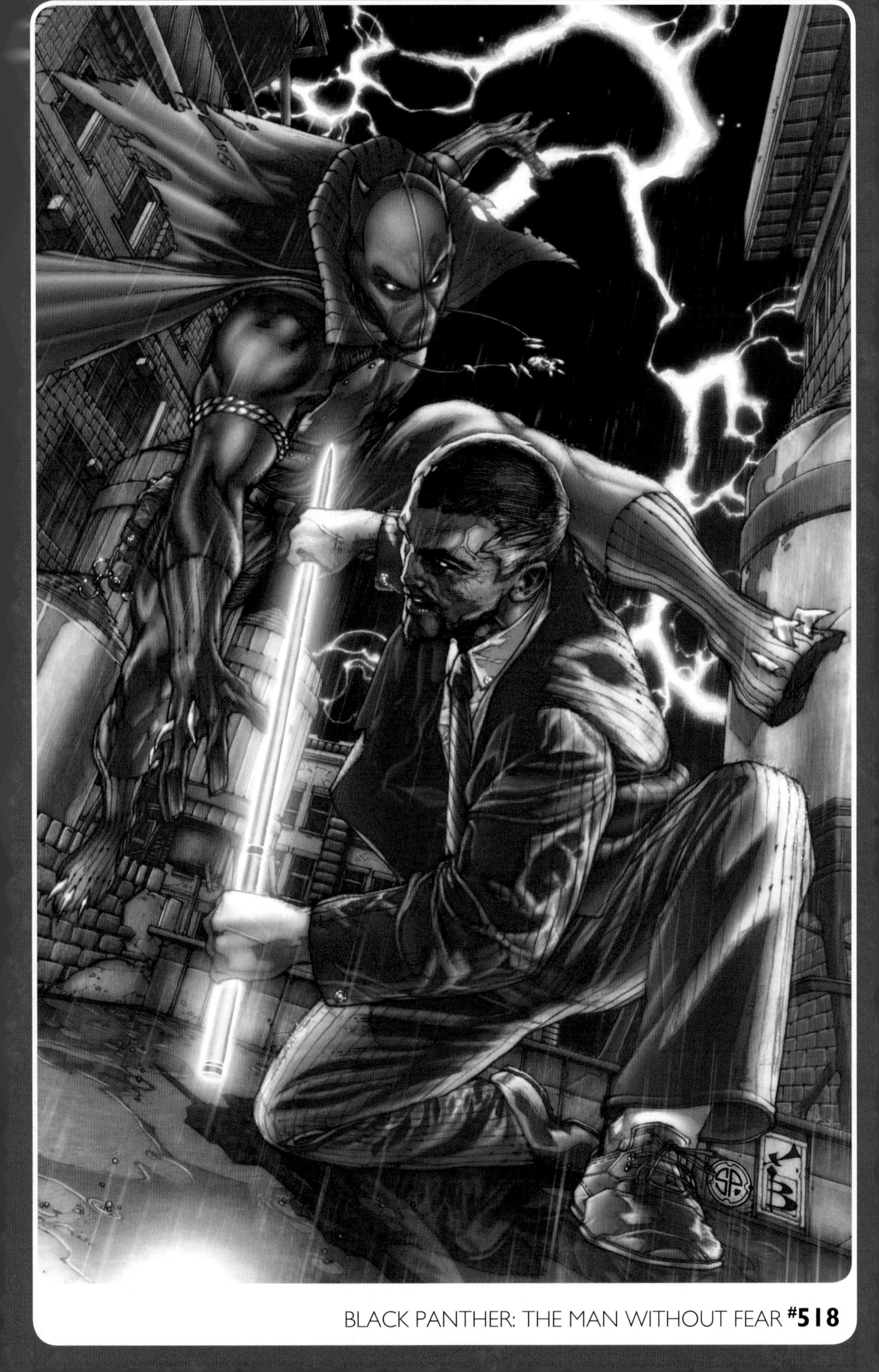

BLACK PANTHER: THE MAN WITHOUT FEAR **#518**

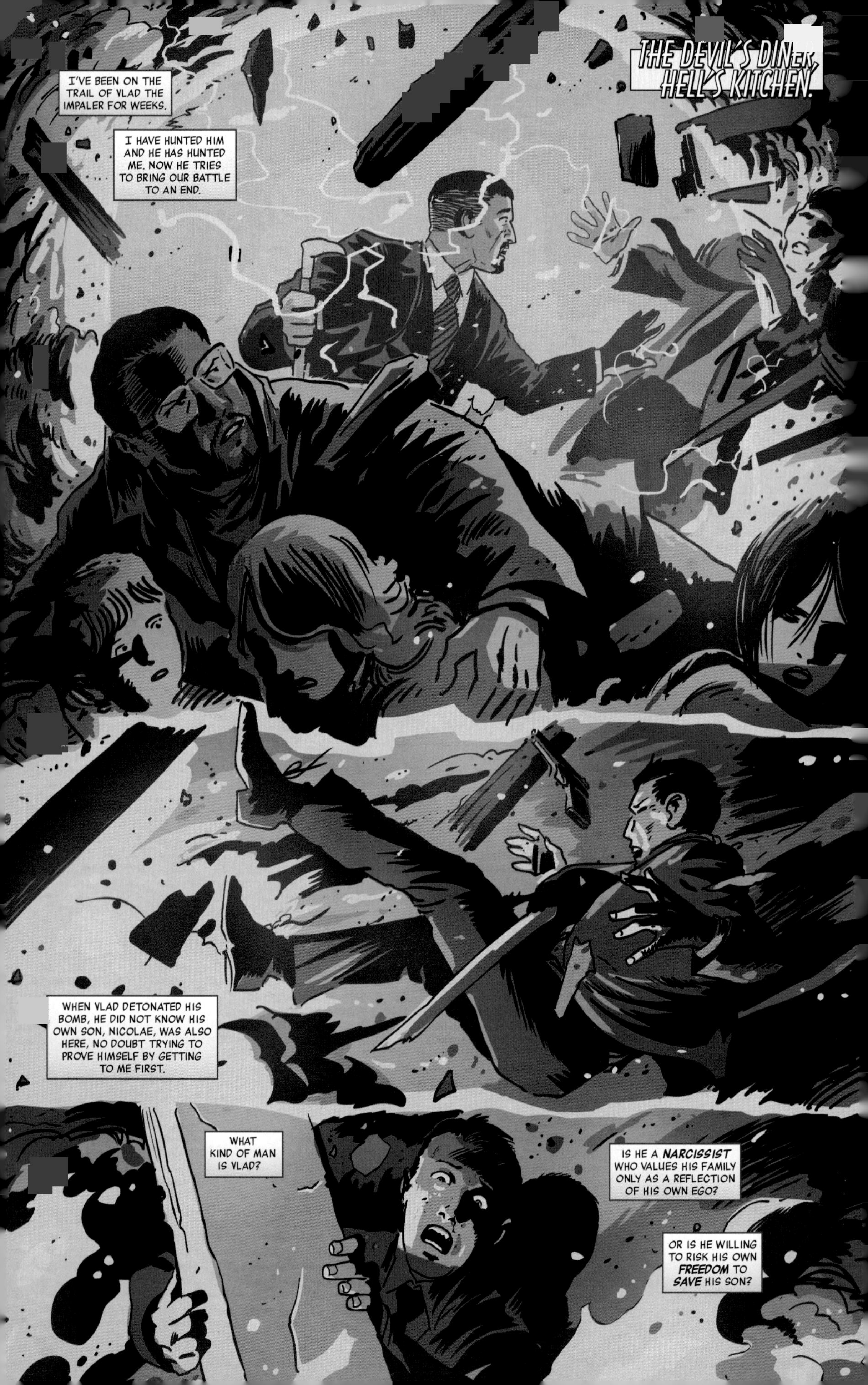
THE DEVIL'S DINER, HELL'S KITCHEN.
I'VE BEEN ON THE TRAIL OF VLAD THE IMPALER FOR WEEKS.
I HAVE HUNTED HIM AND HE HAS HUNTED ME. NOW HE TRIES TO BRING OUR BATTLE TO AN END.
WHEN VLAD DETONATED HIS BOMB, HE DID NOT KNOW HIS OWN SON, NICOLAE, WAS ALSO HERE, NO DOUBT TRYING TO PROVE HIMSELF BY GETTING TO ME FIRST.
WHAT KIND OF MAN IS VLAD?
IS HE A NARCISSIST WHO VALUES HIS FAMILY ONLY AS A REFLECTION OF HIS OWN EGO?
OR IS HE WILLING TO RISK HIS OWN FREEDOM TO SAVE HIS SON?

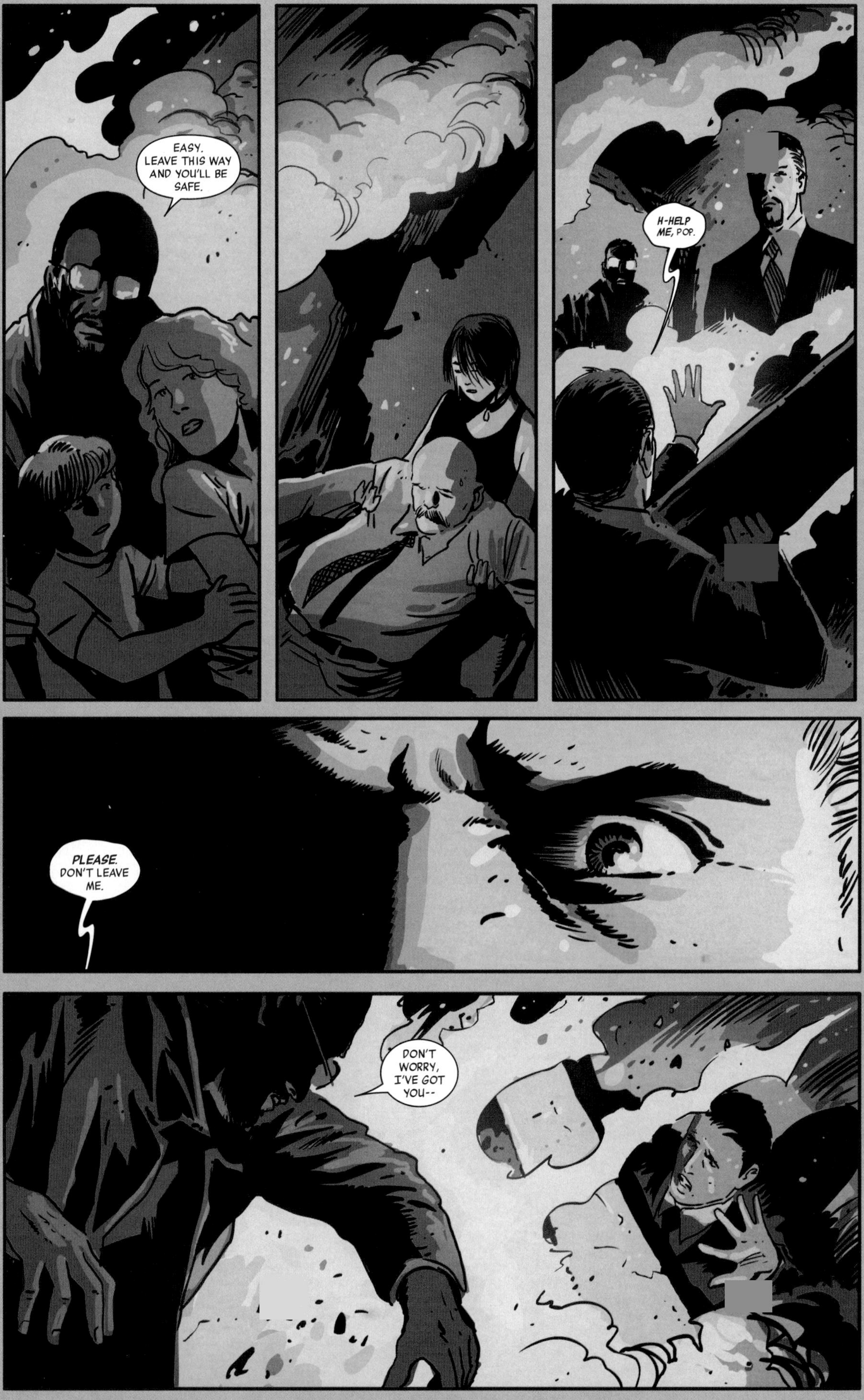
EASY. LEAVE THIS WAY AND YOU'LL BE SAFE.
H-HELP ME, POP.
PLEASE. DON'T LEAVE ME.
DON'T WORRY, I'VE GOT YOU--

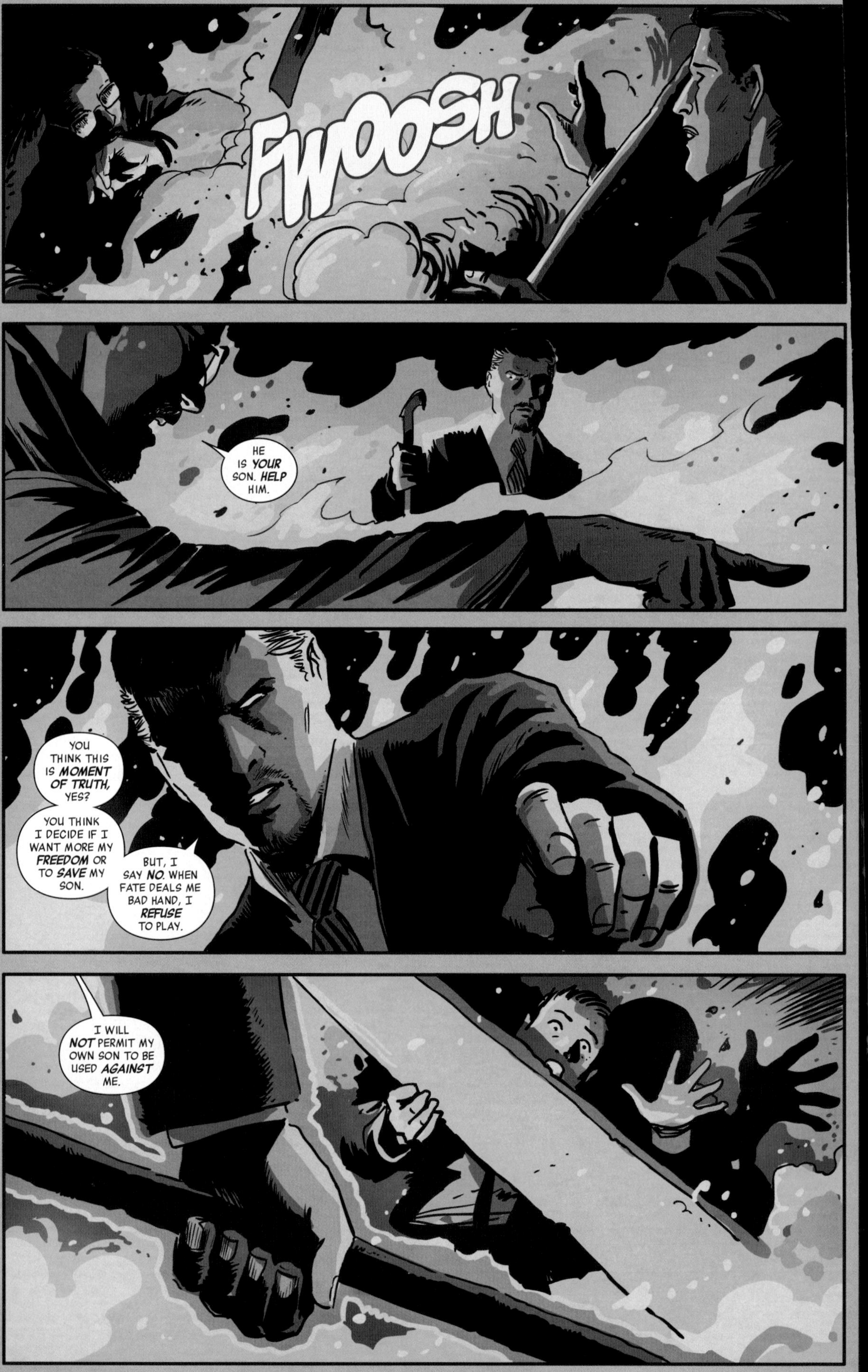
FWOOSH
HE IS YOUR SON. HELP HIM.
YOU THINK THIS IS MOMENT OF TRUTH, YES?
YOU THINK I DECIDE IF I WANT MORE MY FREEDOM OR TO SAVE MY SON.
BUT, I SAY NO. WHEN FATE DEALS ME BAD HAND, I REFUSE TO PLAY.
I WILL NOT PERMIT MY OWN SON TO BE USED AGAINST ME.

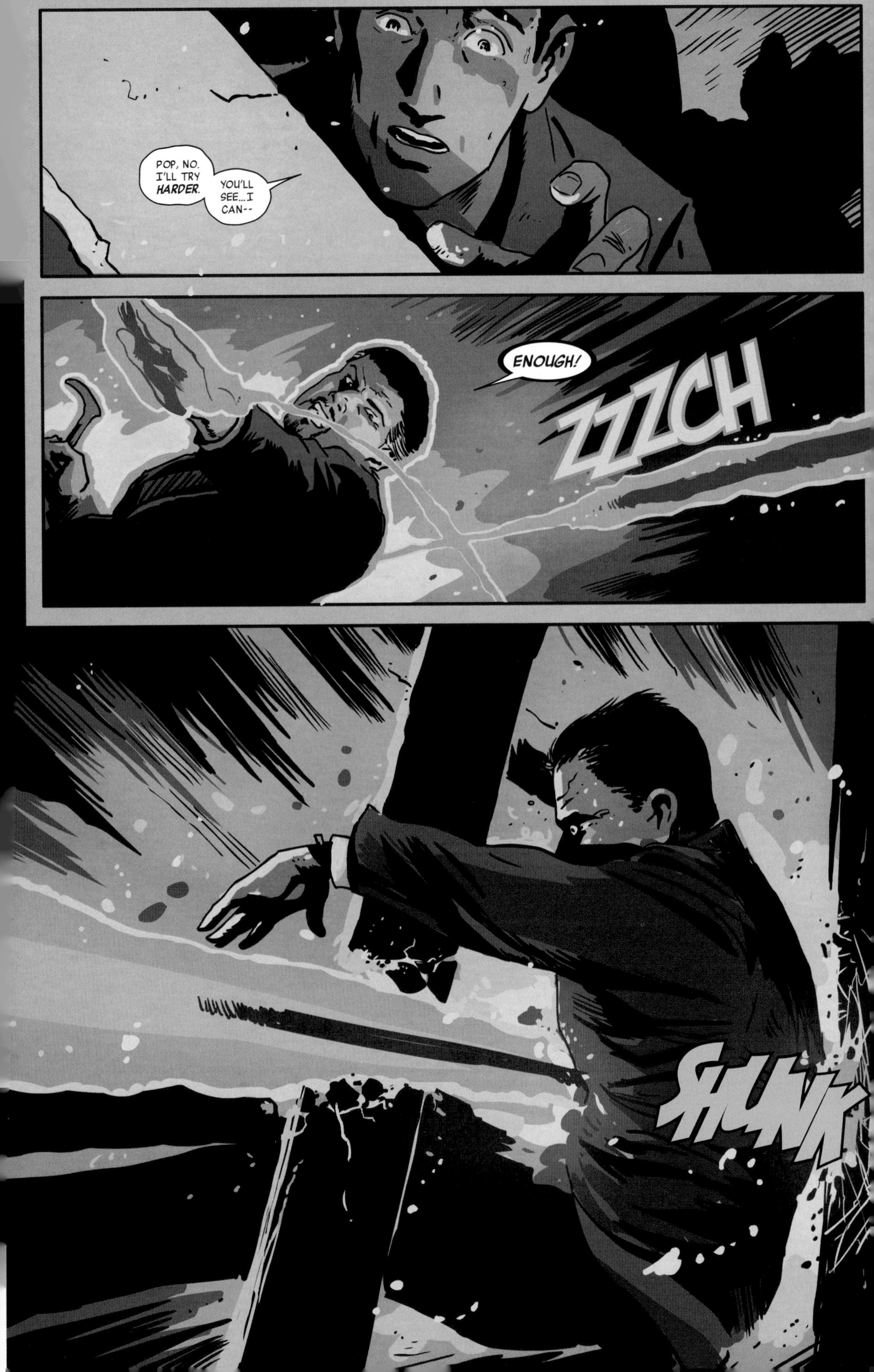
POP, NO. I'LL TRY HARDER.
YOU'LL SEE...I CAN--
ENOUGH!
ZZZCH
SHUNK

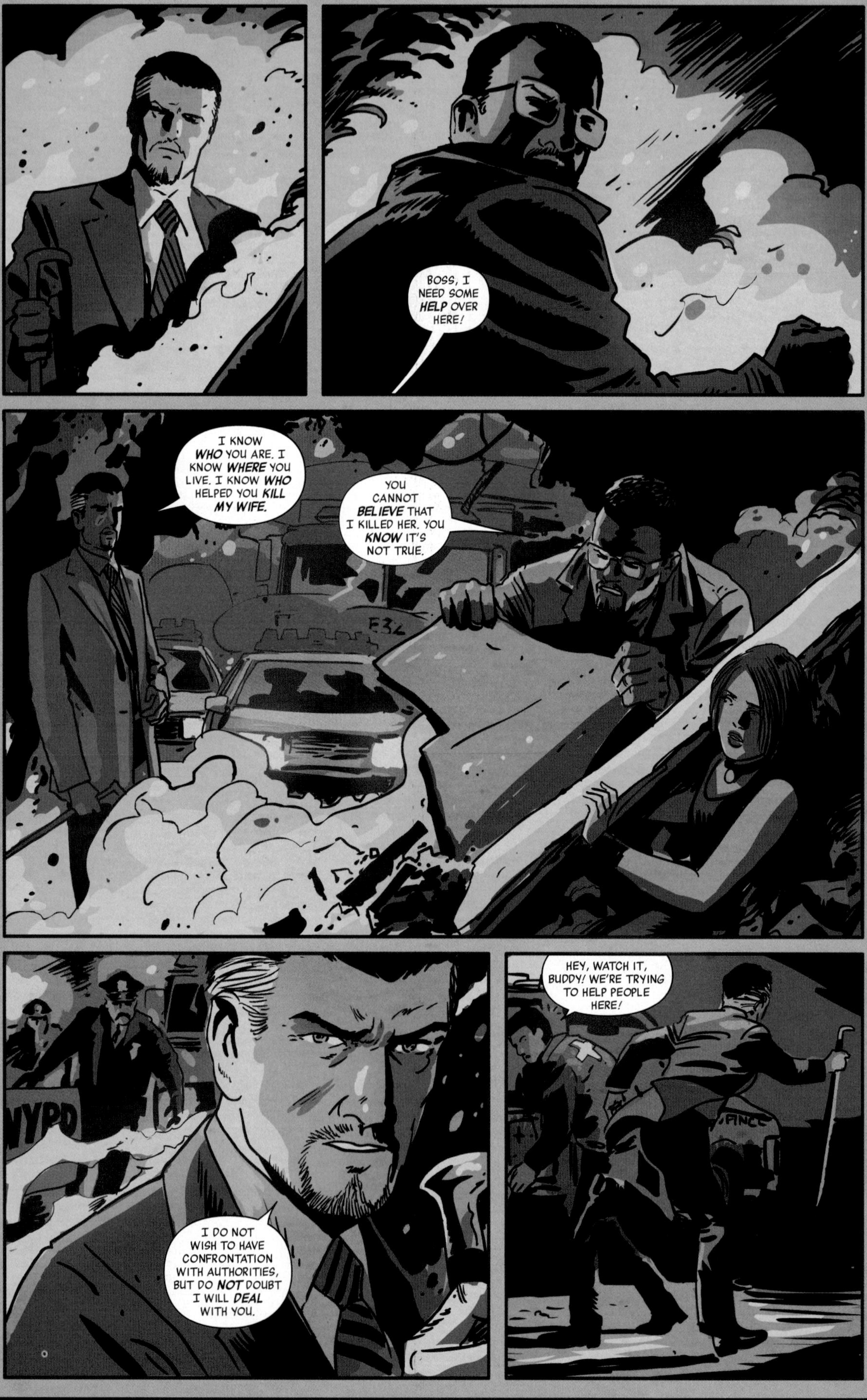
BOSS, I NEED SOME HELP OVER HERE!
I KNOW WHO YOU ARE. I KNOW WHERE YOU LIVE. I KNOW WHO HELPED YOU KILL MY WIFE.
YOU CANNOT BELIEVE THAT I KILLED HER. YOU KNOW IT'S NOT TRUE.
NYPD
I DO NOT WISH TO HAVE CONFRONTATION WITH AUTHORITIES, BUT DO NOT DOUBT I WILL DEAL WITH YOU.
HEY, WATCH IT, BUDDY! WE'RE TRYING TO HELP PEOPLE HERE!

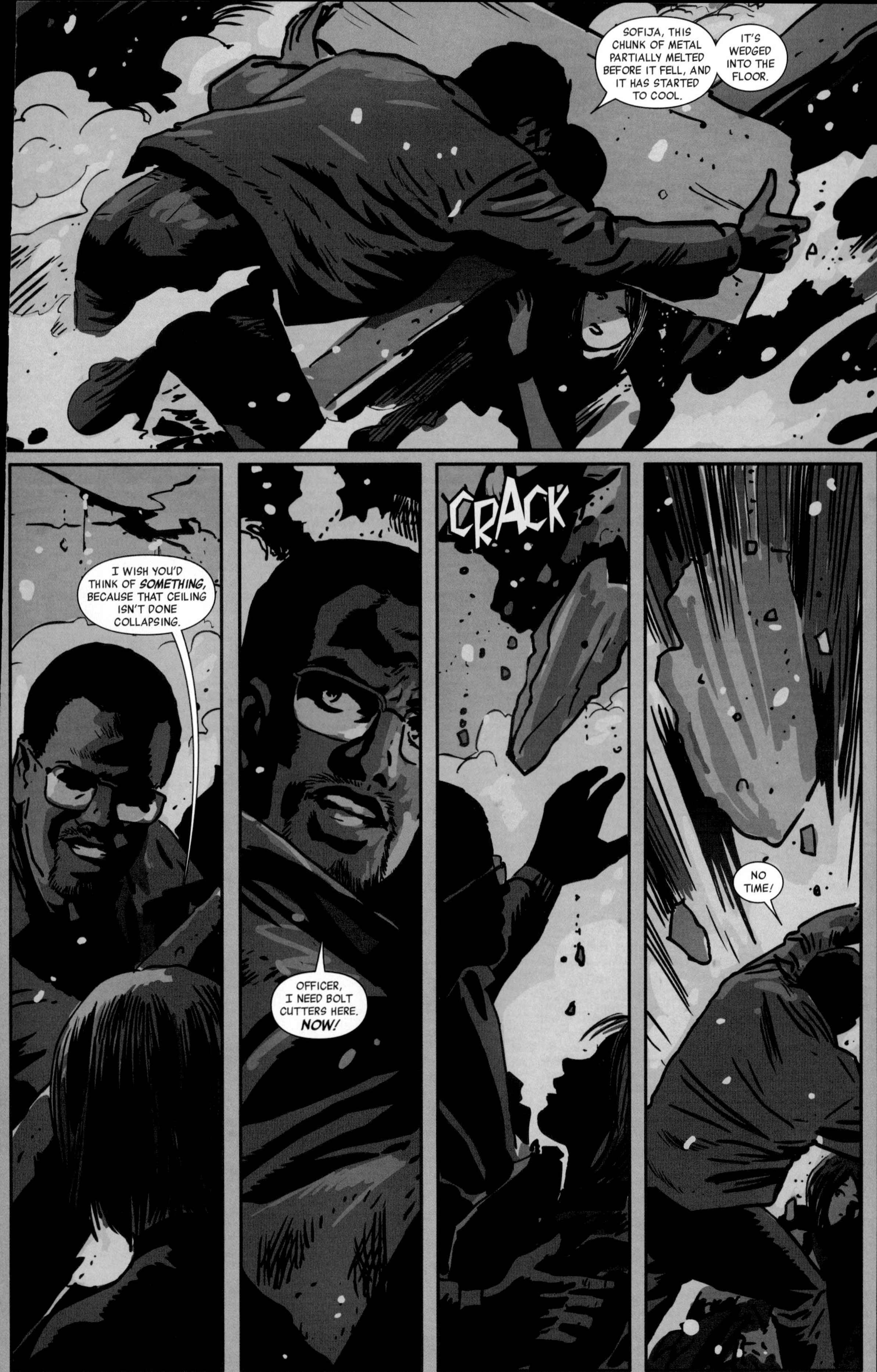
SOFIJA, THIS CHUNK OF METAL PARTIALLY MELTED BEFORE IT FELL, AND IT HAS STARTED TO COOL.
IT'S WEDGED INTO THE FLOOR.
I WISH YOU'D THINK OF SOMETHING, BECAUSE THAT CEILING ISN'T DONE COLLAPSING.
OFFICER, I NEED BOLT CUTTERS HERE. NOW!
CRACK
NO TIME!

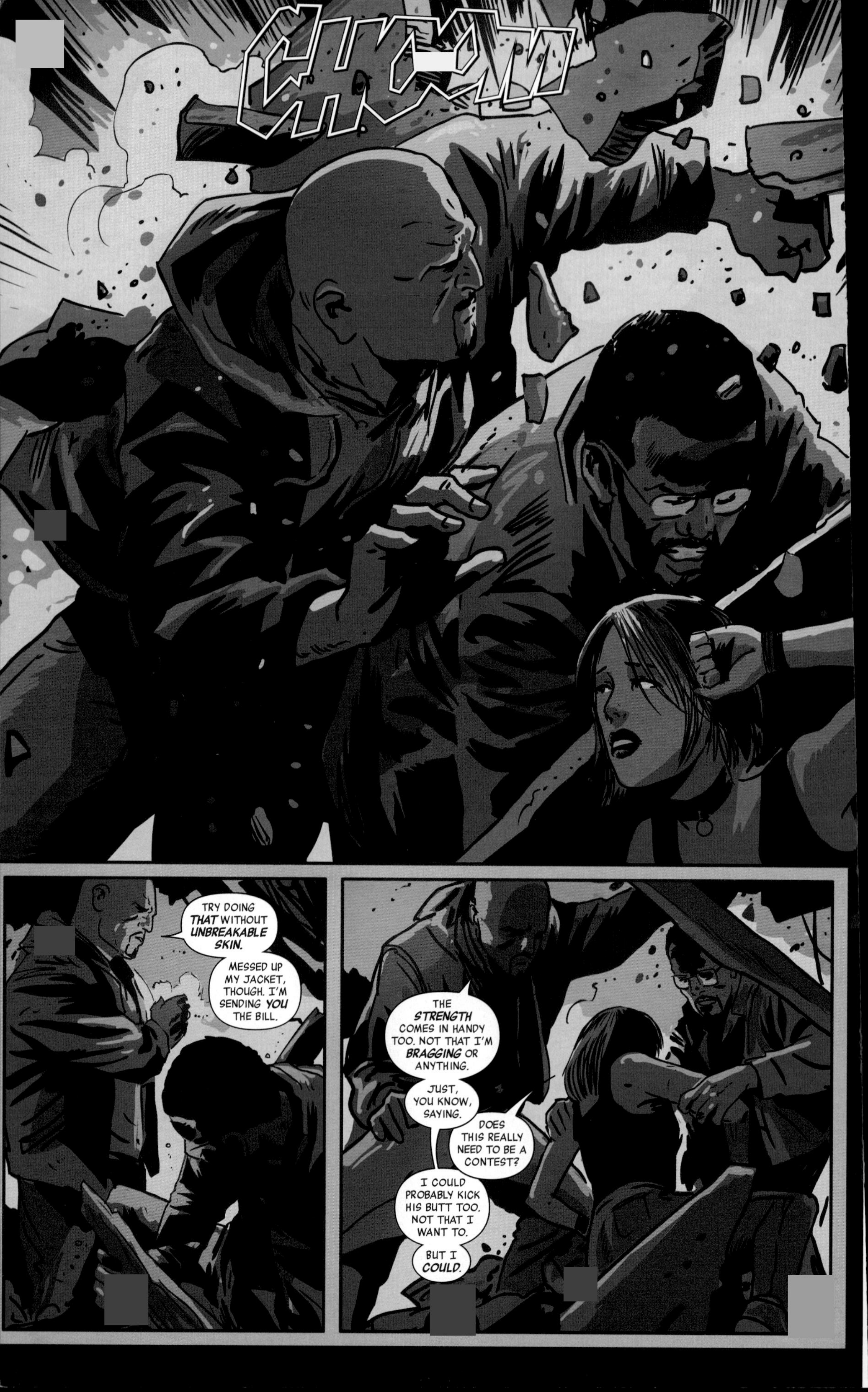
TRY DOING THAT WITHOUT UNBREAKABLE SKIN.
MESSED UP MY JACKET, THOUGH. I'M SENDING YOU THE BILL.
THE STRENGTH COMES IN HANDY TOO. NOT THAT I'M BRAGGING OR ANYTHING.
JUST, YOU KNOW, SAYING.
DOES THIS REALLY NEED TO BE A CONTEST?
I COULD PROBABLY KICK HIS BUTT TOO. NOT THAT I WANT TO.
BUT I COULD.

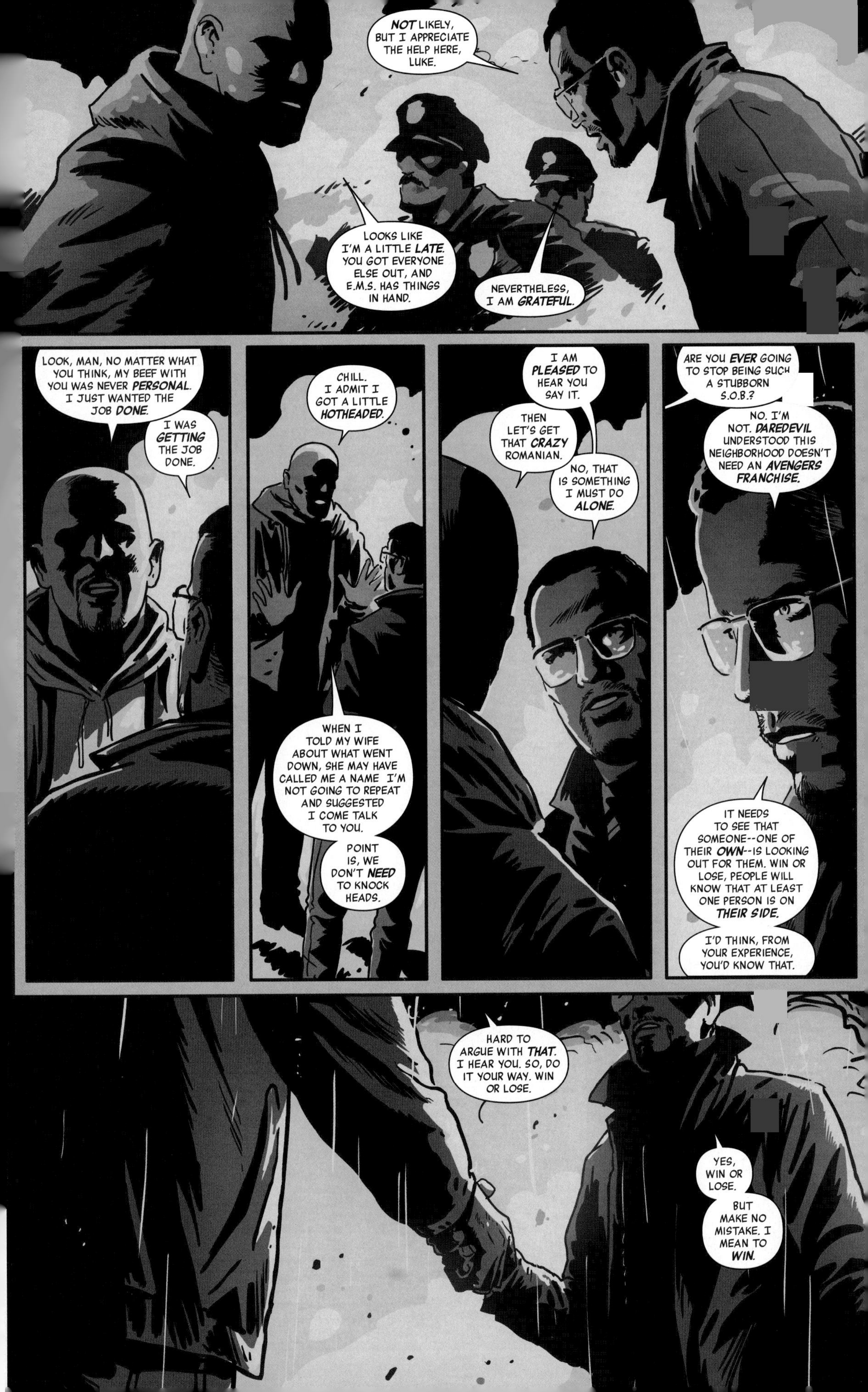

NOT LIKELY, BUT I APPRECIATE THE HELP HERE, LUKE.
LOOKS LIKE I'M A LITTLE LATE. YOU GOT EVERYONE ELSE OUT, AND E.M.S. HAS THINGS IN HAND.
NEVERTHELESS, I AM GRATEFUL.
LOOK, MAN, NO MATTER WHAT YOU THINK, MY BEEF WITH YOU WAS NEVER PERSONAL. I JUST WANTED THE JOB DONE.
I WAS GETTING THE JOB DONE.
CHILL. I ADMIT I GOT A LITTLE HOTHEADED.
WHEN I TOLD MY WIFE ABOUT WHAT WENT DOWN, SHE MAY HAVE CALLED ME A NAME I'M NOT GOING TO REPEAT AND SUGGESTED I COME TALK TO YOU.
POINT IS, WE DON'T NEED TO KNOCK HEADS.
I AM PLEASED TO HEAR YOU SAY IT.
THEN LET'S GET THAT CRAZY ROMANIAN.
NO, THAT IS SOMETHING I MUST DO ALONE.
ARE YOU EVER GOING TO STOP BEING SUCH A STUBBORN S.O.B.?
NO. I'M NOT. DAREDEVIL UNDERSTOOD THIS NEIGHBORHOOD DOESN'T NEED AN AVENGERS FRANCHISE.
IT NEEDS TO SEE THAT SOMEONE--ONE OF THEIR OWN--IS LOOKING OUT FOR THEM. WIN OR LOSE, PEOPLE WILL KNOW THAT AT LEAST ONE PERSON IS ON THEIR SIDE.
I'D THINK, FROM YOUR EXPERIENCE, YOU'D KNOW THAT.
HARD TO ARGUE WITH THAT. I HEAR YOU. SO, DO IT YOUR WAY. WIN OR LOSE.
YES, WIN OR LOSE.
BUT MAKE NO MISTAKE. I MEAN TO WIN.

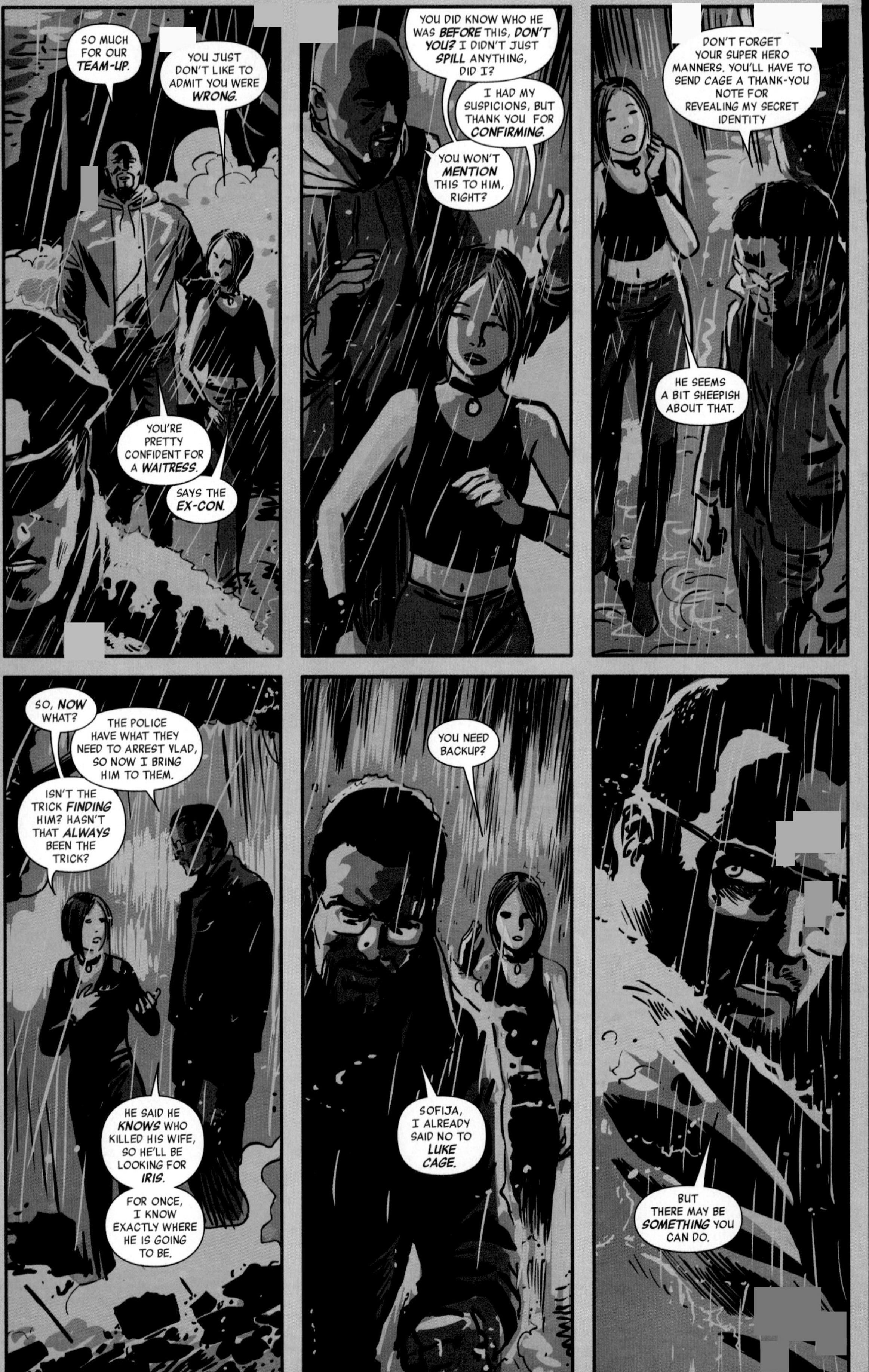
SO MUCH FOR OUR TEAM-UP.
YOU JUST DON'T LIKE TO ADMIT YOU WERE WRONG.
YOU'RE PRETTY CONFIDENT FOR A WAITRESS.
SAYS THE EX-CON.
YOU DID KNOW WHO HE WAS BEFORE THIS, DON'T YOU? I DIDN'T JUST SPILL ANYTHING, DID I?
I HAD MY SUSPICIONS, BUT THANK YOU FOR CONFIRMING.
YOU WON'T MENTION THIS TO HIM, RIGHT?
DON'T FORGET YOUR SUPER HERO MANNERS. YOU'LL HAVE TO SEND CAGE A THANK-YOU NOTE FOR REVEALING MY SECRET IDENTITY
HE SEEMS A BIT SHEEPISH ABOUT THAT.
SO, NOW WHAT?
THE POLICE HAVE WHAT THEY NEED TO ARREST VLAD, SO NOW I BRING HIM TO THEM.
ISN'T THE TRICK FINDING HIM? HASN'T THAT ALWAYS BEEN THE TRICK?
HE SAID HE KNOWS WHO KILLED HIS WIFE, SO HE'LL BE LOOKING FOR IRIS.
FOR ONCE, I KNOW EXACTLY WHERE HE IS GOING TO BE.
YOU NEED BACKUP?
SOFIJA, I ALREADY SAID NO TO LUKE CAGE.
BUT THERE MAY BE SOMETHING YOU CAN DO.

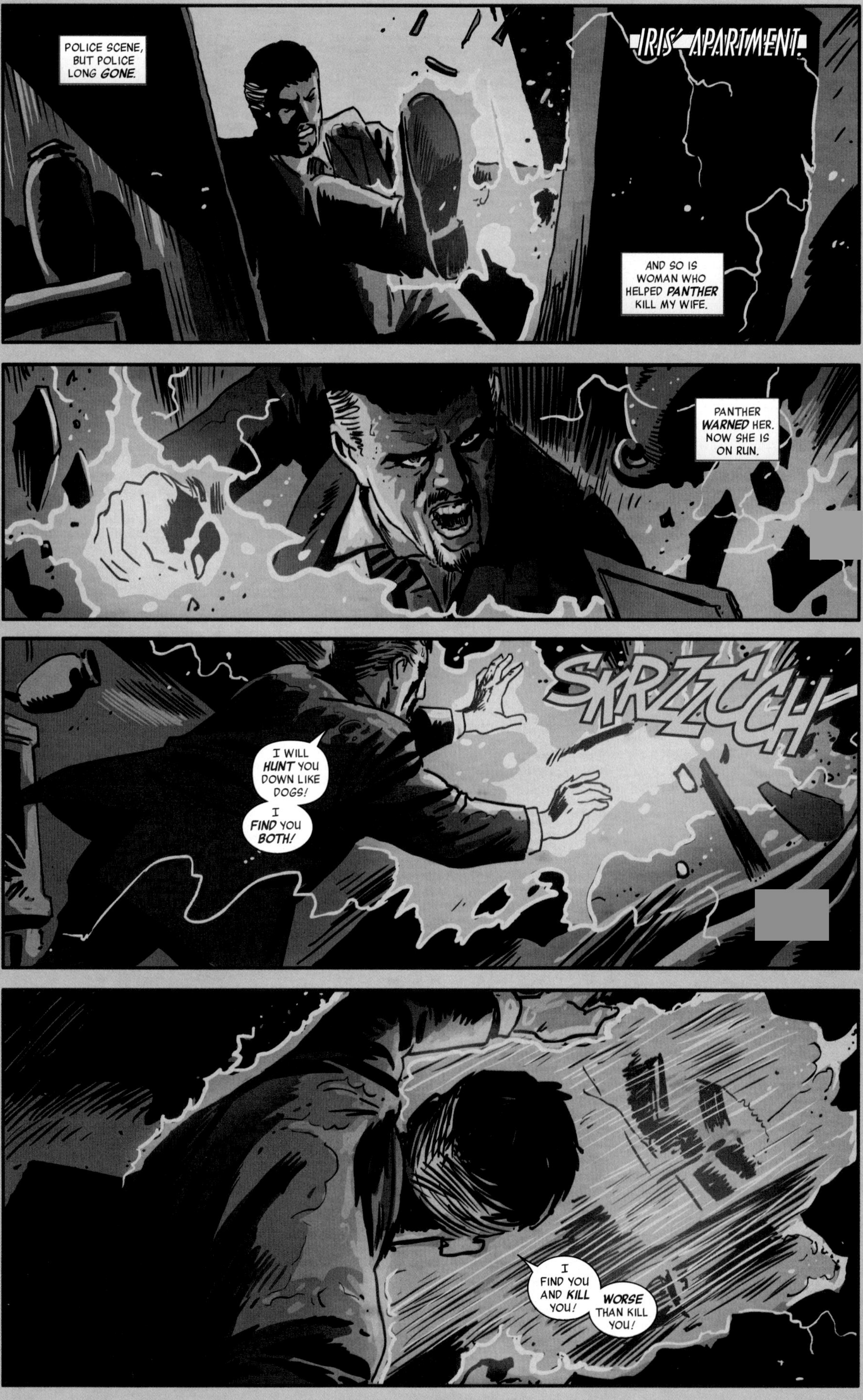

IRIS' APARTMENT.
POLICE SCENE, BUT POLICE LONG GONE.
AND SO IS WOMAN WHO HELPED PANTHER KILL MY WIFE.
PANTHER WARNED HER. NOW SHE IS ON RUN.
SKRZZCCH
I WILL HUNT YOU DOWN LIKE DOGS!
I FIND YOU BOTH!
I FIND YOU AND KILL YOU!
WORSE THAN KILL YOU!

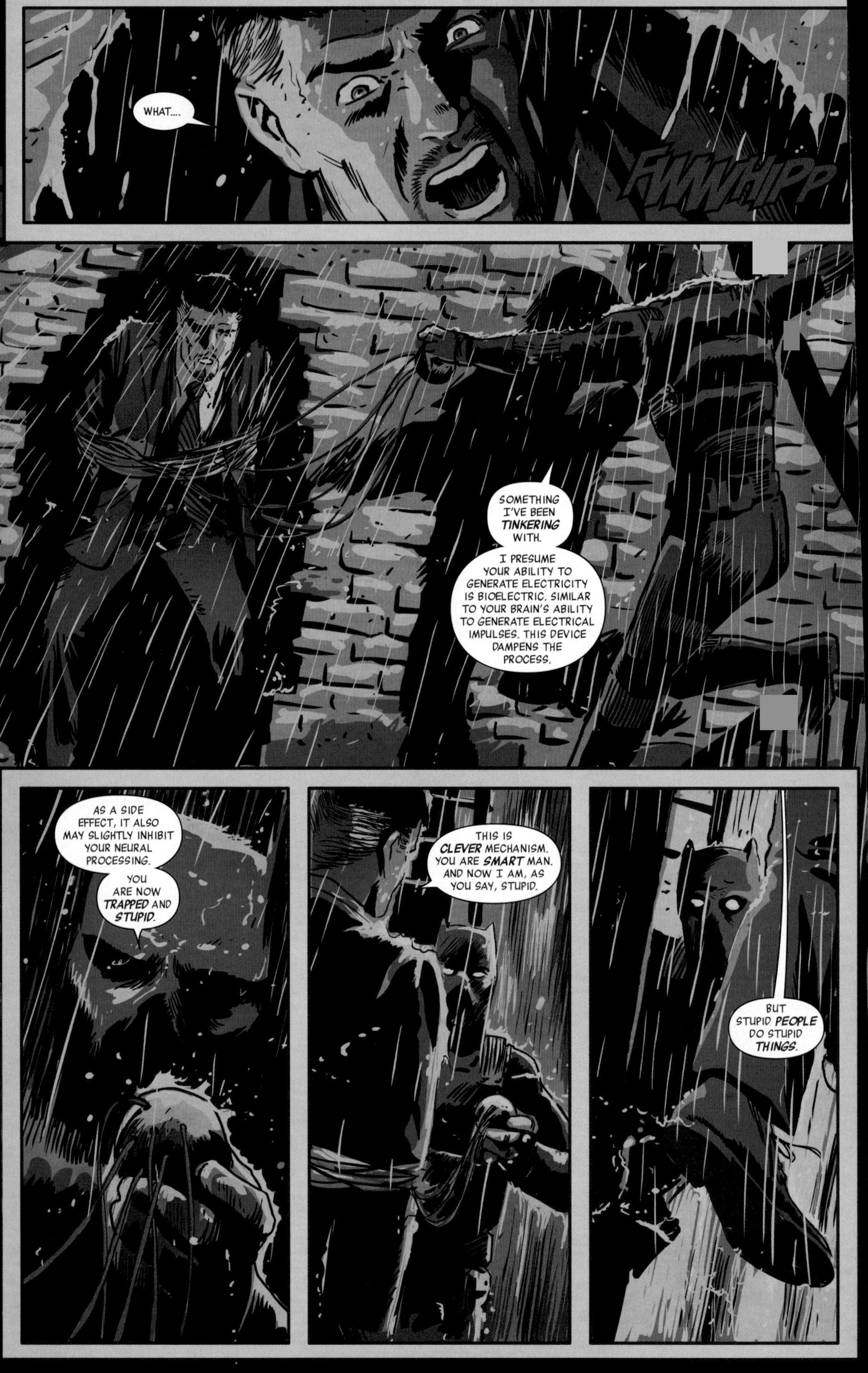
WHAT....
FWWHIPP
SOMETHING I'VE BEEN TINKERING WITH.
I PRESUME YOUR ABILITY TO GENERATE ELECTRICITY IS BIOELECTRIC. SIMILAR TO YOUR BRAIN'S ABILITY TO GENERATE ELECTRICAL IMPULSES. THIS DEVICE DAMPENS THE PROCESS.
AS A SIDE EFFECT, IT ALSO MAY SLIGHTLY INHIBIT YOUR NEURAL PROCESSING.
YOU ARE NOW TRAPPED AND STUPID.
THIS IS CLEVER MECHANISM. YOU ARE SMART MAN. AND NOW I AM, AS YOU SAY, STUPID.
BUT STUPID PEOPLE DO STUPID THINGS.

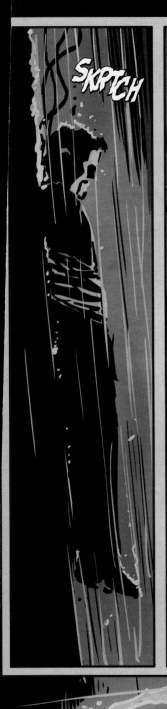

SKRTCH

YOU ARE **SMART** MAN, YES.

KPNCH

BUT NOW WE SEE I AM **NOT** STUPID. NO... I AM **SMARTER.**

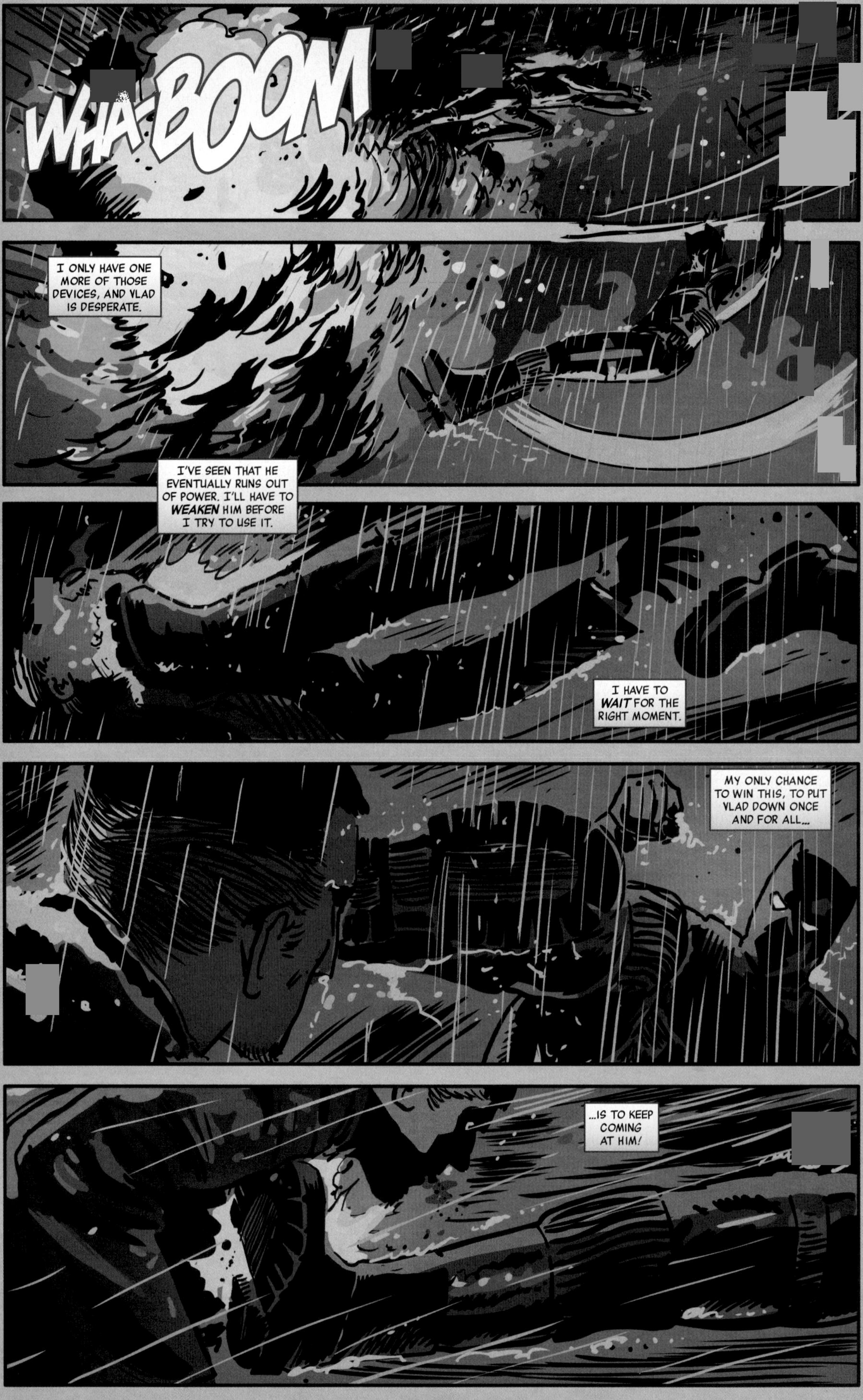
WHA-BOOM
I ONLY HAVE ONE MORE OF THOSE DEVICES, AND VLAD IS DESPERATE.
I'VE SEEN THAT HE EVENTUALLY RUNS OUT OF POWER. I'LL HAVE TO WEAKEN HIM BEFORE I TRY TO USE IT.
I HAVE TO WAIT FOR THE RIGHT MOMENT.
MY ONLY CHANCE TO WIN THIS, TO PUT VLAD DOWN ONCE AND FOR ALL...
...IS TO KEEP COMING AT HIM!

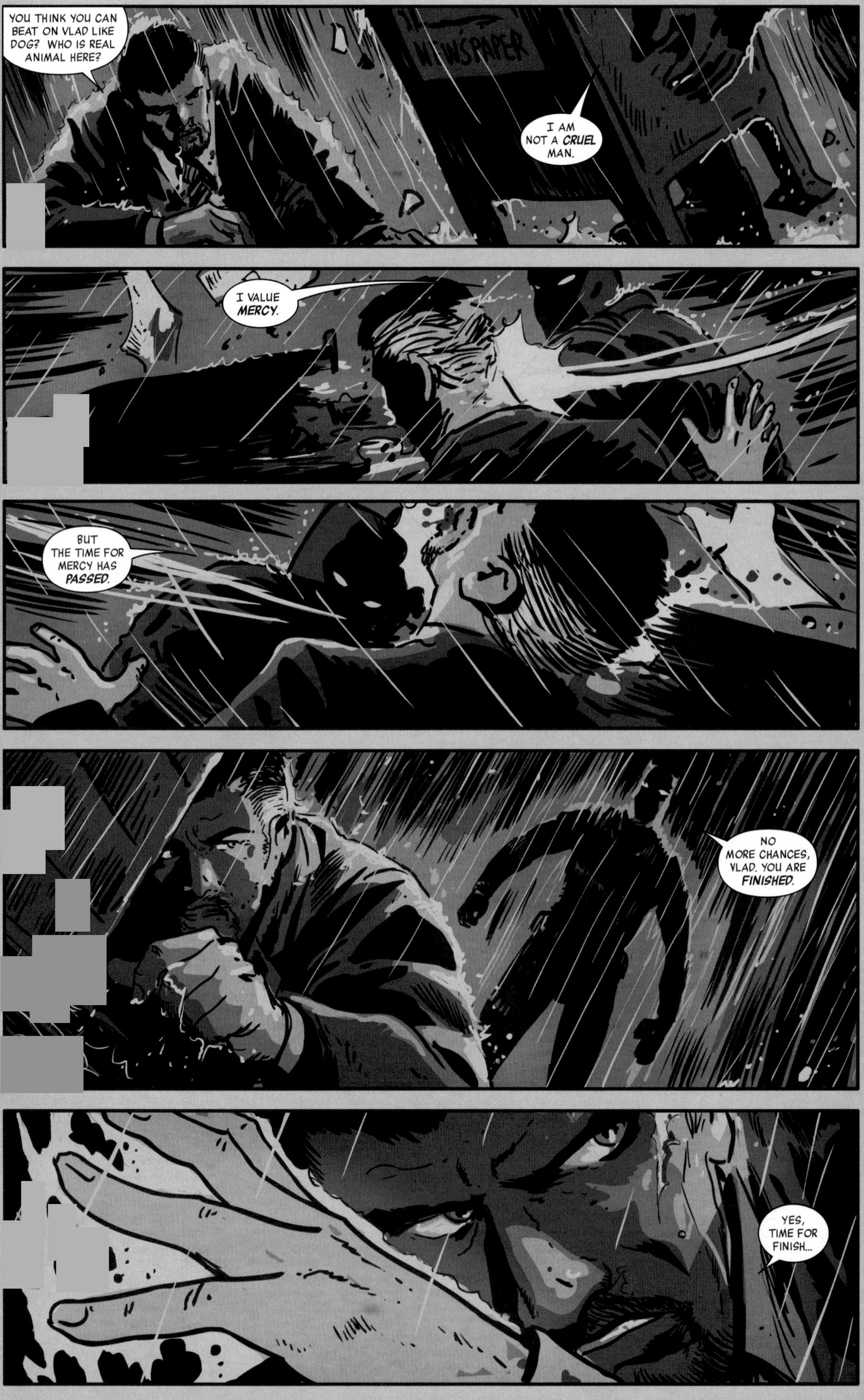
YOU THINK YOU CAN BEAT ON VLAD LIKE DOG? WHO IS REAL ANIMAL HERE?
NEWSPAPER
I AM NOT A CRUEL MAN.
I VALUE MERCY.
BUT THE TIME FOR MERCY HAS PASSED.
NO MORE CHANCES, VLAD. YOU ARE FINISHED.
YES, TIME FOR FINISH...

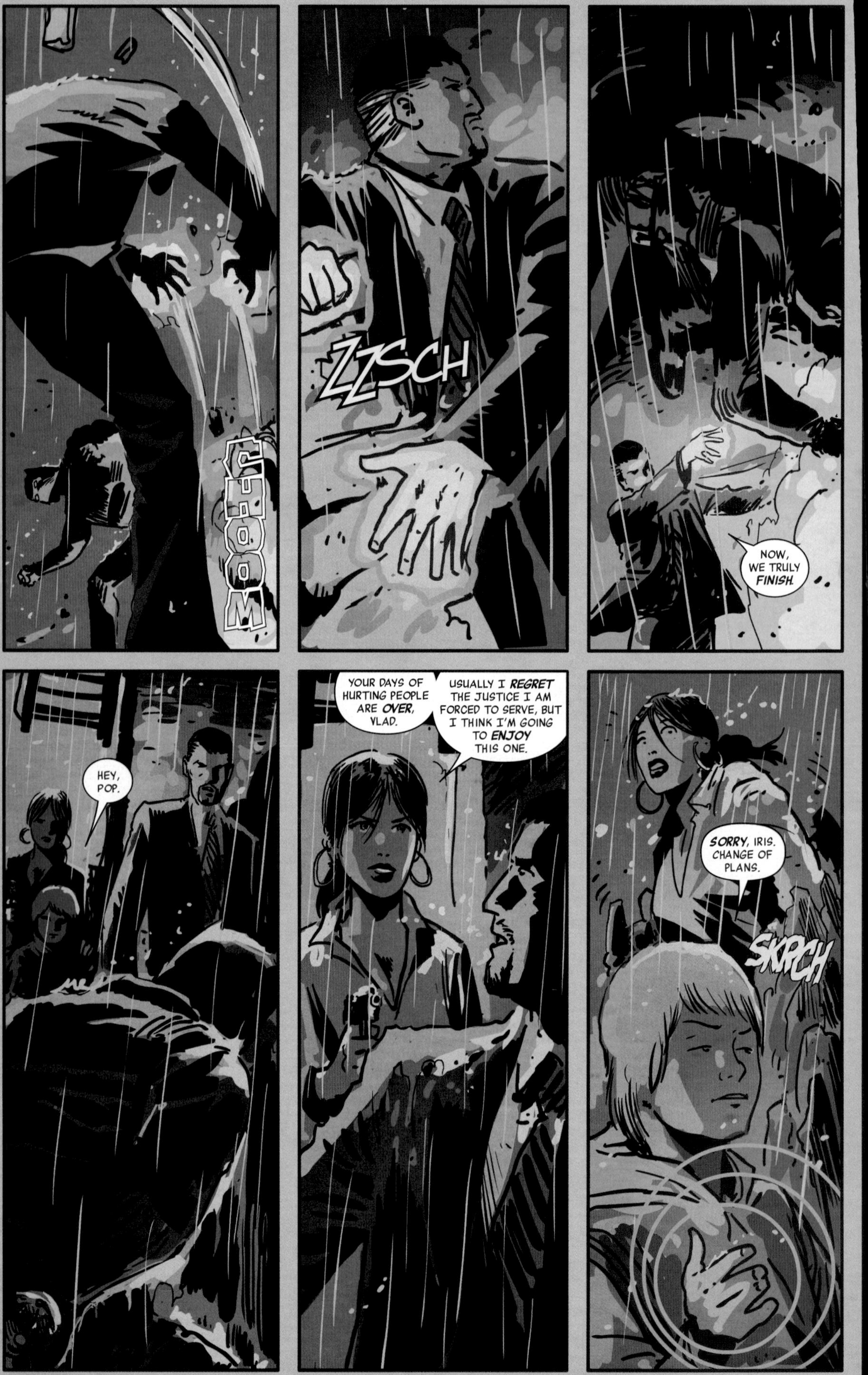
WHOOM
ZZSCH
NOW, WE TRULY FINISH.
HEY, POP.
YOUR DAYS OF HURTING PEOPLE ARE OVER, VLAD.
USUALLY I REGRET THE JUSTICE I AM FORCED TO SERVE, BUT I THINK I'M GOING TO ENJOY THIS ONE.
SORRY, IRIS. CHANGE OF PLANS.
SKRCH

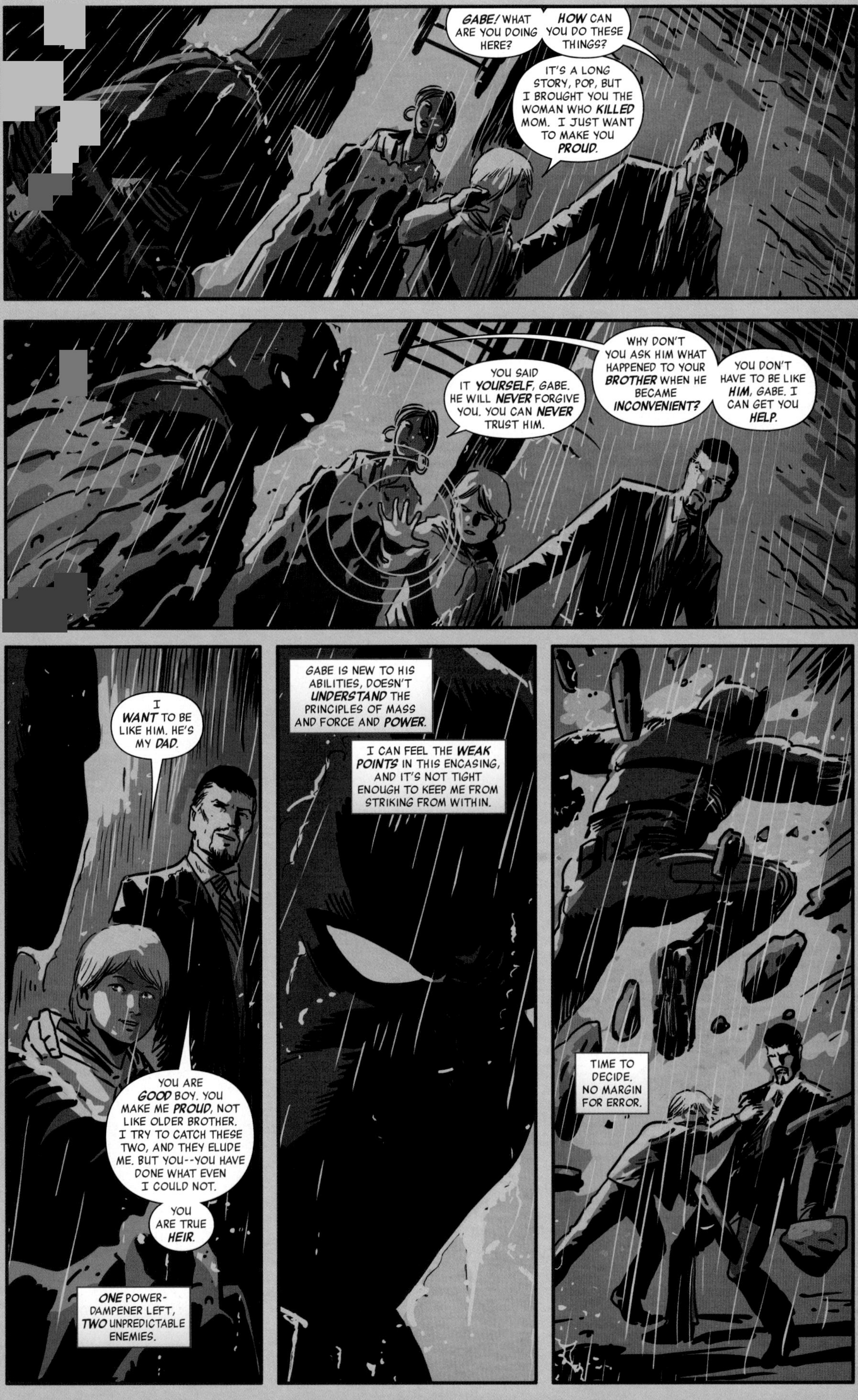
GABE! WHAT ARE YOU DOING HERE?
HOW CAN YOU DO THESE THINGS?
IT'S A LONG STORY, POP, BUT I BROUGHT YOU THE WOMAN WHO KILLED MOM. I JUST WANT TO MAKE YOU PROUD.
YOU SAID IT YOURSELF, GABE. HE WILL NEVER FORGIVE YOU. YOU CAN NEVER TRUST HIM.
WHY DON'T YOU ASK HIM WHAT HAPPENED TO YOUR BROTHER WHEN HE BECAME INCONVENIENT?
YOU DON'T HAVE TO BE LIKE HIM, GABE. I CAN GET YOU HELP.
I WANT TO BE LIKE HIM. HE'S MY DAD.
YOU ARE GOOD BOY. YOU MAKE ME PROUD, NOT LIKE OLDER BROTHER. I TRY TO CATCH THESE TWO, AND THEY ELUDE ME. BUT YOU--YOU HAVE DONE WHAT EVEN I COULD NOT.
YOU ARE TRUE HEIR.
ONE POWER-DAMPENER LEFT, TWO UNPREDICTABLE ENEMIES.
GABE IS NEW TO HIS ABILITIES, DOESN'T UNDERSTAND THE PRINCIPLES OF MASS AND FORCE AND POWER.
I CAN FEEL THE WEAK POINTS IN THIS ENCASING, AND IT'S NOT TIGHT ENOUGH TO KEEP ME FROM STRIKING FROM WITHIN.
TIME TO DECIDE. NO MARGIN FOR ERROR.

POLICE ARE NOW INVOLVED. THINGS ARE GOING TO HAPPEN *QUICKLY.*

NYPD! NO ONE MOVE!

I DON'T WANT YOU HARMED IN THE CROSSFIRE, BUT I AM *NOT* DONE WITH YOU.

IF I CAN ONLY CAPTURE ONE OF THEM, IT MUST BE GABE. HE IS YOUNG ENOUGH THAT HE MIGHT YET BE SAVED.

BUT I DO NOT ACCEPT THAT I CAN ONLY CAPTURE ONE.

I'VE FOUGHT VLAD ENOUGH TIMES NOW TO SENSE WHEN HE GROWS WEAK.

I AM *SORRY,* MY SON. I WILL *AVENGE* YOU *AND* YOUR MOTHER, BUT I AM ALMOST DEPLETED.

I *CANNOT* MAKE MY STAND NOW.

DON'T *LEAVE ME,* POP!

ONE *LAST BURST* IS ALL I HAVE.

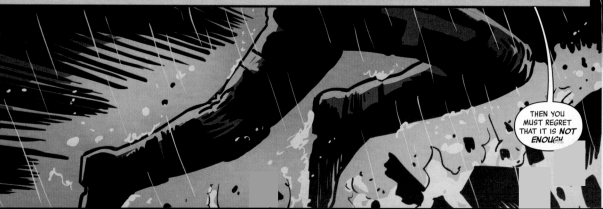

THEN YOU MUST REGRET THAT IT IS *NOT ENOUGH.*

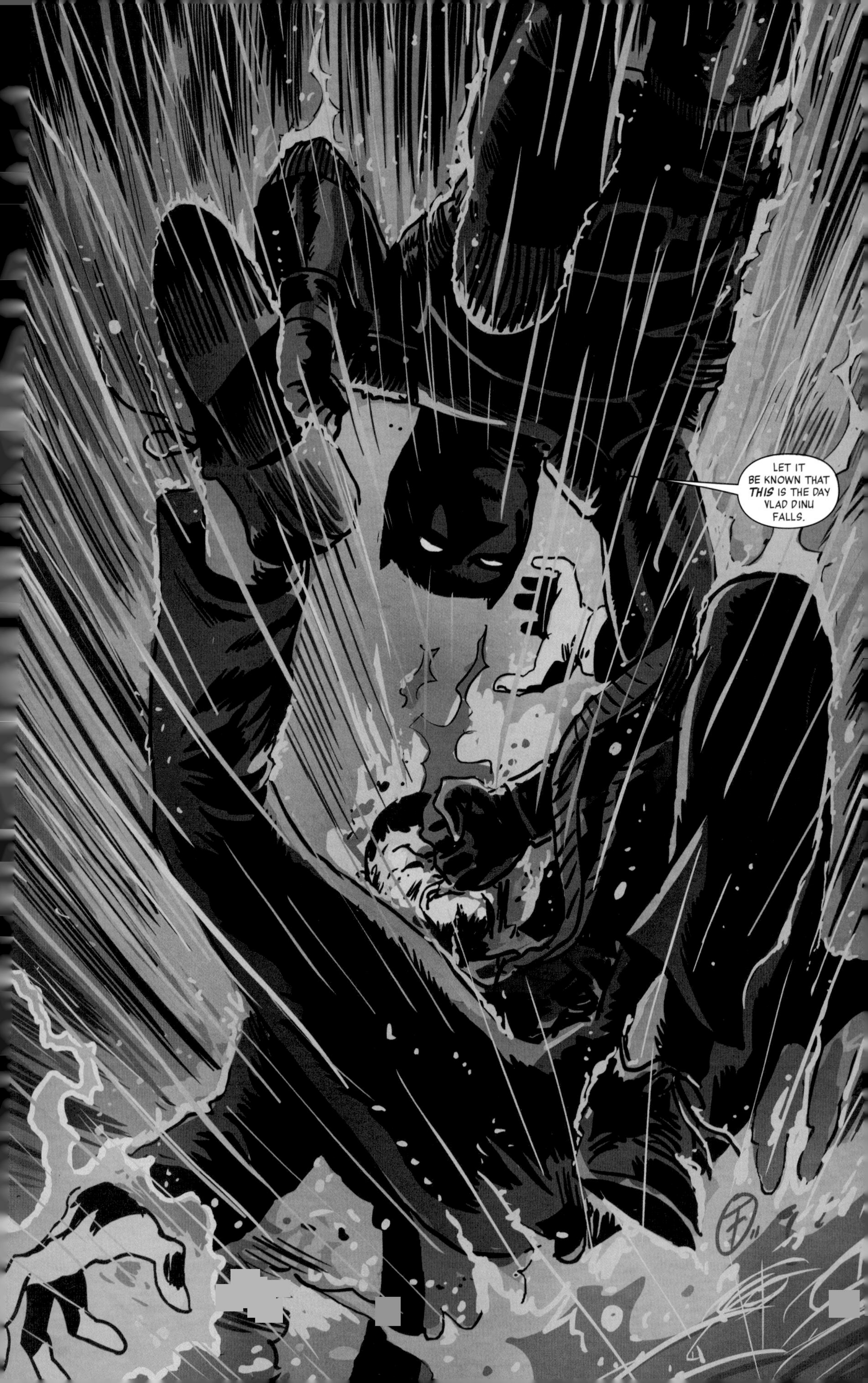
LET IT BE KNOWN THAT *THIS* IS THE DAY VLAD DINU FALLS.

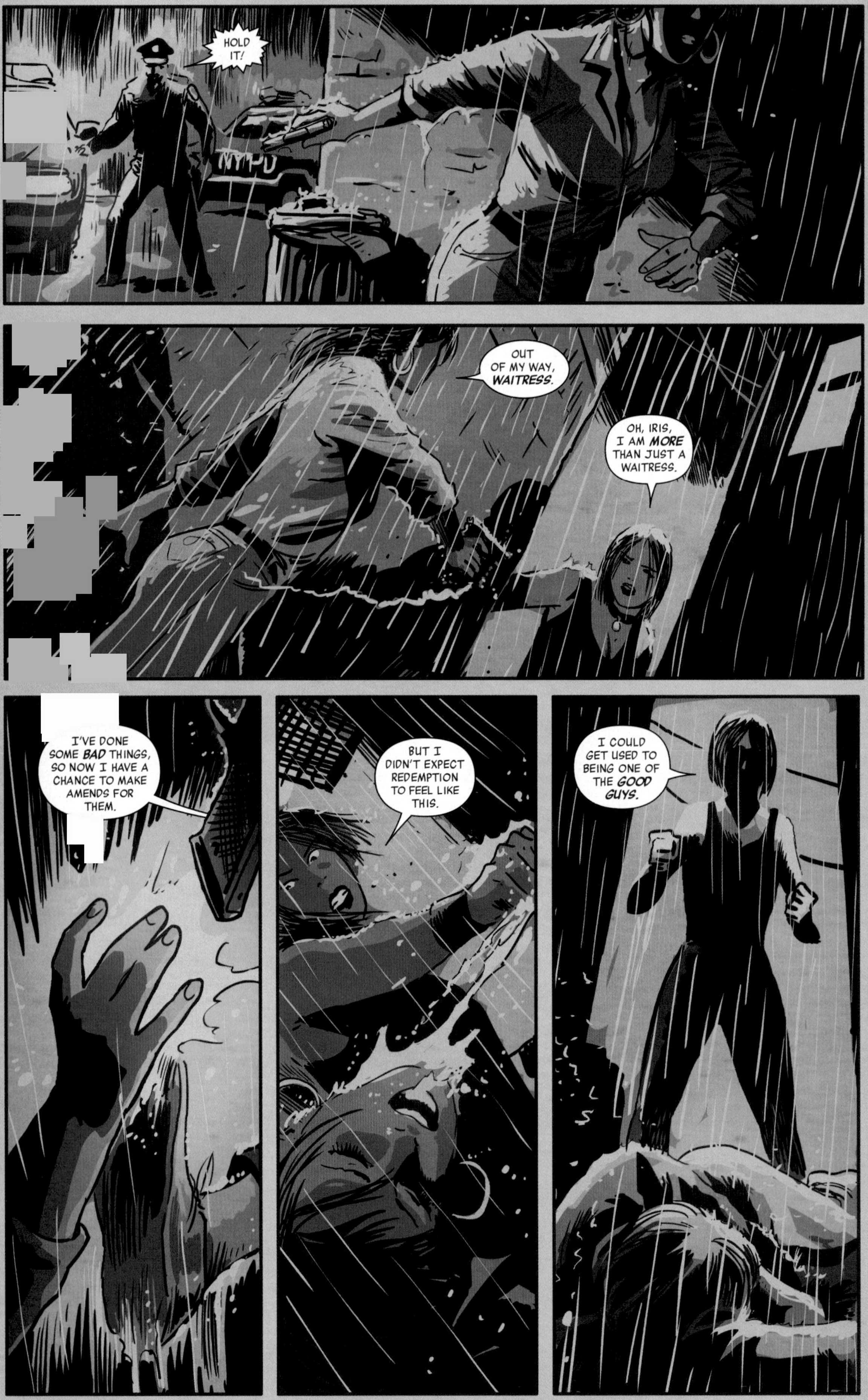
HOLD IT!
NYPD
OUT OF MY WAY, **WAITRESS.**
OH, IRIS, I AM **MORE** THAN JUST A WAITRESS.
I'VE DONE SOME **BAD** THINGS, SO NOW I HAVE A CHANCE TO MAKE AMENDS FOR THEM.
BUT I DIDN'T EXPECT REDEMPTION TO FEEL LIKE THIS.
I COULD GET USED TO BEING ONE OF THE **GOOD GUYS.**

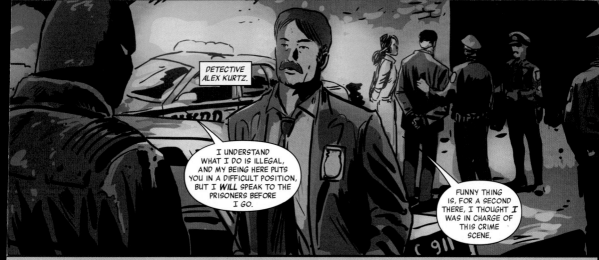

DETECTIVE ALEX KURTZ.

I UNDERSTAND WHAT I DO IS ILLEGAL, AND MY BEING HERE PUTS YOU IN A DIFFICULT POSITION, BUT I **WILL** SPEAK TO THE PRISONERS BEFORE I GO.

FUNNY THING IS, FOR A SECOND THERE, I THOUGHT *I* WAS IN CHARGE OF THIS CRIME SCENE.

I FIGURED OUT WHO YOU WERE, YOU KNOW. A LONG TIME AGO. **SUBTLETY** ISN'T REALLY YOUR THING. BUT I **WON'T** TELL ANYONE.

YOU ARE TOO **TIMID** TO SEEK REAL JUSTICE, BUT I SUPPOSE WHAT YOU DO IS BETTER THAN **NOTHING**.

I CAN ONLY HOPE YOU WILL USE YOUR TIME AWAY TO REFLECT ON WHAT YOU'VE DONE, IRIS. IF YOU CAN, LET GO OF YOUR **RAGE** AND **FEAR**.

NEVER HAVE I SEEN SUCH ARROGANCE.

MY **LAWYERS** WILL MAKE MOCKERY OF THESE CHARGES. EVEN IF THEY DO NOT, **SOMEONE ELSE** TAKES MY PLACE. NO MATTER WHAT YOU DO, HELL'S KITCHEN REMAINS **SAME**.

BUT **MY BOY.** MY GABE. HE WAS NORMAL, HEALTHY BOY. HE HAD **NOTHING** TO DO WITH MY BUSINESS.

NOW HE IS **CRIMINAL**. HE GOES INTO SYSTEM, COMES OUT WORSE.

THIS IS WHAT YOU HAVE ACCOMPLISHED.

PANTHER, YOU THINK YOU HAVE IT ALL WRAPPED UP NICE AND NEAT, BUT YOU **DON'T**. BECAUSE THIS WHOLE TIME, YOU'VE LET YOUR OWN FRIEND DOWN. HOW ABOUT THAT?

THAT BUSBOY--BRIAN. MY BROTHER EXPERIMENTED ON HIM, AND HE'S STILL OUT THERE. AND HE HAS POWERS. LIKE MINE.

BRIAN'S ALIVE?

THE EXPERIMENTS DID SOMETHING TO HIM. TURNED HIS BRAINS TO MUSH. BUT HE'S OUT THERE AND YOU MISSED HIM.

THEN I HAVE AN **OBLIGATION** THAT CANNOT BE IGNORED.

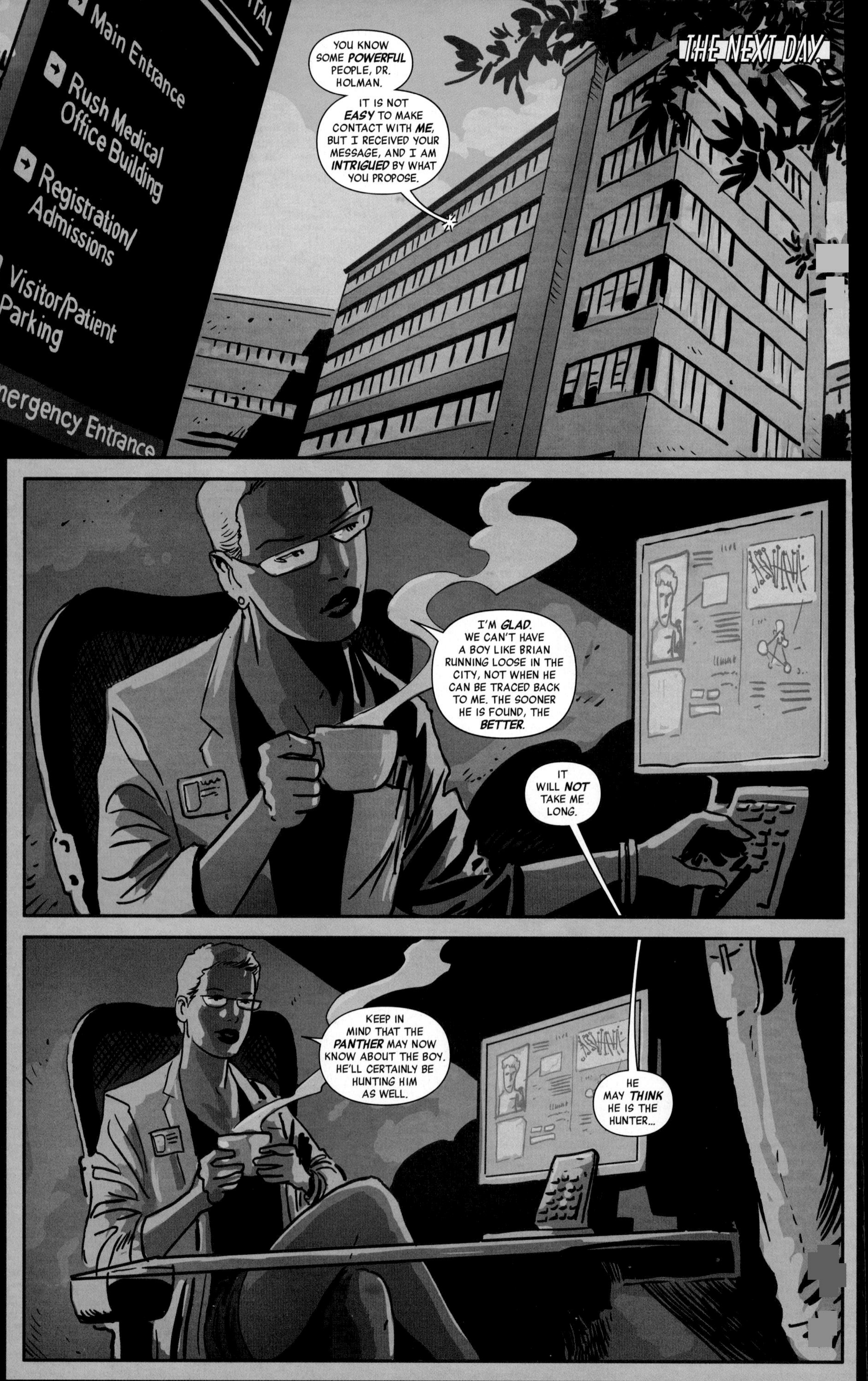
THE NEXT DAY.
Main Entrance
Rush Medical Office Building
Registration/ Admissions
Visitor/Patient Parking
ergency Entrance
YOU KNOW SOME POWERFUL PEOPLE, DR. HOLMAN.
IT IS NOT EASY TO MAKE CONTACT WITH ME, BUT I RECEIVED YOUR MESSAGE, AND I AM INTRIGUED BY WHAT YOU PROPOSE.
I'M GLAD. WE CAN'T HAVE A BOY LIKE BRIAN RUNNING LOOSE IN THE CITY, NOT WHEN HE CAN BE TRACED BACK TO ME. THE SOONER HE IS FOUND, THE BETTER.
IT WILL NOT TAKE ME LONG.
KEEP IN MIND THAT THE PANTHER MAY NOW KNOW ABOUT THE BOY. HE'LL CERTAINLY BE HUNTING HIM AS WELL.
HE MAY THINK HE IS THE HUNTER...

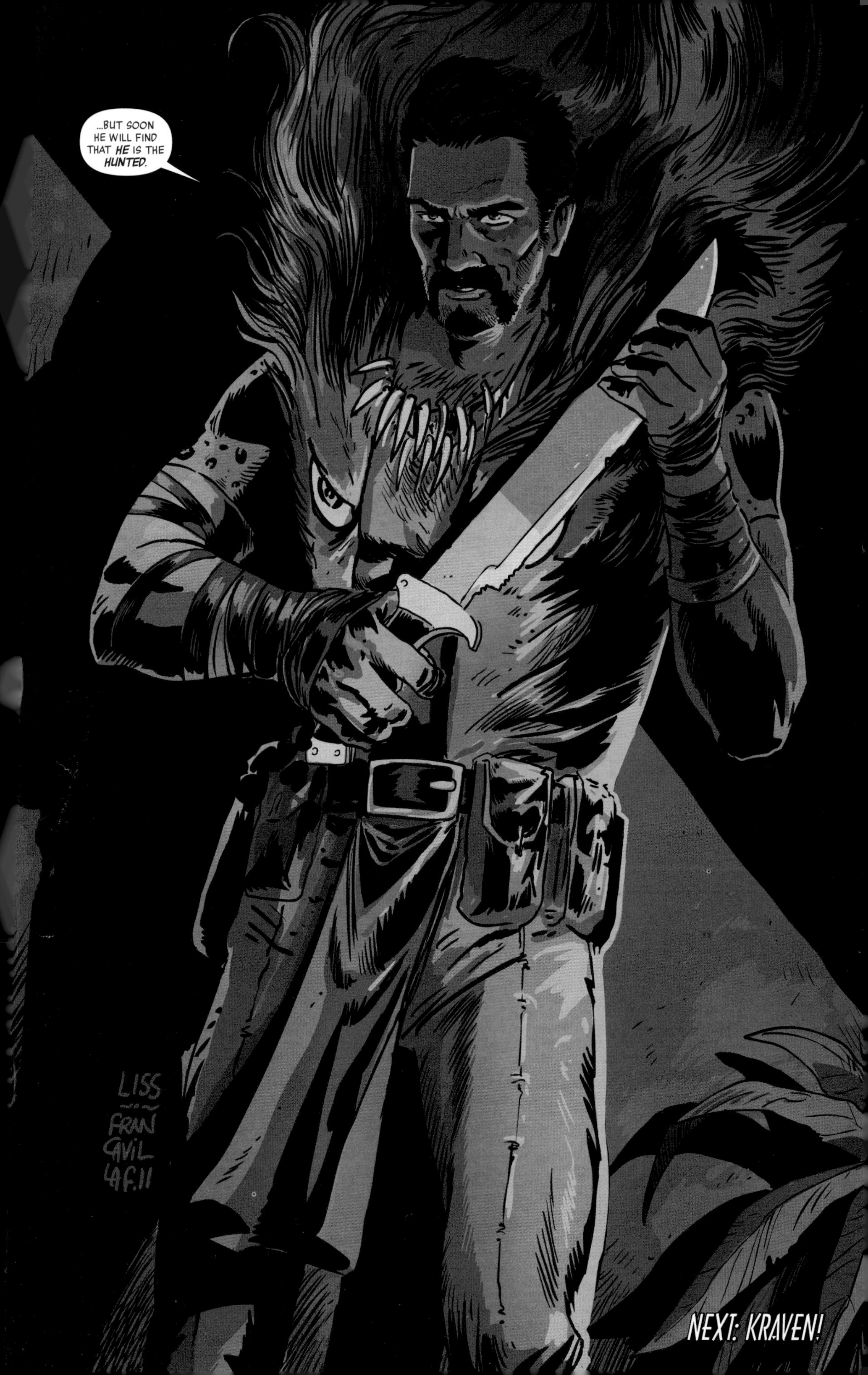
...BUT SOON HE WILL FIND THAT HE IS THE HUNTED.
LISS FRANCAVILLA F.11
NEXT: KRAVEN!

KEEPING THE DEVIL'S COMPANY

There's A New Man Without Fear In Hell's Kitchen, But Who Is He? Novelist David Liss Unravels The Mystery.

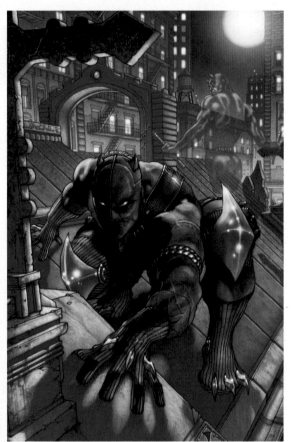

Cover to *Black Panther: Man Without Fear* #513 by Simone Bianchi.

Who better to install one of Matt Murdock's friends as the new guardian of Hell's Kitchen than the best-selling writer of a novel named *The Devil's Company*? Award-winning author David Liss, whose historical thrillers have captivated readers and critics alike, is now turning his attention to a very modern hero in the pages of *Black Panther: The Man Without Fear*. In a title that replaces *Daredevil* with issue #513, David is plucking T'Challa out of the wilds of Wakanda and throwing him into the urban jungle of Hell's Kitchen. It promises to be a Black Panther tale like no other as the new Man Without Fear prowls a neighborhood torn apart by the events of *Shadowland*. With it, David – who last year contributed a Phantom Reporter origin tale to the *Daring Mystery Comics 70th Anniversary Special* – returns to Marvel, so *Spotlight* took the opportunity to welcome him back.

SPOTLIGHT: So what brings a former African head of state to Hell's Kitchen?

DAVID: T'Challa has abdicated the throne to his sister, Shuri, who is now queen of Wakanda and the Black Panther. In the wake of the devastation of *Doomwar*, he is looking for meaning in his life. In the wake of *Shadowland*, crime and mayhem are on the rise in Hell's Kitchen. The neighborhood has never needed a protector more. This is a perfect opportunity for T'Challa, who is trying to figure out who he is without his Black Panther powers and without his kingship.

SPOTLIGHT: And, as things stand, without his title.

DAVID: The Black Panther is a name of cultural, political and religious significance, and there is only one: Shuri. In the first issue, when T'Challa is asked his codename for his costumed persona, he refuses to answer. I'm playing him as not wanting to claim the title of Black Panther – but not wanting to take another name, either. We'll probably have others, and perhaps the newspapers, call him the Black Panther – but he will for now deny that the name is appropriate.

Writer David Liss.

SPOTLIGHT: The loss of Vibranium in *Doomwar* presumably means a return to a low-tech Black Panther and, from the looks of it, the sleek classic look?

DAVID: Yes. T'Challa has no enhanced powers and no tech. He has also walked away from his wealth and has to live off his working man's salary. He will have no tech he cannot buy or build himself.

SPOTLIGHT: What facets of T'Challa's character do you think would appeal to longtime Daredevil fans? What do you think are their key similarities and striking differences? How fitting do you think DD's traditional tagline, the Man Without Fear, is for T'Challa?

DAVID: Like Matt Murdock, T'Challa is a man who lives by a rigorous code of honor. He has committed himself to protect Hell's Kitchen, and that means he'll go to any lengths to do that. T'Challa has spent a lot of time in New York, and he and Daredevil have had adventures before. None of this backstory is necessary to understand the series, however. All that matters is that T'Challa is exactly the right person, in exactly the right situation, to take over as guardian of Hell's Kitchen. I think the most important difference between the two is that Murdock knows the neighborhood inside and out. T'Challa has a lot to learn. As far as being a man without fear goes, the interesting thing to me is that this is a persona they project to the public, not an accurate description. Of course both characters experience fear, but they also possess great courage. The presence of one is perceived as the absence of the other. Part of T'Challa's story is going to be how he tests his own courage

without his Black Panther powers or Wakandan tech to help him.

SPOTLIGHT: Will T'Challa find himself in the sights of Hornhead's rogues gallery?

DAVID: I think it is very likely that the longer T'Challa stays in Hell's Kitchen, the greater the chances he'll have to face off with villains who have made that part of the city their home. That said, we wanted to make this its own story, not try to wedge T'Challa into Daredevil's shoes, so the first arc will not center on a traditional DD enemy. Instead, we're introducing Vlad the Impaler, a Romanian immigrant and longtime enforcer who sees the current power vacuum as the perfect opportunity to become the new crime lord of Hell's Kitchen. Vlad is a family man, dedicated to his wife and sons, an understanding and forgiving boss – to a degree. He is also a ruthless killer, who will stop at nothing to achieve his goals, and this new vigilante who is attempting to take over for Daredevil is going to be a big thorn in his side. Let the contest begin!

SPOTLIGHT: During his time with the Avengers, Black Panther assumed the secret identity of school teacher Luke Charles. Could this be a case of Welcome Back, Mr. Charles?

DAVID: We decided not to go with that secret identity. Besides the fact that the name Luke Charles invites confusion with another hero with a similar name, T'Challa doesn't want anyone to know he's in Hell's Kitchen, including his former associates in the Avengers. He's determined to do what he needs to do alone, so he's taken a new name. With Foggy Nelson's help, T'Challa has created a false identity for himself so he can live in and get to know Hell's Kitchen. He is now Mr. Okonkwo, an immigrant from the Democratic Republic of Congo. He sets himself up as the manager of a centrally located and popular eatery, The Devil's Diner.

SPOTLIGHT: Will readers see much of T'Challa's wife, the

X-Man Storm, in this series? Any other familiar characters in Black Panther's supporting cast?

DAVID: For now, Storm is off in Utopia, doing her own thing with the X-Men. As you'll see in issue #513, she understands that T'Challa needs to be alone right now – and, for his sake, she encourages it. He has asked her to stay out of Hell's Kitchen since he cannot test himself if every time he gets in trouble one of the planet's most powerful heroes comes swooping in to save him. In the early issues, there will not be any characters from BP's past showing up, but who can say what the future holds?

SPOTLIGHT: You are known for your mystery and thriller novels and short stories. Will you be bringing that kind of feeling and approach to *Black Panther: The Man Without Fear*?

DAVID: I like to read and write character-driven stories, and that's what I want *Black Panther: The Man Without Fear* to be. There will be lots of action, exciting sequences and daring adventures, of course – but those things are only successful when the reader truly cares about the characters that experience them. I want to bring that kind of intensity to this series.

SPOTLIGHT: You are the latest in a line of writers from other fields to write in comics, and particularly at Marvel, in recent years – what do you think the attraction of the comics field is right now?

DAVID: I love comics, so that's the principal attraction for me. It is, however, an exciting and dynamic time to be involved in the medium, so I can understand why some writers who may not already be fans would want to get involved. But I'm like one of those rookie baseball players: I'm just happy to be here.

SPOTLIGHT: How are you finding the scripting process and collaborating with an artist, Francesco Francavilla, compared to your "day job"?

DAVID: One of the things I love most about writing comics is that it is so collaborative. A fiction writer is all alone, but in comics it's a three-way collaboration between the writer, artist and editor – and it's incredibly liberating and satisfying to see how great ideas come out of the interplay between different people and different approaches. I love Francesco's pages, and I think his rendering of the script is just right. He gets both the dark noir elements, but also the exciting, action elements. It's brooding, but also dynamic.

SPOTLIGHT: One last question: Is T'Challa a David Liss fan?

DAVID: I like to think that as one of the smartest men in the world, T'Challa is lucky enough to be able to learn his way around Hell's Kitchen, figure out the limits of his new skill set, defeat criminals and villains, *and* still find time for historical fiction.

The Devil's Company didn't just make a snappy title for our Spotlight interview: It's also the name of David Liss' most recently published Random House novel. When you've put down Daredevil #513, go grab a copy from your nearest bookstore! •

Writer: **Jess Harrold**
Design: **Michael Kronenberg**
Head Writer/Editor: **John Rhett Thomas**

PANTHER ON THE LOOSE: The King of Wakanda is now Hell's Kitchen's protector! (Art from *Black Panther: Man Without Fear #513* by Francesco Francavilla.)

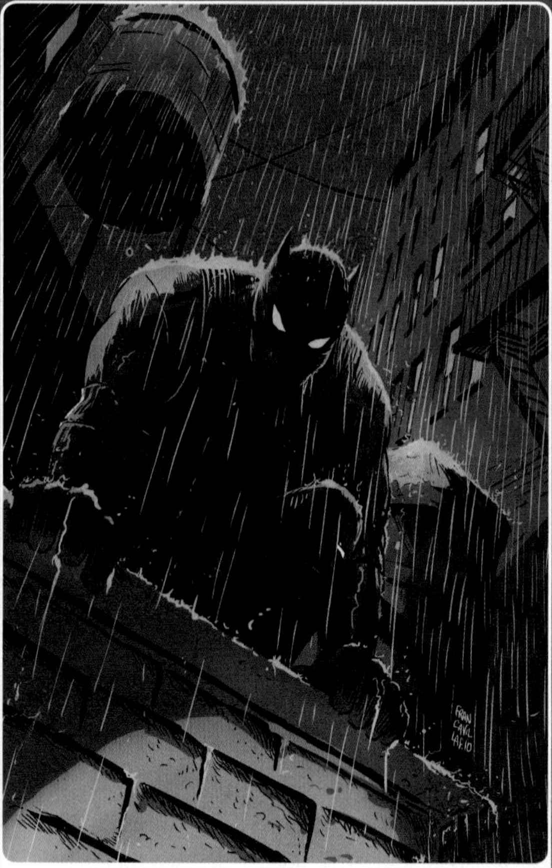

#513 VARIANT BY FRANCESCO FRANCAVILLA

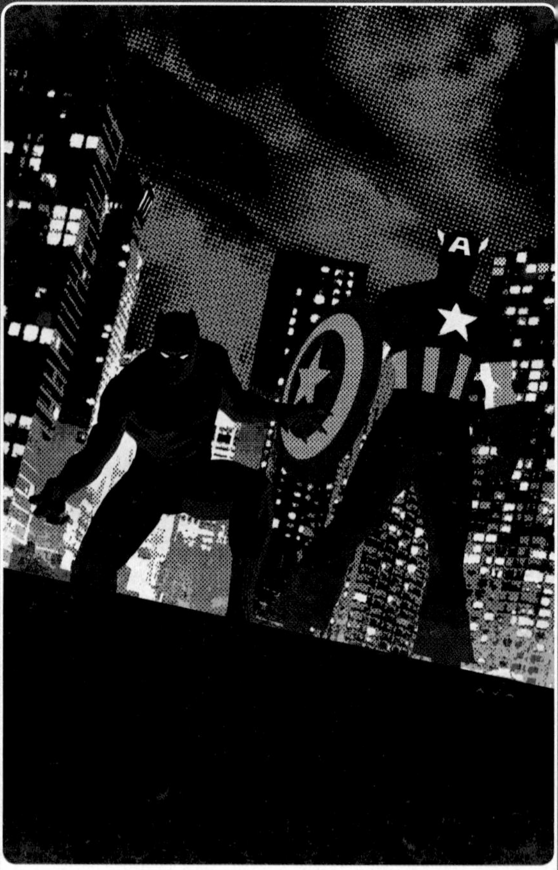

#516 CAPTAIN AMERICA 70TH ANNIVERSARY VARIANT BY DAVID AJA

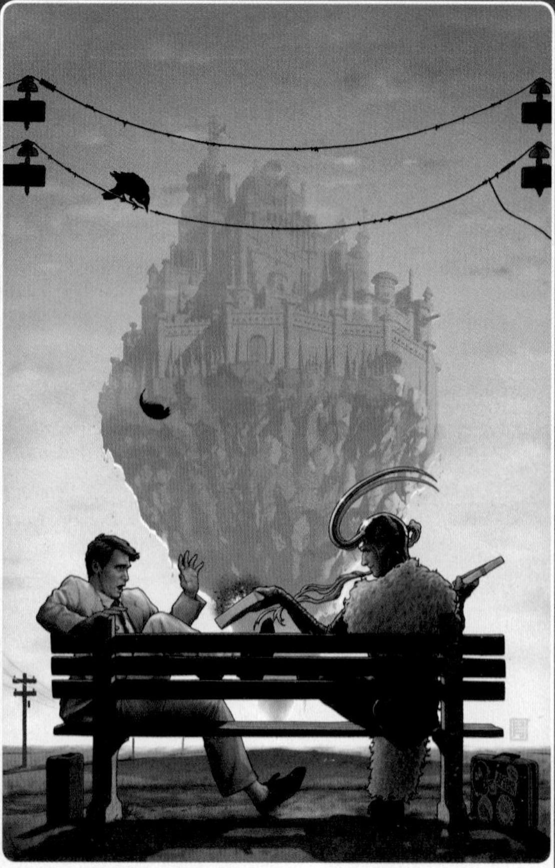

#517 THOR GOES HOLLYWOOD VARIANT BY JOHN TYLER CHRISTOPHER